Advance Praise for Act from Choice

"[Robert] Goldmann thoroughly examines unwanted habits in this helpful book… [It] does an excellent job of describing how humans form and keep bad habits, and it offers a wealth of effective tools and exercises to remedy them. The overall tone isn't one of judgment or criticism, which may be helpful to readers who might be defensive or resistant to change. The guide makes its process a personal one in which the reader is fully in charge. A thorough, conversational guide to aligning one's habits and actions with one's intentions."

—Kirkus Reviews

"Wonderful. A twofer— It is written in a style that any overweight smoker can understand and use, and is a finely crafted though easy to understand text book for professionals. A great gift, especially for people raised on guilt."

—Doug Jarvis. retired former Senior Vice-President,
Cablevision Systems Corp.

"Robert Goldmann dedicates ACT FROM CHOICE to his teachers, including those thousands "who work to benefit others, helping us awaken our innate sanity and compassion for ourselves and others." And in that dedication, he gives away his entire purpose. ACT FROM CHOICE simply dazzles! It synthesizes years of research that Mr. Goldmann has undertaken to make sense of suffering, to develop forgiveness, to instill compassion (starting with himself) in his clients and, now, his readers.

"Goldmann's education and decades working at the executive level do not alone not account for the remarkable insight in these pages: rather, his insight comes from his obvious hunger to effect change—first in himself, then to cultivate it in his clients and students. What he achieves in his pages is a compelling description of recent neuroscientific findings; his purpose: to support us in making freer choices— to benefit ourselves and others, and live the fullest possible life as we define it for ourselves. He never lectures or dictates; he urges us forward. The Method he designs demands our attention and commitment. It does not fail to reward."

—Sara MacDwyer, Attorney at Law & Mediator,
Certified Family Law Specialist

"Robert Goldmann has written a book full of compassion, humor, and wisdom about who we think we are, who we really are, and who we want to be, based on groundbreaking science in neurology and psychology. More than 400 references and 15 years in private practice back up his crystal-clear insights.

"In Part I of his book, Mr. Goldmann recommends we forgive ourselves for the way our habits, our subconscious, and mental laziness drive our thoughts and actions. Part II is about technique. He provides a seven-step mnemonic cost-benefit structure illustrated with dozens of applications to daily life for recognizing and managing those reactions we choose to manage-- from very simple ones easy to master, to highly complex ones that take practice.

—Laird Durham, international consultant, magazine writer, and author of the self-help Prentice-Hall book *100 Careers: How to Pick the One That's Best for You*

"Act from Choice is the book I've been wanting for an embarrassingly long time. It dissolves my usual excuses for occasionally being cantankerous (an understatement) when I wish I'd have been calm and kind.

"This book provides solid, understandable, step-by-step methods for being how I'd like to be, but never knew quite how to do. The clarity is remarkable as must be the breadth and depth of the author's knowledge and experience. The book's introduction of Targeted Mindfulness makes it especially important and a treasure."

—Bob Schwartz, a founder and former Vice President of Kagyu Droden Kunchab (KDK), San Francisco, and Main Coordinator, and Secretary to the Executive Director of Kagyu Monlam, Bodh Gaya/ India

"Robert Goldmann's Act from Choice is really two books: Part 1 describes the theory behind human development and change. It's comprehensive and as good a work as I've found since grad school many years ago, yet easily understandable by the general reader. If you want to know the big picture of human development, read and enjoy Part 1.

"If you're into changing you, and already know the theory, you could go directly to Part 2. It's a systematic guide to changing behavior. If you follow the steps, you will get results."

—Michael H. Smith, PhD, therapist, coach and organizational development consultant located in Oakland California

"A unique amalgam of serious science, Buddhist compassion, and business-coaching directness. Robert Goldmann has brought to Act from Choice his wisdom, deep study and analysis, creating a method appropriate to everyone who wishes to manage themselves better. Do what you mean to do, and avoid acting on regrettable impulses. Robert Goldmann taught me why I think the way I do, and how to act the way I mean to. It works!"

—James Sherman, managing director of Pollinator Partnership, an environmental not-for-profit, and a former CEO

"There's one problem with The Act from Choice Method – it works too well! It leaves me no excuse for continuing my so-called "unwanted habits"; either I have to admit I don't want to quit them or follow the method and lose them."

> — Clyde Grossman, founder and former Managing Director of Interactive Studio Management, a video game business development and consulting company, and founder of DoNoHarm.us

"When you master the tools presented in *Act from Choice*, you'll set aside those feeble excuses you've relied on to justify your misbehavior, self-sabotage, and insecurity. You will be able to own who you are, be who you want to be. Goldmann's book is a glorious tour of oft unexplored and generally inaccessible territory: the "unconscious" drivers of your motives, feelings, and fears.

"Robert Goldmann's material combines a thoughtful review of the research literature with the rich experience of a coach who is clearly dedicated to helping his clients find and follow their own, true path. His insights will help you exchange helplessness, frustration, and fear for hope, action and fulfillment."

> —Steve McElfresh, PhD, Vice President of People, New Relic Inc.

"So often, well-intentioned people with high ideals and compelling visions act in ways that do not benefit them. They (and we!) wonder why they would continue to do such things, and, more importantly, what they can do about it. Enter Act from Choice. Goldmann's book offers a step-by-step guide with handy worksheets and descriptive examples that are accessible to anyone who has struggled to express their values and be as they "mean to be." It works when they are willing to do the work. Willingness is encouraged by Goldmann's explanation of why self-management is so difficult for all of us humans, and his tools for raising a new level of self-compassion and awareness. Act from Choice is straightforward, easy-to-understand and useful for individuals and the professionals (therapists, coaches, teachers) who work with them."

> —Georgianna Marie, transition coach, and founder of The GMarie Group, a training consultancy

ACT FROM CHOICE

SIMPLE TOOLS FOR MANAGING
YOUR HABITS, YOUR EMOTIONS AND YOURSELF
TO BE HOW YOU MEAN TO BE

ROBERT GOLDMANN

CLARITY PUBLICATIONS

Clarity Publications, LLC
P O Box 70008
Point Richmond, CA 94807
ClarityPublications.com

Credits:
"POEM", by Sakyong Mipham Rinpoche, © Mipham J. Mukpo, All rights reserved, used here by permission
Other credits
Developmental Editing, Ingrid Emerick, Girl Friday Productions | Editing and production support, Angie Kiesling, The Editorial Attic |Index, Nancy Kopper |Interior illustrations, Nick Heitzman |Interior design and typesetting, Pamela Trush, Delaney-Designs | Book cover: Mary Schuck, Mary Schuck Designs | Cover concept and original photo: Sita Sherman | Bird photo, iStock.com/Phil Fowler Nature Photography | Author photo, Julie Mikos | Supplementary designs and support for book and website, Anita Goodman, Agoodgirl Design | Website design, Champion Fleming, Champion Design

Publisher's Cataloging-in-Publication
(Provided by Quality Books, Inc.)
    Goldmann, Robert (Robert J.), author.
     Act from choice : simple tools for managing your
    habits, your emotions and yourself, to be how you mean
    to be / Robert Goldmann.
       pages cm
       Includes bibliographical references and index.
       LCCN 2017941440
       ISBN 9780998568706 (pbk. : alk. paper)
       ISBN 9780998568713 (hard cover : alk. paper)
       ISBN 9780998568720 (Kindle)
       ISBN 9780998568737 (ebook)

     1. Choice (Psychology) 2. Self-management
    (Psychology) 3. Habit breaking. 4. Mindfulness
    (Psychology) 5. Emotional intelligence.
    6. Self-actualization (Psychology) 7. Self-help
    publications.   I. Title.

    BF611.G65 2017   153.8'3
                               QBI17-827

Dedicated to

Pema Chödrön

Jon Kabat-Zinn

Stephen and Ondrea Levine

Tsoknyi Rinpoche

...and the thousands of others who, like them, by their example, with ceaseless activity and selfless devotion work to benefit others, helping us awaken our innate sanity and compassion for ourselves and others.

DISCLAIMER

Nothing in this book should be used to diagnose or treat physical or mental conditions that could be clinical in nature. This book presents suggestions for working with common habits that are not clinical in nature. If your behavior or feelings are in the slightest bit dangerous to you or others; if your mental state or behaviors keep you from feeling or being fully functional, or if they are potentially damaging to you, your relationships, your livelihood, or your security; or if you are chemically or emotionally addicted, get licensed professional help, and consult with your health care provider as to the appropriateness of working with this book.

TABLE OF CONTENTS

INTRODUCTION xix

**PART I: UNWANTED HABITS: WHAT WE DO AND
WHY WE KEEP DOING IT**

   1   Habits Make Us Do It 1
   2   You Are What You Choose, Not Your Habits 7
   3   Habitual Impulses 11
   4   Sometimes You Manage Your Impulses............................ 15
   5   The Anatomy of Self-Management 17
   6   Mind, Brain, and Behavior 39
   7   Brain Knows and Decides Before We Do 52
   8   How Mind and Brain Interact...................................... 65
   9   Emotions Make It Possible to Decide 75
   10   How Brains Construct Reactions and Emotions 85
   11   Why You React the Way You Do.................................. 101
   12   Putting It All Together... 127

PART II: HOW TO ACT FROM CHOICE

   13   Introduction to the Act from Choice Method..................... 135
   14   T Is for the Truth of What Happens............................. 142
   15   O Is for Objective... 155
   16   M Is for Motivation 159
   17   Decide Whether to Commit 171
   18   C Is for Commitment 174
   19   A Is for Awareness 178
   20   P Is for Plan 192
   21   Simple Plans for Cold Habits 202
   22   Complex Plans for Hot Habits.................................... 221
   23   How to Cultivate Your Values by Managing
        Unwanted Attitudes.. 231
   Afterword: Be How You Mean to Be 249

THE ACT FROM CHOICE RESOURCE COMPANION 257

ACKNOWLEDGMENTS... 301

NOTES... 307

BIBLIOGRAPHY 319

INDEX 341

THE AUTHOR 359

EXPANDED TABLE OF CONTENTS

INTRODUCTION.. xix

About the Method.. xxiv
   Targeted Mindfulness xxv
Suggestions for Working with This Book xxvi

PART I: UNWANTED HABITS: WHAT WE DO AND WHY WE KEEP DOING IT

CHAPTER 1   HABITS MAKE US DO IT 1
Betrayals, Large and Small 1
   It's What You Do or Don't Do 2
   It's Not Only About Doing and Not Doing.................................2
Emotions Drive Habits...4
   Unwanted Impulses and Habits Are Simply Unwanted, Not Bad 4
   Misdirected, Misguided, and Useless Habits.................................5

CHAPTER 2   YOU ARE WHAT YOU CHOOSE, NOT YOUR HABITS 7
You Are Not Your Impulses 7
You're in Very Good Company..8
   The Apostle Paul 8
   The Dalai Lama 9

CHAPTER 3   HABITUAL IMPULSES..11
Stimulus, Impulse, Action...12

CHAPTER 4   SOMETIMES YOU MANAGE YOUR IMPULSES ...15
Two Well-Managed Impulses...15
   When You Itch, You Decide Whether and How to Scratch....................15
   You Control Your Speech When It's Important.................................15

CHAPTER 5   THE ANATOMY OF SELF-MANAGEMENT............17
Distraction from Self Is the Master Habit.................................17
   Witness the Master Habit in Action 19
   Breaking Free of Master Habit...20

Introducing the Choosing Space 20
What Directs Attention to the Present? 21

Introducing Your Sentinel 23

**In the Choosing Space: Meeting Reactive Brain and
Intentional Mind** 25
Needing More than Awareness 28

Willpower 29

Handling Self-Management Failure 32

Learn to Judge Yourself Fairly 34

Key Takeaways 37

CHAPTER 6   MIND, BRAIN, AND BEHAVIOR 39

Why We Need to Understand Mind and Brain 41

Brain and Mind Are Not What We Experience 42

Mind and Brain Defined 43
Mind 44
Brain 45

What the Subconscious Does 46

How and Why Reactive Brain Acts First 47

Exercises 48
Watch Your Mind Get Distracted 48
Instructions 48
Commentary 49
Experience Your Mind 50
Instructions 50
Commentary 50

**CHAPTER 7   BRAIN KNOWS AND DECIDES
BEFORE WE DO** 52

Priming 55

Priming Can Change Us from Dishonest to Honest. Honest! 57
Priming Can Cause People to Over- or Under-Perform 58
Images of Money Are Powerful Primes 59
Priming with Ideas of One's Mortality Can Shift Political Positions 59

You Doubt 62

CHAPTER 8   HOW MIND AND BRAIN INTERACT 65

Examples of Mind/Brain Unreliability 66

Biases 72

CHAPTER 9   EMOTIONS MAKE IT POSSIBLE TO DECIDE 75

Are Emotions Really That Important? 75
    Emotions Are Deciders and Motivators 75
    Emotions Are Necessary for Making Decisions 76
        The Patient Who Could Neither Decide nor Choose 77

Emotions and Your Gut Feelings Are Mostly Right 81

**CHAPTER 10   HOW BRAINS CONSTRUCT REACTIONS
               AND EMOTIONS** 85

Our Wonderful Brains 85

Brains and Emotions 87
    The Problem 89

Birth of an Emotion 91
    The Stimulus 91
    The Problem 91
    The Brain's Early Warning System 91
    Verdict. Sentence. Enlisting the Body. 94
    Now You Feel the Emotion 95
    Lessons from the Snaky-Shaped Something 98

What's Next 99

CHAPTER 11   WHY YOU REACT THE WAY YOU DO 101

How Habitual Reactions Are Created 101

Personality and Emotional Styles 103
    Personality 103
    Emotional Styles 104

How We Get Our Unique Personality and Emotional Styles 106
    The Role of Genes 107
    Early Childhood Personality and Adult Reactions 110

Characteristics We All Share 111
    Fears 111
    Reactions 112
    Emotions 112
        Secondary Emotions 115

The Individual's Unique Learning and Its Effects 116
    Learning...116
Other Ways Emotional Habits Are Formed 118
Conditioning Produces Misguided Habits...118
Misdirected Habits 121
Useless Habits 122

CHAPTER 12   PUTTING IT ALL TOGETHER 127

Emotions and Reactive Brain 127

Obstacles and Allies..129

Regarding Guilt, Shame and Self-Blame.......................................130

Behavior and Realistic Expectations 131

PART II: HOW TO ACT FROM CHOICE

CHAPTER 13   INTRODUCTION TO THE ACT FROM
                CHOICE METHOD 135

The Challenges of Habit Management 135

How the Method Addresses the Four Primary Challenges 135
    Preliminary Phase...136
    Decision Phase..136
    Committed Phase..137
        Commitment...137
        Train Your Awareness...138
        Plan 138

The Mnemonic for the Method 139

How to Use Part II..140

CHAPTER 14   T Is for the TRUTH OF WHAT HAPPENS 142

What Is It You Do or Don't Want to Do? 142

Important Considerations 143
    What Are You Responsible For?...143
    Looking for Triggers 144
    Misguided, Misdirected, and Useless Habits 145
        Misguided Habits 146
        Misdirected Habits 147
        Are Your Felt Emotions Primary or Secondary?........................148
        Useless Habits 149
    The Source of Your Habits 151
    The Validity and Usefulness of Your Reactions 151

And the Answer Is… 151
    What do you observe? What happens? What's your experience?
    How useful are your reactions? 152

CHAPTER 15   O Is for OBJECTIVE 155
Ask the Questions 157
State Your Preliminary Objective 158

CHAPTER 16   M Is for MOTIVATION 159
Motivation Is Essential 159
The Benefits of Self-Management 159
Sources of Motivation 161
    The Consequences of Your Habitual Reaction 161
    The Benefits and Costs of Self-Management 163
    Your Habits and Values 165
        Defining Your Values 165
Now Evaluate Your Motivation 167
Reconsider Your Objective 170

CHAPTER 17   DECIDE WHETHER TO COMMIT 171

CHAPTER 18   C Is for COMMITMENT 174
An Essential Step 174

CHAPTER 19   A Is for AWARENESS 178
Jackie's Story 178
    The Habit 178
    Managing the Habit 179
    The Technique 179
Sentinels 180
Creating Your Sentinel 181
    Design Your Sentinel 181
    Common Misconceptions 181
    Train Your Sentinel 182
    Train to Your Objective 183
    Be Accurate About the Facts 184
Support Your Sentinel 185

What to Do When Your Sentinel Fails 185

Knowing Mind 186
    Ask the Second Question 187

Conclusion 190

CHAPTER 20   **P Is for PLAN** 192

The Commitments 192
    Commit to a Formal Process 194
    Emotional Profiles 194
    How We Make Things Worse 197
    Validating Feelings Is Effective Medicine 198
    Delaying Response 198
    Next Steps..199

CHAPTER 21   **SIMPLE PLANS FOR COLD HABITS** 202

Managing Unwanted Wanting 202
    The Situation and Plan 203
        Preliminary Phase 203
        Decision 204
        Committed Phase...204
    The Plan in Detail—Commentary 206

Recapping Habits of Wanting 210

Managing Unwanted Habits of Resistance and Avoidance 210
    Two Kinds of Triggers to Resistance 211
    Triggers That Occur Unpredictably 212
    Scheduling When Habits Appear 213
    Routine and Simple Encounters...214
    Managing More Complex and Multi-Session Tasks 216

CHAPTER 22   **COMPLEX PLANS FOR HOT HABITS** 221

What to Plan and Prepare..222

Max and the Boys...222

Rachel and Her True Love 225

CHAPTER 23   **HOW TO CULTIVATE YOUR VALUES BY**
                         MANAGING UNWANTED ATTITUDES 231

Unwanted Attitudes Are Gifts..233

The Method 233
    Preliminary Phase..234
        T-Truth..234
        O-Objective 234
        M-Motivation 234

    Committed Phase 236
        C-Commitment..236
        A-Awareness..236
        P-Plan 236
            The Spot Plan 237
            Example: Patience..237
            Example: Generosity and Openness 239
            The Extended Plan 240
Challenges...244
    Difficulty Dropping Unwanted Attitudes and Manifesting
      the Value Objective 244
    Attributing Too Much to Individual Success.........................245
    Judging Yourself Unfairly..246

AFTERWORD   BE HOW YOU MEAN TO BE 249

THE ACT FROM CHOICE RESOURCE COMPANION

Contents..258

Introduction 259

Highlights of the Act from Choice Method...............................260

Tools to Use During Pause and Choose......................................263
    Find Your Center 263
    Cool Off...264
        Repeat Something Important to You...........................264
        Withdraw 264
    Get More Clarity 265
        Reframe 265
        Disidentify 266
        Investigate...266
        Accept What Is True..267
    Leverage Intentional Mind 267
        Acknowledge Pain and Console Yourself....................267
        "Drop the Storyline"...268
        Figure Out If You Have any Power...............................268
        Communicate and Negotiate 269

Choose Principles and Sacred Values 269
Renounce the Unwanted Action or Attitude 270
When All Else Fails..270
Tell Yourself Why..271
Reexamine Your Commitment 271
Choose Regret Instead of Guilt..272
About Certain Emotions..273
Guilt and Shame..273
Guilt 274
Shame 275
Anxiety 276
Overwhelm: Too Much to Do 277
Anxious That Bad Things Might Happen................................278
Everything Accommodated, but Still Anxious? 280
Negative Self-Talk..280
Introducing Gremlins 281
For Some, the Antidote for Negative Self-Talk 283
Slogans, Mantras, and Aphorisms..285
Developing Greater Awareness 291
The Power of Awareness and Curiosity 291
Knowing Mind 292
Getting to Knowing Mind 294
Tips for Increasing Awareness 294
Tooth-brushing Practice 295
Acceptance Training..297
Practice Becoming Present..298
Set Alarms to Bring You Present..299

ACKNOWLEDGMENTS.. 301
NOTES.. 307
BIBLIOGRAPHY 319
INDEX 341
THE AUTHOR 359

INTRODUCTION

You define who you want to be [by the choices you make]
in the little details of your life.

—*Ingrid Betancourt*[1]

It seems everyone has ideas about *who* they are. Then our behavior tells us, "Maybe you're not that," and we're disappointed in ourselves. Maybe embarrassed.

It doesn't have to be that way.

All of us are subject to occasional, unseemly outbursts, bad moods, and negative emotions like anger, greed, cowardice, jealousy, and resentment. Sometimes they cause us to do things we don't intend to do—or keep from doing things we want to do, and we regret them. Sometimes we tell lies— little white ones and big ones too. Our appetites seem to have a will of their own, and not just for food. Yet, if asked about our values, we claim many of the virtues, like generosity, kindness, patience, and fairness, and get all huffy if told that's not how we're behaving. These situations can undermine our feelings of integrity and make us unhappy with ourselves.

The purpose of this book is to help you act from choice—to make and follow through with choices that reflect your intentions. The foundational choice is whether to act according to your intentions or let your emotional and mindless impulses turn into actions that violate your values.

Years of study, work with coaching clients, observation of colleagues and friends, and personal experience have convinced me that we're defined by the values and behaviors we *consciously choose* to manifest, so long as we're trying to act accordingly. I mean that in spite of our unwanted thoughts and behaviors, we actually *are* who we *choose* to be if we're really working at it. For me that means making a real effort to restrain unwanted impulses, and continuing to feel dismayed when they break through, leading to actions that contradict our values and intentions.

Ultimately, *how* we are is the measure of *who* we are. But I believe that any assessment of how we are must take into account the effort we make to be how we mean to be.

Self-management seems a challenge for almost everyone. How about you? I guess that you may have picked up this book because you're frustrated by some inability to manage yourself consistently, and you want to do better.

Act from Choice will give you tools for managing your emotions, your habits, and yourself so you can be how you mean to be. The tools you'll find here will help you interrupt unwanted habits and emotions, choose what to do, and act more consistently with your values and intentions rather than give in to unwanted impulses.

The phrase *to be how you mean to be* has specific meaning for me. First the goal is about how *you* mean to be, not how anyone else thinks you should be. *To be* refers to the qualities you display when relating to other people, to the situations you face, and to you and your life. It refers to qualities such as patience, discipline, determination, courage, compassion, open-mindedness, and more—whatever you've chosen for yourself. Finally, being *how you mean to be* says there's a commitment to follow through with your intentions so that you have the right to claim the values you've chosen.

I use the word *mean* intentionally. Some are confused by my use of mean rather than *want*. I interpret *want* to be an expression of emotion, like *desire* or *aspiration*. I feel there's little commitment implied by *want*. *Mean* adds to *want* or *aspiration* a commitment to put forth effort in order to achieve what is wanted.

My self-management goals are grounded in meaning to live with integrity, which, for me, means that my values, intentions, and actions are consistent with and complementary to each other, and I can trust the promises I make to *myself*. Of course, your motivations for reading this book may be very different and much more specific. Perhaps you want to relate better with the people who are important to you; to gain better control of a difficult, habitual emotion; to sustain an exercise program; to stick to your diet; or to stop procrastinating.

If your goals are about managing behaviors you feel are inconsequential, my comments about values and integrity may seem too grand, and not relevant to your issue. You may question whether dieting, stopping procrastination, and exercising regularly have anything to do with values and integrity. But it turns out that discipline requires motivation, which we can boost by including in our goals explicit understanding of how we want to feel about ourselves. Think of a time when you did something that was difficult to do. Remember how proud you felt, and for good reason. The point is that your feelings about success or failure are not abstract. They are also about what you've demonstrated about yourself, to yourself.

In contrast, if you feel bad when you succumb to temptation and break your diet, procrastinate, or stop exercising, isn't there an underlying feeling that you're not as *good* or as disciplined as you want to be and think you *should* be? If so, those feelings come from a sense that you haven't lived up to your standards about how you want to be in the world.

I believe we achieve our goals more consistently when we recognize how our performance expresses our values and demonstrates who and how we've chosen to be. In Part II, I'll show you how to use your values to increase your motivation, whether you're trying to stay on a diet or be more patient with your family.

Regardless of how you want to improve your self-management, your behavior and effort are what count. It's what you do and how you work at being the person you mean to be that's important. No good purpose is served in claiming to be kind, compassionate, generous, or disciplined if you're habitually unkind, judgmental, stingy, or unreliable, and you aren't doing something about it.

As you'll discover from reading this book, many obstacles stand between each of us and being how we mean to be, the biggest of which are internally generated. It's impossible to act perfectly all the time. But making the effort to improve and manage oneself should count for a great deal. Better performance can be a source of great satisfaction, reinforcing feelings that we are who we mean to be at root, even though we sometimes fail.

You think it should be so @#$@#$! easy to be how you mean to be. You intend to act or think a certain way, but you don't. Your behavior and the results are regrettable, though not all the time by any means. Most of the time, you're a master of self-management. But there are times when you fail. You keep trying not to react the way you do, and you make some progress, but still you continue to embarrass yourself by what you say, do, or find yourself thinking. You may have thoughts and attitudes that embarrass you, even though no one but you knows about them—prejudice, hatred, and lust are favorites. Maybe you wonder how you can be who you think you are, harbor such thoughts, and be so unable to follow through with your intentions. Maybe you accuse yourself of being weak, a phony, or of not trying hard enough.

It's natural to want to be able to manage yourself, but self-management is unnatural. It's harder than we think it should be because it's not only about you. There are two actors involved: you and your subconscious. Regrettable behavior happens when you and your subconscious disagree about what you should do, and your subconscious wins the battle. The human subconscious is like a separate being that lives inside us.[2] It has its own ideas about how to interpret what's going on around us and what we should do about it, and does its best to make us do what *it* thinks is right, never mind what we think. It doesn't want you trying to manage yourself.

For convenience and effect, I and others talk about the subconscious as if it were an independent person, like a so-called homunculus living within us. In fact, as the therapist and author Timothy Stokes writes in this book, What Freud Didn't Know, we habitually experience automatic processes—scripts, he calls them— that are "activated without purposeful conscious effort and with limited conscious oversight …. when conditions beckon them, not [because] we call upon them." Moreover, as Stokes observes, the subconscious is not hidden from us because we've repressed it, as Freud believed. It's hidden from us because that's how our brains are constructed: it's simply how we're all made.

Part of the subconscious is devoted to looking for threats and opportunities.[3] It scans the environment constantly. Its interpretations of what it finds, and its notions of how we should react produce the impulses we feel. Those impulses are right nearly all the time. But sometimes they are not what we would choose, and they produce regrettable consequences when they turn into action.

The subconscious's interpretations of what it finds, and its decisions about what to do in reaction, are like computer programs. Even though the programs are lodged in our subconscious, are uniquely ours, and influence our actions, we didn't create them. We didn't even get a chance to vote on them. They were developed automatically by the brain, often at a very early age, based on the way our personality traits—influenced by our genetics—affected the way we reacted to what we experienced.[4]

Today those "programs" are set in motion automatically and subconsciously without any intent on our part. Moreover, the subconscious creates the impulse and emotions you feel before you're even aware of what it found—whether it's a person it decides is dangerous, a pretty picture it wants you to buy, or a bag of chocolate chip cookies it wants you to eat.[5]

You and everyone else are sure that's not what happens. You're probably certain you're in charge, that you see something, evaluate it, and only then decide what to do—and that's pretty much what most of the scientific community argued as late as the early 1980s. But the scientific research findings are incontrovertible: the brain perceives, judges, and tries to get you to react before you're aware of what it (and then you) is reacting to. You need to understand this in order to know what you're up against when you try to manage your impulses, and it's only fair to factor those realities in when you find yourself judging yourself. You'll read about the science describing the influence of the subconscious on your behavior in Part I, *Unwanted Habits: What We Do and Why We Keep Doing It*.

Recent discoveries about the role of the subconscious are so significant and so different from previous understandings and intuitions about behavior that they've even sparked renewed debate about free will.[6] The scientific research says that the subconscious does what it does independently of consciousness. The decisions the subconscious makes are based on interpretations and automatic reactions that it creates without our input, and then it tries to get us to enforce its decisions. The *no free will* folks say that if all that is true, the subconscious does it all, and we don't have free will.

But we've all experienced becoming aware of unwanted, possibly unsavory, or dangerous impulses and choosing to do something different instead.[7] As a result, I'm with those who say that whether or not we have free will, we seem to have at least some *free won't*, the ability to block our impulses and decide what to do instead.[8] Nevertheless, though we recognize that we can manage our impulses to some degree, we want to be more effective and consistent at doing it. The Act from Choice Method will teach you how.

The way it is now, when you wake up to knowing you're carrying out an unwanted impulse, you may try to exercise free won't. But often the impulse slips by your awareness, which is your first line of defense, and it isn't until you're well into or have even completed the unwanted action that you realize you're violating your intentions. The impulse may have been about something as minor as wanting to eat the chocolate chip cookie or as significant as wanting to hit someone. What happens then? You try to enforce your better judgment, invoking willpower to resist the impulse.

Contrary to conventional wisdom, the amount of willpower you're able to invoke at any particular moment is not a measure of character. Willpower is like a muscle: it will be weaker than normal right after you've used it a lot—making decisions or doing things you resist, or if you're simply tired. If you try to use it then to battle an unwanted impulse, it may not be strong enough. Or the impulse could be so powerful, and driven by such strong emotions, that no amount of willpower could overcome it.

Putting it all together, when we attempt to manage unwanted impulses, we're confronted with four key challenges:

- The first is to break through distraction and become aware of unwanted impulses when they arise.

- Second is to pause in the face of the impulse's momentum.

- Third is to overcome the impulse's momentum while choosing what to do and imposing our choice.

- Fourth is to deal with the consequences of failure when it happens—to banish guilt and recover the motivation and intention to continue trying to manage the habit after failing to do what we intended.

This book will give you tools to deal with those four challenges. Use it like a handbook. It is divided into three parts. In Part I, *Unwanted Habits: What We Do and Why We Keep Doing It*, I describe how brains produce unwanted reactive impulses automatically and independently, without our involvement. I will show you what you face when you're trying to manage yourself—specifically, how and why you experience the *impulses* you do and why they're so hard to resist. You'll learn that you had no role in choosing what you react to and how you react, and therefore have no reason to feel guilty or ashamed of your impulses. Of course, that in no way relieves us of responsibility for managing our impulses to keep them from turning into unwanted actions.

Part II, *How to Act from Choice*, describes the Act from Choice Method in a linear, step-by-step fashion. Some readers will want to work with the Method as they read through it the first time. Others will want to skim Part II the first time through, and return to work with it later.

The last part of the book, the Resource Companion, contains tools, tips, and ideas for dealing with several specific emotions and situations. Scan its table of contents to find tools that seem relevant to your self-management goals.

About the Method

The Act from Choice Method is a synthesis of practices and ideas from a variety of disciplines and traditions. I've added a number of innovations I don't believe you'll find elsewhere. There are also some significant changes in emphasis compared to many other approaches to habit management.

Though it is now well known that habitual patterns are acquired by the subconscious through happenstance and without input from us, I believe I place more emphasis than others on the consequences of that fact; I believe we are innocent of our impulses and should not feel guilty about having them, as long as we're trying to manage them. This is important because of the habit (!), so common in Western cultures, of turning our mistakes and shortcomings into attacks on ourselves. Unwanted impulses are still called *sins* by many, even when heroic restraint keeps them from turning into action. I believe little is gained by labeling habitual thoughts and impulses acquired through happenstance *sin*, and that such judgments lead to self-destructive attitudes and denial, making it more difficult to make beneficial changes. Further, such judgments make it harder for each of us to recognize that we are competent, far more than adequate, and worthy of our own respect, dignity, and compassion.

Targeted Mindfulness

As mentioned previously, one of the greatest challenges of self-management is becoming aware of unwanted impulses soon enough to interfere with them before they turn into regrettable actions. You've probably experienced the difference between being angry and being aware that you're angry. That's the kind of awareness you need to cultivate in order to manage yourself. When you're aware of your anger, you can judge and manage your actions. When you're the anger itself, you're its victim. Think of awareness of your anger or other emotions, attitudes, moods, and biases as a necessary aspect of being present.

The traditional approach to learning to be present involves mindfulness practices, usually including sitting meditation. The results of meditation practice are extremely durable and effective at improving one's *general* mindfulness. Experienced mindfulness practitioners enjoy many rewards from their practice, including being more present to themselves and others, experiencing less stress, having greater tolerance to stress, and improved mood and equanimity. Even so, many find that their unwanted impulses continue to turn into action without triggering their awareness.

The Act from Choice Method introduced in this book uses an approach I call *targeted mindfulness*. As the name implies, its aim is to train the subconscious to look for and make us aware of specific unwanted impulses soon enough that we can intervene and choose our reactions. The tools that make up the Act from Choice Method are simple to use. They're effective for people with or without experience with mindfulness practices; they are not time consuming, and they are effective right away. You don't have to use them for months or even weeks to get significant benefit from them. They are useful on their own, and also as adjuncts to traditional mindfulness practices.

The benefits of traditional mindfulness training and practice are truly vast. Targeted mindfulness practices have quite limited and different objectives and are no substitute for a regular meditation practice. Nevertheless, many people, those with and without mindfulness training, will find targeted mindfulness to be effective in helping them become aware of their habitual patterns sooner than they otherwise would—thereby making them more successful at managing unwanted habits.

Targeted mindfulness practices rely on the human brain's innate ability to wake us up and bring us to awareness when something important is happening. But we have to train it so that it knows to do it specifically when we want it to. The main targeted mindfulness technique used in the Act from Choice Method is an imaginary lookout I call a Sentinel. It is an extremely effective technique for calling attention to things we want to be sure to become aware of.

The Sentinel technique is a synthesis of elements from a variety of sources. It relies on the general idea of *mind protection* and *protector principle*, which are found in Tibetan Buddhist teachings and practices; traditional memory-training techniques that use the brain's well-known faculty of storing information associatively; and the brain's own error detection and alarm mechanisms that let us know when intention and action don't match. (If any of that sounds like Greek, don't worry. There's a lot of explanation coming.)

You'll find additional techniques for cultivating awareness in everyday situations in the Resource Companion at the end of this book. They can be very effective whether used as standalone practices for those who have no experience of mindfulness practice, or as informal supplementary practices for experienced mindfulness practitioners.

Suggestions for Working with This Book

This is a big book, and there's a lot in it. In fact, it's three books. Readers will have their own way of approaching it. Not everyone will want to read every word or even go front to back. Some will be fascinated by Part I, which describes the way our brains work, and will want to read every word; others will want to get right to the Act from Choice Method itself, or see what might be of interest in the Resource Companion at the end. Still others will want to pick up parts at random. I say hooray to all of you. It is a handbook. Use it like one.

Here are some suggestions about how you might want to approach the book, especially if you like to pick and choose.

Introduction

To get a good sense of the book you could go from this Introduction directly to the Afterword, and then review the *Expanded Table of Contents* to see what tempts you.

To get a sense of Part I read Chapter 12, "Putting It All Together." In my view, the most important thing to get from Part I is an understanding of how much influence the subconscious has over our impulses and behavior. That view will likely convince you that impulses are created innocently, and we're up against a lot when we try to manage ourselves. If you want to get high points about how our brains produce unwanted reactions—including our individual reactive styles—you could read Chapters 4, 6, 7, 8, 10, and 11.

Read Chapter 13, "Introduction to the Act from Choice Method," to get just that—an introduction and overview of the Method. To get a good sample of how the Method works, read the first half of Chapter 21, which contains a detailed description of how to work with it. The second half of that chapter is about managing habits of resistance and avoidance, habits like procrastination.

If your interest is primarily in targeted mindfulness, discussed earlier in this Introduction, read Chapter 19, "A Is for Awareness," which discusses the Sentinel in detail and also the technique *Ask the Second Question*. You might also be interested in some of the material in the Resource Companion at the end of the book, in particular the sections on *Slogans, Mantras, and Aphorisms* and *Developing Awareness*.

Motivation is essential to effecting changes in behavior and attitudes. Chapter 16, "M Is for Motivation," could serve as a standalone method for undertaking anything you find difficult or tend to resist doing.

Have at this book in any way that suits you. It's yours. Use it in the way that best serves your interests and needs.

Please keep in mind that this book is meant to help readers manage habits that are subclinical. It is not suitable for diagnosing psychological problems or disease. Most important, if your behavior is at all dangerous to yourself or others, if it is so durable and disturbing that it keeps you from feeling fully functional, or if you are addicted to substances or behaviors that interfere with your happiness or livelihood, seek licensed professional help, and rely on their recommendation as to whether you should work with the techniques in this book.

My goal is to teach you how to use your insights and innate skills to identify and manage the habits that cause you to do things that run counter to your best intentions and conflict with how you mean to be—habits that make you unhappy with yourself, as a result. There is theory here, but more important, there are techniques—practices you can use to manage yourself and your emotions so you can be how you mean to be.

Robert Goldmann
Richmond, CA
April 2017

PART I

Unwanted Habits:
What We Do and Why We Keep Doing It

CHAPTER 1

Habits Make Us Do It

*Each of you is perfect the way you are ... and you can
use a little improvement.*

—*Suzuki Roshi*[9]

Betrayals, Large and Small

You're a good person.
You have good values—
High standards.
You want to do what's right,
And you work hard at it.
But before you know it,
You betray yourself.

You explode in anger, tell a whopper, eat the whole bag of cookies, or do something else you didn't mean to do and will later regret. Maybe you yelled at a child, your partner, a stranger; or maybe you didn't yell or lie, but you said or did something else you're sorry for.

Maybe you don't realize what you're doing until you're well into it, if then. Or maybe you realize it, and it feels terrific while you're doing it. Nothing feels so good in the moment as towering, self-righteous rage, but when it's over you feel bad and there are consequences. Not only do you feel bad, you feel you *are* bad. You've done this before, and know you'll do it again. *Why can't you control yourself*, you wonder? When you wake up to what you've done, you feel you've betrayed yourself, your values, and what you stand for. Again. It's a habit, and you feel a loss of integrity; you're embarrassed, maybe even ashamed. You made things worse, and now there are apologies to make, a fiction you'll have to remember for the rest of your life, or "... there's all that weight to be lost."[10]

It's What You Do or Don't Do

Maybe you didn't do or say anything, and you're sorry about that. Something happened, and in spite of your best intentions, you crumpled. Courage? You changed the subject to avoid confrontation and left without doing or saying what you wanted, or following through to get it.

Too often, you don't say *STOP*, don't demand respect, explain what you mean, or ask for what you want. You say *yes* when you want to say *no*, or you say *no* when you want to say *yes*. Or maybe you want to say *yes*, *maybe*, *say more*, but the best you can squeak out is a barely audible *no*, making you feel like a wimp, a fraud, or worse.

Not doing what you intend is a habit.

One of the most common habits in this category is procrastination. You have a big project due tomorrow. You've known about it for two months—sixty days of increasing, gut-twisting anguish. Every morning, you've put it off until it's too late in the day to start. And now you're facing an impossible deadline. You still haven't begun; it's still there to do, and there's not enough time left to do it right. It can no longer be the masterpiece you imagined, and you won't win the prize or recognition you fantasized. Or maybe it will cost you financially: you'll owe the government more money because you delayed filing your taxes and didn't have the time to find all of your deductions.

You've suffered on the run-up and will suffer the consequences of the delay. For what? You could have produced something to be proud of instead of just getting by—and maybe this time you won't even get by. Maybe you'll get fired, or disappoint a colleague, or lose hard-earned money. There's no one else to blame, and you feel bad.

You've let yourself down.

It's not enough that you intended to do something different. What you said, or did, or thought contradicted your values, costing you real-life consequences and self-esteem. You realize you need to get this habit under control, or it will keep costing you dearly.

Maybe a book will help. This book.

It's Not Only About Doing and Not Doing

Those habits I just mentioned produce regrettable, observable behavior. But we are also subject to habits that produce attitudes, thoughts, judgments, and moods that may or may not result in unwanted behavior, but whose mere appearance in our minds make us feel out of integrity with our values. They include letting moods cloud or distort perceptions and cause us to punish innocent bystanders, giving license to judgments and prejudices antithetical to our values. These *habits of mind* cause us to act and react differently than we would if not under the influence of the habits. When we're frustrated or in a bad mood, we may say or do things in a tone of voice that we regret, or with aggression that is out of proportion and undeserved by its target. Situations that are positive or unremarkable might produce negative emotions. We might miss opportunities for joy and happiness.

Prejudice and judgment can cause us to think and feel in ways that are inconsistent with our values. For example, humans are wired to be suspicious of strangers and people who are different from us: they're "others." We're all influenced by social mores, even when we're not explicitly aware or approving of them, so it's not surprising that we find ourselves reacting negatively to people we don't know just because of how they look, act, speak, or dress, without any knowledge or interest in what they're really like.

While our innate ability and tendency to stereotype may come in handy when we need to make a quick decision or avoid trouble, it is often the cause of social injustice. Even the act of experiencing such thoughts can feel like a betrayal of our values. Civil rights leader Jesse Jackson famously said, "There is nothing more painful to me at this stage in my life than to walk down the street and hear footsteps and start thinking about robbery. Then look around and see somebody white and feel relieved...."[11]

I feel bad when I catch myself judging someone because of his or her appearance. Having attitudes about people based solely on what I can see or hear violates my values about how I want to relate to people, so, for me, profiling and stereotypical reactions are unwanted habits. But I do have them, so I work at managing them to keep them from turning into behavior.

Thoughts and attitudes that oppose our values are unwanted habits. We do not choose them, yet we experience them repeatedly. They appear automatically, swiftly, without warning, and without our participation, in the same way that we experience urges to physical action.

You do these things, think the thoughts, and have the attitudes that betray your values not because you're a bad person or otherwise of poor character. You do them because the combination of your genetics and experience from womb to the present moment has given you those automatic reactions—habitual reactions to things you encounter in your world.

Emotions Drive Habits

As noted in the Introduction, one purpose of this book is to show you that the automatic ways you react are not of your design, and to teach you how to manage impulses that produce unwanted results. All of them are emotional habits—impulses to act, as well as thoughts and attitudes that appear in your mind—powered by emotions your brain produces subconsciously and involuntarily. The emotions that accompany impulses are usually exactly what is called for in the situation, yet they're often not what you would choose given time and perspective.

Unwanted impulses produce our unwanted actions, thoughts, and attitudes. The challenge is to manage the unwanted *impulses* to keep them from turning into unwanted *behavior*, and to keep unwanted attitudes and thoughts from influencing us unintentionally. It is said that a gentleman is one who never insults someone *unintentionally*. There are times when anger or fear are essential for getting us to take the actions needed for survival. Most of our emotions, moods, and attitudes have a place in our toolkit, but we need to get out of automatic to use them intentionally and skillfully rather than mindlessly.

Unwanted Impulses and Habits Are Simply Unwanted, Not Bad

I hope you'll come to think of your unwanted habits as simply "unwanted," not "bad." Chances are that when I write unwanted habits, you think bad habits; it's how we're conditioned to think. Yet the word bad is unnecessary and gets in the way. There's a tendency to think that if we have bad habits, then we *are* bad. Anything that causes us to think of ourselves as bad can produce guilt, shame, and denial, which keep us from recognizing and acknowledging what it is that we do. If we don't acknowledge what we do, we can't manage ourselves.

Many people believe that calling something bad creates additional motivation for change. That may work for some, but that attitude may make the habit dig in and be more difficult to manage. Carl Jung is credited with the observation that "what you resist persists." That has been my experience, so I'll stick with unwanted.

Of course, there are habits that most of us can agree are truly "bad." They are dangerous to our person, relationships, fortune, and other people. Some bad habits include domestic violence, child abuse, self-injury, and excessive use of drugs and alcohol. (None of these, and others like them, are manageable with do-it-yourself methods. If you struggle with any habits like them, I urge you to seek help from licensed professionals.)

As mentioned in the Introduction, the Act from Choice Method you'll learn in Part II will help you manage a wide variety of unwanted habits that are neither dangerous nor clinical in nature. They are "unwanted" simply because you don't want them.

It's also important to remember that *unwanted* refers to the context in which the habit occurs. Almost all emotions, thoughts, and feelings are neutral in the abstract. Habits become unwanted when they're inappropriate according to your standards and/or are harmful to others, you, or your goals. Consider the emotion of anger. Anger is not the problem, nor is behaving angrily. Anger and other strong emotions can be very useful, and you should know how to use them appropriately and effectively; for example, acting from anger could be decisive in stopping someone from harming themselves or others. But, when moved to anger, consider whether it will be helpful to the situation. When Nelson Mandela was asked why he wasn't angrier about his years of unjust imprisonment and the oppression of his fellow black South Africans, he replied, "If I thought it would be useful, I would be."[12]

Misdirected, Misguided, and Useless Habits

Most of our habits are extremely helpful. They're time saving; they help us avoid danger or take advantage of opportunities; and in most cases, they lead to behavior that is exactly what we'd consciously choose. There are three categories of habits that almost always cause more problems than what they're reacting to. They are misdirected habits, misguided habits, and useless habits.

Misdirected Habits are those in which the impulse the habit creates doesn't address the stimulus that produced it. Something makes us feel bad, and we're moved to eat, or drink to excess, or mistreat the dog. The reaction is misdirected because it does nothing to address what made us feel bad. Maybe the bad feelings go away temporarily, but since the reaction didn't address its cause, the problem remains to be dealt with.

Misguided Habits are those in which we have a significant reaction to something, but there is no objective reason to feel or behave the way the habit directs us to. These habits are caused by conditioning. Conditioning can cause the brain to interpret things incorrectly. Just as Pavlov's dogs were conditioned to salivate when a bell rang, whether or not there was any food coming, something has caused us to mistakenly forecast that the stimulus will produce undesirable (or maybe desirable) consequences; we experience anger or terror, for example, even though the stimulus is harmless.

My principal teacher, Tsoknyi Rinpoche, calls the way we feel and react when influenced by misguided habits "real but not true."[13] The feelings produced are very real; we feel under threat, the impulses and emotions are very powerful, but there is no *true* reason to feel that way. PTSD symptoms are perfect examples of misguided habits. A returned veteran is approached from behind in a supermarket in Minneapolis, and he reacts as if he were being ambushed on a street in the war theater where he served. An innocent remark by an old man produces the same feelings the adult felt as a child when rebuked by his father.

Useless Habits are just that: utterly useless. Of course, it's the habits that are useless, not you. It's normal to get angry when you're frustrated, you witness injustice, or your cultural norms or sacred values are violated.[14] But think how utterly useless it is to get angry in a traffic jam or while watching the latest shenanigans of some politician. Though normal, the reactions are useless if you can't do anything about the situation. Better to use that anger to energize yourself to change the situation when you can do something about it, but it's useless to sit there and honk the horn, bang on your steering wheel, or throw shoes at the person on the TV. You may think your emoting is justified, and certainly, expressing your frustrations makes you feel better in the immediate term, but research shows that all it does is make you feel bad longer.[15]

The antidote for useless habits is the Serenity Prayer:[16]
>*God grant me the serenity*
>*to accept the things I cannot change;*
>*courage to change the things I can;*
>*and wisdom to know the difference.*

My slogan when trying to cope with useless frustration or disappointment at situations I can't change is "Don't make things worse than they already are." It's bad enough to be stuck in traffic, much better to figure out how to adjust for being late; why pile more bad feelings onto the situation and feel worse, longer?

Getting caught up in useless anger is equivalent to *taking poison hoping that someone else will die.*[17] (On the positive side, every time you recognize you're doing this, you have an opportunity to develop a healthy sense of humor about yourself.)

CHAPTER 2

You Are What You Choose, Not Your Habits

*You are neither good nor bad. You are a person who
does good and bad.*

—*Albert Ellis*[18]

All of us do things and have thoughts and attitudes that betray our values, not because we're of poor character, but because our individual genetics and experiences, from womb to the present, have given us a set of automatic, habitual ways of reacting to our experiences. You didn't choose those reactions; they just moved in and took up residence long ago. So now you find that when confronted with certain situations, you may experience unwanted impulses, hold undesired attitudes, or think or act in regrettable ways. And, unfortunately, these habits are stubborn. Even if you can override the impulses and restrain yourself from acting out, you can't simply will the impulses away.

You Are Not Your Impulses

*The problem is not that people have impulses; rather, it
is that they act on them.*

—*Roy F. Baumeister and Todd F. Heatherton*[19]

In many cultures, simply feeling an *impulse* to violate cultural norms and moral imperatives is judged, in and of itself, to be a sign of low character, shameful at best, sinful at worst, even when you successfully interrupt the impulse and no untoward behavior results. This is a cruel judgment because most of our impulses are involuntary. They were programmed by the brain, automatically, at a very early age. That so-young brain was recording the way its genetically influenced traits reacted with its experiences. You never had a chance to vote or otherwise choose or influence your traits or the experiences you were subjected to, and at that age you didn't have the wisdom to know how to choose, if given the opportunity.

In his book *Emotional Intelligence*,[20] Daniel Goleman tells us that many of our emotional habits are formed early in life, even before we have language.

Those comments of his gave me my first understanding that we do not choose many of our regrettable reactions—that the impulses those emotional reactions produce are no cause for negative self-judgment. They're simply what our individual brains innocently programmed us to do.

Since many of our most troublesome, unwanted, automatic reactions were formed in response to situations not of our making, it's no wonder our impulses don't match our adult, values-driven intentions. The mismatch between those intentions and our preprogrammed reactions is what makes us judge the consequences of some habits, and the habits themselves, unwanted. Their existence is not under our direct control, and the fact that we get angry, envious, greedy, or inappropriately lustful is no reason for negative self-judgment, as long as we do our best to stop the impulses from turning into action.

But make no mistake. While *impulses* don't count, *behavior* does. Unwanted impulses will continue to arise, to be sure, but we can't be let off the hook for our behavior. Unfortunately, some of us get so caught up in feeling guilty about the impulses that we go into denial that keeps us from acknowledging that we behave the way we do. Obviously, we will never be able to work on what we cannot acknowledge as fact. If you tend toward denial, I hope you will come to accept that your impulses do not reflect your character. If you can keep that in mind, it will help you manage your behavior regardless of what you think of your impulses.

You're in Very Good Company

"Poem"

I am good
People make mistakes
They are good

—*Sakyong Mipham Rinpoche*

You're not alone in having unwanted habits. In fact, you're in very good company. How about the Apostle Paul? And the Dalai Lama? And billions of other humans living and not.

The Apostle Paul[21]
In Romans 7:18-19, the Apostle Paul writes,
> *... I have the desire to do what is good, but I cannot carry it out.*

For I do not do the good I want to do, but the evil I do not want to do—this I keep on doing.[22]

Paul seems to be decrying his own behavior, later identifying the cause as "sin living within [him]" (verse 20). If Paul could not entirely control his impulses and felt out of control and "bad," it's not surprising that we react to our unwanted habits the same way.

Paul had it right and wrong. He was right to acknowledge the behavior, but in my view he was understandably misguided in seeing it as inherently sinful—that is, a sign of immoral character.

It's perfectly understandable how the Apostle Paul and we, without the benefit of all that's known about human psychology and neurobiology today, attributed out-of-control behavior to supernatural, malevolent forces and bad character. Robert Sapolsky, professor of biology, neuroscience, and neurosurgery at Stanford University, points out that five hundred years ago people with epilepsy were thought to be possessed by the devil, and were often executed.[23] We've come a long way, even though there are parts of the world where such ignorance prevails, and there are even individuals in advanced countries who hold these views.[24]

The Dalai Lama

His Holiness, the Dalai Lama, is a man of peace: compassion is among his highest values. Obviously, anger is not his thing. Nevertheless, he experiences it, and it can even be triggered by something trivial. Asked by an interviewer whether he gets angry, he replied, "Oh yes, if you ask some silly question repeatedly, then I may lose my temper."[25]

While he finds anger regrettable, he seems to believe that it's simply what we humans experience:

Questioner (Kantesh Guttal, Pune, India): "Do you ever feel angry or outraged?"

His Holiness: "Oh, yes, of course. I'm a human being. Generally speaking, if a human being never shows anger, then I think something's wrong. He's not right in the brain. [Laughs.]"[26]

On another occasion, responding to a similar question, His Holiness said, "If someone [says] they never lose their temper [I think] perhaps he comes from outer space."[27]

As you'll see, it's inevitable that humans experience inappropriate impulses. Your habits put you in good, if imperfect and struggling, company. The good news is that we are able to see our habits, acknowledge their existence, judge them inappropriate, and try to bring them under control. Rather than decry the unwanted impulses and blame yourself for them, take credit for your attempts to manage yourself and the effort you're putting into being how you mean to be.

In subsequent chapters, I'll give you evidence to support my claim that we are innocent of our impulses. I hope that evidence will help you view your behavior, and more importantly, yourself, with understanding and compassion. Obviously, habits of action, thought, and attitude are common and durable, but stay with me and I'll show you how to improve your ability to manage them.

But first you need to know what you're up against: how habits work, why they're so durable, why yours are what they are, and what opportunities you have for managing them. These are the topics I present in the remainder of Part I.

CHAPTER 3

Habitual Impulses

Habits are automatic. They don't need you. That's their nature and the source of their benefits and faults. They act whenever we call on them or when something triggers them. We choose to acquire some, for example how to serve a tennis ball, how to form our letters when we write, or how to drive a car. We acquire others unconsciously—how to walk, when and how to smile, what to do when frightened.

The habits we're working with in this book produce their impulses with no help from us. Indeed, they don't want our help. They're programmed to engage automatically. There's no provision for them to be interrupted or otherwise interfered with. A stimulus appears. The brain notices immediately, interprets it, and triggers what Antonio Damasio, professor of neuroscience at the University of Southern California, calls an "emotional action program," a reaction meant to deal with the stimulus or the consequences the brain has forecast (and may fear or desire).[28] If it suspects the stimulus might be dangerous, the emotional action program impels us to fight, flee, or freeze. If it's desirable—a reward or something else of apparent benefit—we're moved to capture it. All of that happens automatically, even before we're conscious of the stimulus's presence.

That's right; the brain notices what's going on, makes its decisions, and orders you to act before you've noticed there's something to react to. It's able to do this because in addition to *conscious* awareness, the brain has a faculty of *unconscious* awareness, which in some of the scientific literature is called *perception without awareness.*[29] You'll read a lot about this faculty in subsequent chapters.

That the subconscious can do this without our involvement or awareness is entirely contrary to our lived experience, as I mentioned in the Introduction. We're convinced that we see something, think about it however briefly, and decide what to do. We believe we consciously choose our reaction. But in fact our reactions are formulated and initiated subconsciously. And *subconsciously* means just that: out of sight of and inaccessible to awareness and conscious interference, as already discussed.

The ability of the brain to do things, see and hear things, and make decisions we're not aware of is one of the characteristics of human behavior that makes self-management and self-judgment so difficult. Ignorant of the role of the subconscious, we give ourselves too much credit for the good things we do and take too much blame for the failures. If you're not already familiar with the many things the subconscious does without our help or knowledge, you'll very likely be skeptical about what I'm saying, as I was when I started studying the neuropsychology of human behavior. I promise to give you a lot of evidence to support these statements.

The brain's automatically and subconsciously generated emotional action programs are key to our survival. The impulses they produce are a call to action—an impulse to act, accompanied by an emotion whose purpose is to motivate us to act on the impulse rather than resist it. The brain systems that produce them make complicated assessments of what's going on and give us near-perfect emotional action programs for dealing with everything that comes our way. We literally could not survive without the impulses they produce. No matter how subtle they are, every change in our environment generates reactions that affect us, often producing an impulse to act.

But the processes that create those impulses are not perfect. While the impulses are overwhelmingly accurate and appropriate, sometimes the processes that produce impulses to perform actions and generate attitudes and thoughts are inaccurate and inappropriate, and undermine our values and intentions. In addition, impulses give us no clues as to whether they're appropriate and what we'd choose to do—even whether they should be trusted or questioned. Left on their own, without oversight, those impulses will turn into action. It's our challenge and responsibility to identify the unwanted ones and interrupt them before they produce regrettable events.

Stimulus, Impulse, Action

Figure 1 is a simple schematic of a habit. Something happens (a stimulus) causing the subconscious to start the process of reaction, and maybe a half-second later we experience an impulse to act and feelings we call emotions. Usually we do what the impulse and emotion want us to do, and that is the right thing to do.

The subconscious constantly monitors and reacts to your external world as it communicates with you through your five senses. (Reactions triggered by thoughts, such as *Maybe I didn't lock the front door*, travel different pathways in the brain. The impulses they produce are not as predictable and may not arise as immediately as they do when triggered by external stimuli.[30]) An external stimulus could be something desirable, pleasant, disgusting, or threatening. It could reach us through seeing or hearing something pleasant or threatening: smelling something unusual, such as smoke, and feeling the impulse to rush to the door, or smelling something enticing and experiencing the impulse (desire) to possess it. It could be hearing something we think is demeaning, producing anger and the impulse to lash out, or feeling something brush against us, causing the brain to forecast something pleasant or dangerous to follow and producing an impulse to act accordingly.

Figure 1

Habit of Reaction

ACTION

Impulse
and
Emotion

Stimulus

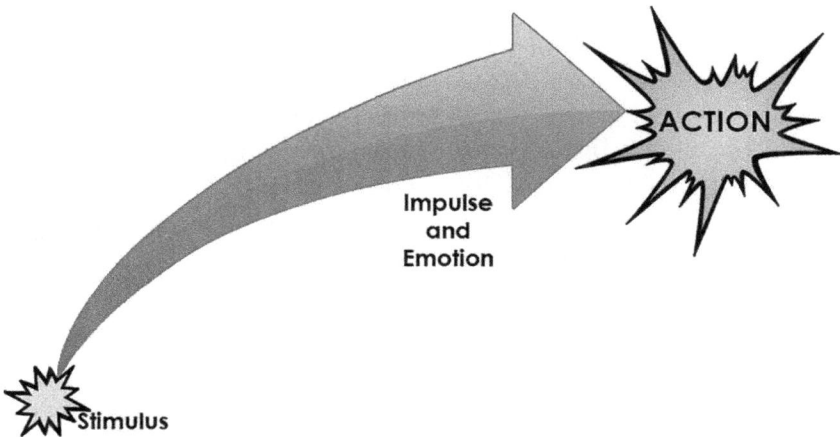

The brain has a lot to do to get from stimulus to impulse, and it does it on its own, without your awareness or involvement. It interprets sensory input, decides what it means, forecasts its consequences, and initiates the emotional action program, which grabs control of the brain structures[31] that set the body up to carry out the action part of the emotional action program, whether that's to hit, scream, freeze, smile, kiss, boast, lie, eat, cheat, hide, or negotiate, for example.

The body made ready for action (or inaction) produces physical feelings we become aware of, even if only subconsciously. But the brain is wired to interpret those physical feelings produced by those body states and turn them into what you and I call *emotions* or *feelings*, such as attraction, repulsion, anger, sadness, and joy. As mentioned before, the specific actions, attitudes, and thoughts that *your* brain wants *you* to perform result from *its* interpretation of the situation and your unique genetics and experience. (Chapter 11 explains how you develop your unique ways of reacting.)

I can't emphasize enough that everything from the sensory perception of the stimulus through production of the impulse and its associated feelings take place subconsciously and automatically. You're not involved. You first realize that something is happening when you experience the feelings and impulse to act (or think) the way the emotional action program wants you to. The processing of sensory information that produces emotional action programs is separate and distinct from the brain pathways that produce the *conscious* experience of those senses. Your emotional brain sees before you do because the processing that takes place for your conscious benefit takes longer than what the emotional brain uses to make its decisions. For example, the feelings and accompanying urges of the emotional action program stimulated by an image become conscious before the brain has processed the image enough for us to be able to *see* it in any detail. Consequently, we often experience the feelings and the accompanying thoughts and urges of the emotional action program before we know what might have caused them. In those cases, we awaken to a process that's flooded with emotion and potentially misguided intention, that's well underway, but not of our choosing. We feel emotion and the desire to act, and only then try to determine what justifies our feelings and the actions we're poised to carry out.[32]

When the brain's interpretation of the stimulus or its consequences is inaccurate, and/or when the action it prescribes is contrary to what you would choose in the circumstances, the impulses you feel will lead to unwanted actions or thoughts, unless you intervene. The emotion and urge to act are intertwined; you become caught up in finding the best way to carry out the impulse, even if the action is something you would not have chosen and will later regret.

CHAPTER 4

Sometimes You Manage Your Impulses

You have a lot of experience controlling your impulses and choosing to do something different. You probably don't realize what you do, don't think of it as a specific skill, or know how to apply it to habits you don't manage as well as you'd like. Here are two impulses you're probably good at managing—excellent examples of successful self-management.

Two Well-Managed Impulses

When You Itch, You Decide Whether and How to Scratch[33]

When you're bitten by a mosquito or get poison ivy (you poor thing), there are moments when you itch like crazy. But you probably pause and choose whether to scratch, and, if so, how. You want to scratch. The impulse is so strong that you want to scratch with abandon, and when you were a baby that's what you did, and your worried parents may have covered or restrained your hands to keep you from hurting yourself. But you're older and wiser now, and when you itch and feel the impulse to scratch, you become self-aware: you know you itch, know you want to scratch, and know (remember) that scratching has unwanted consequences. Not only is the itch present; you are too. And in that state of self-awareness you're of two minds: give in to the impulse, and if so figure out how to scratch and how hard, or grimace and bear it to keep from hurting yourself. You usually control yourself, at least a little.

Sure, sometimes you fail to do the *right thing*, and you scratch, and, if you're paying attention to anything, it's to how good that feels. But then you wake up to what you're doing, consider the consequences, and decide whether and how much to restrain yourself.

You Control Your Speech When It's Important

You probably adjust your words and tone of voice frequently to make them appropriate to whoever is listening, especially if you want something from the interaction. Everyone I've asked remembers a time when they consciously rejected and then changed the words spilling into their minds wanting to be sounded. They edited themselves on the fly rather than let the first words they thought turn into speech.

If you have a tendency to use harsh language or four-letter words to express yourself with close friends, maybe with colleagues and peers too, you're probably less colorful around small children, clergy, and others you're trying to impress, get something from, or not offend. You may dumb-down your language or spice it up in other circumstances. Maybe you can remember seeing yourself manipulating your speech to be shocking, clever, or flirtatious.

In managing this habit, you're trying to monitor and manage your desire to speak what your subconscious is motivating you to say and how to say it. The words could be chosen by an emotional action program reacting to what's going on. For instance, the emotion driving your subconscious choice of words and delivery might be in service of anger triggered by something that just happened, by the need to assert dominance, a desire to show you're creative or clever, a need to get something from the listener(s), or to convey feelings of compassion or desire. This self-editing is a particularly valuable technique for managing how we express emotions.

If we're so good at managing these two habitual impulses, how do we do it? What can we learn from these two? The next chapter answers those questions.

CHAPTER 5

The Anatomy of Self-Management

In this chapter, we'll look at how we experience self-management. We won't be looking at what produces our experiences, but at the stages we go through when trying to manage a habit. Knowledge of those stages can serve as helpful reference points as you try to manage your habits.

We'll start our tour from the beginning stage, before the stimulus appears, and look at successive stages through to the end, at which point we'll have executed our choice and be pleased, or we'll have failed and need to work with the failure.

There's a good chance that some of what you read in this chapter will resonate with your experience. We'll go deeper in subsequent chapters which will describe the psychological and neurobehavioral influences that produce what we experience. I believe the information I'm presenting will give you an understanding of the forces that shape your behavior, both the automatic habitual and the intentional. Knowing how these forces work will make you more likely to recognize when they're in play, equip you to call on forces that can help you, and reject those that oppose you.

We start this exploration of self-management experiences from wherever you and your mind might be before the stimulus that will produce an unwanted impulse appears. There's no itch and no impulse to scratch. There's no impulse to say something that could get you in trouble. Where are you and your mind? Chances are your mind is not tethered to anything in particular and you're not present to yourself. You're probably in the "Master Habit," the habit of being unaware of yourself, your surroundings, and what you're doing—a state of mind I'm about to describe. In Master Habit, you're on full-automatic. There's no awareness of the present moment; you're not present.

Distraction from Self Is the Master Habit

The only problem of our lives is this habit of getting distracted all the time.

—*Dzongsar Jamyang Kyentse Rinpoche*[34]

ACT FROM CHOICE

When we're distracted from full awareness of the present moment, we're deprived of the power to choose. We're not monitoring what we're doing, and certainly not noticing how it compares with our intentions. Instead, we're doing what our habits want us to do. We're trying to perform the habitual action as well as we can, without any concerns about whether the habitual reaction is what we would choose if we had a more global awareness of what was going on and what we're about to do in reaction.

Because habitual impulses come on quickly, forcefully, and are familiar, they proceed without calling attention to themselves. They grab control of the mind and force our attention to their objectives, co-opting us into the emotional action program's impulse and emotion, leaving us still distracted from our intentions and values, unaware there was an opportunity or need to choose what to do.

This habit of distraction-caused ignorance of what we're experiencing in the present moment is what permits impulse to become action. It is the Master Habit, the chief enabler of unwanted impulses. We are often distracted with no sense of where we are, what we're doing or feeling. Even if laser-focused on getting something done, we are usually unaware of ourselves, what's going on in the surroundings, and that it's us that's doing what we're doing. Our body is present but we're not. The Master Habit has many forms. Whether intent on something, lost in mindlessness, or daydreaming, we are disconnected from ourselves. In mindfulness speak, "We're not present."

It is difficult to be present—to be aware of and *fully* experiencing what's going on right now. We're so often off somewhere, mind doing its own thing, working over a past we can't change or recapture, or bouncing between hope and fear of a future entirely made up and usually nothing like what we'll actually face. Maybe instead of overworking the past or future, we're caught up in passive entertainment of some sort. How often have you awakened to realize you were away somewhere, couldn't remember where your mind was, and are wondering why you're now standing in the kitchen? What was it you wanted to get or do? How did you drive from here to there and have no memory of it?

In any of these states of mind, distracted and isolated from ourselves and our surroundings, unaware of what we're feeling, thinking, and about to do, the subconscious is able to get us to do almost anything it wants.

Witness the Master Habit in Action

Erik describes a shame-filled memory this way:

> He is bent over, lips six inches from the ear of his three-year-old daughter Amy, screaming at her as if she were a war criminal. Erik prepared her dinner and was in a rush. He needed to do something that couldn't be done until Amy finished eating. But Amy was just sitting there, food in front of her, showing no sign she'd ever eat it.

He remembers coming to so to speak, seeing himself feeling angry and hearing himself screaming into Amy's ear at the top of his lungs.

Forty years later, he remembers that moment, the shame he felt then, and the regret he feels now. The Master Habit gave Erik license to vent his frustration. He wishes the call to manage his speech had broken through the Master Habit before the screaming began.

Erik can't remember or imagine what could have been so important that he would have treated Amy that way. All of his attention was on extinguishing his feelings of frustration. Nothing else existed. The natural, programmed response to frustration is anger and an impulse to eliminate its cause.[35] In this case it was aimed at getting Amy to stop blocking him from doing what he wanted to do. The emotional power of his frustration was so great that it overpowered any consideration of managing himself, so he stayed in Master Habit and blew his top. Absent from consciousness were any feelings for the daughter he loves, and awareness that he was screaming at a three-year-old. It was only after becoming self-aware that he recognized what he was doing, and to whom; then he was able to see the greater significance of his actions. He says he never would have acted that way if he'd been more aware—of Amy, himself, and the situation.

Being taken over by an emotion is an entirely different experience from *seeing ourselves in the emotion*. When we're *in* the emotion, attention is focused on carrying out the emotional action program's impulse. We may be focused on delivering a mighty blow or the artful wisecrack. Our execution may be a thing of beauty, demonstrating power and skill to be proud of, except we shouldn't do it, and wouldn't have done it if we'd had our wits about us. When we're aware of what we're about to do, and see that it violates our intentions or values, we can interrupt the impulse, as we do when we control scratching and speech. But when we're distracted from the present, self-management is impossible.

Breaking Free of Master Habit

We stay in Master Habit until something breaks through our isolating distraction, at which point the present floods in. We become aware of ourselves and know we're about to act. That awareness opens us into a state of mind I call the *Choosing Space*. In addition to self-awareness, it is marked by the understanding that there is opportunity and need to choose what to do. For a moment at least, we're paused between impulse and action.

Introducing the Choosing Space

Between stimulus and response there is a space. In that space is our power to choose our response. In our response lies our growth and our freedom.

—*Viktor E. Frankl*[36]

Self-awareness creates the Choosing Space (Figure 2). We've caught ourselves "in the act," and there's the possibility to pause the action. When we're fully aware, we can feel the impulse to action or thought, and may be able to understand and appreciate the longer-term considerations too. We experience conflicting emotions. One set of emotions favors our habitual behavior—scratching, or voicing that oh-so-clever epithet. But we also feel the contrary impulses caused by our intention to avoid the damage of scratching, or the social opprobrium and other consequences of speaking inappropriately. In other words, we see the choices available to us and feel the conflicting emotions of each choice. And we feel the opportunity and need to choose.

The Choosing Space is essential to self-management. You can manage yourself, your habits, and your emotions if and only if you're aware of yourself as the actor facing your habits and intentions. It is fundamental that you can only manage what you're aware of. When you're unaware, you don't know there is anything to manage, much less that you can or should. You can manage the scratching and the words you speak only if you know you're moved to scratch or to speak inappropriately. When we're distracted and unaware, we're on autopilot, at the mercy of our impulses.

Figure 2
The Choosing Space

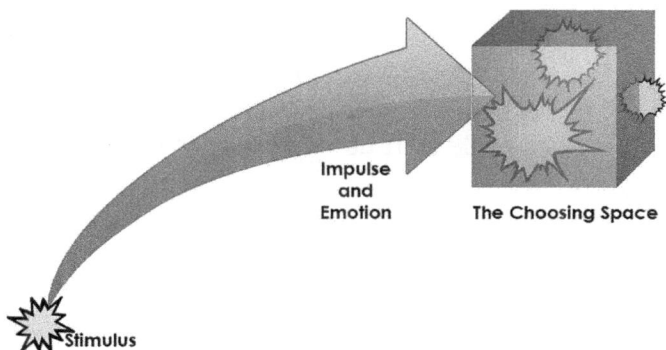

Impulse
and
Emotion

The Choosing Space

Stimulus

I'll have more to say about what we do when we're in the Choosing Space, but first we need to answer a number of questions, in particular what rescues us from Master Habit when we need to manage ourselves—that is, what turns our attention from its distracted state to what's going on in the present? Something has to happen to break through Master Habit and launch us into the Choosing Space. What does that? How does that work? And how can we make that happen when we want it to?

What Directs Attention to the Present?

Attention is one of those qualities of human experience we think we control, but really don't. Remember a teacher or parent telling you to pay attention? You immediately did but then lost it, and went back to Master Habit. The brain directs your attention.[37]

There's an extraordinary amount of scientific literature about attention and what directs it, the aim of which is to understand what makes us attend to one thing or another, exactly as I'm trying to answer the question "What brings attention to the present?"

What I get from the literature is the generalization that the brain decides what we pay attention to, based on its moment-by-moment changing priorities. Brain's many internal signals, each clamoring for priority, compete with each other and with stimuli from the external world that come to it through the sense organs. Internal and external signals compete with each other, and *brain* decides what is most important in the moment.[38] Sometimes internal processes get priority and determine what you should pay intention to, and sometimes external stimuli win the battle for priority, like when you walk into a parking meter or hear a siren.

Erik was rushed, hurrying to get to the next thing and frustrated by Amy's intransigence. His brain assigned its highest priority to reacting to the frustration, which locked out self-awareness and consideration of everything else.[39] Tsoknyi Rinpoche says, "People don't do things they don't intend because they want to.... We do negative things because of lack of attention."[40]

There's a reason that we're usually distracted. As you'll learn in Chapter 7, when the subconscious is in reaction mode, it is incredibly shortsighted. It focuses on the immediate. It bases its decisions entirely on what is directly in front of it. In this mode, it neither knows nor cares what it doesn't know, and what additional information might be desirable or available. It is Google-free! And this makes sense. Reaction mode is about only two things: keeping you from harm and capitalizing on immediately available opportunities. Nothing matters beyond what to do in this moment. Its decisions are devoid of longer-term considerations, of speculation about alternatives, or concern about consequences beyond the immediate effect of what it wants you to do. Your subconscious simply does not care about or consider possible consequences of the emotional action program it wants you to execute. That's long-range stuff. That's your responsibility, not your subconscious's.

Consequently, the first challenge of habit management is to wake you up to what's going on. That requires that we get the brain to turn our attention to the present—to the Choosing Space in which there is the possibility of seeing impulse, intention, alternatives, and consequences all together where they can compete. We make better decisions when we're aware of those considerations. We can decide what to do next. It's that simple—but profound and difficult.

The challenge is to get the subconscious to take us to the Choosing Space. We do that by teaching it which specific habits are contrary to our intentions—that we mean not to scratch or to speak inappropriately. Targeted mindfulness implants those intentions. When the subconscious knows what we do or don't want to do, it will try to take us to the Choosing Space whenever it discovers that we're about to violate our intentions. But the intentions have to be at least as important to us as competing demands for our attention.

First the brain has to know what we do and don't want. Here's the tool that makes targeted mindfulness work.

Introducing Your Sentinel

So the ability to pause and to not act on that first impulse
has become a crucial emotional skill in modern lives.

—*Daniel Goleman*[41]

Your Sentinel calls attention to unwanted impulses and the need to pause, jerking us out of Master Habit and into the Choosing Space.

The brain has a mechanism that can produce a high-priority signal to interrupt Master Habit and bring us to self-awareness when unwanted impulses appear. The brain keeps track of intentions and compares them to current impulses and behavior. When there's a mismatch, it issues that error signal, and if the signal has a high enough priority the brain will wake you up and direct your attention to whatever you're experiencing and feel impelled to do.[42] You become present and self-aware: you're in the Choosing Space. (Interestingly, this same brain mechanism keeps track of your promises and lets you know when you've broken one.)

This error mechanism is like a sentinel that stands watch and raises the alarm when something you're moved to do might be contrary to your intentions or values. Like a good sentinel, it does not tell you what to do, it only raises the alarm. What you do then is your responsibility, not the Sentinel's.

Let's see what brings your Sentinel into the action when you might want to scratch or speak inappropriately.

- The intention to scratch is innate. The intention not to scratch is learned. The learning came from your experience of what happens when you scratch too hard, and was reinforced by your parents' entreaties. That learning planted the intention to resist scratching in your brain's error-detecting alarm system—your Sentinel's inventory of things to watch out for. Consequently, when you're tempted to scratch, the Sentinel, noticing the mismatch between intention and your potential behavior, issues its mismatch signal to notify you to pay attention to what you're doing. If your intention to not scratch is stronger than competing demands for your attention at that moment, you're launched into the Choosing Space.

- I believe the intention to control speech is likely due to our need for social acceptance. Social acceptance is key to survival. As infants we depend on support from our caregivers. Even then, and later in life too, we need to be connected to and accepted by all the groups we associate with. Social acceptance appears to be a normal, high-priority human need—innate even.[43] Our ancestors rewarded those who honored societal norms and punished those who didn't. People who violated them weren't given good spots by the fire or choice products of the hunt, and probably didn't get to mate with the highest-status, most healthy individuals either. In our time, the need to belong feels as compelling. No matter how independent and confident we might feel, our subconscious antennae are always out, ready to warn us if we're in danger of behavior that could lead to ostracism from groups we depend on or want to join, even if we're not conscious of that concern. Indeed, one of our most common and troubling negative emotions is shame, which stems from our fear of people discovering some secret thought or behavior, and ostracizing us as a result.[44]

- Every group has its norms, and we try to conform to each group's norms as we move from group to group—from home, to work, to social activities, interacting with close friends, family, colleagues, customers, bosses and subordinates, and still others—so many disparate groups and their norms—so many groups in a single day. Whether we're seeking validation from a group or looking for a big order from a potential customer, we're launched into self-awareness when there's danger that we won't conform to norms of behavior. The danger of committing social errors makes us wary. Almost no one commits sloppy speech to a high-status person unless they're sick, exhausted, drunk, or drugged. (Fatigue, alcohol, and drugs weaken the prefrontal cortex, the part of the brain most involved in self-restraint.)

My experience and understanding of how the brain chooses where to direct attention is that the error function—the Sentinel function—is effective only to the extent that the intention is important to you, the intention is clearly understood, and the Sentinel has been well trained through frequent experience of disappointment and success. Most important is that you care enough about success or failure to *mean to* conform to the intention, and that you do so because success and failure have emotional significance for you.

Remember that the Sentinel's signal will only be important enough to the brain to direct your attention if the intention is important to you. That's a good part of the reason why you need to be committed to managing the habit if you want to be successful in managing it. If, instead of a strongly held intention, it's a *sort-of* aspiration, something you *might* want to address *someday*—a mild *want*—the Sentinel is not likely to be as effective as you'd want.

You might have guessed where I'm going. If the ability to manage your unwanted habits depends on your brain waking you up to an unwanted impulse, it's essential that you train this error function, your Sentinel, to wake you to the specific unwanted habits you care about. I'll show you how to do that in Part II.

Having given you some understanding of the Sentinel function, let's look now at what happens when you arrive in the Choosing Space. Remember, this is the space in which you'll decide what to do—whether to go along with the unwanted impulse or do something different—whether to scratch, whether to let the words flow unimpeded, whether to scream at Amy.

In the Choosing Space: Meeting Reactive Brain and Intentional Mind

Landing in the Choosing Space you're awake and aware, faced with the competition between your habitual reactions and your intentions. You feel both the unwanted impulse and your resistance to it—the need to scratch, the knowledge that it's dangerous to scratch, and your need to control yourself. Maybe this is a simple unwanted habit, and, as with scratching, you know the *right thing to* do; maybe not. It depends on whether your intention was to act a certain way in these situations or simply to avoid doing what the impulse wants of you; or maybe your intention is simply to pause and decide what to do. Regardless, you're now experiencing two minds—the mind of intention, which is at odds with the forces of a brain-produced emotional action program. I call those opposing forces *Reactive Brain* and *Intentional Mind*. The Choosing Space is their battleground. The stronger force will determine what you'll do next (Figure 3).

Figure 3

Intentional Mind Competes with Reactive Brain

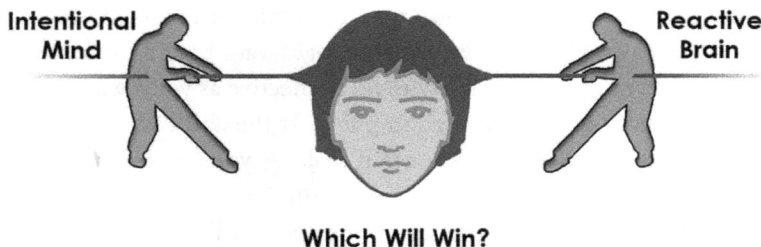

Intentional
Mind

Reactive
Brain

Which Will Win?

Reactive Brain is the collection of brain functions that chooses your emotional action programs and tries to get you to behave the way the emotional action program wants you to; it's everything the brain does, from experiencing the stimulus subconsciously and interpreting it, through formulating a reaction and issuing the emotional action program. Reactive Brain's functions do not include your conscious awareness of the stimulus. Conscious awareness is produced by separate brain functions and almost always appears later than the felt impulse produced by emotional action programs.

Reactive Brain is powered by the emotional center of the brain. Speaking generally, the brain structures implicated in performing Reactive Brain's functions are thought to involve mainly what is often called the limbic system, though not including the frontal cortex.[45] The only things that challenge Reactive Brain's impulses are Intentional Mind and, of course, changed circumstances.

Intentional Mind stands for the collection of brain functions that produce our intentions, attempt to bring them to consciousness, and try to execute them when reaction and intention disagree. It is guided by the actions, attitudes, and thoughts we choose, and therefore are conscious, by definition. When intentions appear in our conscious mind, we recognize they are ours. We believe in them and willingly defend them as the right thing to do.

Intentional Mind also includes brain functions that enable consciousness, including self-awareness and the decision-making processes of choosing and manifesting how we mean to be in action and thought.

To resist reaction, we have to be conscious of what's happening. We have to know our intentions, consciously choose what to do, and have the strength (willpower) to overcome Reactive Brain's impulses. To choose and achieve goals expressive of intention we use what are known as the *executive functions* of the brain. They include processes of self-management such as planning and prioritizing, setting goals, problem solving, modifying behavior, generating strategies, coordinating information, choosing what to do and think about, and sustaining and disengaging attention and effort. Executive functions also include exercising willpower to overcome Reactive Brain. All of these functions rely mainly on brain structures in the frontal cortex, the part of the brain right behind the forehead and eyes.

The competition between reaction and intention is nothing unusual for the brain. Competition is the brain's thing; it literally seethes with competition. The business of the brain is done by neurons communicating with each other and with other parts of the body—muscles, glands, and organs. Neurons receive input from other neurons, from nerve cells located throughout the body that acquire information about our sensory experiences—sight, sound, smell, touch, and taste—and from the bodily systems that report to the brain their position, condition, chemistry, and degrees of activation, and from lots and lots of other neurons in the brain itself.

There are about 100 billion neurons in the human brain grouped in structures that, generally speaking, have particular roles. Even more awe inspiring than the number of neurons is the complexity of their interconnections: those 100 billion neurons make about 100 *trillion* connections with other neurons. While the number of connections neurons make varies widely, the average is about a thousand connections per neuron. Most of their connections are with other neurons, both within their home structures and in structures that compete with their own. Think, metaphorically, of structures that say *no* communicating and competing with structures that say *yes*, and structures saying *more* competing with structures that say *less*.

Each brain structure has its own ideas of what is important and needs to be done. At its best, this competition is our innate system of checks and balances. Among those checks and balances are reaction and intention. They continuously check on each other. Overwhelmingly they agree, or intention doesn't notice until too late, but when Intentional Mind and Reactive Brain disagree, the stronger one dictates what we do.

When intention and reaction disagree and Reactive Brain wins the competition, or when Intentional Mind is offline in Master Habit leaving Reactive Brain in charge, we may mean to be kind but are unkind, to be generous but are stingy, to be calm, patient, and loving but are excitable, impatient, and judgmental instead.

Imagine you are in the Choosing Space feeling you should choose. The battle with the unwanted impulse hasn't been won yet. You're feeling it but haven't given in. Let's imagine that you want to scratch but haven't, you want to shout that oh-so-creative insult but haven't yet; you are in that moment between screaming at Amy and calming down; you are holding the chocolate chip cookie in your hand and thinking you should put it back in the cookie jar. Intentional Mind and Reactive Brain are competing for control. I'll describe the brain mechanisms that make the competition inevitable in subsequent chapters, but for now let's stick with what you're going through.

Needing More than Awareness

Unfortunately, awareness of being in the Choosing Space and seeing the competition between Reactive Brain and Intentional Mind isn't enough to overcome Reactive Brain's impulse. When you enter the Choosing Space, you're feeling the momentum of Reactive Brain's choice. If you want to make this an evenly matched battle, you have to bring all of intention's armaments to bear immediately. Your armaments are all of the considerations that led you to want intention to vanquish the unwanted impulse.

Arriving in the Choosing Space you know your intentions, but your access to the considerations that motivate you is blocked by the momentum of the unwanted impulse. As you'll learn later in Part I, your emotions are actually feelings caused by the chemical changes to your body setup by the emotional action program to motivate you to carry out its orders. These changes are not instantly reversible; consequently, the emotional feelings that are moving you to go along with the impulse don't immediately subside. Your situation is analogous to recovering from a drugged state, or waiting for the pain in a stubbed toe to subside; it takes a short time, and before the chemical effects of the emotion dissipate, it is difficult to consider arguments against the unwanted impulse. In other words, to some degree you are still under the influence of the emotion that is motivating the unwanted impulse.

You make your best decisions when you are aware of your motivations and the reasons for them. Those reasons include your knowledge of the consequences, the costs, benefits, and effects on your values of going with the impulse or choosing something else. In practice, when you're able to access those considerations, they don't come to you as a bunch of details; you simply arrive at wordlessly knowing the alternative values of going with reaction or intention. While wordless, you feel the consequences of your alternatives vividly in a *Knowing Mind*.

Sometimes the consequences of unwanted impulses are so dire and antithetical to your values that this transformation to the more Knowing Mind happens automatically, as perhaps when you're moved to strike someone, or speak the unspeakable, and stopped just short of completing the action. At other times, you might go directly to intention because the unwanted impulse is weak, and the forces of Reactive Brain are easy to overcome. But other times, you're on that diet, there's a cookie in your hand, it's warm, and the smell is so enticing. You know you shouldn't eat it; your motivation isn't fully there yet, and you say something to yourself equivalent to *oh, never mind*, or *not right now*. You eat the cookie and immediately berate yourself for caving in. (In Part II and the Resource Companion you'll learn tools to help you resist impulse's immediate demands while you choose what to do and build intention's strength.)

Let's assume that you're in the Choosing Space, and by one means or another you've decided to reject the unwanted impulse and do something different. At this point it's only a decision. Now you have to activate it. You flip the switch. But will it happen as you've chosen?

Whenever you attempt to do something contrary to your impulses you call on willpower to make it happen. It may involve competition as minor as telling your hostess the food was great when it was awful,[46] or as significant as refraining from hitting someone. Regardless of how easy or difficult the conflict, resolving it intentionally takes willpower.

Do you have enough willpower to enforce your choice? Will you overcome the forces of Reactive Brain, or will Reactive Brain win?

Willpower

Willpower plays an essential role in self-management. It is willpower that blocks the power of impulses, keeps them at bay, provides the strength to overcome resistance, and turns intention into action. Reaction would always win if we didn't have willpower to help us effect our choices. But willpower is not always strong enough to overcome reaction.

The myths about willpower are pernicious. Too often failures of willpower are blamed on weakness of character.[47] But that school of thought is contrary to the scientifically discovered facts about what willpower is and how it works.

Countless experiments by Roy Baumeister, at the University of Florida, his colleagues, and others investigating willpower, have demonstrated that willpower is like a muscle; it is more physical than mental. Like a muscle, its strength and stamina are limited at any point in time.[48] Whatever your level of physical conditioning, you can only lift so much weight when you are at your best; you can only hold a weight above your head for a finite amount of time, or lift it off the floor a limited number of times before the muscles (not you) are fatigued and you simply cannot do it anymore. To be clear: it is mostly your muscles, not you, that give up.

You use willpower whenever making decisions or overcoming physical or mental resistance, no matter how small the effort, even when choosing the colors for your new car, trying to force yourself to go to the gym, or trying to restrain your speech. As in the weightlifting analogy, recent use of willpower leaves you with less strength and stamina to apply during the next challenge. Baumeister calls that state of diminished willpower *ego depletion*.

Other factors determine how much willpower you have, and it helps to keep the muscle analogy in mind. For example, your baseline amount of willpower is influenced by genetics. Consequently, some people have stronger or weaker baseline willpower than others, independent of their differences in *character* or determination. Still, regular use, including purposeful training, makes willpower stronger, and lack of use weakens it.

Age is also a factor. The willpower *muscle* is the prefrontal cortex, which is not fully developed in humans until the mid-twenties, which explains why adolescents are so reckless. According to the National Vital Statistics System, the three leading causes of death for people age twelve through nineteen are accidents, homicide, and suicide. It is also well established that the prefrontal cortex tends to weaken at the other end of life. Consequently, older individuals may have greater difficulty controlling their impulses, simply as a result of normal aging. Disease and damage affecting the prefrontal cortex can also cause changes in behavior; indeed, this was one of the first indications scientists had of the relationship between brain anatomy and behavior, and of the localization of brain functions to specific structures.[49]

Though many factors can diminish the amount of willpower available at any point in time, it is also true that you can increase your baseline willpower through disciplined training, by repeatedly pushing yourself to the limits of your willpower, for example.[50]

All of the factors I've mentioned so far influence how much willpower you might have at some particular moment, but another factor also influences whether you will have enough to carry out your intentions. That factor is the strength of whatever it is you're trying to overcome. Reactions are accompanied by emotions, and emotions vary in the force they exert on us. While you use willpower to overcome all manner of Reactive Brain-produced resistance, the force of that resistance varies depending on the brain's interpretation of the stimulus it's reacting to. You use willpower to decide what to choose for breakfast, to stay up late to finish a report or taxes, to ask to speak to your boss or partner about some touchy subject, and to leave the safety of a battlefield trench to face the enemy's withering machine-gun fire. The first of those examples is trivial; the rest vary in difficulty depending on the situation, training, and your emotional history with those kinds of experiences. In any case, there's no way for anyone to know in advance whether they'll have enough willpower to overcome Reactive Brain when the time comes.

I've taken up your time to introduce you to the nature of willpower and the factors that influence its strength in order to dissuade you from equating character and willpower—more importantly, to ask you to be careful about judging yourself by your occasional failures to manage yourself. If you equate willpower or self-control with your self-worth, you are exposing yourself to potential, unnecessary damage to your self-confidence.

To reassure yourself that this is true, recall the heartbreaking tales of members of the armed forces who, after receiving traumatic brain injuries and PTSD, are afraid to ask for help or to fairly assess their needs. They judge themselves unworthy because of the false beliefs, common in the military culture of old, that willpower, self-control, persistence, and a cool head are measures of character and self-worth, irrespective of any possibility that there might be mitigating factors—including damage to their physical brains. It's a cruel judgment that does not take into account everything we know about how body and brain influence our behavior and thus our ability to function.

Along similar lines, I recommend you think holistically about what is going on when your willpower fails. Please be careful how you judge yourself at those times. As mentioned in the Introduction, I believe that you are who you mean to be when you're sincerely engaged in the effort. So, what then are we to think of ourselves when we fail and unwanted impulses take over? What do we do when faced with failure of will or discipline? How should we handle those situations and ourselves then?

Those questions bring us to the last topic in this tour of self-management experiences, namely, what to do when self-management fails and reaction wins.

Handling Self-Management Failure

When your willpower is strong enough and you are able to act from choice, everything is fine, and you are justifiably proud of your ability to manage yourself—that time. But, no matter how good you are at managing your emotions, your habits, and yourself, there will be times when the impulse is too strong and/or willpower is too weak. How should you feel? How should you judge yourself after you've scratched the mosquito bite, yelled at Amy, eaten the chocolate chip cookie, watched yourself say something outrageous and inappropriate to a disapproving listener? It will happen. Have you failed? Are you a failure?

I believe it's objectively a failure when impulse wins over intention, and it's always best to be honest with yourself: you intended to do one thing but went along with something you didn't want to do, so *objectively* you failed. We profit by being objective about our behavior rather than making up excuses or lapsing into denial. At the same time, I think it's essential that you distinguish between acknowledging failed performance and considering yourself a failure. If you have that tendency, try to overcome it. It's aggression against yourself, and it's not helpful. It will hobble your attempts at self-development.

Here are two pieces of advice about managing negative self-talk when unwanted reactions break through your willpower. The first comes from Stephen Levine, a spiritual teacher who, with his wife Ondrea, has spent a lifetime working with people facing terminal illnesses. The second comes from Pema Chödrön. Both approaches counsel realism and compassion for yourself.

Levine uses a metaphor that goes something like this: you've practiced lifting weights at the gym, aiming to lift 150 pounds comfortably. Maybe you started with 10-pound weights. You're now up to 75 pounds when someone walks through the door and throws a 100-pound weight at you. Levine says, "It knocks you down. Big surprise! Have mercy on yourself."[51] There is nothing to forgive. You hadn't been training long enough to handle 100 pounds. Get up. Go back to the weight bench and keep working with the weights.

And I'll add this: after reaching your goal of handling 150-pound weights with ease, you'll be rightfully proud of yourself. But trust me. Life is full of 1,000-pound weights that you can neither prepare for nor resist. My wish is that they pass you by, but that would make you both lucky and rare.

There are many things you could gain from this book; among the most valuable would be encouragement to judge yourself fairly, to acknowledge your faults when appropriate, without letting them influence your assessment of your self-worth.

Along the same lines, Ani Pema's advice is to choose regret, not guilt.[52] Some define guilt as coming from the sense of having violated one's personal standards.[53] It can lead to feelings of shame and aggression against oneself. As mentioned earlier, shame is an emotion that is actually fear of ostracism—that is, fear that if people found out about our secret thoughts or activities, they'd have nothing to do with us. (There's more about handling shame and guilt in the Resource Companion.) Feelings that we are bad, worthless, and worse are forms of self-aggression we inflict on ourselves. They are harmful and useless.

In contrast, regret is objective acknowledgment of what we did, but without the baggage of self-judgment. If our behavior hurt someone or something, we immediately make things right, apologize, and make amends. We figure out what happened, what we did, and why. We feel regret for what we did without overdoing it, and we resolve to be more careful in the future, and to try not to do it again. Then it's over and we can try to go forward knowing we did what we could do to rectify the error and try not to err that way again.

Chödrön and Levine counsel us to be realistic and compassionate. You may remember that in the Introduction I wrote that you are the person you mean to be if you're working hard at it and are dismayed when impulses break through. Judgment-free, realistic self-appraisal is one of the greatest gifts you can give yourself. And the effort to do your very best should count a lot in your attempts at self-appraisal.

There's one more thing to add to this advice. Take seriously any feelings like disappointment, sadness, and loss. Failure of intention and simple mistakes can lead to bad outcomes. You missed your goal. Other people were hurt physically or emotionally. We endanger a friendship, a job, and then we try to figure out what went wrong.

Make amends.

Choose regret over guilt.

If the failure to manage yourself the way you wanted caused you to feel hurt and sad—any negative feelings like those—take a few moments to acknowledge and honor those feelings. Give them respect. Give yourself the same affection and compassionate care you'd give a friend or child who felt like you now feel. Don't be afraid of turning those feelings into a pity party; your BS detector will catch you out if you do, so you don't have to worry about that. Simply acknowledge that what happened hurt you and made you feel bad.

No one can validate you as fully as you can. It may seem strange when you first do it for yourself, but your respect for your own feelings heals you in ways that nothing else can. So take a moment to apply that balm of self-validation. Then it will feel okay to pick yourself up and move ahead, knowing you've done everything you could have done in those circumstances, and have taken good care of others as well as yourself.

Learn to Judge Yourself Fairly

As I wrote earlier, judge yourself fairly or you will give yourself too much credit for your accomplishments and be too harsh on yourself when you fail, which you surely will do. (By the way, if you know a sure-fire way to grow and succeed without failure, write a book. You'll make a fortune.)

I encourage you to try to judge yourself by the same standards you judge others by. Aim for high but attainable goals, then fairly evaluate your successes and failures. And, in particular, when trying to figure out *who* you are, give fair weight to effort, even if you're unable to carry out your intentions. That's very difficult for many of us to do because we're afraid we'll be too lenient on ourselves. We worry that we'll lower our standards, that judging on the basis of anything other than clear, objective standards is a cop-out.

Many individuals and organizations reject judgments that include consideration of effort, insisting that only results count. That's often appropriate. We expect accountants to total figures accurately; restaurants to pass sanitary inspections; surgeons to amputate the diseased limb, not the good one; pilots to get the airplane from there to here without crashing; and of course, rightly or wrongly, we expect our soldiers to achieve their objectives or die trying. Fair enough, but for me, self-judgment should be based on more than objective standards.

Maybe the following thought experiment will help. Suppose a person is determined to win a gold medal in Olympic figure skating. She trains six hours every school day and ten hours every day there's no school. She maintains this grueling schedule for twelve years. How should she judge herself when she comes in second? Is she out of integrity? Has she violated her standards or intentions when she comes in second? Has she broken her promise to herself when she doesn't win, or is she only guilty of picking an objective whose achievement was not under her control? For sure, she wasn't a *good enough figure skater* on the day she competed in the Olympics, but isn't she a good enough *person* every day? She chose a good objective but not a good standard for measuring integrity or character.

The only thing competitors can control is their individual effort. The results of competition display the competitors' relative skill, but their rankings say nothing about the integrity with which they pursued their goals. Coming in second could represent a greater personal achievement than the winner's. The same could be said for competitors who achieved even lower rankings. Indeed, the person who came in thirty-seventh may have exceeded tests of personal integrity and discipline as demanding as any faced by those who ranked higher. It's a fact that her performance did not measure up to the skill exhibited by the thirty-six people who scored higher, but should she be ranked thirty-seventh in character? Should she rank herself as less worthy or capable as a person?

One can think the figure-skating analogy is off the mark, but only by ignoring the fact that we compete with a subconscious that is powerful and independent. But what about those emotional action programs, you may wonder? Where do they come from? Isn't it a measure of character that when stressed you overeat, that after a bad day at work you're short-tempered with innocents? Aren't those reactions measures of character?

Yes and no. No as to the impulses, because, as you will see, those were created by happenstance; they're simply the results of how your genetic dispositions have influenced your reactions to what you've experienced, and the emotional habits that developed as a result. And, of course, what you experienced was never solely under your control. The subconscious designed your habitual patterns without your input or permission. But, yes, our reactions are a sign of character if they hurt others and we're not earnestly trying to manage them.

Having invited you to value effort as well as achievement when judging yourself, some might think I'm recommending an easy way out that conflicts with the previous sentence's statement of responsibility. That's not my intention.

I encourage you to use every bit of discipline and willpower you're capable of to achieve your objectives. Some people are more highly disciplined than others. Some are naturally so as part of their genetics and experience. Regardless of where we start, effective training can give us more willpower and discipline than we'd have otherwise, and I encourage everyone to work at increasing theirs. The military is able to train average men and women to do things they probably never thought they could, and to *want* to do them. Moreover, there is much evidence from research by Caroline Dweck at Stanford University[54] and Angela Duckworth[55] at the University of Pennsylvania that beliefs about yourself and the importance of what you're trying to accomplish can substantially improve your performance.[56]

Having said that, let me state my views on discipline as clearly as I can. Bring every bit of discipline you're capable of to managing yourself. Don't be shy. Don't be lazy. Don't hold back. Do your best. If you can push your way through to your goals, by all means do that. Failure to use the willpower and discipline you're capable of is a sign of either a lack of commitment to your goals or laziness—or both. Don't feel you have to get fancy about approaching any of the goals you care about. Don't wait to learn something from me or anyone else before starting. The Nike® slogan says it all: "Just do it." Don't creep up on the amount of discipline you use. Apply it all from the beginning. You can always back off if there's good reason to.

The takeaway here is that willpower is a real thing, just as your physical strength is. If you try to override reaction when the emotional action program's impulse is very strong, or your willpower is at a low due to depletion or underdevelopment, you may not succeed in managing your behavior. The state of your willpower reserves could be more determinative of your success in any particular moment than your determination or character. For that reason, be very careful about judging failures of willpower.

Key Takeaways

We've come to the end of this trip through the stages of self-management. Here is an overview of what we've covered, including some key concepts and terms:

- We're usually in Master Habit, distracted from any awareness of ourselves, our feelings, alternatives, and the consequences of what we're doing or preparing to do, even if we're highly focused and concentrating on carrying through with some specific action.

- A stimulus occurs and is perceived by the subconscious, which interprets it and issues an emotional action program meant to deal with its forecast consequences. The emotional action program sets up the body to respond, gives us an impulse to act, and directs our attention to the stimulus. The state of our bodies is fed back to the brain, which interprets those feelings as emotions, which in turn motivate us to carry out the emotional action program's impulse.

- We become aware or we don't. Usually we stay in Master Habit and simply execute the emotional action program's demands.

- Otherwise, our Sentinel, the error mechanism that lets us know when there is a mismatch between intention and behavior, detects the mismatch which, when important enough to us, creates a high-priority signal that overcomes other demands for our attention, bringing us to the present—to awareness of our self and the situation. The Sentinel is effective if, and only if, the intention is important to us and the Sentinel has been well trained (as discussed in Part II).

- Having been launched into being present, we're in the Choosing Space. Our attention is directed to the stimulus. It is usually here that we have the first intimation of the stimulus and our reaction to it. In the Choosing Space, we are self-aware, aware of our feelings, what we're about to do; we may be aware of our alternatives and their consequences. The emotional action program's impulse is paused. We're of two minds, witnessing and managing the competition between Intentional Mind and Reactive Brain.

- Having chosen what to do, we carry out our choice. If we choose to go along with the emotional action program's impulse, it's easy. Resisting the impulse is hard or easy depending on the state of our willpower in comparison to the strength of Reactive Brain's impulse.

- There will be times when we cannot overcome the impulse— when our attempts at self-management will fail. I encourage you to make amends to anyone injured by your actions, and to choose regret instead of guilt. That includes being objective about what happened and your judgment of yourself. Further, be sure to validate any feelings of loss that resulted from the failure to manage yourself the way you wanted. Finally, judge yourself as you would someone who faced the challenge you faced with your level of intention, but who also failed.

That, I believe, is the sequence of events, challenges, and aids we usually experience when a habit arises. With the exception of the discussion of the Sentinel, that description is only about what we experience. It tells us very little about what is going on in the subconscious to produce the specific habits we feel or why they are so difficult to overcome. The rest of Part I describes the underlying forces that created and now maintain your habits. We'll start on those topics in the next chapter, which describes Mind and Brain, the conscious and unconscious you.

CHAPTER 6

Mind, Brain, and Behavior

I made a number of assertions in previous chapters that may have struck you as novel, maybe outlandish, and were almost certainly inconsistent with your experience of yourself. Introducing Reactive Brain, I alluded to the powerful, important, but subconscious processes of the brain that try to get you to do things without your knowledge or agreement. This is in stark contrast to our sense that we direct everything—that we are responsible for everything we think or do. Can it really be true that we are so heavily influenced by aspects of our own being and know nothing about them? Taken together, those assertions about the subconscious activity of the brain indicate that we are not the authors of our actions, thoughts, and attitudes to the extent we think. Moreover, they indicate that our emotions are produced by those same subconscious forces rather than by the rational cognition, judgment, and choice that we're capable of and so proud of.

Here are the basic allegations I'm making and will support in this and subsequent chapters:

- Our subconscious sees what's going on before we do. It forecasts whether what it sees is good, bad, or irrelevant; decides what we should do as a result; and produces emotion-propelled impulses that direct and motivate us to fill *their* prescriptions for action, their emotional action programs. That sequence of events comes from the emotional or Reactive Brain.

- Reactive Brain's choices of how to interpret and react to stimuli depend on, and are formed by, our genetics and experience, not our conscious judgment.

- What we call "emotions" are actually our hard-wired interpretations of the physical feelings caused by the way the brain has set the body up to react.

- We can't decide if or how to react to what we're experiencing until we become conscious of the stimulus. Even when conscious of it, we usually accept Reactive Brain's choice of how to respond, due to inattention or the power of the emotion that Reactive Brain produced.

ACT FROM CHOICE

These statements attribute an enormous amount of power to the subconscious and very little to the "actor" we think we are. And yet it's that actor that we know best. When you think of yourself, you're thinking of that actor, yourself as experienced in consciousness, not your subconscious, which you can't see or directly evaluate. You have no direct experience of your subconscious and therefore no intuition about its role or power as a separate force within you. It's not that you're uniquely handicapped in this way; we all are—every one of us—and that handicap makes it very difficult to accept these statements as true.

We think we do things because we considered what was going on and decided what to do. We yell at the kids because they've broken a rule. Okay. Maybe we overreact, but it's our decision, sort of. Isn't it? We say things to make things—ourselves, in particular—sound better than they are because we want to show we are successful, have value, and are important. Maybe we shouldn't, but it's our decision to say those things, isn't it? We eat the whole bag of chips or cookies because we feel bad and want comfort, but that's our decision, right? Yet for some of us, the fact that we experience these impulses and don't override them makes us think we're weak or "bad." If we have free will, what are we to make of our transgressions? We feel the way the Apostle Paul did. We want to do good but often do the opposite. So we must be weak or bad, right?

Well, yes and no. It's true that we often run out of willpower and can't successfully manifest our intentions, as I explained in the previous chapter. But, as much as it's *yes*, it's also *no*. And it's the *no* part that we'll explore in this chapter. I will explain and support those statements describing the power of the subconscious—of Reactive Brain—to influence our actions, attitudes, and thoughts. It's not all bleak. Our subconscious speaks first and powerfully, but it can be overridden, as I illustrated earlier in discussing our ability to control how to deal with the itch and the urge to say something inappropriate.

Nevertheless, this chapter and the next are meant to give you an appreciation for what you're working against when your intentions and reactions disagree. In these two chapters we'll look at evidence that reveals that our emotions are *primary* influences of our actions, but lack conscious input from us. In this context, primary refers to *when* things occur in time, not which force is ultimately stronger. In other words, primary refers to the fact that the subconsciously produced impulses and emotions come first in time before our conscious appraisal. I'll also discuss the mechanisms we use to override them.

The material I present in this chapter comes primarily from psychological experiments focused on understanding how humans behave. Psychological experiments are often about seeing how people react to certain stimuli, and how those reactions change as a result of changes in the conditions that researchers manipulate. Psychological experiments tend to look at us from the outside, which is to say they don't describe what the brain itself is doing. Understanding the physical operation of the brain is important to round out our understanding of why it's so hard to exert will or choice in the face of reaction, and why reactions are so durable. We'll get to all of that in this and later chapters.

Why We Need to Understand Mind and Brain

While it's important that you accept responsibility for your behavior, you need to understand that there are limits to how much control you can have. Put simply, you need to know how much control you can reasonably expect to have over your behavior, and what could be beyond you. Not knowing leads to confusion and unnecessary guilt, shame, negative self-judgment, and denial, as I mentioned previously.

Studies of people trying to change addictive habits, smoking for example, show that those who relapse—who fail at their ability to abstain from their addictions—"...feel like failures, embarrassed, ashamed and guilty. These individuals become demoralized and resist thinking about behavior change."[57] My experience is that those of us who are trying to change even less addictive habits suffer similarly and tend to give up because we don't understand why our habits are so compelling and hard to manage. I believe that understanding how habits work, and having a realistic knowledge of the limitations of willpower as discussed in Chapter 5, helps us maintain motivation even as we experience occasional failures, as we surely will in our attempts to improve our self-management.

Brain and Mind Are Not What We Experience

Maybe 5 percent of brain activity is conscious; the rest happens in our subconscious.[58] By definition, we can't experience the subconscious in action; consequently, we have no intuition about what it is doing or how it affects us, nor does anything in our experience remind us that there's more going on than what we're conscious of.

We learn about our subconscious by wondering why we do some of the things we do that disturb or amaze us, from inferences about what we do, and from hearing the results of scientific inquiry. Our lack of any "feel" or intuition about the role and power of the subconscious is one of the most confounding aspects of human experience, and a significant cause of the difficulties we experience when trying to manage ourselves. We can read about the mind and the subconscious, as maybe you have, but we can't experience it firsthand because subconscious means just that: hidden from conscious view, inaccessible to direct observation.

Compare that to our understanding of and intuition about our physical bodies. We have direct, conscious experience of the body and know a lot about how it works, its strengths and limitations. We're pretty clear about how injuries and training can affect us. That the body's performance depends on its strength, conditioning, flexibility, and dexterity is obvious. If we have a physical weakness, say an arm injury or a sore hand, we feel the physical sensations, understand the effects, and know how to compensate to keep from making things worse. When we're injured, we mostly accept that we can't return to pre-injury functioning until we heal. We know if we use a muscle a lot it fatigues even to the point of uselessness. (How many times can you bend your arm while holding a twenty-pound weight before you can no longer bend it?) We know and accept that we're too weak to lift the front of a car off the ground, and we know that we have to train if we're to do something requiring great strength or athletic prowess.

But the brain is invisible and largely without physical feeling. To understand the condition of your brain, you would have to consult a neurologist, and even then you would have no feel for what she told you. Unlike an injured arm or knee, an injured brain is hard for us to comprehend or get a feel for. There would just be the symptoms—terrors, mania, irascibility, the inability to put thoughts together, to process certain kinds of information, to control emotions, to think things through, to move the way you want, and/or to speak properly—all so different from before the brain was affected. The resulting feeling would be one of helplessness and maybe anger. "Why can't I control this? I should be able to control it, to will it, but I can't." A person struggling with a brain injury or dementia could have a hard time determining whether something was wrong or different. We know when we've sprained an ankle, but do we know when we're reacting differently to what's going on around us?

Mind and Brain Defined

I would like you to think about, to compare and contrast, two aspects of the human brain that I refer to as **M**ind (with a capital M) and **B**rain (with a capital B). "Mind" stands for the human faculties of being consciously aware—to consciously know what's going on outside and inside of us, to choose and try to enforce our choices of behavior and thoughts. Mind both knows and knows that we know. It knows what we like and don't like, what we want, what we intend, what we've lost and gained, and how we feel. Mind is our instrument of cognition, which is defined as "the process by which we come to know the world.... More specifically, cognition refers to the ability to attend to external stimuli or internal motivation, to identify the significance of such stimuli, and to plan meaningful responses to them."[59]

Mind includes the ability to call upon the *executive functions* I described in the previous chapter in connection with the definition of Intentional Mind. Most executive functions are used consciously, because we have to be conscious in order to choose, otherwise the choice is the result of preprogramming of some sort that runs without our involvement. Consciousness requires the use of working memory, another function of the frontal cortex. When we're conscious of something, it is in working memory. We are not consciously aware of things when they are not in working memory.

I use "Brain" to represent *everything affecting reactive behavior* that is not Mind. The brain activity we'll consider in this book is largely restricted to what is involved in the instigation and carrying out of reactive impulses, both the wanted and unwanted ones. In other words, the formation and activity of Reactive Brain. Much more than that goes on in the brain, but it is outside the scope of this book.

Mind

We experience things consciously and subconsciously. The difference is that we don't know what our subconscious experiences until the results emerge in consciousness. Some things Brain is aware of never rise to consciousness.

Among the most significant things we experience consciously is our experience of ourselves. We know we think. We know when we're angry, hungry, or feeling sexy. If we're paying attention, we know what our physical bodies are doing: picking up the salt, sending a text message. We can consciously decide to bake a cake, then experience ourselves making it, have a judgment about how it turned out, and feel proud or bad about it accordingly. (Of course, often we do any and all of that mindlessly—performing the functions and thinking about something else unless something calls us out of Master Habit.)

Whatever we're doing or experiencing consciously feels like all there is to know of ourselves in the moment. We'd like to think that we have a lot of say in determining what we want, do, and think. Our experience of ourselves as individuals capable of choosing and acting is based on conscious experiences.

In short, we experience ourselves and our Minds like this (Figure 4): Mind is everything that counts. Brain, the subconscious, can't be all that important, can it?

Figure 4
Me and My Mind

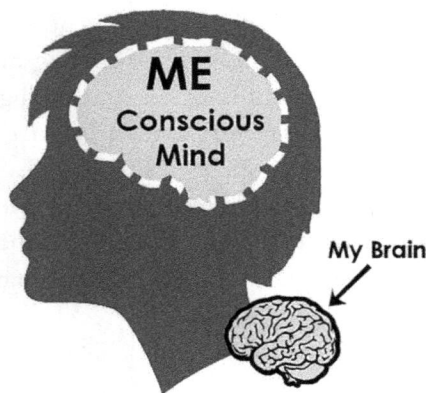

This Is the Way It Seems

Brain

As I use it, Brain represents all the functions involved in reaction formation that we can't consciously witness. Though we can't see Brain in action, we can and do experience its products, the impulses it generates, and what it's trying to tell us or get us to do. But the processes that produce those results are invisible, and we're not able to fiddle with them before Brain pokes something into consciousness that we can be aware of and work with. (Keep in mind that I use small-b brain to refer to the entire physical brain, which includes both Mind and Brain functions.)

If only 5 percent or so of all human brain activity is conscious, the other 95 percent is subconscious: it's busy running the machinery. Consider this: it takes the coordination of about 50 muscles to rise from sitting to standing, and about 300 for you to simply stand still! Mind has no clue how to do any of that. Brain tries to figure out what's going on around us so that it can identify threats and opportunities, and develop responses to what it sees and anticipates.

When you realize that much of that 95 percent of brainpower that is acting subconsciously is trying to save us from threats and give us an opportunity to breed and feed, you can see that the real picture is not the one above (Figure 4), but what we see in Figure 5: not big Mind, little, inconsequential Brain, but little Mind and big, very consequential human brain that Mind can neither see nor understand directly, doing nearly all the work.

Figure 5
Me and Brain

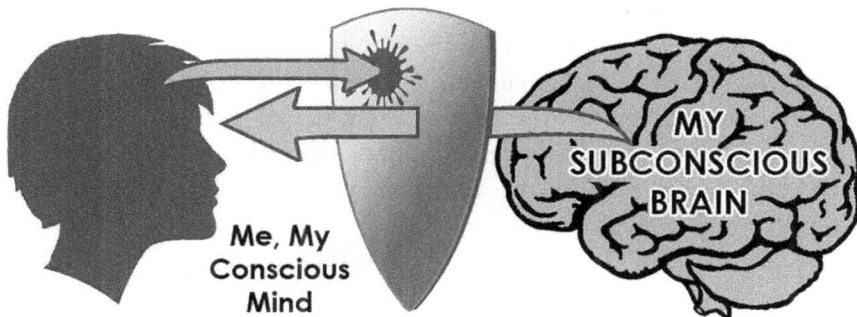

Me, My Conscious Mind

MY SUBCONSCIOUS BRAIN

The Way It Really Is

What the Subconscious Does

Nowadays almost everybody has heard of the subconscious and has ideas about what it does. Freud made it famous, maybe infamous. And no doubt you've had some experience of it yourself, even if not remarking on it. You couldn't remember the name of your sixth-grade teacher, or someone or something else, but suddenly minutes, hours, maybe even days later, it popped into your mind. Your subconscious searched it out and presented it to you.

It can also do more complex and inventive tasks, sometimes referred to as the *creative process*.[60] You're trying to solve a problem—anything from developing the theory of relativity (if you're Einstein), to writing software code, fixing a broken engine, choosing a powerful metaphor for a poem, composing the just-right musical phrase, or figuring out how you're going to get enough money to do something. You use your cognitive Mind to work on the problem, but nothing comes of it. You work on it until you get so frustrated that you give up.

You move on to other things; hours, days, even weeks go by. Then suddenly, with no warning, a pretty good answer appears as if from nowhere. It's just right, or close enough to point you to a great solution. There are many real-life examples of this from history, and here are a couple I particularly like. The benzene ring, a hexagonal diagram representing a chemical structure important in organic chemistry, was first suggested by Friedrich August Kekulé, who said he'd had a daydream of a snake with its tail in its mouth. Another example: the body of mathematics known as analytical geometry is said to have come to René Descartes in a dream. Those are examples of the subconscious doing more than simply reacting. Presumably it's been pawing through everything you know, trying new combinations, checking the results against your objectives, and finally telling you it's found something that might work. It does that because all of your conscious effort let your subconscious know the answer is important to you, and that the question hadn't been answered.

It's all well and good that the subconscious can do all that. But that's not what happens when it's looking out for you in the present. Reactive Brain scans the environment constantly, looking for threats and opportunities. When it finds either, it prepares you to deal with them—to avoid or vanquish threats and capitalize on opportunities. As you'll discover as you read further, Reactive Brain treats physical and psychological discomfort like threats. If you're uncomfortable about what's going on, Reactive Brain will cook up something to squelch those feelings immediately. That's what produces those misdirected habits that alleviate the bad feelings temporarily but don't help the situation. If you do the first of the exercises at the end of this chapter, you'll experience your mind doing just that.

How and Why Reactive Brain Acts First

To get you to address immediately what it considers urgent, Reactive Brain has to be the first in line to know what's going on so it can make judgments and act on your behalf as quickly as possible—immediately, in fact. It will not—indeed it cannot and does not—wait for you to perceive, then analyze, make up your mind, and then act. It's out in front looking for hostiles as well as things you'd like to have.

This is mind-boggling stuff. There is nothing in our experience that supports the view that Brain knows, analyzes, and chooses before we do. As noted in the Introduction, as recently as the early 1980s[61] the conventional view of most psychologists was that we *first* see and *then* decide for ourselves, and that that order of events is the most influential process determining our attitudes—our feelings of wanting and not wanting, of aversion and attraction. What's the evidence that contradicts our experience? What led all those psychologists to change their minds? Maybe more importantly, why should you care?

I present this material to show you that your emotions, your liking or not liking something, are often influenced by factors you have no influence over or awareness of. Knowing that gives you license to examine your automatic reactions and develop your independent evaluations of how you mean to be, what you value, and what those considerations mean for your behavior.

We have feelings of like, dislike, and indifference to everything we encounter. These preferences are what produce our gut feelings. Should we support invading Iraq, or more or less gun control? How should we feel about *those people*? Gut feelings often contradict our values, which confuses us. My purpose here is to open you to the idea that your feelings may not be reliable when measured against your values. So, when it's important, don't trust. Question and verify. But in order for you to be willing to expend the energy to doubt your gut feelings, to rely on them less and make the effort to verify your gut-based decisions, you have to believe that Reactive Brain may be influencing you inappropriately, making you have ideas and impulses that may not be valid according to your personal standards.

Exercises

Before reading further, you may want to try one or both of the exercises that follow.

These exercises will introduce you to aspects of your Mind you may not have experienced before. If you've had some mindfulness training, they may be wholly or partly familiar. Otherwise, these could be your first experience of witnessing your Mind in action.

The first exercise will introduce you to the forces that lead to distraction. You'll see distraction happen and experience the discomfort that results when you try to resist it.

The second exercise will help you watch your Mind at work and introduce you to some of the different levels of awareness you're capable of. You'll see how your Mind jumps from one thing to another. If all goes well, you will get the sense that what's in your Mind might not be all that important or even accurate. As to different levels of awareness, you may see that you can be aware of what's in your Mind and be aware of yourself watching yourself. You might also be able to notice your feelings about what you see when you're watching your Mind, and be aware of your feelings while not only feeling your feelings, but having opinions about your feeling, and seeing those opinions too—all seemingly at the same time. Intriguing?

I recommend you try these when you are able to give them your full attention. If not now, later. They'll keep, and you'll lose nothing by continuing to read ahead.

Watch Your Mind Get Distracted

Do this exercise and you'll be able to see your brain moving your Mind around, even when you don't want it to. You'll witness the forces that distract you.[62]

INSTRUCTIONS

Find a watch or clock that shows the seconds. In this exercise, you'll put down the book and try to pay attention to the seconds as they tick by for five minutes. But read the rest of the instructions first.

While you're trying to pay attention to the clock, notice what is happening in your Mind. When you find your Mind has drifted away, that you're talking to yourself, asking yourself why you're doing this, telling yourself it's hard, you hate it, you want to stop, or anything like that, just notice the mind-talk and the tone of voice. Notice any emotion you're experiencing when you find you're unable to hold your attention to the seconds ticking by. See if you notice the feelings in your body that accompany the Mind wanting to stop watching the clock and think about something else. Try not to get angry at yourself or me and to relax enough to simply notice what's going on with your Mind—your feelings too. If any emotions come up, don't reject them, but don't let them take you away. Just see them.

When you realize you're thinking about something else and not paying attention to the clock, drop what you're thinking about and return your attention to the seconds ticking by. No matter how antsy you feel, try to keep your attention on the seconds for the entire five minutes.

Start the exercise now, if you're up for it.

COMMENTARY

Re-read those instructions and see what you remember of your experience, of the way you talked to yourself, how hard it was to keep yourself focused on the timepiece, the emotions you felt, if any, the way you talked to yourself, if you did, and anything else that seemed important about the experience.

It was probably hard for you to stay focused on the watch. Even if you've been introduced to mind training previously or are an experienced mindfulness practitioner, trying to stay focused probably caused some discomfort—even physical discomfort. Reactive Brain doesn't like to sit still and concentrate on one thing. It wants to move around. It believes it's in charge. The mental and/or physical discomfort you probably felt was the effort of you trying to use willpower to resist what Reactive Brain wanted you to do. It was trying to drag you away, but you were resisting it.

That feeling comes up for almost everyone. If you felt it, you can have some understanding of why our Minds jump around all the time. The subconscious causes that. The only difference between ordinary experience and this exercise is that you consciously tried to hold your Mind still and pay attention to the effort required. Consequently, you were aware of the tug-of-war going on. Any pain you felt was analogous to trying to hold a heavy weight in the air and still for a long time. We don't usually feel that pain of mental resistance because we don't usually resist the subconscious when it tries to take over. We normally let ourselves get pushed around like a mouse being worried by a cat, because we're distracted and consequently don't notice or care.

Experience Your Mind

This next exercise is an invitation to experience your Mind and different levels of awareness.

INSTRUCTIONS

Close your eyes, take a breath or two to relax and become present. When you feel relaxed and present, say to yourself mentally, silently, without using your lips, "This is my Mind."[63] Say it silently, like that, a few times. Then stop and let your attention rest on the space where you heard your silent voice. When you look there, you're watching your Mind. Continue to watch that space.

The purpose of saying something is simply to show you where to look. It is not an attempt to define "Mind." Take a few moments to observe, quietly, that space where you heard the words, without forming judgments about what is there. Try not to be captured by words, thoughts, or ideas that appear there. Try to observe whatever you experience, without judgment.

Let what appears in your Mind, what you see there, be like the crawler at the bottom of the TV screen on CNN—that running series of headlines, one after the other, incessantly appearing. Simply notice, without getting involved in what appears there.

You may want to set a timer for three to five minutes so you give it enough time that you'll get the full experience.

Start the exercise now.

COMMENTARY

The words "this is my Mind" appeared in your Mind. You used your Mind to hear the words that appeared there, and without trying to do anything special you used your conscious awareness, sometimes called your "observer self," to witness you—your awareness, your Mind—experiencing itself. Simultaneously you might have noticed that you were aware of what was in your Mind, and you were aware of yourself observing your Mind, each as seemingly different things: Mind, contents of Mind, and yourself as observer. They weren't separate, of course, but being aware allowed you to see your Mind's activity in a way that you could consciously experience and know that you were also observing your Mind. You were also more open, more objective, less carried away by what was in your Mind—also less judgmental than you are when you are *being* the emotions you feel and your thoughts, without any self-awareness. The difference between *being* Mind and *being aware of* Mind is similar to the difference between being angry and knowing you are angry, as discussed before. And what a difference that makes.

I hope you were also able to notice that you are not your Mind, in the same way that you are not your anger when you know you're angry. You begin to have a different relationship with your Mind when you see that you can choose what to think about, can observe the thoughts and moods that appear unbidden in your Mind. And having observed them, you can choose whether to join them or not, rather than automatically become them.

That more open, less subservient relationship to your Mind makes it possible to evaluate what you're thinking and feeling rather than just going along with and being taken over by whatever pops into your Mind. The objective is to have the same kind of relationship with your Mind that you have with almost any other body part you're able to control consciously—your arm or fingers, for example.

Don't be concerned if you don't get all of that or even any of it yet. If you did get it all, don't turn it into something concrete. It's enough to have an inkling that the relationship between you, what's in your Mind, and your Mind itself could be different than it habitually is, and that you can exert more choice over it than you normally do.

There's no need to dwell on any of that now. I simply want you to recognize that you can see the contents of your Mind as an almost separate thing that is apart from your sense of you, or of reality. (If you didn't do the exercise but were intrigued by what you just read, I encourage you to go back and do it sometime. Be sure to wait until you can give it your full attention.)

CHAPTER 7

Brain Knows and Decides Before We Do

Pretty much everything we encounter is evaluated,
unintentionally and unconsciously, as either good or bad
immediately after we encounter it
(i.e. within 250 milliseconds).

—*John A. Bargh*[64]

You really do have a subconscious and it really does influence you, moment by moment, without you having the slightest awareness of its influence.

Your Brain is able to know, to judge, and be aware when you are not. And on the basis of what it knows, it can influence you without your knowing because it is organized to see, know, and form an opinion before you are physically able to access the information it's perceived. The description of this activity of the Brain—your subconscious—is now well accepted.

In 1980, psychologist Robert Zajonc (pronounced Zî-yontz or Zî-yonc[65]), then at the University of Michigan (later at Stanford University), published a paper proposing that the brain makes affective judgments of things it's exposed to unconsciously; that is, we form judgments when merely exposed to something, even when we're not aware that we've seen it; also, that cognitive and affective processes of the Brain are separate from one another. (When scientists and others working in psychology and related fields say "affect" they're referring to emotions. If you're not familiar with that usage, just substitute "emotions" for "affect" and you won't be far off.)

In other words, Zajonc's proposal was that 1) emotions and cognition (thinking) are separate functions of the brain, and 2) that the subconscious produces feelings of liking, not liking, and indifference toward objects and images before the conscious mind is aware of and can evaluate the object. Though well supported by data when Zajonc's 1980 paper was published, it was still only a proposal, and the prevailing view of psychologists then was, "Before I can like something I must have some knowledge about it, and in [sic] the very least, I must have identified some of its … features." Continuing in psychology speak, that common view was that "Objects must be cognized [known or seen] before they can be evaluated,"[66] and by implication, our feelings about objects must result from cognition, which is conscious. The theory Zajonc proposed in the 1980 paper turned all of that on its head, producing "agitated opposition."[67]

We have preferences—positive, negative, and neutral feelings, no matter how subtle—about every person, thing, and idea we encounter.[68] Many factors can influence those feelings, but regardless of how they come about, the feelings are important. To quote Zajonc: "Preferences ... give our lives direction and our actions meaning. They influence ideological values, political commitments, the marketplace, kinship structures, and cultural norms. They are sources of attachment and antagonism, of alliance and conflict."[69]

So what are some of the ways we develop preferences? Here are just a few examples: we inherently like or dislike certain things virtually from birth, like sugar or horseradish—that is, sweet or bitter, respectively. Other preferences are created by conditioning—something good happens when you're in a certain place, and that place becomes a preferred location; someone compliments something you're wearing, and you develop a preference for similar items. Social norms demand we give preference to some things or behaviors, and of course we learn to prefer them in others and ourselves. Preferences can also emerge from seeing how an item's objective characteristics compare with our desires: price, horsepower, color, size, and apparent durability, for example.

Those means of preference development were well understood when Zajonc issued what seems to be his first paper on the subject in 1968. We seem to rely on conscious appraisal to form some of our preferences. But there were other mechanisms of preference creation that were less understood when he began his research in the late 1960s.[70] From that time through the early 2000s, he and colleagues, including Jennifer Monahan at the University of Georgia and Sheila Murphy at the University of Southern California, published the results of a prodigious amount of research aimed at understanding the nonconscious mechanisms of preference formation, in particular the relationship between what he called "mere exposure" and preference.

At the time of Zajonc's first paper, there was plenty of evidence that *conscious* familiarity with something creates a preference for it and that more exposures lead to a stronger preference. The truth of that statement is what compels insurance, perfume, and car companies, among many others, to show you the same ad six times during a one-hour TV program, and why you buy the products even though you object to seeing the ads so often.

While the fact that exposure creates preference was well established, most of the evidence was based on the recipient not only being exposed to the stimulus—the image or advertising jingle—but being aware that they had seen or heard it.

Zajonc and colleagues researched the effects of *subliminal exposure* on preference—that is, what happens when people are exposed to images but have no awareness of the exposure. There are a number of techniques for reliably exposing an image subliminally to a subject. They include equally well-developed and accepted techniques for verifying that a subject has, in fact, no memory of any image they've been exposed to only subliminally.

The research Zajonc and his colleagues performed had the following basic structure. First, research participants were shown various images subliminally, generally for four or five milliseconds (1/250 or 1/200 of a second). Afterward, they were shown a group of images comprised of those they had been exposed to subliminally mixed with images of a similar sort that they had never seen before (*novel* images). Exposures in the second round lasted one or two seconds—enough time for subjects to know what they were seeing. Then they were asked to express their preference for each image.

In some experiments the images looked like Chinese characters (ideographs); in others they were nonsense groups of characters that might be suggestive of Turkish words (for example, IKTITAF, and AFWORBU). Of course, neither the images nor the nonsense word groups had any particular meaning. They weren't real Chinese characters or Turkish words, and the participants were not Chinese- or Turkish-language competent. In some cases, the researchers used images from a college yearbook. Sometimes research participants were *shown* the subliminal images several times, sometimes only once.

The conclusions were very clear. There was a decided preference for those images the participants had seen previously, though subliminally, and the more frequently they had been exposed to them subliminally, the greater the preference. Interestingly, there were other experiments in which the first exposures were for one or two seconds, creating conscious awareness of those exposures. When shown those same images mixed in with images they had not seen before, participants again showed a clear preference for those shown previously, but the preference was not as strong as when the first exposures were subliminal. The researchers theorized that when we see something long enough to know we've seen it—one to two seconds, for example—we're also making cognitive judgments about it, which *reduces* the preference effects of mere exposure, which develops subconsciously.

These two types of experiments and their variations, repeated in countless labs since Zajonc began his work, show that there is indeed a subconscious, that it is alert to stimuli we're exposed to before we're consciously aware of them, and that it creates potentially strong preferences without our conscious consent.

Priming

A vast body of research-based evidence shows that subliminal exposure can influence our behavior very significantly, just as Zajonc's research subjects developed preferences after subliminal exposure alone. The term used to describe creating unconscious awareness for something is "priming." The thing that one has only subconscious awareness of is called a "prime." The objective of this kind of research is to see if people who've been primed with something behave differently than people who haven't.[71]

There are two basic forms of priming experiment. In one, the image is primed subliminally, which means the subject is shown the prime in a flash lasting between 4 and 25 milliseconds (one-250th to one-40th of a second), so short an exposure that it cannot be consciously apprehended. Often the subliminal exposure is followed immediately by certain masking techniques— for example, a strong, competing image that saturates the visual centers of the brain, keeping the brain from processing the subliminal image and bringing it into consciousness. Researchers are very diligent about testing participants after priming experiments using well-established and validated methods to make certain that subjects have no awareness of the priming stimulus.

In another type of experiment, the stimulus is not exposed subliminally. Instead, the prime is in plain view but there is no mention of it and no reason for the subject to be conscious of its presence or to think it has any relevance to the purpose of the research. As with the priming experiments, the behavior of subjects who have been exposed to the prime is compared with those who haven't been primed, to determine the differential effects of the priming, if any.

Here's an example of an experiment that demonstrates the effects of priming that is not done subliminally. In this experiment by John Bargh, Mark Chen, and Lara Burrows, then at New York University,[72] subjects were told the research was about something entirely unrelated to its real purpose.

They were then presented with several five-word groups and asked to rearrange four of the five words in each group to make grammatically correct sentences. For example, "*bread, car, slowly, she, ate*" should be turned into "She ate bread slowly." There were two groups of experimental subjects; each group was given a list of words to rearrange, but the lists shown to each group were different. One group's five-word collections included respectful words such as *respect, considerate, appreciate, patiently, yield, polite,* and *courteous.* The other group's collections included more aggressive words: *aggressively, bold, rude, bother, disturb, intrude,* and *infringe.*

After performing the word arrangement task, subjects were directed down the hall to the investigators' colleague, who supposedly would give them their next assignment. When the subjects arrived at the colleague's office, they found access to the colleague blocked by another person who was gossiping with him. The experimenters predicted that people primed with the more aggressive words would interrupt more quickly than those primed with the respectful ones.

And that's what happened. Those exposed to aggressive words interrupted in five minutes, on average, while 82 percent of the respectful-word subjects waited the whole ten minutes allotted to the experiment. (No one knows how long they would have waited if time hadn't been called.)

Here's another example. Did you ever imagine that a funny video clip could turn you into a heartless killer?

I exaggerate, but here's the setup. In this experiment the subjects are told that an out-of-control trolley is barreling down the tracks headed for five people unaware of its approach. They'll all die if something isn't done. In one version of the problem, there's a lever you can pull to divert the trolley to another track where there's one unsuspecting person who will die instead of the five. Do you pull the lever causing one person to be killed rather than five?[73]

In another variation, instead of a lever there's a fat man standing on a bridge over the tracks. If you throw the man off the bridge, the trolley will hit him and stop, thus sparing the lives of the five people. (You are too skinny to make a difference, so self-sacrifice is not a practical option.)

So it's the same deal, only in the second case you have to actually push someone to their death, versus just pulling a lever. Time and time again (this is a popular research question), participants asked if they'd pull the lever, killing one person to save five, were almost unanimous in saying they would; but only 10 percent would push the fat man off the bridge. Why the difference when the outcome is the same? Imagine yourself pushing a frightened man to his certain death. Imagine touching him, pushing him. Imagine his emotions and feel yours. Compare those to the emotions you might feel by simply pulling a lever. The emotions you imagine you'd feel pushing the man to his death make the decision for you. The emotions are so powerful that they're almost impossible to overcome for most people, even though, at some rational level, the right thing to do is the same as pulling the lever: push him and save five others.

Now let's change the situation.[74] In another set of experiments by the same researchers, before participants were confronted with the fat-man-on-the-bridge version of the dilemma, one group was shown a TV documentary about life in remote Spanish villages—a really boring film, they say. The other group was shown a comedic clip from a *Saturday Night Live* TV episode. Only 10 percent of the boring documentary viewers said they would push the man off the bridge, the same result as previously. But *Saturday Night Live* viewers were more than *three times* as likely to say they'd push him. So, no joke (no pun intended), bore people and only 10 percent would push the poor guy; make 'em laugh and a full 30 percent would—at least in that set of experiments. Do you think the 20 percent of the sample influenced by the comedy skit think humor made them more willing to kill the fat man? I wonder how they would feel if they knew they could be manipulated so easily.

The conclusion reached in these studies is that we can be influenced subliminally in a way that affects our preferences, values, and behavior. So how widespread are these effects? After all, these are sterile lab experiments that have no practical applications in the real world, right? And, in any case, you yourself couldn't possibly be influenced through subliminal messages or things you didn't *know* (realize) you'd seen. Right? Well, that's the normal reaction, but the evidence of countless studies is overwhelming: subliminal messages can influence us in significant ways. And no one is immune.

What follows are more examples, some of which may startle and even shock you.

Priming Can Change Us from Dishonest to Honest. Honest!

Many applications and documents, some you've probably completed, have a section in which applicants must attest to the accuracy of the information they've provided by signing their names. It's usually the last thing on the form, but research shows that reporting is more honest if that section is placed at the beginning of the form.[75]

In a test where the participants were asked to report on the volume of work they performed, 37 percent of those signing at the beginning cheated compared to 79 percent who signed at the bottom. The number was 64 percent for those whose forms did not require a signature. (Given the sample size, 64 and 79 percent were statistically identical.)

In a similar experiment by the same researchers, participants were asked to report their expenses driving to the lab so they could be reimbursed. Those who signed at the top reported $5.24 in expenses; those who signed at the bottom reported $9.62; no signature, $8.45. (Again, $9.62 and $8.45 were statistically the same.)

The researchers believe that placing the signature block at the beginning stimulated attention to the participants' self-image. Those who were not primed, because they didn't see the signature block until *after* they filled in the rest of the form, simply took greater advantage of the lack of verification and reported more dishonestly than those who were primed.

Priming seems to have a rather clear impact on honesty. In another test of priming's power, there was a 300 percent improvement in collections at a self-service café. Students and faculty could avail themselves of the self-service coffee and tea bar at a certain British university. This service ran on the honor system.[76] There was a list of suggested prices and a box to put the payments in.

One day, without notice, someone placed a photo of a pair of eyes above the price list. Every week the photo was changed, alternating between flowers and eyes. No one commented on the signs; there was no explanation. In week one, with eyes, the average contribution was 70 pence; in week two, with the flower picture, the contribution dropped to 15 pence. Over the ten-week period, eye-weeks produced three times the contribution of flower-weeks.

Priming Can Cause People to Over- or Under-Perform

People tend to feel anxious if they sense their actions might be interpreted as confirming a negative stereotype of a group they're identified with. That anxiety, called *stereotype threat*, will often result in poor performance. In a study by Claude Steele at Stanford University and Joshua Aronson at the University of Texas at Austin, African-American students were given a test made up of twenty questions from the graduate record exam. Half of the students were never asked to indicate their race before taking the test. (In other words, they were given no priming.) The other half were first given a questionnaire that included a place to indicate their race (the prime). The latter group performed at half the success rate of the unprimed group.[77]

Images of Money Are Powerful Primes

According to work done by Kathleen Vohs, Nicole Mead, and Miranda Goode,[78] people are more independent and will persevere longer before asking for help if first primed with images of money. But priming with money also makes people more independent, more selfish, and less charitable. The prime can be real currency or Monopoly® money, and it only needs to be visible. You don't need to call the participants' attention to it or connect it to anything they are being asked to do. Researchers also use something more subtle, for example a word-rearrangement task involving money similar to Bargh's aggressive/respectful word-rearrangement experiment.

What they found was that "handling money, compared to paper, reduced distress over social exclusion, and diminished the physical pain of immersion in hot water."[79] But participants were also "more selfish and much less willing to spend time helping another student who pretended to be confused about an experimental task."

When an experimenter clumsily dropped a bunch of pencils on the floor, the participants with money picked up fewer pencils. In another experiment in the series, participants were told that they would shortly have a get-acquainted conversation with another person and were asked to set up two chairs while the experimenter left to retrieve the person. Participants primed with money chose to stay farther apart than their non-primed peers (38 centimeters compared to 15). Money-primed undergraduates also showed a greater preference for being alone.

"The general theme of these findings is that the idea of money primes individualism: a reluctance to be involved with others, to depend on others, or to accept demands from others."[80]

Priming with Ideas of One's Mortality Can Shift Political Positions

I was finishing an early draft of this book in December 2015, around the time of the San Bernardino, California, terrorist attack in which fourteen people were killed and twenty-two were seriously injured. Immediately afterward, poll results favoring presidential candidate Donald Trump surged along with increased speculation that he could actually become the Republican Party's 2016 nominee. Not surprisingly, this spike in popularity produced much discussion in the press as everyone tried to explain why someone who was so aggressive, so demeaning to all Muslims, women, immigrants, and others—one who shatters conventional standards of political rhetoric and behavior—could garner such widespread support, even among the right-wing base of the Republican party. A possible explanation is that being reminded of one's mortality—in this case, sparked by the San Bernardino terrorist attack—shifted political preferences.

Apparently, it doesn't take much to produce a shift like that. Jeff Greenberg, Tom Pyszczynski, and Sheldon Solomon, now at the University of Arizona, University of Colorado, and Skidmore College, respectively, have studied how people's attitudes change when they are primed with the idea of their own death—not death in general, but their own death.

At some point in the research interaction, participants are asked a question that causes them to consider their own mortality. For example, buried among other questions might be something like "What is your reaction to ideas of your own death?" For comparison, a control group might be unprimed, or asked about their personal experience with something else that is disagreeable, for example, experiencing pain at the dentist's office or taking exams. In addition to numerous journal articles, their research is summarized in the book *The Worm at the Core: On the Role of Death in Life.*[81]

In short, people primed with reminders of their own mortality, whether in a subliminal or non-subliminal way, become more identified with and defending of their cherished beliefs and cultural values,[82] and are more attracted to strong and charismatic leaders[83] and to people who validate and share their beliefs and feelings about those who threaten them.[84] They were also more aggressive—more willing to adopt extremist solutions to conflict, including self-martyrdom, and were more willing to kill those who threaten or violate their cultural norms or safety than were unprimed study participants.[85] They were also willing to exact greater punishment for those who violate their cultural norms: for example, male and female municipal court judges who were primed with their own mortality and then asked what bail they would demand from a prostitute asked for nine times the amount demanded by unprimed judges ($455 compared to $50).[86] Consistent with those results, primed participants were also willing to give greater rewards to their heroes.[87]

People primed with disagreeable events other than death, say, dental pain, for example, do not exhibit this desire for aggression against culture violators, indicating that the reaction primed by mortality is not simply retribution or revenge, but a reaction uniquely stimulated by recognition of one's own mortality.[88]

Still another disturbing effect of being reminded of one's mortality is that those primed with their mortality become more stereotypic in their thinking.[89] In other words, they are more likely to consider people they see as *others*. And these others are all lumped together, all posing the same threat or being seen as undesirable in the same ways and for the same reasons as individuals who have proved to be real threats: admitted or proven terrorists, for example.[90] You'll recognize this attitude as the misguided force behind much of the vandalism, physical attacks, and harassment aimed at people resembling whatever group we're currently afraid of.

It doesn't take much to remind people of their own mortality and stimulate these attitudes. After the September 11, 2001, attacks, priming effects could be demonstrated by *subliminally* showing research participants images of "9/11" or "WTC."[91] The overblown fears that individuals have that they could be killed in a terrorist act obviously were heightened by the San Bernardino attack in December 2015. (I say "overblown" because at the time of this writing, the odds of being killed or injured in a terrorist attack in the US are less than those of being struck by lightning. Whereas the odds of being killed in a gun incident are thousands of times higher, and even still greater are the odds of dying from a tobacco-related disease—more than 12 times higher than dying from a gun-related injury.) We've seen similar reactions in France following the terrorist attacks in January 2015 that killed 14 at the magazine *Charlie Hebdo*, and 4 people and a policewoman at a Jewish supermarket the next day, and, of course, after 130 were killed and over 360 were wounded in attacks that took place at several locations in Paris the following November.

In experiments conducted in late September 2004, about six weeks before the US presidential election that pitted John Kerry against incumbent George W. Bush, two groups of undergraduates at Rutgers University were asked to read an essay favorable to actions taken after 9/11, including the launch of the Iraq War. Participants in the mortality-primed group were two-to-one in favor of George Bush for president; the unprimed group favored John Kerry, four-to-one.[92] There were similar differences in participants' opinions of support or rejection of the Patriot Act, legislation that greatly increased government surveillance of individuals and their communications.

Not everyone reacts the same way to thoughts of their own death. The reactions I've cited are greater for people with lower income and education, as well as for people who hold to more conservative ideals. On the brighter side, it seems that the higher your self-esteem the more immune you are to fear-based priming. Research shows that people who have been primed in this manner, but measure as having high self-esteem, are less likely to be defensive of their worldview.[93]

You Doubt

The examples I've given in this chapter are meant to establish for you as fact, that we humans do indeed have a subconscious, a Reactive Brain, that becomes aware of what is going on around us before we do. This Brain also forms judgments (preferences) about things that we are not yet conscious of and motivates us to act according to its ideas of what should be done. I urge you to accept the idea that your brain does exactly the same things for you and to you. I understand that's not your experience, nor is it mine. But all of those things are undoubtedly true for each and every one of us at times. What is most significant about these characteristics of the subconscious is that they cause us to react in ways we might not have, independent of the subconscious's influence. If you're thinking, *Maybe those research subjects did that, but surely not me!* you're not alone, and I'll have more to say about that in a few pages.

I was guided to some of the preceding research by reading *Thinking, Fast and Slow* by Daniel Kahneman, who was awarded the Nobel Prize for the work he did with his longtime research partner, Amos Tversky,[94] that was influential in launching the field of behavioral economics. In case you're not familiar with his work or this field, behavioral economics attempts to describe the way we *actually* make decisions. *Predictably Irrational* is the title of a book by Dan Ariely, another behavioral economics researcher.[95] The title alone is a handy summation of the way we actually behave. Basically, we are not the rational beings on which much of economics theory depends. Instead, we are highly emotional in our judgments, and our decision making is often and predictably faulty when judged by the standards of rationality. In fact, we frequently act contrary to our personal interests and fortune. More of Kahneman's observations are coming in a few pages.

On this question of our doubting caused by our inability to observe the effects of being primed (by definition, without our knowledge or awareness), Kahneman writes:

When I describe priming studies to audiences, the reaction is often disbelief. This is not a surprise: [Mind] believes that it is in charge and that it knows the reasons for its choices. Questions are probably cropping up in your mind as well: How is it possible for such trivial manipulations of the context to have such large effects? Do these experiments demonstrate that we are completely at the mercy of whatever primes the environment provides at any moment? Of course not. The effects of the primes are robust but not necessarily large.... The idea you should focus on, however, is that disbelief is not an option. The results are not made up, nor are they statistical flukes. You have no choice but to accept that the major conclusions of these studies are true. More important, you must accept that they are true about you.[96]

John Bargh, the lead researcher in the experiments showing the impact of being primed with aggressive or respectful words, in a book chapter appropriately titled "Being Unaware of the Stimulus Versus Unaware of Its Effect," addressed the difficulty researchers have in convincing people of the effects of priming:

Inasmuch as people check such a proposition against their own phenomenal experience to test its validity, we will never be persuasive [that priming can have such influence] because by definition one can never have any ... experience of perception without awareness.[97]

Kahneman states clearly that understanding the hidden powers of priming on the subconscious does not make one immune to them. Despite performing the research and knowing how the brain works, he is still subject to these influences. The difference between the researchers and the rest of us is that they're more watchful; specifically, they are more likely to try to validate what appears in their Minds before taking actions that have significant consequences.[98]

That watchfulness is one of the keys to managing unwanted habits. I'm convinced that the intention to be watchful promotes self-awareness. It trains our error-detecting Sentinel described in Chapter 5. The training starts with being skeptical about quick-acting gut feelings. That's why I recommend *Don't trust. Question then verify*, rather than "Trust, then verify." We need to be on guard whenever the stakes are significant, and the longer we wait before taking out the magnifying glass of cognition, the greater the likelihood that Reactive Brain will take us over before we can course-correct.

The experimental results I've presented about the influence of the subconscious on our behavior raises some obvious questions:

- Is it really possible I'm doing things I don't agree with?
- Is my subconscious really that powerful in relation to me?
- Am I really in Master Habit most of the time, allowing my subconscious to have its way with me and my world?

The answers to these questions will come from your understanding of how the subconscious Brain communicates with the conscious Mind—in other words, how Reactive Brain and Intentional Mind interact.

CHAPTER 8

How Mind and Brain Interact

Before beginning this chapter, please answer this question: How many animals of each kind did Moses take on the ark?[99]

I'll ask you about your answer in a little bit.

One of the most important things to understand when trying to manage oneself is the relationship between Mind and Brain, specifically their individual roles and how they interact when they disagree about how to interpret or react to some stimulus.

This topic is enormous in scope: countless scientists and philosophers have labored for millennia to figure us out. Fortunately, in this book we're interested in only a small piece, just the basics of how and why Reactive Brain and Intentional Mind relate to each other, what each does, and how to help Intentional Mind win more often when it disagrees with Reactive Brain. This chapter explains what Brain does and how Mind reacts or ignores what Reactive Brain does. We're still looking at this from the outside in—that is, at evidence from psychological studies rather than the neurological findings presented in the following chapters.

As mentioned earlier, a terrific resource describing the interaction between Mind and Brain, particularly between Reactive Brain and Intentional Mind, is Daniel Kahneman's *Thinking, Fast and Slow.*[100] The book focuses in particular on the relative roles of the subconscious and conscious, how they interact, and how their relationship produces biases that cause often-costly mistakes, just as unwanted habits do.[101] It's a rich collection of research findings from Kahneman and other researchers.

Whereas I talk about Reactive Brain and Intentional Mind, Kahneman describes two collections of brain functions he calls System 1 and System 2. System 1 is the fast-acting, habitual subconscious that judges and reacts; it is the home of automaticity and habits—the desirable, accurate ones, and the unwanted ones too. It initiates emotional responses and constructs emotional action programs.[102] It produces interpretations of reality that it feeds into conscious, cognitive mind (his System 2). System 1's interpretations are usually accurate, but many are biased or simply inaccurate, as you'll learn.

As I understand Kahneman, when functions of the brain are concerned with deciding how to react to external stimuli, his System 1 corresponds closely to what I call Reactive Brain. His System 2 corresponds closely to what I call Mind. When his System 2 (my Mind) is deciding what to do in reaction to stimuli, it corresponds to Intentional Mind. To minimize confusion in what follows, when using Kahneman's nomenclature—System 1 and System 2— I'll follow each with either Mind or Brain in brackets.[103] (You may find it annoying but it will save you the effort of remembering which is which.)

Examples of Mind/Brain Unreliability

Let's start with your answer to the question about Moses and the ark that led off this chapter. Did you answer two? Or did you remember that it was Noah, not Moses, who built the ark?

Kahneman says the percentage of people who answer the ark question correctly is so small that it has been dubbed the *Moses Illusion*.[104] Inevitably, when I ask this question during a workshop, I hear a chorus of "two" followed by groans and the sound of hands smacking foreheads when I point to the error. After stumping them with this one, it's difficult to trick the group again. Having been this embarrassed, Mind is no longer as willing to accept everything I say without thinking about it. (*Don't trust. Question then verify* in action.) Mind will do that if given sufficient motivation. (I hope this little experiment either amuses you or starts you on the road to creating a sense of humor about your mental foibles. You're not alone.)

Since you weren't forewarned that I was going to try and trick you, you probably answered "two" because, as Kahneman demonstrates through these and numerous other examples, System 1 [Brain] is gullible and biased to believe what it hears, while System 2 [Mind] is lazy; the ark question is an example of that. (Of course, you're not lazy, but your Mind is. It prefers a low-energy resting state in which it accepts rather than checking what Brain tells it.) To gullible System 1 [Brain], the ark question seems cogent because, Kahneman says, Noah and Moses share a vowel sound, have two syllables, and both feature in the Old Testament. Since the stakes are small, and there is cogency (it sounds sorta right, right?), Brain accepts the question as stated. (Keep in mind that Mind's preference for being in a low-energy state—half-asleep, if you prefer—is a significant factor in maintaining the Master Habit of distraction.)

Kahneman summarizes the roles and interactions of System 1 [Brain] and System 2 [Mind] as follows.[105]

> …Systems 1 [Brain] and 2 [Mind] are both active whenever we are awake. System 1 [Brain] runs automatically and System 2 [Mind] is normally in a comfortable low-effort mode, in which only a fraction of its capacity is engaged. System 1 [Brain] continuously generates suggestions for System 2 [Mind]: impressions, intuitions, intentions, and feelings. If endorsed by System 2 [Mind], impressions and intuitions turn into beliefs, and impulses turn into voluntary actions. When all goes smoothly, which is most of the time, System 2 [Mind] adopts the suggestions of System 1 [Brain] with little or no modification. You generally believe your impressions and act on your desires, and that is fine—usually.

Nevertheless, one of System 1's [Brain's] additional functions is to determine whether it needs help from System 2 [Mind], which happens whenever System 1 [Brain] doesn't have an immediate answer to a question or doesn't understand what it finds (sees, hears, smells, tastes, touches) in your environment. Answer these two questions and you'll experience System 1 [Brain] acting alone, and System 2 [Mind] being roused to solve a problem.[106]

$2 \times 2 = ?$

$36 \times 15 = ?$

Don't want to bother with the second question? That's okay. You've experienced what I wanted you to: System 2 [Mind] knows the answer to 2×2. It's something Brain knows. It's right there, effortlessly accessible, and, in contrast to the most common response to the ark question, it happens to be right. System 1 [Brain] knows it doesn't know the answer to 36×15. It stops your System 2 [Mind], so to speak—wakes it up, letting it (you) know you have to get involved.

Similarly, pronounce these words:

Cat

Pneumosilicosis

System 1 [Brain] knows what *c-a-t* means and effortlessly gives it sound. In fact, when it sees *cat*, it can't shut out its understanding of it because "System 1 [Brain] cannot be turned off."[107] But it doesn't know *pneumosilicosis*, and because System 1 [Brain] doesn't recognize the word, it gets System 2 [Mind] involved. Your System 2 [Mind] wakes from the Master Habit and starts sounding it out. (Obviously, if you use *pneumosilicosis* frequently, your System 1 [Brain] will learn it and respond to it as easily as to *cat*.)

System 1 [Brain] is far more important to us than those simple examples illustrate. Referring to the relationship between System 1 [Brain] and System 2 [Mind], Kahneman elaborates:

> When we think of ourselves, we identify with System 2 [Mind], the conscious, reasoning self that has beliefs, makes choices, and decides what to think about and what to do. Although System 2 [Mind] believes itself to be where the action is, the automatic System 1 [Brain] is the hero of the book [Kahneman's]. I describe System 1 [Brain] as effortlessly originating impressions and feelings that are the main sources of the explicit beliefs and deliberate choices of System 2 [Mind].[108]

A substantial part of the 95 percent of Brain activity that takes place in System 1 [Brain] is trying to figure out what's going on around us so it can protect us and help us get the good things in life, particularly the opportunity to reproduce. It does that by "provid[ing] a continuous assessment of the main problems that an organism must solve to survive: How are things going? Is there a threat or a major opportunity? Is everything normal? Should I approach or avoid?"[109] Or, as Zajonc might put it, "Do I like it or not?"

It makes perfect sense that we have a System 1 [Brain] and System 2 [Mind], and that they're organized the way they are. Quoting Kahneman again:

> The division of labor between System 1 [Brain] and System 2 [Mind] is highly efficient: it minimizes effort and optimizes performance. The arrangement works well most of the time because System 1 [Brain] is generally very good at what it does: its models of familiar situations are accurate, its short-term predictions are usually accurate as well, and its initial reactions to challenges are swift and generally appropriate.[110]

Unwanted habits are disagreements between Reactive Brain's automatically generated emotional action programs and Intentional Mind's desires—disagreements caused by the systematic biases produced by Reactive Brain [System 1] that we did not choose or invent—that we can influence only *after* Brain has started us toward fulfilling *its* desires.

Our Brains are determined to protect us, and the mechanisms that permit that rapid interpretation of the environment are error prone. Brain *means* to jump to conclusions so it can prepare us for threat or opportunity. We survive because we have a subconscious that is aware of what's going on before we are, that makes judgments about what is happening, that prescribes a solution, and then sets up the body to respond before we know what's going on. In order to do all that, Brain has to be adept at jumping to conclusions, making decisions based on very little information, and being paranoid. It needs to *act* instantly, and therefore to *decide* instantly. Consequently, it is built to be paranoid, to decide that anything that *could* be dangerous *is* dangerous, and to initiate action consistent with its beliefs immediately and without questioning itself. We then accept System 1's [Brain's] snap judgment and act on it unless something gives us reason to question what System 1 [Brain] is trying to do, and we're motivated to intervene.

Here are two more examples that may help you experience this Brain [System 1]/Mind [System 2] interaction.

Solve the following problems:

- A bat and a ball cost $1.10 in total. The bat costs $1.00 more than the ball. How much does the ball cost? Answer: ___ cents

- In a lake, there is a patch of lily pads. Every day, the patch doubles in size. If it takes 48 days for the patch to cover the entire lake, how long would it take for the patch to cover half of the lake? Answer: ___ days

These two questions are from the Cognitive Reflection Test (CRT) developed by Shane Frederick, then assistant professor at MIT's Sloan School of Management and presented in Kahneman's book.[111] Maybe you took the time to solve these problems, or maybe you didn't. Regardless, each has an intuitive answer, an answer that appears in your Mind immediately, with no prompting or thinking. In the bat and ball problem, the intuitive answer is ten cents. In the lake problem, it's twenty-four days. There is almost no way to keep those answers from popping into your mind, and they're both wrong: the correct answers are five cents for the ball and 47 days for the patch to cover half the lake.

What's particularly interesting here is that these questions are not meant to test mathematical abilities, but rather to show whether one tends to trust their intuition or to deliberate and verify its accuracy before making a decision. To a degree, the CRT is a measure of over-confidence. Everyone is injected with the intuitive answers. People who deliberate will check them against the terms of the problems. Notice that if the ball costs 10 cents (the intuitive answer), the bat would cost $1.10, and together they would cost $1.20, not the $1.10 stated in the first line of the problem. (The ball costs 5 cents; the bat then costs 5 cents plus a dollar, and the two together cost $1.05 + .05 = $1.10, which meets the terms of the problem. Regarding the lake problem, if the lily pads double in size every day, covering the entire lake in 48 days, on the previous day—day 47—they covered half the lake.)

I gave you those problems so you could experience your intuition giving you wrong answers. You'll have to judge for yourself whether you were ready to accept the answers and put them forward as your work, or whether you would have spent more time to verify them if you had more time to give and/ or the stakes were higher.

You have a lot of company if you would have settled for the intuitive answer. In one study of the test, it was given to 3,428 people, mostly students from various universities. Over 50 percent of the students from Harvard, MIT, and Princeton, and 80 percent of students from less selective schools got the bat-and-ball problem wrong.[112] Looking at the results from all schools on all three questions combined, half the students missed two of the three questions, on average[113] a third had no right answers, and only 17 percent got them all right.[114] While this performance indicates that only a small number of participants check their work, the tests were pretty low-pressure affairs with little at stake. One can only hope that we're more careful when having the right answer might be critical to fortune, health, or relationships.

Here's another example of System 1 [Brain] asking for and getting help from System 2 [Mind]. According to Kahneman, forty Princeton students were asked the same three questions from the CRT. For half of the students, the printed font was small and a washed-out gray color. The font was clear for the others. Ninety percent of those with the clear font made at least one mistake, but only 35 percent of those with the hard-to-read font made a mistake. That result seems to be counterintuitive, but what it demonstrates is that when System 1 [Brain] found the font difficult to decipher, it engaged System 2 [Mind], and its involvement reduced the number of errors. The moral is that it pays to pay attention to what one is doing. (I'll bet that's not the first time you've heard that.)

While the lack of care many give to solving problems is interesting, more important is the demonstration and confirmation that System 1 [Brain] gives us answers that can be wrong, and there is a tendency for System 2—conscious, cognizant Mind—to accept what System 1 [Brain] tells it. The lesson we can take from these examples, as with others you'll encounter in these pages, is to be alert and wary, especially when the stakes are high.

What is really going on between System 1 [Brain] and System 2 [Mind]—between Reactive Brain and Intentional Mind? According to Kahneman, System 1 [Brain] is very good at jumping to conclusions. He and I are commenting about what the subconscious does on the spot, immediately upon encountering something. It's important for Reactive Brain to be very fast, worried about threats and anxious to capture anything that appears desirable. So, of course, if it's to be effective, it must make decisions rapidly. Because it's trying to jump to conclusions, System 1 [Brain] doesn't care about information it doesn't have or about the quality of the information it has; if what it sees is coherent—it sorta makes sense—Moses built the ark, the ball costs 10 cents. It goes with that and asks no further questions. It doesn't know and can't afford to care about information it doesn't have. It doesn't stop to ask questions and consider the answers. It relies solely on information in front of it, in the moment. Kahneman calls this characteristic of System 1 [Brain] WYSIATI—standing for *What You See Is All There Is*. In the next chapter, you'll learn that the physical construction of the human brain supports this jumping to conclusions. It's not a fault; it's the way the brain is wired. It's the way it has to be if we're to survive. But! As you'll see, that need, and the brain's excellence at fulfilling it, inevitably produces errors.

To summarize, System 1 [Brain] is satisfied with coherence—is gullible—and System 2 [Mind] is lazy and often locked in Master Habit. Consequently, System 2 [Mind] tends to accept and endorse what it gets from System 1 [Brain], making some level of error inevitable.

Biases

Kahneman presents many more examples of Brain [System 1] churning out its opinions about what we're encountering that we (System 2 [Mind]) adopt without question. Many of our opinions are biased because they arise from systematic distortions. WYSIATI (what you see is all there is, where "you" refers to System 1 [Brain]) is the cause of many biases. It causes System 1 [Brain] to form preferences and aversions as soon as it sees or hears something. And that's what we (System 2 [Mind]) normally accept.

Consequently, $9.99 feels like nine dollars, not ten. People are more likely to agree to a surgical procedure when told that the survival rate in the first month after surgery is 90 percent, but refuse one in which the likelihood of death in the same period is 10 percent. Ninety percent fat free feels good, but 10 percent fat feels unacceptable. And Subaru automobiles feel good because "Love is what makes a Subaru a Subaru."[115]

Because of WYSIATI—Brain's built-in rush to judgment—Brain puts out $9 feelings without waiting to include the 99 cents that follow. Even after $9.99 sinks in, our "gut" still tell us it's $9. Similarly, 90 percent linked with survival produces a good feeling, while 10 percent linked with death sounds bad. And regardless of your interest or the value of Subaru cars, you feel good about them because they're associated with the word *love*, and what could be better than that?

We humans are loaded with biases; this is a well-documented fact. The Subaru example exploits one of the most common biases, called the halo effect, in which we color our feelings about living and inanimate objects by the first thing we hear or see about him, her, them, or it. The halo effect is one of advertising's most potent tools of persuasion.

Biases distort reality and cause us to react or relate to situations, people, and things in ways that are not rational. Kahneman's book says much about this, but, as encyclopedic as it is, his examples cover only a tiny percentage of the literature describing the biases and distortions we're prone to. Fun fact: Wikipedia has a well-sourced list of 117 biases.[116] Mind you, some are only slightly different from others in the list. While you certainly don't have all of them, you surely have some.

Here are six common biases:

Bias Blind Spot Bias is thinking you are less biased than others. Need I say more about this one? You would be rare indeed if you're not experiencing right now at least a touch of denial. You might find yourself trying to convince yourself that indeed you have no biases, and as a result this bias does not describe you. And maybe you're right.

Confirmation Bias is the tendency to seek out information that confirms what you think and to ignore, misremember, or reject without any consideration information that contradicts your position. Most conservatives don't seek out opinions of liberal writers and media, nor do liberals want to hear conservatives' opinions.

Fundamental Attribution Error Bias: This one's especially pernicious. It's the belief that other people's actions are caused more by their personalities, values, and character than by the facts of their situations. For example, you might believe that a person is poor because he or she is of low character, unambitious, lazy, and looking for handouts, and that the person's situation or history or environment has nothing to do with their poverty. Conversely, you may believe that all rich people are more worthy than poor ones.

Social Projection Bias is the assumption that other people think, feel, and have values just like yours—that they share the same likes, dislikes, preferences, and prejudices. Did you ever feel disappointed or betrayed when a friend showed you they didn't share a point of view you value in terms of politics, religion, or judgments about people you both know?

Representativeness Bias is the tendency to think that all the members of a definable group share a particular characteristic—in other words, stereotyping, namely "All _____s are _____."

Loss Aversion Bias is the fear of losing things we have. We tend to be more concerned about losing what we have than we are about getting something we don't have. For example, most people are more willing to sell stocks in which they have a profit, compared to selling stocks in which they have a loss (which would solidify their loss). This one can cost you real money.

Why are biases important? Why is it important to recognize our biases? Biases distort our understanding of and reactions to the world as it really is. Moreover, they keep us from looking past intuition to find the facts and weigh them in light of a more accurate view. Consequently, biases can cause us to make decisions we might not make if we had accurate information and an open mind.

As I mentioned in the Introduction, we constantly face opportunities and difficulties. Many situations are pleasant, but others are challenging, disappointing, and even threatening. We are afraid that X will happen in the future. Maybe it does; maybe it doesn't. We think we won't be able to stand it if X happens, but when it happens, we deal with it as well as we can. We deal with things best when we see what's going on, clearly, free of bias. Moreover, the more confidence we have that we're seeing and dealing with reality, the less fearful we are, *even if what we see is painful and threatening.* To quote an ancient Buddhist text, "When there is no obscuration of mind, there is no fear."[117]

Get curious about your biases. First, did reading about those biases trigger your bias blind spot bias—your denial button? Did you find yourself saying to yourself, "Not me"? Would it help if I told you that, as familiar as I am with this material, writing it and reading it makes *me* feel defensive, even though I'm absolutely certain I have biases? I don't need to be defended from that fact; what I need is a healthy dose of skepticism to remind me to be open-minded when presented with information I don't like.

To deny bias is to try to protect an unrealistic opinion of ourselves. Try to cultivate openness to unbiased self-examination and compassion for what you find. Learn to see yourself as a product of the unique combination of nature and nurture that you've experienced.

To create a window into those causes and conditions that influence how and why you behave and believe as you do, we'll now turn our attention to understanding how the physical brain works.

First we'll look at emotions. One of the most interesting recent findings in brain research is that without emotions we are largely unable to make decisions. This is another statement you'll find hard to believe or relate to before you've seen the evidence, but the fact is that in order to make even the simplest of decisions, we need emotions to confirm our choices, and we're helpless without them.

Before leaving this chapter, consider this quote from one of my favorite authors. It sums up this chapter pretty well, I think.

> *That was the thing about thoughts. They thought*
> *themselves, and then dropped into your head in the hope*
> *that you would think so too. You had to slap them down,*
> *thoughts like that.*
>
> —*Terry Pratchett*[118]

CHAPTER 9

Emotions Make It Possible to Decide

Are Emotions Really That Important?

Your first reaction to the statement that emotions drive our decisions could easily be that you're not the emotional type, and you're unaware of any significant emotional influence in your decision making. If that's you, you have a lot of company, and you might be asking, with a good deal of skepticism, "Are emotions really that important? What is their role in managing the habits I'd like to manage better?"

In this chapter I'll show you some of the scientific evidence that says it doesn't matter whether you are unemotional or emotional, or whether we're talking about insignificant or highly fraught decisions. Emotions influence all of us continually and profoundly, all the time, even when they're at such a low level that we're unaware we're experiencing them.

Emotions Are Deciders and Motivators

The scientific literature points to the conclusion that emotions are present in everything we do: they are always right there, expressing preference, avoidance, and indifference, and trying to motivate us to act the way they want. We act in accordance with them and have to overcome them to act a different way.

We experience our preferences through physical feelings that correspond to degrees of attraction, aversion, and indifference. The feelings may be strong or imperceptible. Sometimes there's just a gut feeling that guides us. Regardless of how strong or weak the feelings, or how conscious or unconscious we are of them, the emotional underpinnings of like, dislike, and neutral are always there. Sometimes we're drawn to one thing, one course of action, one product, one person. At other times it's "I want both so much that I can't decide." Feelings and impulses of attraction and aversion can be powerful, even debilitating. Consider the power of addictions as examples of the strength of such feelings.

At other times our feelings are so faint that we're not aware of them; nevertheless, we do indeed feel them, and they nudge us toward *their* choice of what's best for us, even when what they want is disastrous to our interests. Want a cigarette? A fight? A second (or third) cookie? The forbidden fruit in glass or bottle? Something on a plate, in a store, or sitting at the bar?

One of the reasons that Zajonc's research on priming discussed in Chapter 7 is so important is that it shows that preferences are created before and without the benefit of conscious thought. As previously discussed, we don't analyze, weigh, and then choose. Brain expresses its preference before Mind knows there's anything there to have an opinion about. If we're going to do something different based on conscious choice, we have to use willpower to overcome the emotional preference our subconscious chooses for us.

Since emotions are so much a part of our response to everything we encounter, it stands to reason that habitual unwanted reactions come from a contradiction: Reactive Brain wants what Intentional Mind wouldn't choose. It's not that there's an error. Reactive Brain is doing what it's been programmed to do, even when the result doesn't align with our values or intentions.

Emotions Are Necessary for Making Decisions

Two well-established, research-based findings underlie the conclusion that we need emotions to help us make decisions. The first finding is that preferences are often formed as a subconscious function of the brain, as just mentioned. The other important finding is that humans unable to physical feel emotions are literally unable to make most decisions. That finding grows out of research results first published by Antonio Damasio, whom I cited earlier as the originator of the term *emotional action program*.

There's plenty of opportunity for anyone reading this to be confused. Chances are when I mention *emotions* it brings to mind the more florid ones like anger, despair, and ecstasy. But most of our emotions are more subtle than those. Recall that I said earlier that when the Brain has formulated its prescription for how to react to a stimulus—the emotional action program—it sets up the body to respond. We feel the way our body has changed and call the new feelings *emotions*, even though most of the time the physical feelings are so subtle that we're not consciously aware of them. Nevertheless, they are there, and they do influence our decisions.

If this is a new concept for you, you might wonder how it is that you've gotten to your age, whatever it is, without someone telling you about this.

The reason is that most of the information I'm about to discuss was almost entirely unknown, and certainly not accepted, before the late 1970s and as late as the mid-1980s. Even then it was resisted by some researchers, practitioners, and students of psychology. In fact, research into the nature of emotions and their importance used to be frowned on. Thankfully, the function, role, and importance of emotions has become much clearer of late due to the increased research on emotion performed by psychologists and neuroscientists, with both disciplines relying increasingly on advanced brain-imaging techniques that tell us so much about how our brains work.[119]

So back to that all-important assertion that humans require emotions to guide their decisions. Think about it. People who can't feel emotions are often unable to make even the simplest decisions. I'm not speaking about all those who are ignorant of their feelings, but rather people who, because of a physical abnormality, have brains that cannot process emotions.

Antonio Damasio works with such people. His findings help us understand emotions and their influence on behavior and thinking. When you compare the behaviors of people who can't feel emotions with those of us who can, you have a good basis for determining what emotions do for us—which human characteristics depend on them.[120] Damasio's patients typically have experienced accidental or surgical insult to the prefrontal cortex which severed the physical connections between the parts of their brains that create emotions and the frontal cortex. Sometimes this surgical procedure is performed to correct life-threatening or debilitating disease, in which case it's a lesser-of-two-evils choice. Keep in mind that their unusual behavior was caused by a physical event: physical separation of parts of the brain, not by mental deficits caused by the person's experiences.

"Elliot" was one of the first patients to spark Damasio's interest in this research area. He had lost a significant part of his prefrontal cortex as the result of surgery to remove a tumor and adjacent damaged tissue. Damasio describes Elliot this way.[121]

THE PATIENT WHO COULD NEITHER DECIDE NOR CHOOSE

Prior to surgery Elliot was a successful, happily married man. "He had a job with a business firm, and had been a role model for younger siblings and colleagues … [and] had attained an enviable personal, professional and social status." As his tumor grew, he developed severe headaches. It was harder for him to concentrate, and as his condition worsened "he seemed to lose his sense of responsibility and his work had to be completed or corrected by others."

After the surgery to remove portions of his prefrontal cortex, which he survived well, Elliot underwent a "radical change in personality." He could no longer hold a job and was "living in the custody of a sibling."

Everyone could see that Elliot was "intelligent, skilled and [an] able-bodied man who ought to come to his senses and return to work. Several professionals had declared that his mental faculties were intact."

Damasio describes the radical changes in Elliot's personality and how "astonished" his family and friends were by the changes. He needed to be prompted to get out of bed to go to work. At work, he couldn't manage his time and couldn't meet scheduled commitments. He lost the ability to stay on task and to choose among alternative courses of action.

After losing one job, then others, he gave up regular employment and went into a number of ill-fated ventures. His family couldn't cope with the new Elliot. There was a divorce, then a series of other marriages that failed. In spite of these changes, and the deterioration of his standard of living, his memory and ability to reason were intact. Damasio recounts "being impressed by Elliot's intellectual soundness." Elliot tested in the normal, even superior, ranges in every test related to intelligence he was given. All of these showed his "perceptual ability, past memory, short-term memory, new learning, language and ability to do arithmetic were intact. Attention…the ability to focus on particular mental content to the exclusion of others was also intact, and so was working memory…."

Damasio writes that Elliot was given every test of mental ability that could reasonably apply. In addition, he was given a battery of tests to judge his knowledge of social norms and moral judgments, all of which he completed with a superior level of performance. But still, he couldn't manage his life.

So here was a man who had superior intellectual and reasoning abilities, but who could not make sensible judgments about his life. It's no wonder that government agencies and insurers stopped supporting him, believing that he was at best lazy and at worst a malingerer who should simply return to work.

But he couldn't.

Damasio writes that a significant clue came to him from Elliot's admission following a particular battery of tests. Elliott was presented with a number of scenarios and asked to analyze the consequences, propose alternative solutions for arriving at particular goals, and resolve any moral dilemmas. He performed above average in all of these. According to Damasio, Elliot "produced an abundant quantity of options for action, all of which were valid and implementable." And then Elliot smiled, apparently satisfied with his rich imagination, but added, "'And after all this, I still wouldn't know what to do.'"

It was apparent to Damasio that while Elliot's analytical abilities were intact, *he had no ability to make a decision*. Elliot was unable to move from an objective analysis of alternatives to a decision as to which one was best because he was missing an emotional signal attaching to one of the outcomes that would indicate to him that he preferred one over the others. *The analytical information alone didn't give Elliot enough reason to decide one way or the other.*

Here are two more examples involving another Damasio patient with prefrontal cortex damage, who, because he was unable to feel emotions, could drive on icy roads quite well, but couldn't make the simplest scheduling decision.[122]

This patient, with prefrontal cortex damage similar to Elliot's, happened to come to Damasio's lab on a day when there had been freezing rain, resulting in slippery road conditions. When asked how the trip had gone, the patient described the conditions and the fact that they called for using "the proper procedures for driving on ice." He recounted seeing a driver in front of him go into a spin on a patch of ice that he calmly drove over.

If you've ever had to drive on slippery roadways, someone taught you or you discovered that the best way to get out of a skid is to turn your wheel in the direction of the skid—in other words, to go with rather than against it, which lets you regain traction and control so you can exit from it. But your instincts when you start to skid will be a mini-panic (emotion!) directing you to get out of the spin right away by turning the wheel opposite to the direction of the skid, which will likely make the skid worse.[123] The patient's prefrontal damage had left him without the ability to feel that mini-panic, which is why he was able to drive according to the cold logic he had learned.

But there's more to the story.

The next day, the patient was given a choice of two follow-up appointments, just a few days apart. It would be a shame to deny you Damasio's description of what happened:

> .... for the better part of a half hour [he] enumerated reasons for and against the two dates: previous engagements, proximity to other engagements, possible meteorological conditions, virtually anything that one could reasonably think about concerning a simple date. Just as calmly as he

had driven over the ice, and recounted that episode, he was now walking us through a tiresome cost-benefit analysis, an endless outlining and fruitless comparison of options and possible consequences. It took enormous discipline to listen to all of this without pounding on the table and telling him to stop, but we finally did tell him, quietly that he should come on the second of the alternative dates. His response was equally calm and prompt. He simply said, "That's fine."

Damasio observed that someone with an intact prefrontal cortex would have seen the whole episode in a larger context, which would have given him an emotional bias toward choosing one of the dates or asking Damasio or his staff to choose one. Comparing the patient's behavior with *us*, he writes, "None of us would have spent the amount of time the patient took with this issue.... We would picture the waste of time and have [felt it] as negative; and we would picture the minds of others looking at us, and [marked that] as embarrassing."

The preceding comments are emblematic of Damasio's conclusion that emotions are required to make even the most inconsequential decisions. Indeed, the overwhelming evidence from Damasio's work is that humans need emotional confirmation—some *gut feel*, some felt physical sensations—that an alternative is right before we can choose it. It's these gut feelings that guide our choices.

Our real-life behavior reliably defies all those theories built on the presumption that humans rely on cold hard logic alone to make economic and other decisions. We can't and we don't. The faulty emotional reactions we experience, like those I mentioned in the previous chapter, often produced by cognitive biases, are driven by the identical forces that Kahneman describes—that is, by the imperfect information processing in System 1 [Brain] reacting to stimuli, and the failure of System 2 [Mind] to notice their inappropriateness and attempt to intervene.

As the research done by Damasio, Zajonc, Kahneman, and hundreds of other investigators has shown, emotions are critical drivers for human behavior. And, while we might describe some people as more emotionally driven than others, we all feel and respond to emotions, because for healthy brains "Affective [emotional] reactions are inescapable," as Zajonc puts it. To paraphrase Zajonc on this subject: unlike our judgments about the objective characteristics of stimuli, *emotional reactions that accompany our judgments cannot always be voluntarily controlled.* Most often these experiences occur whether we want them or not. Zajonc further points out that many institutions, like law and science, keep trying to devise ways to make judgments *objective* because "we wish some decisions to be more independent of these virtually inescapable [emotional] reactions."[124] And yet emotions are inescapable, automatic, and *essential* because the physical construction of the human brain requires it, as you'll see.

Emotions and Your Gut Feelings Are Mostly Right

Much of this chapter and others is about how wrong gut feelings and intuition—manifestations of emotions—can be. But it's important that this be placed in context. We have to depend on emotions and intuitions; we're helpless, literally stuck without them. That's what Elliot's lack of emotions, and many more cases like his, have shown. If we didn't have them, we surely would not have survived as a species and couldn't as individuals. Emotions are an essential part of systems that constantly monitor the environment to determine what is needed to protect and maintain us. To repeat: the systems that make up Reactive Brain constantly scan our bodies and environment to see what is going on and what should be done in response. They are on the lookout for threats, mates, food, and various other rewards. When they spot something they interpret as harmful, they choose a course of action, prepare the body to respond, draw our attention to the threat, and impel us to act. It's absolutely clear that those emotions and gut feelings are right most of the time.

Reactive Brain is essential to our well-being. It is worthy of our esteem. Still, it's not infallible, and it gives us no clues as to whether it's right or wrong. Remember how right ten cents felt as the answer to how much the ball cost? The only way we can detect Reactive Brain's errors is to break free from Master Habit and do our best to evaluate its messages independent of the strength of its impulses and accompanying emotions. That's very difficult to do because our emotions and intuitions feel so right, whether they are right or wrong. System 1 [Brain] never ever indicates to System 2 [Mind] that its idea, instinct, or gut feeling may be faulty.

Emotion and intuition are so frequently right that some people consider it unseemly to question them. Some cultures glorify intuition and people who proudly *trust their guts*. Those same cultures tend to denigrate people who take their time to ponder before deciding. How un-wo/manly it's considered to pause, consider, analyze, and choose!

Gut feel is so handy, so easy to come by—so *us*—that we want to believe it's right. It's a sign of wisdom, even of grace or some other spiritual intervention, some think. Besides, it's so much easier to go with the gut than to think things through and wrestle with the uncertainties that thinking often exposes.

But gut feel is created by the emotional brain, as you'll see in the next chapter. It is a product of emotional action programs, and essential for getting their work done, as Damasio and his colleagues have shown. Maybe wo/manly boosters of gut feelings would reconsider if they recognized that what they're describing is emotion by a different name. The desire to trust, even to glorify, intuition is so strong that many of the people I know who've read *Blink*,[125] Malcolm Gladwell's bestseller describing the work of the subconscious, believe it is an uncritical validation of intuition, and are seemingly oblivious to the contrary evidence that Gladwell presents in its opening pages.

Its very first tale illustrates how fallible intuition can be. It describes the Getty Museum's attempt to determine whether a statue it acquired at great expense was real or fake—a tough assessment. The museum staff responsible for the purchase was certain, in their guts, that the statue was genuine; not so the outside experts asked to opine on its authenticity. It's not surprising that the museum folks, their credibility at stake, *felt* it was genuine. Was that their need to be right or their expert judgment? The outside experts, with no skin in the game, believed the statue was a fake. Obviously one group was right; the other was wrong. Given the interests of the two groups, which is more likely to have had accurate guts?

And yet so many people read that story and still think that *Blink* is an unqualified endorsement of intuition. I believe that to be nothing less than a mass demonstration of *confirmation bias*, the common twisting of some facts and ignoring of others, done subconsciously to protect and defend what one wants to believe. Believing in our innate ability to intuit the right decision by gut feel is so much easier, much more desirable than having to wrestle with every choice. Remember that I support the view that intuition plays a valid role *most* of the time. It's just that its record of success is not perfect, and it needs to be checked, especially when the stakes are high.

As a species, we're constantly making personal and business decisions that turn out to be objectively unwarranted, economically unsuccessful, and against our interests, though they feel like the right thing to do at the time.

Consider the leap of faith that CEOs and Hollywood studio executives take when green-lighting a new hire, a new acquisition, or a high-budget movie project. You may think these important decisions are based on careful analysis, but research shows that they are often driven by gut instinct.

It is said that a full 80 percent of new products and corporate acquisitions fail to meet their objectives; 80 percent of new hires are said to be disappointing, and before DVDs (or VCR tapes) and television royalties, only about 6 percent of Hollywood movies made a significant profit; 15 percent broke even, and 50 percent were never distributed, and therefore were total losers.[126] In partial support of Kahneman's observations on the loss aversion bias—the reluctance to sell losing stock, for example—he cites research on 163,000 stock transactions that took place over a seven-year period in 10,000 individual brokerage accounts. It showed that when people sold one stock and bought another, the stock they sold did better after the transaction than the one they bought to replace it.[127]

It's tempting to ridicule *those people* who make those poor economic decisions—irresponsible, clownish, and confident-for-no-good-reason are some of the descriptors that come to mind—but the fact that so many people make these bad decisions means that it's a human flaw, not an individual one. We're all subject to these biases. We all rely on feelings that, at times, are simply not trustworthy. You do. I do. We all do. It isn't *those people*. It's us too.

So what are we to do?

When it's important, pause. Ask questions. Look for objective confirmation. Then decide. If it matters at all, don't trust. Question and verify.

In an article in the *Harvard Business Review* recounting the poor record of business investment decisions, Kahneman and co-author Dan Lovallo recommended that executives discard their optimistic biases and inject greater objectivity and diligence into project reviews. They recommended comparing project assumptions with real-life results obtained by themselves and others in comparable situations, and scrutinizing their intuitions and biases.[128] They remark also on the need to withstand the societal norm in many companies that requires that everyone applaud the newest initiative rather than question it.

I'd be doing less than half my job in this book if I simply let it all go with the cheery admonition to be careful! You need more than that to have a chance at discovering when your emotions are leading you astray, and there will be more in Part II, which describes the Act from Choice Method.

Before we go there, let's first look at how emotions really come about: how does the Reactive Brain transform perception of a stimulus into an emotional action program? After looking at that, I'll describe how individuals get their unique patterns of reactive response.

CHAPTER 10

How Brains Construct Reactions and Emotions

Our Wonderful Brains

Take a moment to pay homage to our wonderful brains before delving into the whys and hows of emotion making and the mistakes our brains make as a result. After all, the errors they make are very small in number compared to the uncountable decisions the brain makes spectacularly well.

We know that the brain keeps us alive. It's not something we think about a lot, but we've been told—taught—that it runs the pumps, the chemical machinery of the body, and initiates and controls physical movement. We know we depend on it, if for no other reason than we've been told repeatedly that only brain-dead is dead-dead. Moreover, the brain is the one part of our body that we indisputably and uniquely rely on, because while an increasing number of machines can substitute for other body parts, a brain-machine doesn't appear to be on the horizon. (And, by the way, whose brain would substitute for yours or mine, and who or what would we be then?)

In addition to running the machinery, the brain does much to inform, delight, and protect us. Our sensory systems capture the sights, sounds, smells, tastes, and physical feelings that come with touch. Its conveyance and interpretation of sensory information are what allow us to understand what's going on around us, the things we need to learn about, enjoy, and fear. Without sensory information, we'd have no idea what was going on in the world, and we couldn't learn anything.

Our senses are the source of pleasure and pain and provide us with the information from which we can determine what is there that we want, and what is out to get us. We're blessed with the ability to turn experience into learning, and to form timesaving habits so we don't have to consciously reconstruct how to drive a car or to walk each time we do it. We even know how to read faces and body language, giving us insight into what people are thinking.

The Brain infers these things and learns others, usually unprompted by Mind. Contemplation of what our senses bring us informs poetry, philosophy, science, religion, art, and so much more. We can think, reason, and judge; analyze, argue, write poetry, perform complicated tasks, do business, and so much more because we have cognitive systems that allow us to think things through and decide whether people, situations, and things are good or bad for us.

Seeing connections between things is the spark for ingenuity, innovation, invention, and problem solving. It is the key to enjoying the myriad fascinating people, places, things, and relationships we encounter. All those things we do, and much more, are made possible by the brain elaborating and finding meaning in the raw sense data we encounter.

There's so much more still. Our memory systems record things we've learned and experienced, the pleasant and unpleasant—objects, encounters, situations, and people we'd like to be with and those we want to avoid. We've learned that bears, while furry and cute, are predators that we need to be wary of, and some of us remember how to read music and speak another language years after learning them.

We have at least three distinct memory systems: one for facts, one for procedures, and another for emotions, and we have brain mechanisms that tie them together. When something happens, the first two systems, our declarative and procedural memory systems, store facts and procedures that we can explicitly recall or that are simply there, fully embedded, and are called into use without conscious thought. "Emotional memory" stores the emotional impact of situations and how strong (important and affecting) they were. One of the really neat things about our memory systems is the way they link related things together so that one thing can remind us of another. This facility is called "associative memory." It is what makes memory management possible. It also accounts for why our minds seem to jump from one thing to another, often uncontrollably, it seems.

For example, suppose you get a message that your Uncle Charlie called. You've always felt kindly toward him. Maybe you remember the bicycle he gave you when you were a child. And then you recall that he is balding, has no eyebrows, and is overweight. His pear shape might call to mind Alfred Hitchcock, which might lead you to recall his film *The Birds*, and from that, how much you hate pigeons and what they once did to your car. Then you wonder if it's time to get your car inspected, and how much you hate that the government makes you do such things. Or maybe you recall a recent time in church (the ch- sound in church is similar to the ch- in Charlie), or your first love, Charlotte. Maybe the bicycle reminded you of the time you fell off, leading you to remember you have to renew your car insurance or check your tires for wear. A progression of memories like that might bubble up into your conscious Mind from your subconscious, completely unbidden.

Brains and Emotions

In order to understand how the Brain produces emotions, let's go at it from the perspective of what is needed to protect us and get us the opportunities we humans require. Besides running the body's systems so that we're able to cope with changing situations, our brains need to cope with threats and capitalize on opportunities; this is true for humans and all living entities. Every other concern is superfluous to those imperatives. In fact, when the body is preparing to deal with threats, it shuts down every system not central to protection, including the digestive and reproductive systems, so it can focus all of our energy resources on dealing with the threat.[129] That's what the brain does; that's what it's wired to do. The brain is wired to do all that and more.

Besides making available all the energy we're capable of coming up with, the human brain has to do a number of other things to deal with threats. (Capturing opportunities is also of high importance to Brain, but threats generally place greater and more immediate requirements on reaction than opportunities do, so that's what this discussion will focus on.)

To mount effective responses to threats, Reactive Brain has to:
- Continuously update and maintain an instantly accessible catalogue of everything that could threaten you physically and psychologically. It's obvious that physical threats are important, and these are usually easy to identify. The importance of psychological threats is less obvious until you recall the last couple of things that made you really angry or sad. Recall, for example, your reaction when you felt your ego or social standing was threatened, or how you felt when being falsely (or even rightly) accused of something. To develop the required catalogue of threats, Reactive Brain must have access to your complete emotional and declarative history— memories of everything that ever happened to you, including the consequences and the emotions.

- Be on the lookout for and recognize threats instantly and always. No matter what you're doing, no matter where your attention is focused, Reactive Brain has to be on guard. As long as you live, it should not ever be bribed into distraction by pleasures or a shiny new anything. It must be on guard every instant you're awake, and even when you're asleep, to a degree.

- Be paranoid and decisive. If there's even the remotest possibility that something could be a threat, Reactive Brain must label it so. No shillyshallying. No internal debate. Whether high or low probability, it's a threat!

- Prescribe and initiate a response immediately, without waiting for anything else—especially you—to agree! There can be no doubt or delay in choosing your response. Out of its library of potential responses, Reactive Brain must choose and execute the one that's most appropriate for dealing with the threat. Choice and execution must be automatic and instantaneous. No waiting; no second thoughts. Reactive Brain must put you in motion to deal with the threat in the way it has prescribed. Maybe you'll adjust your response when (and if) you catch up and figure out what's going on, assuming you can figure it out and come up with a better idea. But you could be wrong, so you'd also want your Reactive Brain to stay in there trying to enforce its solution until you've shown you're strong and determined enough to get Intentional Mind to take over.

- Prepare your body to respond and get it into action immediately. It would be disastrous if Reactive Brain had to negotiate with you before responding to threats. Some of Reactive Brain's solutions will require immediate action: duck, hit, freeze, plead, apologize, run, scream, or grab a weapon. Even before calling your attention to what's going on, Reactive Brain must prepare your body to execute the action it prescribes and put your body and you in motion: to get your heart pumping, open your veins to carry more blood, pump you full of energy and alertness-producing hormones, shut down unnecessary body systems so you'll have available all the resources of your body to cope with the situation, and direct your attention (eyes and ears) to the threat.

There's not a single thing in that list that you or I can do without if we're to survive. I can't emphasize enough the importance of *immediate* action—even if the prescribed response is only to freeze in place. Reactive Brain has to do it all immediately, rapidly, and automatically. Many predators can move at over 30 miles an hour. Doesn't sound like much until you realize that at 30 miles an hour they're moving at 44 feet—about three car-lengths—per second. Most people can throw a rock or ball faster than that. If ten feet of warning could be decisive in saving you, a delay of a quarter of a second might mean the difference between death, injury, and escape. Truly, there is no time for thought, no room for delay.

But is it possible that Reactive Brain could be wrong? Could it misread the situation or prescribe an ineffective response, or one inimical to your values or to some relationship that might be affected by your response? Of course it could and does, which is exactly how we get unwanted habits.

Remember that Reactive Brain, Kahneman's System 1 [Brain], cannot know its own errors. It only knows what's immediately in front of it, and it's incapable of bringing other considerations into its decision processes. That's what you want from a survival perspective, and you have to admire the degree of control taken away from you by Reactive Brain because, right or wrong, its speed gives you a greater chance of survival. The need for survival wins in the design criteria of Reactive Brain: better alive and wrong than dead for really good reasons.

Reactive Brain has a real problem fulfilling its role: it takes time for the Brain to generate the accurate, fine-grained details that are necessary to make really good decisions. That is more time than Reactive Brain can tolerate. What is Reactive Brain to do? How can it be fast enough to meet the priority of protection to still give you time for the information processing and cogitation necessary to produce good decisions?

The answer is it can't.

The Problem

So much of what we humans do requires us to consciously apprehend what's around us. That's a fancy way of saying you can't do much with your conscious mind unless you have a conscious experience of what your sense organs detect.

As discussed previously, Zajonc's work, as well as the results of countless priming experiments by others, shows that Brain can see, create, and respond to preferences before we can. But if we're going to participate in our lives in a meaningful, fact-based way, we have to have consciously accessible experience of what our senses detect. We need to experience the images that come to our eyes. We need to know the details—the shapes, the colors, the variations in contrast that produce the image. We need to know the identity of the person, see the expression on his or her face, hear the tone of voice, and understand what we hear. There are analogous details in the other senses. We have to consciously experience sense information for it to be useful to us. And, of course, the Brain does ultimately present to Mind the details of sight, sound, taste, touch, and smell. The problem is in the word "ultimately."

It takes precious time, on the order of a half-second or more, for Brain to turn data captured by our eyes into a complete, consciously accessible and understandable visual image—the same conversion time, more or less, for other sense data. (The variation in the length of delay is dictated by how complicated the images, sounds, and so on, are.[130]) That's too long a delay in Reactive Brain time. Remember, it's not simply a matter of seeing or hearing what's happening; in order to make an informed choice about what to do, you have to know what is *really* happening. Was it factually what Reactive Brain thought it was? Do you care about what's happening and its consequences? Whether you care a lot or a little, what would you prefer to do? Understanding what is happening, forming judgments accordingly, and then choosing to respond takes time—maybe a second or two—but Reactive Brain needs to respond faster, in a quarter-second or so.

How can Reactive Brain make a choice and respond more rapidly than we can? It does this by tapping into the brain's sensory information stream long before the information is fully processed and gets to consciousness. While the conscious brain is processing the data we ultimately *see* or *hear* in consciousness, Reactive Brain is already deciding what's there and what to do about it. During that interval before you are conscious of what's going on, Reactive Brain is working with the raw, unprocessed, imprecise sensory data. It monitors the data, looking for anything at all like what it has in its general catalogue of threats. If it finds anything that could be threatening, it puts you in the action.

To see how it works in practice, let's take a walk together outside, at twilight.

Birth of an Emotion

Walk with me.

Somewhere up ahead on the ground there's a snaky-shaped something. Maybe it's actually a snake. Maybe it's a rope or a twig. Maybe it's just the way the light reflects off the ground. Let's imagine what your Reactive Brain does with this image. You haven't seen it yet, but Reactive Brain has.

The Stimulus

The snaky-shaped something is the stimulus. Photons reflecting from the image arrive at your retinas and are turned into signals that will eventually go to the visual centers of your brain to be processed into an image you will *later* become conscious of and be able to *see* and understand. That processing takes time. Our experience of sight—the images we're conscious of, that we know we consciously experience—are put together from processes that take place in four visual processing structures (cortices) in the brain. Some structures deal with straight lines, and others with colors, light values, movement, contrast, and spatial organization. The visual cortices work together to process the information. There's lots to do. It takes time—precious time if you're about to step on a snake.

The Problem

Reactive Brain, always at work, is on the lookout for threats and opportunities. Perfection is you seeing what's there, examining it, and deciding what to do about it. Good is being warned right away and prepared to react even if it turns out to be harmless. This is an example of perfection being the enemy of survival.

The Brain's Early Warning System

A Quick but Sloppy Response: The emotional mind is quicker than the rational mind, springing into action without pausing even a moment to consider what it is doing.

—*Daniel Goleman*[131]

In the brain, everything is going on at once; visual signals—like that from the snaky-shaped something—are processed simultaneously with signals from other senses. Many bodily functions proceed at the same time: food is digested, air is breathed, body temperature is held constant, hormone levels are monitored and adjusted; the body is responding to other ongoing input, and you may be lost in Master Habit, thinking about the meal you just ate, or how welcome sleep will be. In other words, the brain is nothing like a single computer running a single program where things happen sequentially; rather it is more like an enormous collection of computers, each doing its own thing. Each communicates and is influenced by and competes with others. In short, it's really busy in there.

Still, Reactive Brain's priorities are clear: protect and maintain our bodies and help us exploit opportunities for procreation and nourishment. Everything else is a bonus. Time is of the essence. Speed may determine the difference between life, injury, or death. Basically, you have to deal with threats first thing. There'll be time for your neuroses after threats are dealt with.

So, back to the snaky-shaped something. The image lands on your retinas causing signals to be produced in the optic nerves (left and right), which terminate in a brain structure called the thalamus—the visual signals' first stop in the brain.[132]

Data for four of our five senses—all but smell—stop first at the thalamus, which is a central switching point for sensory data arriving at the brain.[133] After the thalamus, sense data go in two main directions: one direction takes the data to the specialized centers that make the sense data useful to Mind. The other goes directly to the emotional processing parts of the brain, in particular to the amygdala.[134] (Smell bypasses the thalamus almost entirely and goes directly to the amygdala, a path that is thought to be left over from our evolutionary heritage. Our animal relatives ate or starved, lived or died, bred or didn't, depending on their ability to smell threats and opportunities, and going through the thalamus wastes precious time when all of that is at stake.)

The amygdala is a key member of the constellation of brain structures important in producing emotions and their action programs.[135] As already mentioned, those brain structures are often referred to collectively as the limbic system, which is considered to be the emotional processing center of the brain. The amygdala reads the sensory information coming from the thalamus, looking for signs of threat and opportunity. Along with the hippocampus, a brain structure involved in memory creation and retrieval, the amygdala has access to information about innate and learned threats, what we've experienced in the past, and how emotionally important those experiences were. The amygdala uses this information to determine if a threat could be present. If so, it prescribes its reaction in the form of an emotional action program consisting of an impulse and instructions that prepare the body for the action the impulse will goad you into performing.

Figure 6
Development of an Emotion

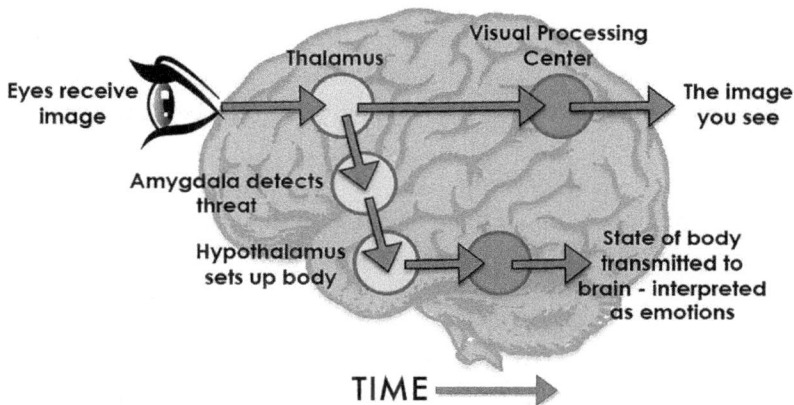

All the while, the amygdala continually receives data, not only from the thalamus but also from every other part of the brain that could have useful information about what is going on. Simultaneously the amygdala tells those brain structures to get aid and/or to stand-down and not interfere. The amygdala is a very big deal, indeed.

Joseph LeDoux, professor and researcher at New York University's Center for Neural Science, discovered the bypass route that information takes from the thalamus to the amygdala that allows the amygdala to do its work while the rest of the brain is extracting details from the information.[136] He is truly Dr. Amygdala. While much of his work is about fear in its many aspects, LeDoux notes that "the amygdala has also been implicated in emotional states associated with aggressive, maternal, sexual and . . . eating and drinking . . . behaviors as well as the processing and use of rewards to motivate and reinforce behavior."[137]

At this point, the copy of the sensory information that goes to the amygdala is unprocessed; it is missing the clarity and nuance that higher-order visual processing centers will extract. You and I couldn't make much sense of what the amygdala sees. If you could see it, you would want more detail before forming a judgment about what was being seen. Like the amygdala, you would see there was a snaky-shaped something up ahead, but would not know if it was a snake, a twig, or a trick of light. In another situation where animals could be present, you might see enough of an image to suspect there was an animal present, but have no idea what the animal was and whether it was dangerous. If you had reason to be afraid of animals, that fuzzy information might make you freeze or run. If you were less anxious, you might wait for a better image to develop before acting. But the amygdala isn't like that. The amygdala will make a decision based on this fuzzy, low-resolution image. For this reason, among others, the conclusion the amygdala jumps to can be quite faulty.

Nevertheless, that low-resolution data is what the amygdala bases its moment-by-moment decisions on. It compares its conclusions with emotional memories and models of dangerous situations to decide if what it sort-of sees is a threat, an opportunity, or a never-mind; and, based on that decision, whether and how it needs us to respond. If it decides that what it sees could be a threat, it goes into full threat mode, initiating the emotional action program it wants you to respond with.

Notice that you didn't tell the amygdala to look out for snakes. You and I are just out there for a walk. *Snake* is far out of Mind. Fear of snakes is something we're born with because we're human, so the amygdala, Reactive Brain, is automatically on the lookout for them along with countless other threats it thinks it knows about, both innate and learned.

Verdict. Sentence. Enlisting the Body.

Now things move very fast. Having decided to act, the amygdala does everything possible to arm the body and motivate us to act. It's ideally suited to do that because it has a close physical connection to the body's main control center, the hypothalamus—in many ways the most important enabler of emotional action programs and much else besides.

The hypothalamus's job is to adjust the body to the ever-changing demands placed on it by the environment and its internal conditions. It's responsible for the body's maintenance and survival. Its two most important pathways are to the pituitary gland and the autonomic nervous system, which includes the programs for arousing the body (fight or flight) and relaxing it (rest and digest). The hypothalamus controls just about every function important to sustaining life: breathing, heart rate, blood pressure, hormone levels, body temperature, digestion, elimination, ovulation, levels of sexual arousal, and much more. If you want to make the body safe, you must give it the resources to act, and you do that by giving it control of the hypothalamus. In any instant, whichever brain structure controls the hypothalamus controls the state of the entire body and its key functions. As Sapolsky puts it so cogently, "Every part of the limbic [emotional] system is fighting for control of the hypothalamus."[138]

The amygdala's prescription for reacting to what it found goes directly to the hypothalamus. The physical path is short and fast. The hypothalamus translates the message and immediately issues commands to the body. Heart rate and blood pressure increase. Muscles in blood vessels relax to allow greater blood flow. In the snaky-like something situation, the face is set in an expression of fear and engorged with blood so that everyone who sees you knows there's trouble. The adrenal, pituitary, and other glands release stress hormones. Attentional circuits in the brain stem open the pupils to give you greater visual acuity, and the eyes and head are turned swiftly to where the snaky-shaped something lies. Ovulation and digestion, as well as other functions that will only be needed if and when you survive, are shut down to make the energy they'd consume available where it's most needed, as already mentioned.

Still, you don't yet know if what's ahead is actually a snake, because you haven't seen it yet. You're behind the action that the amygdala and hypothalamus have initiated. Their program is running, and *you* are not yet behind the wheel.

Now You Feel the Emotion

The body's been set up by the hypothalamus. The body's state is communicated back to the Brain, which translates the state of the body into the sensation of fear. While this translation from physical feelings to an identifiable emotion happens automatically, that's not what we think we experienced. The way we remember it later, we think *we* (Mind) saw the snaky-shaped something, and that made us frightened; but in fact, subconscious Reactive Brain saw it first and did all this work. Mind sees it later. It was the feelings in the body caused by the hypothalamus preparing it for action that produced the physical feelings we call fear. Those feelings arrived *before* we "saw" the snaky-shaped something.

In 1890, William James, philosopher, psychologist, physiologist, and physician, proposed something like what is now accepted as the real order of things in the way emotions develop. In his book *The Principles of Psychology*, published long before the advent of the advanced tools of neuroscience and psychology in use today, he stated the following:

> Common-sense says, we lose our fortune, are sorry and weep; we meet a bear, are frightened and run; we are insulted by a rival, are angry and strike…. [T]he more rational statement is that we feel sorry because we cry, angry because we strike, afraid because we tremble, and [it is] not that we cry, strike or tremble, because we are sorry, angry or fearful…. Without the body states following on the [unconscious] perception [of the stimulus], the latter would be purely cognitive in form, pale, colorless, destitute of emotional warmth. We might then see the bear, and judge it best to run, receive the insult and deem it right to strike, but we should not actually feel afraid or angry.[139]

James's last sentence accurately describes Elliot's situation: the condition of having accurate cognition devoid of emotion, which situation makes it virtually impossible for us to choose what to do.

We're not done with the snaky-shaped something, so let's get back to the trail.

Your Reactive Brain knows there's something to pay attention to, and we still have to bring you (Mind) into the picture. Reactive Brain directs your eyes to the snaky-shaped something, and you feel the fear. If you're close to it, you probably jump away from it. If it's farther away, you probably freeze, afraid to move, and when you compose yourself enough to look carefully to figure out what's really there, you decide what to do. Depending on how much you habitually fear snakes, you may have felt terrified in those first instants. With less fear of snakes, you'd be less fearful.

The point is that after the body is set up to react, information describing its physical state goes to the brain, which turns that information into the feelings we call emotions. At the same time, Reactive Brain points our eyes to the stimulus, which is when Mind can first begin to form its own opinion about what's happening and what should be done in response.

The linkage between the body and the emotions is effective because the emotional action programs set up physical feelings that are unique to the particular emotion the emotional action program means to convey. A recent study by Lauri Nummenmaa and colleagues, in which the feelings created by thirteen different emotions were mapped by the study's subjects themselves, showed that each emotion had a unique signature that was common among study subjects.[140] A groundbreaking study of human emotions by Paul Ekman, that we'll look at later, showed that seven basic emotions produce, involuntarily, unique facial expressions that are recognized and produced by people of many different cultures, both primitive and modern.[141] The Nummenmaa study mapped Ekman's seven basic emotions—anger, fear, disgust, contempt, sadness, surprise, joy—and six related ones: anxiety, love, depression, pride, shame, and envy.

Interestingly, the relation between body and emotion works both ways.[142] When we're lighthearted we smile, and when we smile we feel lighthearted. Try this for yourself. Take a moment to think of something mildly disturbing. It could be someone or something that makes you angry. Work up a little emotion. Relax your face; then, using your facial muscles, raise the outer corners of your mouth into a half-smile. It doesn't have to be a real smile. Notice what happens to your emotions.

The key takeaway here is that the feelings of anger, fear, sadness, guilt, shame, anxiety, and happiness, even, are caused by and felt only *after* the body has been set up to fulfill Reactive Brain's emotional action program. We (Mind) do not participate. This is all involuntary, automatic, and fast. And, again, we're the last to know. That's the way it is, but it's not what we think we experience.

Once Mind, in particular the prefrontal cortex, gets involved we have options. Speaking generally, when we become aware there's something to deal with, if the product of the prefrontal cortex's cognizance decides the amygdala is wrong in its assessment of the situation, or doesn't accept its prescription for action, the prefrontal cortex attempts to override the impulse created by the amygdala's instructions to the hypothalamus. The prefrontal cortex uses its connections to the amygdala to block the latter's orders to the hypothalamus.[143] When the prefrontal cortex, acting as Intentional Mind, doesn't intervene, the hypothalamus will continue to support Reactive Brain's commands.

Lessons from the Snaky-Shaped Something

There are four lessons I'd like you to take away from our twilight walk in the woods.

Lesson 1. Our recollections of what we experience can be very unreliable. We think we were in charge, but sometimes we aren't. It isn't that we saw the snaky-shaped something and became afraid; instead Reactive Brain saw it first, chose what to do, and set up the body to execute its orders. The state of our body combined with seeing the snake made us feel fear. We couldn't be in charge until we became conscious of the stimulus—the image—and possibly couldn't get control even then.

In short, we weren't in charge. Reactive Brain was.

Lesson 2. The amygdala bases its evaluation on the *unprocessed* information it gets from the thalamus.[144] This reliance on unprocessed information creates the possibility of error. The snaky-shaped something did not have to be a snake to produce the preprogrammed impulses and the feelings of fear. It only had to look sort of like one. If the amygdala had been able to wait for more detailed data, it would have discovered what the snaky-shaped something actually was, avoiding the possibility of error caused by its necessarily hasty judgment. But Reactive Brain is set up to protect; it can't wait and decide. It can't provide for alternative interpretations of unprocessed data. It has to act now. And that's exactly what you want it to do.

Similarly, something you hear might make you feel you've been insulted, but it might not have been an insult. Even if it was an insult, it might not have been worthy of a response. There may be many different interpretations of what you heard and alternatives for responding. Regardless of the possibilities and alternatives, Reactive Brain will treat the insult as a threat because the stimulus *resembled* a threat, and, as we know, Reactive Brain doesn't consider alternatives.

Lesson 3. Reactive Brain is very fast and creates a great deal of momentum. Finally awake to what it's doing, if we want to do something different from what Reactive Brain has prescribed, we have to be very fast and strong enough to extinguish or redirect the momentum of the impulse it produced.

Lesson 4. We can't modify the emotion or the emotional action program until we're aware of it and the stimulus. You only enter the Choosing Space, becoming aware of the mismatch between Intentional Mind and Reactive Brain, if your Sentinel has noticed the mismatch, and the error signal was powerful enough to break you out of Master Habit, all as described in Chapter 5. The impetus that launches us into self-awareness, the Choosing Space, may come late or never. If we don't leave Master Habit, there's no opportunity to choose.

LeDoux speaks directly to the problem:

> The fact that emotions, attitudes, goals, and the like are activated automatically (without any conscious effort) means that their presence in the mind and their influence on thoughts and behavior are not questioned. They are trusted the way we would trust any other kind of perception.... When one is aware of biases and possesses values against having these [thoughts and behaviors], he or she can exercise control over them. However, the ability to do this depends on being aware of the unconscious influences, which is quite another matter.[145]

If we're to recognize unwanted impulses *before* they turn into regrettable actions and attitudes, we need to know what triggers us and how we react. Once you understand why you react the way you do, you can turn your attention to the tools you'll need to make and enforce your choices. The Act from Choice Method will give you the tools for increasing and speeding up your awareness of your unwanted unconscious influences and for working against their momentum so you can impose your choices—your intentions—on the situations you face.

What's Next

There is one more question to answer before exploring the Method itself. In this chapter you've seen how the emotional brain's systems, working with the thalamus, amygdala, hippocampus, and other brain structures, grab sensory data before it's been fully processed, decide what it means (jump to conclusions, that is), and try to get you to fulfill Reactive Brain's prescriptions for action. We have yet to explore how *your* emotional Brain figures out what is threatening, and how it comes up with *your unique* set of preprogrammed reactions.

We're all different. Perhaps your friends are afraid of spiders, and you keep pet tarantulas. Perhaps when you've been insulted you shut down, whereas some people go into a towering rage and maybe get physically violent. So how come our individual definitions of what is threatening and the way we react to threats are so different? And, if your habitual responses are mellower than someone else's, are you more virtuous than they are, or should you think yourself a pushover compared to their brave, warrior-like behavior?

Of course, it's neither necessary nor appropriate for you to form such opinions. You react the way you react. As I've mentioned in several places already, our habitual responses are products of our individual genetics and experience, and we've acquired our habitual impulses innocently. The next chapter explains how that works.

CHAPTER 11

Why You React the Way You Do

How Habitual Reactions Are Created

Habits are cobwebs at first, cables at last.
—Chinese proverb

The preceding chapter showed how the machinery of our brains engages automatically to protect us. Every healthy human being has this same machinery, but our individual machines are run by programs created by our individually unique genetics and experience, as you'll learn in this chapter.

Reactive Brain is constantly looking, seeing, learning, and responding. The main question we'll focus on in this chapter is why our Reactive Brains react to stimuli differently. Specifically,

- How does Brain decide that some person, situation, or object is good, bad, or neutral?

- Once it decides, what makes it pick a particular emotional action program?

- Why is my Reactive Brain's understanding of threats, and its responses to them, different from yours?

Why does one parent yell at the recalcitrant child, while another coaxes her to do her homework? Why do some people go for the cookie when anxious, while others go into full gotta-control-everything-in-and-out-of-sight mode? And why do each of us have a different tolerance for stress and different ways of responding to it? Why do some people compliment their neighbors on their new golf-club membership, their children's grades, their spiffy new anything, while others feel diminished by another's success and need to make up a story to show they're successful too? The answers to questions like these will help you understand that you acquired your most unwanted habitual impulses innocently—as a matter of pure happenstance, not character.

We develop defense and coping strategies to protect ourselves in situations that make us feel threatened, bad, or anxious. Many habitual emotional reactions are formed very early in life as a result of the way our personalities and emotional styles lead us to respond to what we experience. Personality and emotional styles, terms I'll define in a few pages, are significantly influenced by our genetic inheritance.

As Damasio writes, "The internal preference system is inherently biased to avoid pain, [and to] seek potential pleasure...."[146] Those biases shape our reactions: Daddy shouts at brother and we become frightened. How do we react? Maybe we cry. Maybe we go to Daddy and try to soothe him, or we hit brother; or maybe we hit Daddy and soothe brother. Maybe we run to Mommy for comfort. Maybe we run and hide. Maybe we bury ourselves in the cookie jar, or go find our blankie. Maybe we pull the cat's tail, hit it, yell at it, or comfort it.

If what we did reduced our discomfort, even for a tiny moment, it's automatically remembered (learned), used the next time, and every time thereafter when we feel the way we did the first time we tried that reaction and it made us feel better. Those reactions, or something similar, become lifelong habitual responses to the kinds of feelings we had when Daddy yelled at brother—until we decide they're unwanted and make an effort to change the way we react.

Why did we react the way we did? Maybe it was a random choice. More likely, in my view, we had a preference due to our toddler-personality traits and emotional styles, both of which were informed by our genetic inheritance and in-utero experiences. What will we do in the future when confronted by a similar stressor? We'll do whatever worked before.

As we've already seen, Reactive Brain does not think ahead. It does not think about alternatives. It does not think about consequences or values. It reacts in ways meant to deal with threats, get rewards, reduce fear, and banish discomfort. Reactive Brain grabs at what worked in the past. It wants the pain to stop right now. For Reactive Brain, it's now that counts; that's all that counts. If you do something more lasting, or choose something based on its ability to solve the bigger problem, you've broken through Master Habit and made a well-considered adult choice that weighs consequences, which Reactive Brain never does.

I'm making four main points here:

- First, we are born with behavioral dispositions (traits) that comprise our personality and emotional styles.

- Second, those traits, and the way they're expressed, change as we age and learn, but at any particular time they are what we are born with, modified by our experiences from conception to the then-present.

- Third, when confronted with stimuli as infants or toddlers, having no consciously chosen values, no perspective, and no language, we react in ways that reflect those early traits and the urgent need to banish discomfort and threat and get rewards. The introvert will not get up and dance. The agreeable one will not hit Daddy. She is more likely to take him a favorite doll and try to calm him.

- Fourth, if what she did relieved her anxiety or fear or sadness, or got her what she wanted, it becomes her habitual way of responding to situations that feel similar. She'll do the same thing ever after, wearing a groove in her behavioral repertoire that will be difficult to avoid or escape from. If it didn't make her feel better, she'll keep trying until she finds something that does, and then continue to do that. It seems likely that she'll settle on whatever gives her relief rather than gambling on something untried.

As in infancy, sometimes the habitual responses solve the real problem—trying to calm Daddy and oneself, for example. Other responses—gobbling up the cookie jar—may only give short-term relief from discomfort and cause other problems.

Personality and Emotional Styles

Earlier I mentioned that personality and emotional styles influence Reactive Brain's choices of how we respond to stimuli. But what are they, and how do we get our individual, unique personalities and emotional styles? First, let's define the terms.

Personality

Psychologists describe personality in terms of five traits, or dispositions, called the Big Five or the Five Factor Model. The Five Factors are consciousness, agreeableness, neuroticism, openness, and extraversion. Think of each trait as having a range of variation. For example, while one pole of the extraversion dimension is extraversion itself, the opposite pole is introversion (see Table 1).

Table 1 Big Five Personality Dimensions	
Extroverted vs. Introverted	Bold, assertive, positive
	Withdrawn, timid, reserved
Conscientious vs. Uninhibited	Reliable, wants to achieve, organized
	Impractical, lazy, negligent
Agreeable vs. Antagonistic	Warm, altruistic, trusting
	Cold, suspicious, stingy
Neurotic vs. Emotionally stable	Anxious, impulsive, resentful,
	Relaxed, content, unflappable
Open minded vs. Closed minded	Emotionally aware, thinker, challenges convention
	Uninquisitive, rigid, dogmatic

Psychologists are able to measure these traits with useful accuracy. Personality assessments produce values for each of the five dimensions, and psychologists use them to diagnose personality disorders.[147] (If you're interested in knowing what your personality profile looks like, you can take a computer-based personality test that is said to be close to the professional version, but is free, at http://www.personal.psu.edu/faculty/j/5/j5j/IPIP/ipipneo120.htm, hosted by Pennsylvania State University.

Emotional Styles

Emotional styles, as a concept, was introduced to the general public in a 2012 book by Richard Davidson and Sharon Begley.[148] Davidson is a professor of psychology and psychiatry at the University of Wisconsin-Madison. Begley is a highly respected and widely published science writer who has authored or co-authored two other books on brain science. In their book, they describe six emotional styles that emerged from Davidson's thirty-year study of the brain and behavior. The six emotional styles are resilience, outlook, social intuition, self-awareness, sensitivity to context, and attention. Their principal characteristics are shown in Table 2.[149]

Table 2 Emotional Styles		
Style	*Contrasting Poles*	*Definition and Examples*
Resilience	Fast to recover vs. Slow	How quickly one recovers from emotional experiences. How long one holds on to anger and stays in a bad mood.
Outlook	Negative vs. Positive	Whether one has a positive or negative outlook. Maintaining a positive, sunny disposition regardless of what's going on; alternatively, usually gloomy and seldom enthusiastic.
Social Intuition	Puzzled vs. Socially Intuitive	How sensitive people are to nonverbal cues given by others, and to the requirements of various social situations. Does one recognize that the person they're talking with isn't interested in them, and is looking everywhere except at them? Does one notice the person in the crowd who is in distress?
Self-awareness	Opaque to self vs. Self-aware	Knowing if, how, and what one is feeling in any given situation. Not being surprised when told how they appear to be. Knowing it first.
Sensitivity to Context	Tuned out vs. Tuned in	Awareness of the context one is in and what roles, expectations, and actions are appropriate in the circumstances. Is this the place to tell one's favorite off color joke, to play Angry Birds, or to accept a cell phone call?
Attention	Unfocused vs. Focused	The ability to focus in the face of both internal and external distractions.

One could look at Davidson's emotional styles and wonder what the big deal is. Can't we just be more sunny and upbeat instead of hanging on to upsets? Can't we just stop being self-absorbed? Putting it differently, if you don't possess some of these maybe less-desirable characteristics, you might think they simply represent bad habits, self-indulgence, or worse—no doubt the result of bad or inattentive upbringing, right?

No.

And that's what is so remarkable about Davidson's results.

Where one's emotional styles lie on the spectrum of each of these emotional dimensions is the result of competition between different parts of the brain that experience and genetics have strengthened or weakened. For example, one's degree of openness depends on the relative balance between the left and right hemispheres of the brain. When the right is stronger, the person is more closed. Openness increases as the left strengthens.[150] Davidson and Begley present practices to selectively strengthen parts of the brain to shift emotional styles.

Here, as with personality, we have a set of measurable characteristics that influence how one responds to stimuli. For example, it's clear that people who have a negative outlook will respond to novel ideas differently than those with a positive one. Likewise, people who are self-aware will be more attentive to their emotions, and therefore more likely to attempt self-management than those who are less aware of what they are experiencing. (If you're interested in seeing where you stand on each of these emotional style dimensions, you can find an assessment for each in Chapter 3 of the Davidson/Begley book.)

If you want to satisfy yourself that personality traits and emotional styles influence how one reacts to various stimuli, you might find it useful to look over the tables that describe personality and emotional styles, and imagine how people with various styles might react when confronted by a physical threat, a loss, or challenges to ego, social position, or competency.

How We Get Our Unique Personality and Emotional Styles

Research shows that genes influence 40 to 60 percent of each of the Five Factors that describe personality,[151] and influence 20 to 60 percent of emotional styles.[152] That leaves a lot of room for experience to work on and shape us: 60 to 40 percent for personality characteristics, and 80 to 40 percent for emotional styles.[153] Still, what does it mean to say that genes and experience influence behavior?

Since genes determine much about the physical development of the human body, it's not surprising that they influence the way our brains develop physically, which in turn influences the brain's capabilities and our behavior. While this view has been working its way to acceptance over the last fifty to seventy years, it still shocks many people. How can genes influence behavior? Or, for that matter, how can the mere structure of the brain influence behavior apart from the individual's character-influenced choices? We question the connection between genes and personality traits because of our lack of understanding and feeling for the relationship between ourselves and our physical brain, much less the relationship between us and our subconscious. Besides, we hate the idea that we're not in control.

The Role of Genes

Until recently many scientists and lay people believed that we are born as blank slates; that nurture—experience—is far more important than nature; that there is no such thing as human nature; that little if anything other than physical characteristics are innate; that we make ourselves what we are by using will, stamina, and insight guided by morality; and, finally, that any differences in outcomes are due to those considerations or what our poor mothers and fathers did or did not do for and to us. Some believe that any differences among us can be accounted for by a transcendent soul or past-life experiences. Aside from the influences originating from those sources, if there are innate characteristics, they must be due to the influence of our genes and in-utero experience.[154]

But even then we have a hard time imagining that gene-produced variations in the physical brain could influence behavior—the things we like to do, our dispositions and personality traits, much less anything on which morality and values might bear. We also want to believe we have free will. For many, it's just too challenging to reconcile free will and genetic influences on behavior. Of course, when insisting we're free agents, we're forgetting, or attributing to personal weakness, all of those times when we, like the Apostle Paul, have been unable to override our impulses and have done the opposite of what we think we should have done.

As to our inability to comprehend the connection between genes and behavior, it's simply that we have no experience of it. Sure, parents notice that each of their children have different personalities, and many simply wonder at the difference, attributing it to things that happened after they were born.

Political, religious, or philosophical beliefs may be even greater impediments to accepting the idea that genes play a role in shaping behavior. It is often assumed that acknowledging the central role that genes play in our personality and behavior undermines the obligation to take responsibility for our actions. If our genes are the reasons we do things, then what can we take credit or feel responsible for? Is there any reason to try at all? Won't our genes take care of it for us, or, conversely, doom us? Moreover, it's clear that for society to survive, we must act as if we have free will, and hold everyone to that standard. Otherwise, concepts of good and evil, and the efficacy of effort, can have no role in shaping morality.

Parents sometimes doubt the influence of genes, believing that their children should be more similar because each child shares their genes. This is a simple misunderstanding. While each child has 50 percent of each parent's genes, they don't each have the *same* genes from each parent. At conception, except for identical twins, a mixing and matching of DNA gives each child a unique combination of each parent's contribution.

Finally, there is a well-justified fear that giving too much attention to the importance of genetic influences will promote theories of racial or ethnic stereotyping and eugenics—the belief in racial or ethnic superiority, inferiority, or immorality and that the world can be improved by encouraging forced breeding, sterilization programs, and even genocide.

While the influence of genes is important and well demonstrated, they are by no means the full picture. Davidson makes the distinction succinctly:

> [The] mere presence of a gene is not sufficient for the trait for which it codes to be expressed. A gene must also be turned on, and studies of both people and lab animals have shown that life experiences can turn genes on or off.[155]

Another version of that idea is,

> Genes [or heredity, or nature] load the gun, but it takes the environment [or nurture, or experience] to pull the trigger.[156]

Steven Pinker, Johnstone Family Professor in the Department of Psychology at Harvard University, is the author of *The Blank Slate: The Modern Denial of Human Nature*,[157] which does a thorough job of discrediting the blank-slate hypothesis. The simplest argument in favor of the idea that we're born with important innate characteristics may be Pinker's remark that:

> *Something* in the mind must be innate, if it is only the mechanisms that do the learning. Something has to see a world of objects rather than a kaleidoscope of shimmering pixels. Something has to infer the content of a sentence rather than parrot back the exact wording. Something has to interpret other people's behavior as their attempts to achieve goals rather than as trajectories of jerking arms and legs. (The author's emphasis.)[158]

(Pinker sometimes uses "mind" to refer to the entire brain, which I call small-b "brain.")

There's a great deal of evidence that something mental comes along with babies' cute bodies and smiling faces. The best evidence of genetic influence on behavior comes from numerous studies comparing the behavior of siblings who share known variations in their genes and environmental experiences, including their upbringing. By comparing the degrees of relatedness of siblings, whether they were raised together or apart, and what their experiences were, one can determine how much of the variation (or similarity) in their behavior is due to genes and experience. The gold standard is study of identical twins (from a single egg, who therefore have identical genes) who were separated at birth and reunited as adults. Pinker writes:

> My favorite example is the pair of twins, one of whom was brought up as a Catholic in a Nazi family in Germany, the other of whom was brought up by a Jewish father in Trinidad. Nonetheless, when they met each other [for the first time] in a laboratory in their 40s, both walked in wearing identical navy blue shirts with epaulets. Both of them kept rubber bands around their wrists. Both of them, it turned out on questioning, flushed the toilet before using it, as well as after, and liked to pretend to sneeze in crowded elevators to watch the other people jump.[159]

Here is a sampling of the ways in which identical twins are alike, even those separated at birth and therefore free of the influences of a shared upbringing and other early experiences. Again, from Pinker:[160]

> Testing confirms that identical twins, whether separated at birth or not, are eerily alike (though far from identical) in just about any trait one can measure. They are similar in verbal, mathematical, and general intelligence, in their degree of life satisfaction, and in personality traits such as introversion, agreeableness, neuroticism, conscientiousness, and openness to experience. They have similar attitudes toward controversial issues such as the death penalty, religion, and modern music. They resemble each other not just in paper-and-pencil tests but in consequential behavior such as gambling, divorcing, committing crimes, getting into accidents, and watching television. And they boast dozens of shared idiosyncrasies such as giggling incessantly, giving interminable answers to simple questions, dipping buttered toast in coffee, and—in the case of Abigail van Buren

and Ann Landers—writing indistinguishable syndicated advice columns. The crags and valleys of their electroencephalograms (brainwaves) are as alike as those of a single person recorded on two occasions, and the wrinkles of their brains and distribution of gray matter across cortical areas are also similar.

And, as to the relationship between siblings with different degrees of genetic similarities, he writes:

> Identical twins are far more similar than fraternal twins, whether they are raised apart or together; identical twins raised apart are highly similar; biological siblings, whether raised together or apart, are far more similar than adoptive siblings. Many of these conclusions come from massive studies in Scandinavian countries where governments keep huge databases on their citizens, and they employ the best-validated measuring instruments known to psychology.

What I'm getting at here is the idea that genetics and experience influence personality and emotional styles, and that those two characteristics shape how we respond to various stimuli. Regardless of what you or I would *like* to be true, we're past the point of uncertainty: genetics and experience shape behavior, and they produce traits that are both admirable and unwanted and that we had no role in choosing or shaping. There simply can no longer be any doubt.

Early Childhood Personality and Adult Reactions

Earlier in this chapter I gave an example of how a toddler's personality, emotional styles, and experience could shape its reactive patterns. While adult personalities change throughout life, I believe the reactive patterns of the child shape many of the habitual, automatic ways we react as adults. But the maturing of values, personalities, and preferences makes us want to change those childhood-influenced reactions.[161] Another way of saying this is that Intentional Mind is often an adult mind that has consciously decided it wants to overcome impulses that were programmed originally and automatically to accommodate the child.

I have not found any scientific authority saying explicitly what I just wrote, but this concept is consistent with research on the relative pace of development of the emotional-reactive and cognitive-intentional faculties of the human brain.

Characteristics We All Share[162]

While genes may give unique shape to our individual characteristics, there are many characteristics that we all share. Start from the most basic of evaluations the brain makes for us: how does Reactive Brain decide that what it sees is good, bad, or neutral? Antonio Damasio answers the question: "The brain classifies things or events as 'good' or 'bad' because of their possible impact on survival." In other words, ". . . [it] has a basic set of preferences or criteria, biases or values."[163]

And this from Joseph LeDoux:

> . . . our brains are programmed by . . . evolution or by memories established through past experiences. In either case, though, the initial responses [reactions] elicited by significant stimuli are automatic and require neither conscious awareness of the stimulus [by the individual] nor conscious control of the responses.[164]

In other words, it's all about survival. Survival is of such paramount importance that the brain gives it its highest priority. We're born with a starter set of definitions of what specific things and experiences are pro- and anti-survival. All of us are born with various other universal characteristics that help us learn to engage in, watch, and learn from our interactions with the world, with people, objects, and situations. In addition to giving paramount attention to survival, we have the innate ability and desire to experiment, to learn from experience, and to add that knowledge to our definitions of what is helpful or not. In short, we are born to survive on the basis of what we know, to experiment, to learn as a result, to remember what we've learned, and to change as a result of experience.

Here are some other basic characteristics that help us survive and thrive, and that we share.

Fears

Our starter set of fears varies to be sure, but for most of us it includes fear of snakes, spiders, predators, heights, storms, thunder and other loud noises, lightning, darkness, blood, strangers, social scrutiny, separation, death, embarrassment, and loss of love. Not all of these fears appear at birth. Fears appear when normal development says we might need them. For example, babies develop their fear of heights when they begin to walk. You'll notice, of course, that many of these innate fears are pretty much what any conscientious parent might teach. If a stimulus produces fear, it's because Reactive Brain codes the stimulus as threatening.

Notice that some of those innately fearful stimuli threaten psychological rather than physical survival: social scrutiny, separation, embarrassment, and loss of love. While psychological, each of those fears alerts us to possible loss of support from or status in relationship to others. And, since humans are dependent on support and status for most of our lives, one could argue that these fears are actually about survival.

Notice too that while snakes and spiders might be regarded as particular examples of "predator," many other definitions of predator—bear, wild dogs, piranhas—are not innate and must be learned.[165]

Reactions

We're provided with a set of automatic reactions to each of the fears I just listed. We freeze or run from snakes and spiders (or smash them when we're older and not paralyzed by fear). We automatically step back from the edge of cliffs or other heights; find shelter from thunder and lightning; cower and search for the cause of loud noises; crouch, slow our movements, and search for light when in darkness; physically withdraw from blood and rotten matter; and become wary around strangers.

While children tend to have these innate fears and responses to varying degrees, some adults learn to manage most of them. Otherwise reasonable people become herpetologists, entomologists, or even amateur snake and spider fanciers. Mountaineers overcome their fear of heights, but not enough to get careless. Few adults freak out at the sound of thunder and lightning, though most seek appropriate shelter. Medical professionals become inured to blood and other bodily fluids that may disturb the rest of us. In contrast to those innate reactions that many are able to change, some other fears never lose their emotional power for many of us—for example, losing loved ones, losing social status, separation, leaving home, embarrassment, and death, of course.

Emotions

Humans also come with a basic set of emotions that are triggered by relatively predictable stimuli. To be sure, not everyone is convinced that there are such things as "basic" emotions, and those who do have differing views of how many and which are "basic." For our purposes, it is enough to understand the general mechanisms of response in order to understand the process of emotional action program formation.

As mentioned in Chapter 10, Paul Ekman, longtime professor, now emeritus, at the University of California at San Francisco, did truly ground-breaking and remarkable research on emotions in the 1960s, demonstrating that each of seven basic emotions produces a characteristic facial expression that is involuntary, automatic, and recognizable across a broad range of cultures—Western, Asian, modern, and primitive.[166]

Those emotions are fear, anger, sadness, disgust, contempt, joy, and surprise.[167] In this book I focus on the negative emotions, particularly fear and anger, not because I'm a grump, or that joy and its close relative happiness aren't desirable and important, but because I believe that the negative ones are the close relatives of most of the emotions that drive unwanted habits. And, of course, they are the most extensively researched and the best known, though a lot of work is currently going on to understand happiness in particular.[168]

Table 3 Basic Emotions, Triggers, and Goals		
Emotion	**Trigger (Stimulus)**	**The Impulse's Goal**
Anger	Obstructed or frustrated goal, perceived injustice, violation of norms or sacred values	Remove trigger; punish norm violation; achieve frustrated goal
Fear	Physical or psychological threat	Avoid or reduce harm
Disgust	Offensive, decayed, rotten object	Repel, avoid, eliminate the source
Contempt	Immoral action	Assert one's superiority
Sadness	Loss of something valuable	Call for help; recoup loss
Surprise	Sudden, novel something	Reorient, get information, call attention
Joy	Goal has been attained	Motivation

As mentioned so often before, emotions appear for a reason. A stimulus produces them, and the purpose of the resulting emotion is to motivate us to do something to deal with the stimulus. Table 3 describes the triggers (stimuli) and goals of Ekman's seven basic emotions.[169]

It's important to recognize that while the stimuli for each emotion appear straightforward, the specific actions that constitute a trigger vary according to one's beliefs and values, as well as one's personality, emotional styles, and mood of the moment. For example, anger is triggered when we feel obstructed or frustrated, when we perceive an injustice or observe a violation of social norms or sacred values. Obstruction of goals might be something as trivial as being blocked by a human or object when trying to get to the Rice Krispies® in the cereal aisle, being interrupted when engrossed in some activity, being denied a promotion, or being cut off by some yo-yo driving through a stop sign. Perceived injustice might include anything politicians in the other party say or do. Violation of norms refers to the norms of your societies—plural: your family, culture, religion, country, and even your company.

So a trigger could be not wearing (or wearing) a tie to work, desecrating the national symbol, irreverent speech or disrespectful behavior toward someone, and, of course, in some cultures, seeing someone with an unapproved member of the opposite sex, or other violations of tribal rules. In other words, stimuli that produce anger in one person or culture might be unremarkable to others. Or they might react to the same things with different degrees of upset.

In addition to normal variations in what triggers emotions, it seems obvious that the context in which we encounter a trigger determines whether it triggers us at all, and if so, which emotion it produces. For example, hearing *no* could produce either anger or sadness for the rejected lover, depending on his or her personality and other details. Teenage courtship is common in America and Europe, and generally accepted. But elsewhere in the world simply seeing it can produce a range of from delight to mild disapproval, to rage, and even to murder in some places. So it seems that while we all have roughly the same *emotional toolbox*" there is wide variation in when and how it gets triggered and manifested.

SECONDARY EMOTIONS

Sometimes we make an almost instantaneous transition from one emotion to another, the transition occurring so rapidly that the individual, and everyone around him or her, is aware of only the secondary one. For example, while a physical threat might produce fear, it could instantaneously turn to anger if one were moved to respond aggressively. For many, fear, uncertainty, and doubt can elicit a need for control, and the attempt to get it can be very aggressive. As to all of these secondary emotions, I'm persuaded by Pema Chödrön's comment that "Beneath anger there is fear, and beneath fear there is a tender heart."[170] This isn't always the case, of course, but it's true frequently enough that we should stop and consider what the person screaming at us might be experiencing. Even more important, why are *we* screaming, cowering, boasting, lying, or binging?

To this point I've discussed mostly those characteristics that influence how we react to stimuli we're subjected to: our behavioral dispositions captured under the terms "personality" and "emotional styles," further influenced by the pursuit of survival and reward—all shaped in part by our genetic inheritance and experience. At the start of this chapter, I suggested that we might react differently to a stressful stimulus (Daddy is angry) depending on our behavioral dispositions, and that a lifetime habit is likely to result when a reaction on our part reduces short-term discomfort. Remember that we automatically adopt a reaction because it works: we're stressed, we do something, it relieves emotional discomfort, however briefly, and a habit is born. This is the typical result of experience and genetics combining to create a habitual emotional response: an emotional action program that produces both the impulse to action and the emotion that motivates us.

But there is more to say about the role of experience.

ACT FROM CHOICE

The Individual's Unique Learning and Its Effects

LEARNING

> *Under [the] influence and the agency of experience, the repertoire of things categorized as good or bad [pro-survival or threatening] grows rapidly, and the ability to detect new good and bad things grows exponentially.*
>
> —*Antonio Damasio*[171]

A small child is likely to be afraid of spiders and snakes and want to cuddle with those cute bears until he's taught that bears are predators. Just as we learn that *bear* equals *predator* (predator is an innate fear), we are born with the need to be accepted, to find a safe home in society. Babies cannot survive without the shelter, nourishment, and care others give them. A child in grade school, a teen, a young adult who is bullied or scapegoated can face lifelong difficulties as a result of such treatment, because acceptance by peers is so essential to learning to be a competent adult. Our hunter-gatherer forebears had no place for people who did not conform to their culture. We are very much social animals; we need to belong, and the anxieties we have around being accepted or rejected are innate.

We have to learn the rules of each social system we want or need to join, or that we depend on, and we do learn them. For babies that is the immediate family (or institution). As we grow older, we have to learn the rules of the other groups we encounter as we move from playground, through the schools we attend, to workplaces and our larger communities. Since we need to demonstrate a modicum of conformity to survive as humans, it's not surprising that one of the things we're good at is learning to assimilate and conform to social rules.

Whether the home, community, and workplace are sane or neurotic, kind or malevolent, supportive or rejecting, we learn to cope. Our parents' reactions teach us the family culture. If their culture is not exactly the same as the community's, we figure that out when we go to school. It's not that we sit down with pencil and paper and write down what we've observed, what works and doesn't, what the punishments and rewards are. We absorb all that implicitly, and the result is learning which behavior can get us what we want and help us avoid punishment, including unwanted indifference or aggression from other members.

The prefrontal cortex is the storehouse of social mores (or norms).[172] If you'll recall, while the amygdala is working to classify what's going on around us, choosing an emotional action program and telling the hypothalamus to get us into its program, the prefrontal cortex has a role too. If the prefrontal cortex sees things differently than the amygdala, it can influence the amygdala's actions, even cancelling its orders. It appears that the prefrontal cortex can also take the initiative, and its voice is especially powerful when it's working to enforce social norms.

When the prefrontal cortex recognizes we're on the verge of violating a norm, it sends powerful signals to the rest of the Brain, and everyone pays attention. It is as if social norms have a very high place in the amygdala's views of what is important, and it is thus very attentive to the prefrontal cortex's norm-related instructions. I suspect this is the reason that almost everyone is sensitive to the appropriateness of their speech. Sapolsky says that the prefrontal cortex is what makes us do the "hard thing."[173] How else can you explain young warriors' willingness to risk death by coming up out of their safe trenches, or fathers and brothers murdering their children and sisters because of a breach of tribal custom?

How, too, does one explain the all too common unethical behavior of people in business and other organizations who deliberately deceive their customers, behavior they would never justify to their families and spiritual communities? Just think of the thousands of people, not just business managers and owners, whose participation in the mortgage debacle caused the 2008 Great Recession, not to mention people who in apparently good conscience labor to get more teens to take up smoking. Similarly, it is common for so many of us to hear individuals and groups—particularly minorities—disparaged and say nothing for fear of social reproof.

Somehow we find a way to make all this work for us. Yet it's important to call attention to the fact that our values are often tested by our need to be part of groups whose norms, and the behaviors they dictate, conflict with our values. The internally created emotional pressure to accede to the demands of normative behavior can be powerful enough to compel us to risk our lives, freedom, and self-respect.

Other Ways Emotional Habits Are Formed

Most of the examples I've used so far to illustrate emotional habit formation describe behaviors aimed at dealing with real threats; the impulses are aimed at dealing with the stimuli that trigger them. You might call those well-formed habits. In addition to those, most of us have a number of other habits that are misguided, misdirected, and just plain useless as described in Chapter 1. Misguided habits, you may remember, are emotional reactions to stimuli that will not produce the consequences the reaction is meant to deal with. Being terrified by mice is an example.

Misdirected habits produce impulses that do not address the consequences of the stimulus: kicking the dog after a bad day at work. Useless habits also include excessive negative energy expended on things we can't change: much ado about nothing we can fix.

CONDITIONING PRODUCES MISGUIDED HABITS

Conditioning can make us very upset when there's nothing to be upset about. The feelings are very real, but whatever triggered them will not produce the consequences the habit is meant to deal with.

Something happens today. Some time ago something emotionally significant happened. Some of the characteristics of today's experience were present then, but only present; they had no causal relationship to the emotionally significant event. In other words, the trigger that sets you off today was not the cause of what happened in the past. The trigger was not unique to that situation, didn't cause it, and won't produce a replay of that event. Maybe the weather was the same, or somebody was wearing a striped shirt; whatever happened long ago involved different people and circumstances, and neither the weather nor the striped shirt caused the very real problem experienced then. Nevertheless, that common characteristic produces the emotion of the past. The root cause of this misguided habit is that memories are stored associatively. Brain doesn't realize that the characteristic it sees today was not a *cause* of what happened long ago.

No doubt you've heard about Pavlov's dogs. In the early part of the twentieth century, the Russian physiologist Ivan Pavlov did experiments in which he rang a bell immediately before giving food to his dogs. After many repetitions of bell-then-food, the dogs began to salivate when the bell rang, even if food didn't follow the bell. This is known as *classical conditioning*. The bell is called the *conditioned stimulus* because, though it has nothing to do with food, it is linked to food in the brain of the dogs. You could ring a bell often and forever, and a dog *not* conditioned to associate bells with food would not salivate; not ever.

PTSD, or post-traumatic stress disorder, can be caused by conditioning that occurred during a traumatic event. The National Library of Medicine defines PTSD as "a type of anxiety disorder. It can occur after you have gone through an extreme emotional trauma that involved the threat of injury or death."[174] It's not confined to warriors. In fact, it is surprisingly common: "… [It] is now recognized that repeated traumas or traumas of long duration such as child abuse, domestic violence, stalking, cult membership, and hostage situations may also produce the symptoms of PTSD in survivors. A person suffering from PTSD experiences flashbacks, nightmares, and daydreams in which the traumatic event is experienced again. The person may also experience abnormally intense startle responses, insomnia, and may have difficulty concentrating."[175]

In the case of PTSD, the brain associates almost any feature of the traumatic event with the trauma itself, turning these reminders into highly charged, conditioned triggers (stimuli): on the battlefield these might include the air temperature, loud noises, people shouting, the sight of wounded or dead, time of day, state of fatigue, foreign faces, colors, trash on the side of the road which, in the war zone, might have concealed an explosive device. Because the brain stores memories associatively, all characteristics of the event are linked to the factual (declarative) and emotional memory of the trauma and its emotional impact. For victims of sexual abuse, it might be seeing a place resembling where the abuse occurred, the time of day, people resembling the abuser.

Thereafter, the sight, sound, smell, taste, touch, or thoughts of any and each characteristic of the traumatic situation may fool the brain into thinking the trauma is repeating. Reactive Brain then recreates the impulses and emotions originally experienced, and intended to defend against the assault. Even though the triggering event was no more serious than someone approaching from behind in a grocery store checkout line in Minneapolis, the danger feels present to Reactive Brain. In consequence, all of the emotions of the original trauma repeat in some form in the same way that ringing the bell made the dogs' Brains initiate salivation, as if food were coming.

It's easy to say there's no logical reason for someone to react to a conditioned stimulus, but in fact, there's little the victim can do to control the symptoms without undertaking extensive desensitizing, which typically involves cognitive or other therapies administered by trained mental health care professionals.

PTSD is an extreme example of conditioning that produces emotional effects that are inappropriate to the stimulus. Here's an example that is less extreme and perhaps more common.

> Mari's father expected her to have all the answers. When she didn't, his reaction felt to her like anger, derision, and loss of his esteem. Maybe this didn't happen all the time, but it happened enough to have a significant impact on her. Mari is well into middle age. If her partner asks her a question that's not phrased just right—no matter how inconsequential—she may react with anger. He says he's learned not to ask, "What do you want to do about dinner?" but rather "Have you had a chance to think about dinner?" The latter question doesn't presume she has an answer ready, and she can simply answer yes or no. There's no challenge implicit in the question.

Even though Mari knows that the question what do you want for dinner is not meant to harm her, it feels like an implicit assumption that she should have a plan in mind. If she doesn't have a dinner plan, or hasn't even thought about dinner, the question makes her feel in danger of being judged, and she reacts defensively. Her past experience pairs an innocent question from a loved one today with her fear of losing the questioner's esteem based on her interactions with her father in her childhood. This evokes her anger. It's automatic.

The key thought here is that we can be afraid of (or conversely, attracted to) things that are like things that were merely present at a time in the past when we were frightened of or attracted to something.

The objective for managing a conditioned habit is to accept the impulse, acknowledge it, and train the Sentinel to make you aware that you're experiencing a conditioned response that, however powerful, may not be a justified response to the stimulus. (There is more about conditioned reactions in Part II.) When called to mind, Tsoknyi Rinpoche's slogan, or mantra, "Real, but not true," introduced earlier, is particularly helpful in draining the emotions from conditioned responses.

MISDIRECTED HABITS

You'll recall that misdirected habits reduce discomfort but do nothing to improve the situation or address the trigger. If you kick the dog or yell at the family after a hard day at work, you risk damaging your relationships, and have done nothing to fix the problem at work that made you angry. At best, these reactions lead to additional, needless discomfort as you try to make amends. Moreover, expressing anger uselessly prolongs the anger itself, and the discomfort.

Common examples of misdirected habits are nervous eating, procrastination, and misplaced aggression. When we let the misdirected habits turn to anger, we're often left worse off than before.

Pema Chödrön has an excellent description of misdirected habits in Chapter 11 of her book *When Things Fall Apart*.[176] I find her description of these ancient Buddhist teachings a handy way of thinking about these habits. According to her, there are four general ways we try to escape discomfort:

- We seek pleasure—food, drink, drugs, and sex, for example.

- We go to ego—proclaim our goodness, our status, our separateness, our *rights*

- We exaggerate our emotional reactions—wind ourselves up to get ever more angry, try to enlist others to feel our outrage, for example.

- We become more controlling, especially when confronted by uncertainty or concern about our own mortality.

Here are two specific examples:

- Roxanne, a former smoker, tells me that when she examined her smoking habit, she realized that each cigarette was not the friend she had previously imagined, but was instead "a sacrifice to the demon-god of anxiety, who is insatiable." That observation led her to find other ways to deal with her anxiety.

- Consider Billy, who, when faced with anxiety, would go for control—not control of whatever was causing the anxiety, but control of everything else he could think of. He would fill up his schedule, taking on extreme goals for physical and intellectual development, for achieving more aggressive business goals, for reconnecting with friends and family—all in a frenzy of planning. Though he filled all available time with scheduled doing, it never resolved his anxiety. The goals and plans were worthwhile, but there were too many, and the motivation to do them wasn't there. His real motivation was to feel in control, and so banish his anxiety. Over-scheduling himself worked for only a very short time. His anxiety returned and was more intense because of his failure to achieve all those goals he adopted to ward off the anxiety.

We think we're going to lose something really important to us—job, love, money—and we're terrified, maybe jealous too. We may start a fight with someone who controls the outcome. Maybe we sulk and do the sour-grapes thing, or bury ourselves in the stamp collection rather than prepare contingencies against the worst. All of those divert us from working with ourselves and others who might help us face the situation and change the outcome.

We hold on to our misdirected habits because they temporarily relieve our discomfort. They become ingrained even when we know they are not good for us. They go against our values or best interest, or we've simply outgrown them. They are very hard to root out. The key to managing them is to identify what triggers them and train the Sentinel to break you out of Master Habit and direct your attention to the underlying problem when their triggers appear.

USELESS HABITS

Useless habits are a subset of misdirected habits. Something triggers us, and we put a lot of energy into the reaction—typically angry frustration. Acting out the reaction is taxing, maybe even harmful to ourselves and others, and has no impact whatsoever on what triggers us. Sitting in your car screaming and winding yourself up because of a traffic jam is a typical useless habit. This statement by Nuala O'Faolain, the Irish writer, says everything that needs to be said about why these habits are useless: "If only I could stop wanting the impossible, I'd be happy as a lark."[177] The Serenity Prayer is a powerful reminder that useless habits are just that: useless.

If you find yourself caught up in a useless habit, getting all worked up—angry even—when your emotions can't make the situation better for you, you might ask yourself, "Do you really want to make this worse than it already is?" If you prefer, you could make that a command instead: "Don't make this situation worse than it already is." *Making it worse* refers to winding yourself up, when all you're doing is feeding yourself the poison of negative, useless emotions. Many find this simple question very effective at quickly bringing down their temperature and getting them to be practical about the situation right away. Asking yourself questions is often exactly what is needed to break through the power of some habits. The technique, called *Ask the Second Question,* is covered in detail in Chapter 19.

At this point, you might have a number of questions. Based on my work with clients and meditation students, I'm guessing that one or more of these four might be among them:

First, what is the relationship between your personality and emotional styles today and what they were when you were very young? We'd hate to think we still had that infantile personality, or that our values were the same, even the same as they were in high school. You can take comfort in what studies say on this point. The research says that our personality, values, and preferences change throughout our lifetimes. You're probably not the same today as you were even ten years ago.[178] That's one of the reasons why you may find your old habitual reactions are no longer acceptable.

Second, if our personalities and emotional styles have changed from when we were very young, why haven't our habitual reactions changed? It's likely that quite a few habits you had when you were younger have changed. Some haven't, and their ability to undermine your values and/or intentions makes them seem prevalent and important. A sense of humor helps when dealing with the familiar, old, stubborn habits. Some of those may produce the same unwanted impulses for the rest of your life. Notice how familiar they are; how easily and quickly recognizable they've become; and how, in many cases, they're easier to overcome. Ask yourself if it isn't just the impulses—not what you do in response to the impulses that distresses you. If that's the case, greet them as if they were old but deluded friends.

It often takes conscious effort to change the durable old habitual patterns, which is what this book is about. But there's also a natural process that extinguishes habits through simple learning. The prefrontal cortex learns that a stimulus is not, indeed, as harmful as it once thought. Having fully absorbed that learning, the prefrontal cortex is able to shut down the amygdala's orders to the hypothalamus. When that happens, the amygdala's prescription is short-circuited; it stays below consciousness, and you may never realize there was a competition that your learnings won. You just didn't get as riled up as you used to.[179]

Third, why don't we remember the events—often traumatic—that cause some of our more extreme reactions? The answer to this question has to do with the structure of memories and when in life our memory systems develop. Two types of memory systems important to answering this question are *explicit memory*, also called *declarative memory*, and *emotional memory*. Explicit memory stores and retrieves facts: who, what, where. Explicit memory includes your telephone number, the Pythagorean Theorem you learned in high school, the circumstances of your first kiss, or where you were when you heard about other emotionally significant events. The explicit memory system is slow to develop in humans, which is why most of us can't recall anything that happened before we were three or four.

Emotional reactions to events are stored in a separate emotional memory system, which is well developed virtually from birth. If the childhood trauma occurred early enough in life, memory of the events themselves were not stored in the explicit, then-undeveloped memory system, but the emotional reaction was captured by emotional memory. As in the case of PTSD or other conditioning, when anything suggestive of the early trauma appears later in life, the emotional memory of the childhood event is triggered. Lacking access to memory of the originating event, the emotional reaction seems inexplicable. The principal difference between these experiences and those of people who acquired PTSD later in life is that the events of the childhood trauma can't be remembered, while the events of adult trauma can.

And, fourth, why is it so hard to change our habitual emotional responses? It's just the way the brain works. Many emotional responses are rooted in experiences that have great emotional significance, and so they require a strong opposing force to keep them in check. Research shows that the brain never forgets any negative experiences. For example, when PTSD sufferers are able to reduce their reactivity to the conditioned stimuli that bring on their symptoms, it's not that the brain has forgotten or that the strength of conditioning has been diminished; the symptoms are interrupted because the learning is strong enough that the prefrontal cortex can shut down the amygdala's response.

Even so, if the person is exposed to conditioned stimuli that were not part of the therapy that desensitized him or her, the PTSD symptoms will reappear. And if the person stops being exposed to those stimuli whose effects were "extinguished," the learning will be lost and the reaction to those stimuli will likely reoccur in the future.[180]

I speculate that another factor in the difficulty of changing some emotional habits is the high degree of importance the brain gives the need to conform to social mores, in particular. Recall that values, personality traits, and preferences change as we age.[181] It's likely that some habitual reactions, attitudes, and thoughts, particularly those you once felt you had to honor to conform to social norms, no longer fit your personality and emotional styles, your code of conduct, or your social situation. Still, the emotional importance of the need to conform may continue to exert a powerful influence in the same way that triggers of PTSD do.

For example, many words now heard regularly on TV or in public conversations were taboo, say, 25 years ago. As those previously taboo words became acceptable, I've become an enthusiastic user, but they never fail to give me a twinge of conscience—not when I hear them, only when I use them. You might want to take a moment to think about this issue: If your standards and beliefs have changed over time, ask yourself whether you've modified how you judge things and whether your judgments reflect your new standards. Could it be that some feelings of guilt or shame are aligned with obsolete beliefs?

The purpose of this chapter is to open you up to the idea that the formation of our habitual reactions is influenced by the way our experiences interact with our personality and emotional styles, both of which are significantly influenced by our genes. There is almost nothing we could have done to cause or change what we experienced. Nor did we choose the temperament, or mores, or beliefs of our families or our early playground friends. In other words, none of the factors influencing what we learned, what we learned to react to, and how we react were under our control. Our habitual patterns of reaction and behavior were formed by happenstance, not by choice or character. They just happened.

Our personalities do change, stabilizing to a great degree around age thirty, though they continue to change, albeit more slowly, throughout our lives.[182] While adult personalities change, I believe our childhood personality traits shape many of our habitual, automatic impulses (reactions) that we experience as adults, and that it's our adult values, personality traits, and emotional styles that make us want to keep those unwanted impulses from turning into action. In other words, your desire and motivation to manage your habits are expressions of the values you've chosen, either explicitly or implicitly. Your mature, adult Intentional Mind is trying to overcome the impulses programmed in childhood by a then-appropriately immature Reactive Brain.

Part II describes how to manage those impulses.

CHAPTER 12

Putting It All Together

Part I has been about the forces that stimulate and maintain reactive behavior. In particular, we've looked at how Reactive Brain chooses the impulses and emotions it presents us with, and the great influence emotional action programs have on our behavior. You've also read about the importance of self-awareness in managing habits, and the fact that the amount of willpower we have at any moment is a limited resource, not controllable by character and desire alone. In addition, there has been much about the fact that we are innocent of our impulses and need to judge ourselves fairly—to take into account the causes and conditions that influence our reactions, many of which are not subject to our control.

We've covered a lot of material, and I imagine a summary is in order before we launch into Part II.

Emotions and Reactive Brain

The bedrock of everything I've presented so far is made up of research findings that describe the ever-present and powerful influence that subconsciously produced emotions have on our decisions and behavior. The research says that *all* of our decisions depend on having a preference for one action, one thing, one person, one situation over the alternatives. Those preferences are developed unconsciously and automatically by the emotional systems of the brain that I call Reactive Brain. Reactive Brain interprets the stimuli we're exposed to and produces emotional action programs to deal with them. Emotional action programs produce an impulse to action (or inaction). The brain sets up the body to carry out the action. Brain systems interpret the way the body has been set up as emotions, gut feelings, and intuitions. Whatever we call them, their purpose is to motivate us to act the way Reactive Brain and its emotional action programs want.

Emotions are essential to how we react and what we do in response. If our brains were unable to translate body-feelings into the emotions we feel, we, like Antonio Damasio's patients—Elliot and others—would not be able to make the simplest decisions. Damasio's research was foundational to our understanding that emotions are always attempting to guide us, and that we'd be lost without them. These emotions, that are so essential, are not just the florid ones that come to mind when we hear *emotions*. They are often quite subtle, like the intuitions that make us want to choose one alternative rather than another when there is no clear reason to favor one or the other.

Much of the reactive programming that directs our automatic response took place automatically, without choice, when we were very young. We are born with some behavioral dispositions that are influenced by our genetic inheritance—for example, dispositions toward introversion or extraversion, having a negative or positive outlook, being open- or closed-minded, being fast or slow to recover from disturbing emotions. Those dispositions influenced the way we reacted to opportunity and threat, to things we wanted and things we wanted to avoid. When the way we reacted got us what we wanted or alleviated discomfort, even for just a moment, the reaction was adopted and became a lifelong habitual reaction. We didn't choose those reactions. They just happened.

Reactive Brain is always watching, judging, and reacting. It sees, hears, smells, tastes, feels, decides, and instigates reactions to what it encounters before we're consciously aware there's anything out there to deal with. In other words, it is your Reactive Brain acting subconsciously, programmed in advance by your genetically inspired traits and past experience, that decides for you how stimuli might affect you and how to respond. Moreover, in most cases, it completes that work before you're consciously aware of the stimulus. When we try to modify unwanted impulses, we are working against the habit-inspired programming of Reactive Brain.

The emotional action programs that Brain produces are usually exactly what are called for: the stimuli have been accurately perceived, and the emotions and actions the subconscious prescribes are acceptably close to, and often exactly, what we would have chosen if we had the opportunity to choose. Unfortunately, the processes that produce those *perfect* responses are not foolproof. They often result in impulses and emotions that urge us to behave in ways we would not choose, are not in our best interest, and may violate our values and intentions, producing regrettable consequences. Which is how we get our unwanted habitual reactions.

Obstacles and Allies

We encounter many obstacles when trying to manage our habits. First among these obstacles is that we can't see habitual reactions as they're working up to launching impulses to act. Impulses appear unannounced. Blind to the actions of our subconscious, we think *we* designed and chose our emotions and the actions that emotional action programs command us to execute.

Our challenge is to become aware of impulses as soon as possible and to bring our best cognitive mind to deciding whether we want to execute the emotional action program's wishes or make our own choice. If we're to manage ourselves, we need to exercise *free won't* to interrupt the impulse, then go on to choose and exercise our intentions. Those objectives require us to become aware of the impulses we feel and become present to what's going on as quickly as possible, so that we can see what we're doing and bring our intelligence and intentions to bear. I've introduced you to the Sentinel, a function of the brain, a tool you'll use to help you become self-aware more quickly than you might otherwise.

The Sentinel will be your main tool for effecting targeted mindfulness, the more reliable triggering of mindfulness of situations you mean to manage.

Self-awareness wakes us to unwanted impulses in progress, breaking through the Master Habit of distraction and putting us in the Choosing Space. We see what's happening and can attempt to override the unwanted impulses—to impose the wishes of Intentional Mind on our behavior, thoughts, and attitudes.

Reactive Brain has injected you with strong feelings which it chose based on what was immediately in front of it. It didn't—in fact it never does, and can't—analyze the situation to figure out what is most likely to work and be of value to you and the situation. It can't offer up alternatives and evaluate their consequences either.

We are the only ones who can judge whether what Reactive Brain wants us to do is of value—whether there are different, possibly better responses to the stimulus. Does the stimulus deserve any response? If so, what response would best serve our interests? Is Reactive Brain's response a complete solution, or a short-term panacea that will leave us to face the identical stimulus over and over again? Will the prescribed action promote our interests, help or hurt the situation? Is it consistent with our values? We need the faculties of Intentional Mind to make these kinds of determinations.

Many influences can affect Reactive Brain and undermine Mind's judgment in favor of accepting Reactive Brain's impulses. Those influences include transient moods, Reactive Brain's error-prone processing of sensory data, the myriad biases that Kahneman and many others have written about, the powerful influence of stimuli received only subliminally, our natural desire to believe our gut feelings, the effects of conditioning that have no relevance in the immediate situation, even our intuitive discounting of the role and power of the subconscious.

One of the factors that will influence whether we're successful is the state of our motivation and willpower. You've seen that willpower is a limited resource that can be strengthened through training, but whose strength at any moment depends on how much, if any, has been depleted by recent use.

Regarding Guilt, Shame and Self-Blame

Habitual, unwanted impulses can make us feel guilt, shame, and self-blame, leading to denial, even when we don't act on the impulse. One of the most durable and universal of unwanted habits is believing we're autonomous, that we have control, should always exercise it, and are therefore totally responsible for our self-management failures.

The facts do not support that blaming.

I've urged you to consider that there is no reason to judge or blame yourself for unwanted impulses because the mechanisms of reaction—how Reactive Brain interprets stimuli, the emotions it incites, and the actions it prescribes—are the results of habits, mostly formed very early in life, and always involuntarily.

We are not responsible for our impulses, because they were acquired innocently—by happenstance. The genes and experience so important in determining what we react to, and how we react, are not under our control. Our genes influence personality traits and emotional styles, which dispose us to react to stress and opportunities in certain ways. Neither genes nor experience are under our control when we are young. The brain is forming then, and we are least autonomous and wise. Experience presents challenges and opportunities, and our dispositions influence how we respond. The introverted child will not argue with an angry parent. The extraverted child is less likely to back down.

As for experience, at such early ages we have little choice in what we'll experience. We are not responsible for the temperament of our parents, whether our childhood is hard or easy, or what kind of experiences we had when trying to find a place in our earliest societies: family, playground, and school. It's neither fair nor logical to judge ourselves for having habits that were formed so early in life, so accidentally and without conscious choice.

Often habits acquired early in life are slow to catch up with our values. The old Reactive Brain programming might have made sense to us in the past, but no longer, and this mismatch can be a source of self-generated and inappropriate shame and guilt. You never sat down with your Reactive Brain to tell it how you preferred to respond to stubborn children, your own anxiety, or to physical threats. Neither did you tell it what you object to, nor that, when in difficult situations, you want to react with your fists, with your voice, by negotiating, by attempting to please, or by withdrawing.

Behavior and Realistic Expectations

Behavior is what counts. We are responsible for doing the best we can to manage our behavior—to bring it in line with our standards and values as best we can. Powerful impulses and emotions and inadequate willpower can make that extremely difficult at times, no matter how sincerely and power-fully motivated you are. If you work with the techniques I recommend in Part II of this book, you will certainly improve, but working with habits is analogous to lifting weights. Repeating Stephen Levine's metaphor, you begin the program with ten-pound weights. That becomes easy, so you move up to heavier weights. You get to seventy-five-pound weights. Then one day someone throws a hundred-pound weight at you. You fall down. "Big surprise!" No problem. No fault. Pick yourself up and go back to the weight bench.

There will always be weights too heavy to deal with, and they will knock you down. But with practice and time, it will take more and more to knock you off balance, and you will stop reacting negatively to those inevitable failures. Realistic expectations are the key to shaking off disappointment and maintaining your efforts to manage yourself. Understand that sometimes you will be tested beyond your capabilities. Accept those failures. Objectively they are failures, and there's no sense in sugarcoating them. But keep going. If you are disappointed that you didn't reach your goals, didn't meet your standards, suffered some loss, by all means validate those feelings; grieve the losses, but do not let them turn you against yourself. Choose regret, not guilt.

Judge yourself according to reasonable expectations using the same wisdom and compassion you would use to judge a friend. If you're willing to keep going back to the weight bench, to keep working at it, you're a star and you deserve your acclaim and support.

And, yes, when you fail, when you drop the weights on the floor, clean up any mess you made. Make amends. And choose regret, not guilt, because as long as you are working to manifest your values, you are being *how* and *who* you mean to be, and are entitled to claim those values as your own.

Those are the takeaways that I'd like you to have as you start reading Part II and learn how to use the Act from Choice Method.

PART II

How to Act from Choice

CHAPTER 13

Introduction to the Act from Choice Method

The Challenges of Habit Management

As mentioned in the Introduction, there are four specific challenges we confront when trying to manage unwanted habitual impulses:

- Breaking through distraction and becoming aware of unwanted impulses when they arise.

- Pausing in the face of the impulse's momentum.

- Overcoming the impulse's momentum; choosing what to do, and imposing the choice.

- Dealing with the consequences of failure when it happens— that is, banishing guilt and maintaining the motivation and intention to continue trying to manage the habit after failing to do what was intended.

Of course, you face these challenges only when you're making a conscious effort to manage your impulses. The fact that you're reading this book is a sign that you're on that path.

How the Method Addresses the Four Primary Challenges

Here is what you will need to do to overcome these challenges:

- **Becoming aware** requires that you've identified what you want to manage, have an objective in mind, and have trained your subconscious monitor—your Sentinel—to wake you when the impulse first appears.

- **Pausing** requires that your Sentinel has launched you into the Choosing Space, and you have made the commitment to manage the impulse.

- **Overcoming the impulse's momentum** requires you to have enough motivation and willpower, in that moment, to resist the impulse as you make and follow through with a different choice than Reactive Brain's emotional action program.

- **Dealing with the consequences** of the inevitable failures requires that you understand what you're up against when trying to change, particularly how determined Reactive Brain is. That understanding will help you extend compassion to yourself and begin to trust in the integrity of your effort to manage yourself.

The Act from Choice Method gives you techniques and tools for developing and fostering these skills. It will give you insight into the attitudes and perspectives you'll have to have in order to motivate yourself to succeed.

The Method consists of three major phases: **Preliminary**, **Decision**, and **Committed.**

Preliminary Phase

The Preliminary Phase will help you get clear about what you habitually do or feel that is unwanted, how you want to change what you do, and whether you have sufficient motivation to do what you want rather than go along with the habitual and unwanted. There are three steps in this plan:

- Identify what it is you do, and how you do it.
- Pick an objective for what you want to do instead.
- Identify the considerations that motivate you to manage yourself, and understand how strong your motivation is.

Decision Phase

After completing the Preliminary Phase, including the motivation portion, you will have all of *the objective* information about you and your unwanted habit that you're capable of assembling at that time. That information and your *gut feelings* will tell you whether you're motivated enough to change in the ways you've identified. If you decide you are, then you'll explicitly decide to continue into the next phase of the Method. If you feel you don't have sufficient motivation, I recommend you accept that you're not yet ready to proceed, and think of it as an aspiration. That's not a problem, because if and when the objective becomes important enough, it will tug at you and ask you to commit.

Committed Phase

You've decided to work at self-management and have identified the objective you want to work on. You're committed. Now it's time to make some additional commitments to make your decision actionable. There are three steps in this phase:

- Commitment
- Awareness
- Plan

COMMITMENT

You're asked to make two commitments: to **pause** your action when you first become aware of the unwanted impulse, and then to **choose** what to do, and attempt to follow through with your choice—more specifically, to follow a *formal*, pre-planned decision-making process, which you'll design. Both commitments—to pause and then to choose—are commitments to yourself. I'll show you how to design that decision-making process, using the tools I provide here.

Jumping ahead just a bit, I want to point out that in the Act from Choice Method, the word "Choice" is taken literally. You are entirely free to choose the habitual unwanted impulse after going through your formal decision-making process. Your commitment is simply to follow the process you design. If you weren't allowed to choose habit over intention, there would be no room for choice, and the idea of committing to a process for choosing would be a transparent fiction. Having the permission to go either way will give you a well-deserved sense that you are acting from choice, rather than from an arbitrary rule, and you will have the freedom and responsibility of real choice.

The commitment to *pause* and *choose* is a commitment to two distinct steps, because habit management requires two exercises of willpower. The first is to stop the impulse's momentum as soon as you're aware of it. The second is to make, and attempt to follow through, with your choice.

You'll sometimes find that it's hard to hold off the momentum of the impulse while you try to follow your plan on how to choose what to do, and act the way you've chosen. Putting the brakes on the unwanted impulse as soon as you become aware of it helps enormously. But if you don't take that initial action to pause, you'll be running to catch up as the impulse continues to act on you. If you're *unwilling* to make the commitment to pause, you're done, at least for now. Again, if you're unwilling to take this step, acknowledge that's where you are just now, and put the desire to change in your aspiration box. The changed behavior is not yet "how *you mean* to be." It's how you'd *like* to be.

TRAIN YOUR AWARENESS

Having made the necessary commitments to yourself, the next step is to begin to train your awareness, of which you'll need two kinds. The first is awareness of yourself in the situation: awareness of what you're about to do, how and what you feel, and what you intend to do. Your Sentinel performs those awareness functions. So you begin creating the ability to become aware by creating—hiring—your Sentinel and starting to train it so that it will be ready to wake you up when the impulse appears. This is an ongoing process, as I'll explain.

The Sentinel will open the Choosing Space for you, but as mentioned in Chapter 5, when first entering it, you will still be feeling the power of the emotional action program, which may deprive you of complete access to your motivations. Consequently, to be maximally effective you'll need a second kind of awareness. You'll need the ability to know and appreciate, in that moment, all of the factors that created your motivation: knowledge of the consequences of following the impulse, the costs and benefits, and the effects on your values that come with managing or not managing your unwanted impulse.

The technique for bringing those motivating factors to awareness is called "Asking the Second Question." The Second Question technique is described in Chapter 19, which also describes the Sentinel.

PLAN

Finally, you'll need to have a plan for what to do when you find yourself in the Choosing Space confronting the Reactive Brain's unwanted impulse. Each habit is different, comes about in different environments, and calls for different action plans. For instructional purposes, I find it's helpful to present three types of habits and their respective plans. So in separate chapters I give examples for creating simple plans which address *cold habits*, complex plans for addressing *hot habits*, and plans for cultivating and enhancing your values by managing unwanted attitudes.

Cold habits are unwanted impulses involving how one deals with oneself, or habits involving others too, but in situations which do not require an immediate response. When dealing with cold habits, we can let things cool before reacting because we're the only ones involved, or others are involved but we can take our time to respond. Either way, we have time on our side. Examples of cold habits include procrastination, not maintaining a consistent exercise program or diet, and deciding how and when to reply to an infuriating email.

Hot habits are unwanted impulses that come up when one or more other people are involved and present; emotions may be powerful and hot, and an on-the spot response seems necessary, even if it's just to leave the room. Hot habits often arise when dealing with intimates—family, for example—and in chance experiences of aggression and disrespect. Hot habits require the more complex plans that are necessary for handling the flash of anger directed toward or from another person, as well as feelings of helplessness and fear.

Cultivating and enhancing your values by managing unwanted attitudes is about using unwanted attitudes, thoughts, and judgments that are contrary to your values as tools to cultivate the values they undermine. You might think you're open-minded, but realize that you're occasionally closed, or feel that you're generous, but find you're often stingy. Discovering these contrary attitudes and tendencies in your mind can feel like a rebuke, a challenge to your beliefs about which values you hold. But, instead of seeing these contrary experiences as a source of guilt, you can learn to see your reaction to them as validating your chosen values. That validation provides the trigger for being aware of the unwanted attitudes, and the motivation to manifest the values you mean to claim as your own.

The Mnemonic for the Method

Here is a mnemonic that can help you remember the steps that make up the Act from Choice Method, and a table that summarizes the principal features of each step.

- The mnemonic for the Preliminary Phase is TOM, for Truth, Objective, and Motivation.
- The mnemonic for the Committed Phase is CAP, for Commitment, Awareness, and Plan.
- Decision is the gateway between the two phases.

The Afterword contains remarks meant to help you follow through on your commitments by executing your plans—doing what you've planned and mean to do.

How to Use Part II

As you read about the Act from Choice Method you might feel overwhelmed by detail, and not interested in parts that don't seem to relate to your situation. The detail is here because I want to make this book as complete as possible for a broad spectrum of readers who have an equally broad variety of habits they'd like to manage. Naturally, you will be most interested in what is relevant to you.

It's important that you don't let detail superfluous to your interests keep you from getting to the material you'll need. So here's my advice: skim Part II if you want. See what resonates with you. Then go back and spend time on the parts that seem to hold promise and that you might be willing to work with. If you find that a particular chapter or section requires more effort than you want to give it just then, by all means skip it. Come back to it later if you think it can help.

That said, there are three chapters you should definitely pay attention to. The first is Chapter 19, *A Is for Awareness*. It describes two essential requirements of the Act from Choice Method. The first requirement is hiring and training a Sentinel. You'll need a well-trained Sentinel to help you wake up to unwanted impulses in time to execute your plan before impulses turn into unwanted actions.

The second requirement is that you're able to marshal your motivation to act against the force of the impulse. The technique for opening the mind and the decision-making process to the full force of motivation when we enter the Choosing Space is to *Ask the Second Question*. The technique, and how it works, is described in the second half of Chapter 19.

Chapter 20, "P Is for Plan," describes the elements needed for plans to be effective.

Chapter 21, "Simple Plans for Cold Habits," is a necessary read because it contains the most detailed examples of plan elements that are applicable to most habits. The plan descriptions in other chapters assume you're familiar with the first plan in Chapter 21, which is about Charlie's chocolate chip cookie habit.

Let's go now into a detailed discussion of the Act from Choice Method, beginning with the Preliminary Phase.

The Act from Choice Method
Principal Steps

Preliminary Phase

T — **Find the Truth**
What is it you do?
Misguided, misdirected, useless?
Secondary emotion? Other? — 14

O — Choose your preliminary **Objective**
Specific thing to do or not do
More general—quality of behavior — 15

M — Evaluate your **Motivation**
Consequences of habitual behavior and attitudes
Costs and benefits of change
Values affected by changing or not changing — 16

Decision Phase
Finalize your objective
Do you mean to change, or simply want to?
Is it something you're committed to do, or is it an aspiration?
Decide — 17

Committed Phase

C — Make the **Commitment** to Pause then follow your
plan for choosing when first experiencing the impulse — 18

A — Train your **Awareness**
Hire and train your Sentinel
Design a Second Question — 19

P — **Plan what you'll do when first aware of the impulse** — 20
Simple plans for cold habits — 21
Complex plans for hot habits — 22
Cultivate your values by managing
unwanted attitudes — 23

ACT FROM CHOICE
Follow Your Plan

CHAPTER 14

T Is for the Truth of What Happens

Never underestimate the power of compassionately
recognizing what's going on.

—*Pema Chödrön*[183]

What Is It You Do or Don't Want to Do?

What is it you do that you don't want to do, or don't do but want to do and mean to manage? You probably have a general idea already, but you'll profit by recalling the details: your actions and experiences, the characteristics of the situations in which they appear, and your best guess as to what the unwanted impulse is trying to accomplish.

The habit that made you pick up this book may be so simple that there's no need for extensive analysis: you know what happens, when it happens, maybe what triggers the impulse, and even what you want to do or how you want to feel instead. Still, I recommend you read through the topics that follow and see if any make you want to dig more deeply. Pay attention to any tendency to make excuses for yourself. While thinking about what you do and the stories you tell yourself about your unwanted habits, try to be discerning. Recollections can be teachers, and like all good teachers they will be effective to the extent they are factual and free of judgment and self-justification.

Describe and acknowledge what you do. Accept your understanding of the causes and consequences of the unwanted habit. Accept responsibility without blaming others or without allowing yourself to fall into the traps of shame, guilt, or denial. Accept, too, that if you're new to this type of work—to looking deeply at what you do, and figuring out how much of it is your responsibility—it may feel a lot like peeling an onion, tears included. The more you pull back the layers, the closer you'll get to core issues that have been hiding from you, and the more you'll learn about yourself. It takes time to make discoveries like that and digest them. That's inevitable, so accept that whatever you understand at this moment is the best you can do, even if you think it's not. Though you'll be older and wiser tomorrow than you are today, able to see and understand more, don't wait for further discoveries. Start the work now with whatever you know now. You have at your disposal all the insights you've experienced from birth to this minute.

There are many ways to get insight about your unwanted habits, a number of ways of looking at habits, a number of considerations that will clarify what it is you do. Knowledge of them will make them easier to manage. I'll discuss those considerations first. Following that discussion there is a list of questions that can help you think more deeply about what you do. Finally, there is a form you can use to describe for yourself the habit you want to manage.

Important Considerations

What Are You Responsible For?

It is critical that you identify the truth of the situation and take responsibility for what you do when the habit is triggered. The event that triggers you might be caused by someone else, but your reaction is your responsibility alone. It's important not to blame others for it because that will deny you clarity about what you do and dilute your resolve to manage the habit. To avoid the impulse to blame others, think back to the most recent time this happened. Do you find yourself telling stories to explain that someone else was responsible for the way you feel?

Here's an illustration of this type of responsibility shifting. (Notice that in the example that follows, the actors, Pat and Alex, do not have gender-specific names. I didn't give them those names to be politically correct. I gave them those names so you can imagine that Alex and Pat are whatever gender you want them to be, thus reducing the likelihood that gender stereotyping might interfere with your understanding of the example.)

Pat screams at Alex when Alex doesn't do the dishes. Pat doesn't want to do that anymore. Pat could describe the situation like this: "I scream at Alex *because* s/he doesn't do the dishes. S/he doesn't do enough around the house in general. S/he's lazy."

Certainly, part of Pat's story is true: the part about unwashed dishes and Pat's screaming is accurate. But the rest of the story is Pat making him- or her-self feel less guilty about his/her reaction. His/her description lets Pat off the hook. It's another way of saying, "I would be a good person if Alex weren't bad." (Of course, if this were a real-life situation, it might be that Pat's screaming stems from feeling that Alex isn't worthy, and the screaming comes from his/her guilt from feeling that way, or from fear that the relationship won't last. But let's not get carried away. That's too much ground to cover in this tale. We'll just take it as I've written it.)

If Pat's description just stuck to the facts, s/he might put it this way: "When Alex doesn't do the dishes, I get angry and scream at him/her." When Pat tells it that way, s/he's fully accepting responsibility for the screaming and the way s/he reacts to his/her emotion. It's all about Pat. Full stop.

Here are some other examples of how our stories attempt to absolve us of responsibility:

> *I tried to cut him/her off because s/he cut me off first.*
> *I ate a gallon of ice cream because s/he didn't call me back.*
> *I cheated on my spouse because s/he travels too often.*
> *I went on a bender because I didn't get hired for that job I wanted.*
> *I didn't speak up because I knew those people would judge me if I did.*

Statements like these may be good descriptions of the trigger, but the speaker is avoiding responsibility. Unstated but implied is, "Someone or something else made me do it, and you would do this if someone did that to you. I'm a good person."

Don't buy it. Get in the habit of accepting responsibility for everything you did that went wrong (but *nothing* else, ever). You'll feel better. You'll be conducting yourself with more integrity. And you'll even feel liberated because it will make you feel good about yourself. In addition to feeling more worthy, you might be more courageous. And you won't be so tired from carrying around that defensive shield.

Looking for Triggers

What are the triggers (stimuli) that produce your unwanted behavior or attitudes? What are the behaviors and/or attitudes that you're trying to manage, and the emotions you're feeling?

Remember that you are the only one qualified to opine on what is unwanted. Spend some time identifying what triggers you. The more you know about what sets you off, the better able you'll be to anticipate your unwanted impulses and the situations that pose the greatest danger for you.

Some people are triggered by specific combinations of stimuli. For instance, advice or judgment from a parent or other authority figure might stimulate anger, though the identical advice from a friend or colleague doesn't; or maybe a strong craving for a cookie arises most frequently after a stressful experience. The source of the advice might be key in the first example; in the cookie example, the stress is what matters.

Some people are not so concerned about their regrettable actions as much as they are about feeling uncomfortable emotions. There are many who simply don't ever want to feel anxious, angry, or fearful, for example. There are some who don't want to experience feelings of self-doubt or judgment or prejudice against individuals or groups. The challenge is to *manage* these emotions and attitudes. We're not likely to banish them completely, and there is no shortcut to keeping them from arising.

If you're having difficulty seeing what you do, you might want to review the five characteristics that describe personality that I introduced in Chapter 11. See whether you're motivated to be more or less expressive of these characteristics than you naturally are. For example, are you highly motivated to be more open-minded or extraverted than you usually are?

Here are the Big Five Characteristics of Personality[184]
- Extraverted vs. introverted
- Conscientious vs. uninhibited
- Agreeable vs. antagonistic
- Neurotic vs. emotionally stable
- Open-minded vs. closed-minded

Having suggested that you might want to work on some aspects of your personality, I feel the need to remind you that personality changes over time, but slowly. Consequently, don't expect rapid change. Be careful how you evaluate your progress.[185]

Misguided, Misdirected, and Useless Habits

It will help to figure out whether your unwanted reactions are appropriate to the stimuli that trigger them. Ask yourself whether the actions or thoughts the emotional action program prescribes are useful to the situation; in other words, will your reactions affect the situation or its outcome? For example, when facing a confrontation, does your reaction make it easier for you to communicate with the other parties? Are you able to express yourself accurately and negotiate a satisfactory outcome? When you're angry, is the anger aimed at correcting what is causing the frustration or the affront that triggered it? Is the anger aimed at the perpetrator?

ACT FROM CHOICE

Here are the three kinds of inappropriately structured habits I identified in Chapters 1 and 11. As you read further, see whether the habit you want to work on is like them.

MISGUIDED HABITS

Habits are misguided if there is almost no possibility that the stimulus could produce the consequences the impulse is aimed at mitigating. For example, though there is no causal relationship between X and any negative outcomes, when encountering X, we react as if the negative outcome were sure to follow. PTSD produces misguided habits. A PTSD sufferer is afraid of noise because the battlefield was noisy; consequently, the noise of the crowd at the football stadium frightens her. I believe that most misguided habits are caused by faulty conditioning, like that of PTSD.

I gave you two illustrations of misguided habits in Part I. Mari's harsh reaction to almost any question asked by a loved one when she doesn't have the answer, is a conditioned reaction, probably caused by her history with her father. To my way of thinking, misguided habits can also include over-reaction—that is, the stimulus can have negative consequences, but not so significant as to produce such strong reactions; the person is far too angry, fearful, or indignant for the situation. Another way of considering whether a habit is misguided is to ask whether the reaction is objectively appropriate to the likely consequences of the stimulus.

While reactions like these are not *objectively* warranted, they nonetheless feel very real and compelling. It's no good saying, "You shouldn't feel that way." In his book *Open Heart, Open Mind*,[186] Tsoknyi Rinpoche describes freezing in fear when attempting to cross a forty-story-high glass bridge connecting the Petronas Towers in Kuala Lumpur, Malaysia, a popular tourist attraction. Loads of tourists passed by as well as people pushing hand trucks piled high with goods. It took him three tries to cross that bridge, and in the course of dealing with his fear he hit upon the thought that his fear was "real but not true." In other words, his reaction, fear that the bridge would fall, taking him with it, was very real. It was indistinguishable from how he would have felt if the danger were real. But it was not true because the likelihood that the bridge would collapse under him, sending him falling forty stories to the street below, was essentially zero.

Real but not true is a powerful slogan or mantra because it describes so many experiences of mind that are real but not true. They include feelings of

146

attraction to things that might be worthless and even harmful, or unsubstantiated fears that keep us from crossing bridges essential to our well-being and happiness.

Strong reactions that feel real, but are not true are more manageable when the person understands what causes them, though knowing the cause often isn't enough to override the emotional action program's impulses. Often these habits can only be managed after getting help from skilled mental health professionals.

Some conditioned responses produce reactions that conflict with one's values and intentions. Most people have so-called implicit biases or implicit attitudes that result from automatic, involuntary reactions to others, triggered solely by their superficial appearance. The most troublesome of these reactions are to people identifiable by race, ethnicity or religion, disability, social class, culture, and sexual orientation or identity. These are learned reactions. If you believe these kinds of reactions or judgments are justified, they are explicit. It's our ignorance of our reactions and the fact that we would not for a moment try to justify them that makes them implicit. Most of us have them. They're examples of habits we acquired accidentally and innocently. (If you're interested in finding out about your implicit attitudes, you can take a free online assessment at Project Implicit, accessible at https://implicit.harvard.edu/implicit/.)

Another class of misguided habits is caused by reactions to violations of cultural norms that show up even after you've ceased to honor them. Violations of cultural and community norms produce anger. That's how we're built (see Table 3). But, over time and with experience, our values may change, and what we once thought true or sacred may no longer hold the same meaning for us. We might no longer care to observe certain rituals or hold certain values. Yet we might continue to feel anger or disgust when they're violated even though we no longer value them consciously.

MISDIRECTED HABITS

While misguided habits are characterized by a stimulus that is not "true," stimuli in misdirected habits are real and true, but the impulses prescribed by their emotional action programs are false because they do not address the stimuli. The classic examples are eating the cookie or kicking the dog after an argument with your boss or spouse. The argument makes you feel bad; that part of the habit is true. But the impulse pushed by the emotional action program in no way deals with what caused the difficulties at work or home.

So many of our habits are misdirected. Recall from Chapter 11 Pema Chödrön's description of the four ways we distract ourselves from discomfort, leaving us to face the stimulus another day, even in the very next moment. The modes of distraction she described are seeking pleasure (the cookie); going to ego (our status and being "right"); exaggerating our emotions (for instance, getting angrier and trying to enlist others to feel these emotions too); and finally, attempting to get control over everything.[187]

Procrastination is an example of a common habit that is usually misdirected. There are any number of things that stimulate procrastination. Fear of failure is a common one. We don't want to do something; maybe it's hard or boring, or we think we don't know how to do it, so we postpone it until we're forced to deal with it in the future under far more stressful circumstances, because we frittered away much of the time we could have used to just do it.

ARE YOUR FELT EMOTIONS PRIMARY OR SECONDARY?

The emotional action program produces a primary emotion that your Reactive Brain might quickly exchange for a secondary one. Recall Pema Chödrön's observation that "underneath anger there is fear, and underneath fear there is a tender heart." Going to the secondary emotion is a type of misdirected habit.

It's important to know what you're experiencing before you choose what to do, especially when those strong emotions lead to escape from discomfort that is only short-term and does nothing to address the stimulus and its consequences.

Ani Pema tells a story I'll try to summarize here, though I can't tell it nearly as well as she does. It goes something like this:

> A corrections department official was alone in his office with a policeman whom he'd just told that his son was going to be jailed. The policeman became furious. His rage was so powerful that the official had good reason to be frightened.

Ani Pema said the official told her that, surprisingly, he was able to remain calm, saying nothing for quite a while as the father ranted. Finally, the official said, "You must love your son very much," at which point the policeman's anger dissipated immediately, and he dissolved into tears.

I know of no clearer example of a secondary emotion in action. See how the father's anger kept him from experiencing what he was feeling; see how useless it was and how poorly it served him. More than any other example I've heard, this story illustrates the importance of getting to the truth of how you react and what you do in situations with strong emotions. The invitation for the policeman/father to feel what he was feeling, though offered by the very official who had made him so angry in the first place, opened him to feelings his rage hid from him. When his feelings were revealed, grief, not anger, was shown to be the emotion to feel and respond to.

When emotions run hot, try to determine whether the emotion you feel is a secondary one whose main purpose is to keep you from feeling the primary emotion and any self-judgments that might go along with it. Fear, anger, guilt, and shame can easily lead to secondary emotions and misdirected impulses that take us further from our true feelings.

USELESS HABITS

Useless habits are a form of misdirected habits because they serve no useful purpose. Keep in mind that the habit is useless, not you.

The reaction may be true. Frustration is a hard-wired stimulus of anger. But indulging it can be so useless. How often have you gone on a rant, annoying everyone around you, pumping up your blood pressure when you were *absolutely powerless* to make things better. Do you like to get angry at the other drivers in a traffic jam, including those way up ahead who are invisible and anonymous? And just what is it you'll do to the frail elderly person whose slow walk is blocking you? How upset do you want to get about him or her?

Look at your unwanted habits and see if your reactions make sense to you. Does your reaction address the problem that incited it? Are you stuck in traffic and want to get home faster? Maybe you're worried about being late for that important appointment. Will yelling at another driver, or the red light, or the elderly person crossing at the intersection get you on your way faster? What good will anger do you? Yes, you're disappointed, blocked, frustrated, and humans are designed to react to those situations with anger, but you can be better than automatic you. A better strategy would be to use anger's energy to figure out what to do to mitigate the consequences of being late.

A popular justification for frustration-induced rage or other disproportionate and impotent anger is that it is cathartic—a necessary blowing off of steam, a demand for justice. There is an outsized belief in the cathartic power of anger, that it's good to express our *truth*. But, in fact, catharsis only extends anger.[188] As I've indicated before, the slogan that comes to mind for me in these situations is, "Don't make things worse than they already are." *Worse*, in this case, refers to feeling worse than I feel before turning my frustration, disappointment, or judgment into anger. The situation and its consequences are bad enough. That is pain; making it worse causes suffering—my suffering. This is an example of what it means to turn pain into suffering. A great slogan to remind you of this teaching is, "Pain is inevitable; suffering is optional."[189]

As a foreshadowing of what I'll say about both misdirected and useless habits later, when you're hurting, instead of going to exaggerated emotions, pleasure, or control—none of which will cure the situation or make you feel better for long—first acknowledge and validate what you're feeling, whether disappointment, despair, loss, hurt, frustration, or anger. Then extend compassion to yourself by accepting that you're in pain and it hurts. Do that, and you'll find the emotion you're feeling—in most cases a secondary one—will fade. And you'll no longer be motivated to distract yourself with misdirected or useless habits.

Getting back to your specific situation, what do you tell yourself about the purpose of your useless habits? Do they provide catharsis or some other release? Do they serve you some other way? Do they create unintended consequences that cause more suffering later? Can you let go of your rationalizations around why expression of these useless habits is good for you? What else could you do that would make you feel better in those situations over which you have no control, but in which you react with exaggerated emotions?

What is your mode of operation? How do you deal with discomfort— anticipating the difficult conversation, experiencing troubling emotions, anxiety, and other fears? Are the things that make you angry or fearful likely to produce the consequences you're armoring yourself to handle? Think about it. Get curious about what you react to and how you react. (Discover as much as you can about *how* you react before spending a lot of time on *why*. If you're not careful, time spent on *why* can divert you from working on managing how you react.)

If the habit you have chosen to work on is misdirected, see if you can identify the discomfort you're avoiding: fear; loss; feeling the work is too hard, too boring, or unpleasant; anxiety; powerlessness; attacks on your ego; uncertainty; helplessness; sadness—something else?

If the habit is misguided, label it so. When it arises in the future, tell yourself that what you're feeling is *Real but not true.*

The Source of Your Habits

Knowing the source of habits is a real gift. But be realistic about your ability to find out what caused the habit that's troubling you. Mari knows that her father expected her to know things she couldn't know and made her feel bad when she didn't. She's unusual in her ability to readily understand the cause of her untoward reaction to being asked questions she can't answer. But her inability to remember the events that produce her reactions is not at all unusual.

If you know or can surmise the source of your habits, you'll be better able to distance yourself from them—that is, to undermine any idea that they are solid, valuable, and wise. You'll know that the feelings that accompany your reactions, while *real*, are not *true*. By all means get curious about the source of your habit, but don't let any lack of understanding slow you down. Exercise your curiosity on your own time while you work to manage the habit as it is.

The Validity and Usefulness of Your Reactions

As a final step in this exploration of your habits, examine the validity of your reactions to the stimuli that trigger them.

Are you reacting to a stimulus that's true? Are the potential consequences of the threat real?

Is your reaction appropriate to the potential consequences? Can your reaction mitigate the potential consequences of the stimulus?

- Does your reaction make the situation better or worse?

- Who does your reaction help? How?

- Who does it hurt? How?

And the Answer Is...

The questions below are designed to help you think about and describe what you do. Use them to stimulate thought, not as if they were part of a questionnaire. They're meant to help you. Spend time with the ones that seem to apply to you. Skip the others.

After you've gotten what you can from your answers, see if you can fill out Form 1 that follows immediately after the questions. (You can download copies of the forms used in Part II from ActFromChoice.com.)

What do you observe? What happens? What's your experience?

How useful are your reactions?

1. What is the unwanted habit you want to address? Once you have that in mind, try to answer the following questions:
    a. What happens most often to trigger this unwanted habit?
    b. What do you do in response?
    c. Is your unwanted response an action or some habit of mind, like an attitude or thought, such as judgment, prejudice, or unkindness? What are its consequences?
    d. What is unwanted—the feelings, the way you act/react, the fact that you react at all, or something else?

2. Recall a recent incident in which this habit caused you regret.
    a. Who was involved?
    b. Where were you?
    c. What preceded your reaction? If you know the trigger, what was it?
        Did anything happen before the event that might have influenced your state of mind, your mood, or sensitivity?
    d. What do you feel when this happens?
    e. How do you feel right before your reaction?
        Is your reaction hot and impulsive (anger, jealousy, fear), or cold and contained (close-mindedness, shame, judgment)?
        Do you have time to consider your response, or do you respond immediately?
    f. How do you feel immediately after you've reacted?
    g. How do you feel later when you reflect on what happened?
        Is your habit caused by a secondary or primary emotion?
    h. What emotion are you feeling when you act?
    i. What's your best guess: Is that the primary emotion, or is it a way to make you feel better in the moment?
        If there's a primary emotion that is different from what you're feeling when you react, what is that primary emotion?

3. Who and/or what are your reactions directed at? Do you believe the reactions are appropriate to the stimulus that causes them?
   a. Who or what is the object of your reaction?
   b. Does your reaction directly address the cause of your feelings, or might it be misdirected?
   c. Are the feelings valid? Is it likely that there is good reason for your emotion—that the thing you're afraid of could do you harm, that the thing you're angry at has caused an injustice, frustrated you, violated your sacred values?
   d. Are the feelings you feel and the actions you want to take directed at making things better, or are you simply expressing your feelings?

Form 1
This Is My Unwanted Habit

When _____
_____happens, particularly when _____ does it, or it happens
at _____ [where, or what's going on
at the time], I _____
_____ [what you do, to what or to
whom].

The emotion I feel when the habit begins is _____.
If I react habitually, I feel that _____ will
happen if I don't react.

I believe my habitual reaction _____ [will or will not] help me
deal with the consequences of what could or actually does happen as a result
of the stimulus that triggered it.

This is a [choose: misguided, misdirected, useless] _____
habit because [choose all that apply]:

❏ I realize the stimulus can't produce the results or consequences the impulse is trying to help me deal with.

❏ I realize my reaction might make me feel better but it doesn't help with the stimulus. My mode of reaction in this case is [choose: pleasure, ego, making the reaction bigger, control] _____.

❏ I'm reacting to things I can't control, and my reactions are useless.

If there are primary and secondary emotions involved in this habit, I think the primary emotion is _____, aimed at or to _____, and the secondary emotion is _____, aimed at or to _____. [If there is only a primary emotion, provide only that information.]

Instead of reacting as I do in these situations, I wish I would/could _____ and/or not _____ _____.

CHAPTER 15

O Is for Objective

In this chapter you'll use what you've learned about your unwanted habit to pick your preliminary objective. You'll choose specifically what you want to manage, and how you want you and your reactions to be different.

The objective you create in this chapter is preliminary. The next chapter deals with motivation, which you can best examine when you have an objective in mind. When examining your motivation, you might find that you're not as strongly motivated to pursue your preliminary objective as you might be pursuing another. Consequently, the Act from Choice Method recommends that you finalize your objective only after examining your motivation, at which point you might accept the preliminary one, change it, or abandon the entire program.

The objective to pick might seem obvious to you at first, but looking deeper often produces something more fitting. By way of illustration of how fruitful this investigation can be, let's go back to Pat and Alex:

Remember that Pat screams at Alex when s/he doesn't do the dishes. Pat doesn't want to scream at Alex anymore. Pat has identified a reaction s/he wants to control. S/He could choose as her objective to stop screaming at Alex when the dishes aren't done, and nothing more. But s/he could also choose a broader objective. For example:

- Don't scream when angry at Alex.
- Manage your emotions around Alex.
- Don't scream when angry.
- Manage your anger.
- Don't let your emotions trigger unwanted behavior.
- Always be compassionate.

See how these go from being narrow and specific to a particular situation to being more about how Pat could be more general. The first two objectives are variations on his/her behavior toward Alex; the next set focuses on his/her anger; and the final two are big-picture objectives that focus on any (and all) emotions and any (and all) unwanted behavior aimed at and about everyone, everywhere, all the time.

These cover a broad range of objectives, but any of them could have emerged from Pat's recognition that screaming at Alex about dirty dishes is unwanted habitual behavior that is not consistent with how Pat means to be.

If a narrowly defined habit can produce such a variety of habit-management objectives, how are you to choose?

We vary in how well we understand ourselves. Our motivations and goals differ and change as we gain experience.[190] Pat's choice of objective would be driven by insights about what stimulates the outbursts, his/her dissatisfaction and motivation to act differently, and whether the desire for change should be limited to Alex and the dishes or to change his/her reactions more significantly.

The best you can do in framing your objectives is to incorporate what you know about yourself, how widely the unwanted habits affect you and your world, and how big the variance is between how you are and how you mean to be. Objectives are well selected if they clearly state what needs to be managed and are realistic in relation to your level of skill, experience, motivation, and willpower, and are consistent with your values—your values today, not the values you expect to have in the future when you're all-wise and perfect, and certainly not the values others may have laid on you.

Many people, maybe even you, seeing the broad array of possible objectives for Pat might want to go for the biggest, broadest, most all-encompassing objective you could propose—one that is not only consistent with the primary objective (not screaming at Alex), but is also big enough to make you proud of yourself; something you might imagine a spiritual advisor, parent, or high-status person would admire; something that might earn you a prize. That objective could be summarized as, "Don't let any emotions trigger unwanted behavior" or "always be compassionate."

As admirable and praiseworthy as those selections might be, I recommend erring toward a narrower focus, especially if a structured approach to self-management is new to you. Don't try to be a hero or heroine; set yourself up for success. Narrower objectives are easier to accomplish and measure because they focus attention, which makes it easier to plant the subconscious triggers needed to make you aware of your impulses.

If you choose an objective that is too broad, you'll discover more and more situations you're unprepared to manage. This will reduce your sense of accomplishment even when you manage some situations very well. You can always expand the scope of your objective as you gain skill and confidence, and I'd encourage you to do that as soon as you feel ready.

Ask the Questions

Here is a list of questions whose answers may help you arrive at this preliminary objective. They won't all apply to you. Consider the ones that seem to apply to your situation.

What do you want to manage?

1. What is the habit you want to manage (from Chapter 14)?
    a. The action
    b. The attitude/feeling
    c. Both

2. Is your objective about you in general (e.g. be compassionate), narrowly focused on a particular situation (e.g. Alex and the dishes), or something in between?

3. If your objective is about how you want to act—the values you want to enhance and display—what are those values?

4. If your objective is situation-dependent (e.g. about people, a place, or an issue), what is the situation and its important characteristics?
    a. Certain people (e.g. bosses, significant others/spouse, children, strangers)
    b. Certain challenges (e.g. loss, challenges to ego, not getting what you want, uncertainty, confrontations)
    c. Certain contexts (e.g. work, home)
    d. Certain subjects (e.g. money, love, loss, disrespect, blame)

5. What outcome do you want from the immediate situation and longer term, if applicable? Are some outcomes absolute requirements (e.g. you must not crash the car, hurt your children, endanger your livelihood)?
    a. What do you *not* want to do that you do now, or *want* to do that you don't do now?
    b. What actions/attitudes toward others, situations, or yourself do you mean to reject or enhance?

6. How do you mean to be when triggered? In other words, how do you want to be seen by others, and how do you want to be internally (e.g. open, closed, determined, flexible, helpful, friendly, stern, judgmental, open to problem solving, emotional, vengeful, forgiving)?

7. What do you want your role in the situation to be (e.g. to help, to impede, to be neutral, to be collaborative, to be open and accommodating to others' views and feelings, or more determined to get certain results)?
8. Do you want a specific outcome? If so, what?
9. What other objectives, psychological and material, might you want others and yourself to gain from these situations.

State Your Preliminary Objective

Extract what is most important to you from your thoughts and notes. Use them to describe what you want to manage and your objective in managing it. Go with your best judgment. You can change it later. Add any detail that will make the objective meaningful for you. Try to make your objective consistent with your values and what you want to accomplish.

By way of example, here's what Pat might say at this point: "I want to manage my habit of screaming at Alex when s/he doesn't do the dishes. I don't want to scream at him/her anymore. I don't have anything else in mind."

At this point, not knowing is plenty good enough. If your primary objective is to rouse certain feelings, attitudes, or values in the way you react to the stimuli that set you off, simply write or say that. For example, Pat could have chosen as his/her objective, "Always be compassionate," or "Display my love for Alex in all of our interactions."

The next step in the Act from Choice Method is to describe the source of your motivation and discover whether you're motivated enough to work at achieving your objective.

CHAPTER 16

M Is for Motivation

Motivation Is Essential

It takes motivation to accomplish anything that's challenging. There has to be a reward, a valuable payoff—psychological, spiritual, material. Motivation provides the power to overcome the forces of Reactive Brain. If you're motivated enough, you'll work at it. If you're not, you won't; if you're not intent on gaining the benefits of managing your reactions, or don't think there are any benefits, you won't have the power to overcome Reactive Brain. You have to believe there are benefits from managing yourself better, and that those benefits outweigh the costs in terms of your effort, but also the costs associated with giving up what is comfortable and familiar. For example, many people want to manage their anger better but are reluctant to give up the thrill and power anger gives them.

THE BENEFITS OF SELF-MANAGEMENT

+ Benefits of better self-management:
– Loss from giving up the habit
<u>– Cost of the effort of self-management</u>
= Net benefit of better self-management

It's easy to falter if you lose sight of the benefits and costs, or find the costs of improving self-management are greater than its benefits. Consequently, it's important to define what you will gain and what it will cost you. *Your* answers to these questions are the only ones that matter. Others may have opinions, but your motivation will come exclusively from *your* values and preferences.

In this chapter I'll offer an approach to discovering the benefits and costs of changing how you manage yourself. But first let's review a little of what we have already learned about the ways our brains work.

Asking you to try to identify the objective sources of your motivation is tantamount to asking you to be rational. But recall that Daniel Kahneman got his Nobel Prize for demonstrating that there is no such thing as an entirely rational person—one who makes decisions solely by balancing the objective pluses and minuses of consequences. We're seldom if ever entirely rational because Reactive Brain casts a powerful emotional vote that biases our feelings when judging potential outcomes.

Though we have to try to be rational, Reactive Brain often has different agendas because it's focused on considerations limited to immediate reward and threat. The impulses and emotions it produces feel compelling even when they make no sense in the moment and can't stand up to rational judgment. Remember, too, that Reactive Brain has been at this a lot longer than Intentional Mind has. Reactive Brain was ready and operating, more or less fully, from birth. Intentional Mind wasn't fully armed until you were in your mid- to late twenties.

When there is disagreement between Reactive Brain's prescriptions and Intentional Mind's desires, the competition between those two parts of the brain is the root cause of internal conflict. A strong motivational case built from a rational review of the alternatives helps to strengthen Intentional Mind as it engages with Reactive Brain.

I believe we gain an additional benefit by being explicit about the sources of motivation. Explicit understanding of motivation demonstrates to your Sentinel the importance you place on your intention. This probably increases the likelihood that the Sentinel's signal of a mismatch between intention and behavior will have more force and be more likely to snap you into the Choosing Space. That vote could be decisive in your ability to leave Master Habit and become present.

The steps I describe in the rest of this chapter should give you deeper insights into the benefits of managing yourself and what, if anything, you'll give up by abandoning the unwanted habit. You could find that increased insights give you more or less motivation, a different focus, or a different way to state your objectives. You might even decide that what you had in mind to manage really wouldn't be worth the effort. There is no right answer. Whatever you decide is right.

Sources of Motivation

In the previous two chapters, you described the unwanted habit you want to manage and the objective you want to achieve. In this chapter we'll use three approaches to uncover the sources and amount of your motivation to manage the habit: I'll ask you to:

- First, list **the consequences** of the habitual unwanted reaction you want to manage, regardless of their costs or benefits. In other words, you'll describe the effects on you, on other people, and on the situation, of acting the way the unwanted impulse wants.

- Second, list **the benefits and costs** of managing the unwanted habit, as well as those of *not* managing it—that is, the benefits and costs of changing how you react, or of letting your reactions play out as they do now.

- Third, describe **which of your values are enhanced or undermined** by managing and *not* managing the unwanted habit.

The Consequences of Your Habitual Reaction

In this first step, let's look at what happens when you go along with the habit, *not* what would happen if you reacted differently. Start by making a list of people affected by your unwanted reactions. Don't forget to include yourself right at the top. You don't have to name everyone. You could just name the groups affected, as characterized by their role in your life—for example, self, significant other, children, other immediate family, co-workers, employees, etc.

For each individual or role, list what you believe are the consequences they experience when you execute the habitual, unwanted reaction. Again, start with yourself, and be sure to include your feelings about yourself and the effects of those feelings on you. The consequences should include current and future effects both tangible and psychological, positive and negative.

To aid in this exercise, let's return to Pat and Alex and imagine what Pat might put on this list of consequences:

- I'll feel I expressed myself.
- I'll feel bad that I was out of control.
- I'll worry that I've damaged our relationship.
- Maybe Alex won't skip the dishes next time.

- The mood will be terrible the rest of the night.
- Dinner might not get made or served.
- I'll have to sleep on the couch.
- The neighbors will complain about the noise.
- I'll be in a terrible mood tomorrow.
- So will Alex.

You get the idea. You're only limited by your memory, how much time you want to spend on this, and your willingness to record your observations.

Form 2, referring to a limited number of those most affected, might look like this example for Pat.

Record your insights on Form 2, which you can download from ActFromChoice.com, or make up one of your own.

Form 2: Consequences of the Unwanted Habit			
Consequences of screaming at Alex when s/he doesn't wash the dishes	**Those Affected**		
	Me	**Alex**	**Others**
I'll feel I expressed myself.	+		
I'll feel bad that I was out of control.	−		
I'll worry I've damaged our relationship.	−		
Maybe Alex won't skip the dishes next time.	+		
The mood will be terrible the rest of the night.	−	−	
Dinner may not get made or served.	−	−	
I'll have to sleep on the couch.	−		
The neighbors will complain about the noise.	−	−	−
I'll be in a terrible mood tomorrow.	−		−
So will Alex.		−	

The Benefits and Costs of Self-Management

Next, look at the benefits and costs of managing or not managing the habit. It's fairly common to evaluate a decision by using an approach sometimes called the Benjamin Franklin balance sheet. Suppose you want to buy a new car. You take a piece of paper, draw a line down the center, and write the benefits of buying the car on one side and the drawbacks on the other; or you might compare two or more cars that way. Maybe you already use this technique to decide which job to take or where to go on vacation.

The method we'll use goes a step further. I'll ask you to draw two lines on that piece of paper instead of one: a vertical one, from top to bottom, and a second, horizontal one across the middle. You now have four boxes made up of two rows and two columns (see Form 3). The left and right columns are for benefits and costs, respectively. In the top row, fill in the benefits and costs to you of managing the habit; in the bottom row, fill in the benefits and costs of NOT managing it. You can make this form easily, or download a copy from ActFromChoice.com.

Form 3:
Benefits and Costs of Self-Management

Habit _____

Objective_____

	My Benefits	My Costs
Benefits and costs of managing the habit		
Benefits and costs of NOT managing the habit		

Example:

Form 3:
Benefits and Costs of Self-Management

Habit _____I am eating too many chocolate chip cookies_____

Objective _____I want to limit my chocolate chip cookies to one a day_____

	My Benefits	My Costs
Benefits and costs of managing the habit	Gain less weight, maybe take off some Feel better, look better Feel more in control, more powerful	The struggle to resist temptation Will miss cookies with coffee Will miss sharing them with family
Benefits and costs of NOT managing the habit	Won't have to be on guard all the time Can do what I want, when I want Won't have to miss them	I'll feel I've betrayed myself I won't lose the feeling that I should control myself, and that feeling will nag at me, upset me, make me feel bad

If Pat were filling out this form, in the top row s/he'd write the benefits and costs of managing the habit of screaming at Alex when the dishes aren't done. In the bottom row s/he'd write the benefits and costs of *not* managing the habit—that is, continuing to scream at Alex.

If you've never taken the additional step of looking at the benefits and costs of *not* doing something, you may be surprised at the insights this gives you. The benefits of doing something are not always equal to the costs of *not* doing it; in other words, the two rows are not mirror images of one another, though there may be some duplication.

List the benefits and costs for managing and not managing your habit. Take all the time you want, because these steps have the potential to deepen your understanding of the source and strength of your motivation, or the lack of it. You may believe that you already know a lot about the strength and source of your motivation and that this level of detail won't help, and you may be right. But there's a good chance that you'll learn something from doing this exercise.

The next approach can give you still more insight.

Your Habits and Values

If you worked with the benefits and cost form (Form 3), you've already expressed some ideas about what is valuable to you, what is difficult, what costs money or time, pleasure or discomfort. Now I'll suggest that you go through this again, but this time think about how managing or not managing your habitual reactions relates to the values you hold. But first you'll need to define your values.

DEFINING YOUR VALUES

As discussed earlier, most of us want to be in integrity, feel bad when we're not, and can feel insulted and misunderstood if someone accuses us of being out of integrity. Being *in integrity* means acting, thinking, and feeling in a way that is consistent with our *stated* values. When someone accuses us of acting in a way that conflicts with them, we may react with anger or other strong feelings, saying or feeling, *That's not who I am.* Some, when out of integrity, go into denial and twist the facts in an effort to redefine the values they've transgressed, or they search for excuses to justify why it was okay to violate their standards that time.

This next approach to defining your motivation creates the opportunity for you to see if your unwanted habit produces actions, attitudes, or thoughts that contradict or undermine your explicitly held values. Are your unwanted habitual reactions in agreement with your values, or do they contradict or undermine them? If they undermine them, better management of the habit will reinforce your values and demonstrate your commitment to them. The desire to act and think consistently with your values can provide powerful motivation for controlling the behavior, attitude, judgments, or thoughts that an unwanted habit violates.

Use Form 4 for this part of your motivation inquiry. You can make it yourself or download from ActFromChoice.com. Once again, as in Form 3, you draw a vertical line down the page and a horizontal one across the middle, giving you four boxes—two rows and two columns—to write in. You use the top row to describe the way managing the unwanted habit will affect your values, while the bottom row describes how NOT changing it affects them. You write in the left column the values enhanced by managing or not managing the habit, and in the right column, the values undermined by managing and not managing the habit, respectively. It's possible you've included something about values in the preceding table (Form 3). If you have, please repeat in Form 4 anything in Form 3 that belongs here too.

Form 4:
My Values Manifested / My Values Undermined

Habit _____

Objective_____

	My Values Manifested	My Values Undermined
Values affected by managing the habit		
Values affected by NOT managing the habit		

Example:
Form 4:
My Values Manifested / My Values Undermined

Habit _____I am eating too many chocolate chip cookies_____

Objective_____I want to limit my chocolate chip cookies to one a day_____

	My Values Manifested	My Values Undermined
Values affected by managing the habit	Healthy behaviors Self-control Not giving in to temptation Manifesting dignity and pride in myself	Unlimited right to pleasure Not caring what people think of me Loving my body no matter what it looks like
Values affected by NOT managing the habit	Can do whatever I want What I think is what counts Go with the flow, be happy-go-lucky all the time	Being dignified Show the world I am in control of my urges Truly caring about myself

It's important that the values you identify represent how you mean to be. It's useful to make explicit the values you're trying to uphold, and that might not be obvious from the way you filled out the table. For example, Pat might say:

Screaming at Alex undermines the idea that I'm in control of myself.
Screaming at Alex undermines the trust we have in each other

Though those statements may be good enough for these purposes, neither are clear value statements. So it might be useful for Pat to clarify the values that are implied by what s/he wrote down. Pat might be satisfied with the first statement about control. Or s/he might be more specific, such as, "I should always be in control of how I relate to others." That statement would add clarity about the specific areas of life in which s/he values control. Similarly, Pat might expand the second item about having trust "in each other" to "I should never do something that makes someone important to me feel I'm untrustworthy."

Whether or not you decide to do this extra work to make your values more explicit, test what you've written to see if you really believe what's there. Satisfy yourself that you've described your values, not someone else's, and that you're committed to them—that you *mean* for your behavior to be consistent with them. One way to test your commitment to a specific value is to ask yourself how you would feel if someone challenged your commitment to it. For example, if you felt you were committed to being careful, would you feel insulted or deeply hurt if someone said you were careless?

Now Evaluate Your Motivation

You've put on paper pretty much everything you know about the sources of your motivation to manage the habit or to leave it alone. The next step is to review your work and try to come to a conclusion about whether you're motivated enough to work on the habit.

This is a very subjective process. Inevitably, you'll do it your own unique way, but here are some suggestions.

Start your inquiry with Forms 3 and 4. Pay particular attention to the rows. For example, first compare the costs and benefits of managing the habit—the upper row on Form 3. As you weigh what you've put in the boxes that are for and against managing the habit, where do you come out? Does the balance of benefits and costs tip toward managing or not managing the habit? If the benefits are more valuable to you than the costs, place a check mark in the top-left column. If the value of what you'd give up by managing it is more important to you than the benefits, put a check mark in the upper-right column.

Then look at the bottom row. Once again, if benefits are more important than costs, place a check in the lower left; if the costs are more important, put the check mark there.

Now let's see what you might learn from those two check marks. A check in the upper left says the benefits of managing the habit are more important to you, which means that you prefer working to manage the habit than leaving it alone. If the check was in the upper right, it would indicate that the benefits are not that important compared to the costs of what you'd give up by managing the habit, and you'd prefer to leave the habit alone.

Next look at the check marks for the lower row. If you checked the lower left box you've said that the benefits of leaving the habit alone are more valuable to you than the costs you incur from leaving the habit as it is. You could find, for example, that the enjoyment of your morning cookie—a benefit no change gives you—is much greater than the cost to you of ballooning weight.

After making your check marks for Form 3, do the same for Form 4.

The combination of check marks that indicates strong and clear motivation favoring managing the habit looks like this—for managing the habit, against leaving it unmanaged.

	For	Against
Manage	✓	
Don't Manage		✓

If the check marks were reversed—checks in upper right and lower left—the motivation is against managing the habit. Obviously, if the check marks are in the same columns you have mixed signals.

You'd be on really solid ground motivationally if the diagrams for Forms 3 and 4 were identical: like the example above—favoring managing the habit, or the reverse, saying, *don't bother*. Everything in between is an invitation to look more deeply at your motivation.

Here's an approach to getting still more insight. First, go back to Form 2, which describes consequences of the habit, and see if what you see there adds weight to managing or not managing it. You could look at your list of consequences and conclude you were not willing to suffer those consequences yourself or to put them on others. That conclusion could tip you toward managing the habit. But the reverse could be true. You could conclude there was nothing there that you care about.

Nevertheless, having looked at Form 2, and allowing whatever you did on Forms 3 and 4 to sink in, see if you can feel which way your motivation tips—toward managing or not managing the habit.

When you have the direction of your motivation identified, ask yourself if you're satisfied with that conclusion.

If you're not satisfied, see if you can find more evidence for how you feel in Forms 3 and 4. You're looking for anything you put on those forms that contradicts your gut feelings. If you feel you should manage the habit, but the written evidence isn't consistent with that, look at what you've written on those forms that says that managing the habit would cost you more than it's worth, or undermine values you find more important than those you'd enhance.

Having identified those contradictions, see if you mean them. See if you want to reframe them. See if you want to change any of them, possibly remove them from the negative side.

Keep looking at the evidence and re-evaluating it until you are comfortable with your conclusion.

It's pretty obvious that if you've had to do a lot of work to figure out the direction of your motivation, there probably isn't much motivation there, and you'd be better off either looking at another objective or dropping the project. Still, it would be fair to let it all sit for a week or two and come back to it later. But be honest with yourself. All the judging here is about you judging you. Be especially careful to make sure that any gut feelings that want you to work on a habit are not due to left-over indoctrination—a feeling that you "should" do this or that, even though you don't want to.

If you feel your motivation is weak, it's likely you won't stick with your efforts, which could lead to frequent failures, becoming demotivated, and giving up. My advice to you is to take this work on when your motivation is clear and powerful. Then you'll be successful. And your success will motivate you to take on even bigger challenges.

Reconsider Your Objective

If you decide there's nothing here you care enough about to pursue, or that the objective you came up with in the last chapter is too grand or too narrow and should be changed, honor that conclusion. If you want to change your objective, do that now. Consider how the new objective would change what you'd put in those last two forms. Keep doing that until you've found an objective you're motivated to pursue, or have decided there's no objective important enough to try to manage better than you already do. When you find an objective you're motivated to pursue, move to the next chapter.

CHAPTER 17

Decide Whether to Commit

In this chapter you'll make a formal commitment to yourself to work on the objective that you set in the preceding chapter. But you'll do that only if you've defined an objective you're adequately motivated to pursue. Again, the ultimate test is whether the objective supports how you mean to be, or is something more aspirational—the way you'd *like* to be, *maybe someday*.

If you've been following along and thinking about what you're trying to manage, the costs and benefits of managing or not managing it, and the values that give your objective its importance, you know what you would gain or lose from better management of this habit. You may have increased your understanding of how you benefit by not changing anything—what you may be holding on to by allowing this unwanted habit to run its course. You've identified the impact of these changes on your health, happiness, and values, and hopefully you've realized that aligning your behavior with your values makes these changes worthwhile. All in all, I hope you've been able to decide whether managing your habitual reaction represents a net benefit or loss to you.

If there's not enough benefit to you—including the psychological value of doing better for yourself and others—there's no need for you to continue reading other than to satisfy your curiosity. But if the potential impact of change is important to you, there are still two explicit decisions to be made:

- Do you really want the results of change, including whatever you give up by changing?

- Do you believe it will be worth the effort?

You won't know the full level of effort this will entail until you finish Part II, so let's leave a definitive answer to that question for later. The more important question at hand is whether you will be happier, feel more fulfilled, and be more satisfied with your life and yourself when you are doing, behaving, and thinking the way you imagine you will be when you're managing yourself well.

It's so hard to know. If you delight in your anger, are you really willing to give it up? If being a workaholic and spending less time with your family is fulfilling, will adjusting your work/life balance be something you'll enjoy? If you're a gadfly, unable to stick to just a few key activities, will you be happy attending to fewer ones? Presumably, you worried enough about those questions in the last chapter. But how does it feel right now? Do you feel ready for this work, excited for the possibilities, or exhausted by the prospect? Don't be surprised if you feel hesitant and doubtful.

Here is a test I use when trying to distinguish between true commitment and mere aspiration to a goal—particularly the big goals about how to be. I imagine that there is a switch on my desk. It has two positions. If I leave the switch in the current position, things stay as they are. In the other position, everything will be the way I think I want it. All I have to do to have things the way I think I want them is to flip the switch: I'd be that person, doing those things, expressing those values, achieving those rewards, but giving up all the things that stand between me and that goal. What would that feel like? Am I willing to flip the switch and give up what I have now and know so well?

This is a simple but deceptively powerful exercise for me, and it takes no time at all to engage with. Sometimes I know I'm willing to flip the switch, and I make that commitment. Other times, I know I am not willing, and in that case I take the goal I've been considering and put it in the aspiration box (in the Not Now or Too Hard file). I don't abandon it altogether because it means something to me; it represents values I want to embody. I respect the wanting, the yearning, but accept that I'm not ready to put it in the Now file. Having made that conscious, deliberate decision, the yearning changes: it becomes a quiet, though present, aspiration instead of something that gnaws at me. Since I've taken it on as an aspiration, it colors my future behavior. I've claimed the value and feel obligated to express it when I can, but I can still forgive myself when I'm not willing to rise to its demands.

I realize that might sound like I'm deciding matters of great weight all the time, but I assure you I'm not. Sure, I'd love to lose another fifteen pounds, exercise regularly, become fluent in French, publish an essay every week, and so much more. These are aspirations, all of them. I respect the desire, but they truly are in the Not Now pile. And having made that decision, acknowledging where I am with my priorities, my available energy, and the competition for my attention, I am comfortable with them as aspirations, not commitments. I don't have to do anything further about them until I decide that I have the motivation and resources to give them the effort they require and deserve.

So now I'm asking you to decide. Do you want to try to manage one or more of those habits you've been thinking about all this time? If so, write a more complete description of the habit and the key things that motivate you to manage it better. Here's an example, again imagining Pat:

I want to manage my habit of screaming at Alex when s/he doesn't do the dishes. Managing this habit will enhance our relationship, give me practice for improved management of my emotions in other areas of my life, and eliminate my sense of being out of control, out of integrity, and of acting contrary to the way I mean to be in this relationship. I will feel better about myself and feel even more powerful than any feelings of power I get from screaming at Alex.

If you don't write down your objective and summary motivations right now, please try to say them out loud. Choose words that will help you remember what's important about this objective, what you'll gain, why it's a good thing; weave together the consequences of the habit, the benefits of managing it, and the values you'll enhance when you're being the way you mean to be. Be specific so that reading, hearing, or simply recalling it will bring to mind the most motivating factors. Recalling it from time to time when you're not faced with the habit is an important supporting practice that will nurture your intention and make your Sentinel stronger. You might want to make up a slogan or choose one of mine to support you. Maybe Pat would like "*The less anger, the more me.*" (You may find a slogan that reinforces your intentions in the Resource Companion or at ActFromChoice.com.)

If you've made the decision to pursue the objective you've created for managing this habit, we'll leave the Preliminary Phase of the Method and move into the Committed Phase and the work of turning your decision into action.

CHAPTER 18

C Is for Commitment

An Essential Step

Imagine this: something has happened to produce the unwanted impulse. Your Reactive Brain has become aware of the stimulus (trigger), appraised it, concocted an emotional action program, and set your body in motion. Your Sentinel, realizing this is not what you intended to do, broke you free of Master Habit and thrust you into the Choosing Space. You're in Intentional Mind, aware of the unwanted impulse and your intentions. But the feelings of the impulse have not subsided. Reactive Brain is still fighting for control while you're trying to engage the full force of Intentional Mind.

What do you think you'll do? Will you try to manage the unwanted impulse or let it take over? You've been going along with this impulse for a long time. It's pretty powerful, and it's not easy to break the pattern. Sure, you've now decided that what the impulse wants for you is not what you want. You want to manage it, but it is powerful and has some ongoing benefit to you even if the habit is misguided, misdirected, or plain useless. So what will you do? Are you motivated enough to follow through with your decision?

Reactive Brain doesn't want you to think and will stop you from thinking if it can. Reactive Brain wants you to do what *it* wants you to do without question, without further thought. *Hurry up and do what I told you to do!* Reactive Brain screams. Whether it's alerting you to a crouching tiger in the bushes or an unclaimed cookie in the break room, it takes a conscious act of will to pause in the face of the impulse's momentum and choose what to do. As I pointed out in the overview of the Method, managing habits is a two-step process. When you encounter the impulse, first you have to interrupt the habit's momentum, then you have to choose what to do and follow through with your choice.

In this chapter, I'm asking you to make two explicit commitments essential to managing your unwanted habits, and to make those commitments in a way that feels "formal" to you. Make it feel like a promise you're making to yourself, and will hold yourself accountable to.

The first commitment is that every time you become aware of the unwanted impulse you will do your best to pause the action. Simply stop what you're doing and pay attention to what's going on outside of you and in your Mind.

The second commitment is that having paused the action, *you will choose what to do by following a formal, pre-established procedure*, one that you will have designed to fit your specific needs—that you'll follow your plan, step by step, to its conclusion.

I'll explain. As to the two-step nature of this self-management process, you probably have experience with other two-step processes. For example, suppose you need to have a difficult conversation with someone. You don't know if you can handle yourself well, and you're concerned about the other person's reaction to what you'll say, how difficult it might be, and whether you can expect a good outcome. Regardless, to make any progress, you have to overcome that initial fear of confrontation so you can open the door to the subject. You have to make the appointment and face the other person. Having done that, you have to begin and then manage your part of the conversation. A simpler, if less common, example is this: You see your car start to roll downhill. First you stop it. Then you decide what to do next.

Managing unwanted impulses works the same way. You may be unsure how it will work out, but you have to start, so you start with an act of will that blocks the momentum of the impulse so you can begin the internal conversation that will lead to your choice. That's the pause. You're holding the car, keeping it from rolling downhill. I can tell you from my own experience that the car sometimes feels like a fully loaded 18-wheel tractor-trailer. No matter how determined you are to pause and choose what to do, if the habit has any force at all, there will be times when it will be nearly impossible to make that pause stick. Yet, without it, there is almost no possibility of success. Failure to pause puts you at the mercy of the impulse and the forces it's exerting on you. If you don't interfere with the habit's momentum, away it will go on its own, taking you along with it. Consequently, the commitment to pause is essential. It is the first of the two commitments you must make if you're to succeed at managing yourself.

As for the second commitment, the commitment to choose by using a specific procedure: You're in the Choosing Space. You've paused the habit's momentum, but it's still working against you. You want to eat the cookie, to hit the guy who insulted you, to walk away from working on your taxes tonight. It's so easy to relax your effort and let the impulse take over as it has hundreds, maybe thousands of times before. To strengthen your resistance, you make that explicit commitment to *yourself* that having paused the habit, you will hold yourself accountable to make a choice by using the tools available to you, following the procedure you design.

It is easier to begin the choosing process when you have a plan in place. Moreover, the Choosing Space will naturally stay open while you are working the plan. If you don't know how to choose before you're launched into the Choosing Space, or you haven't prepared yourself to choose, your resolve could weaken, making it harder to keep the Choosing Space open. For these reasons, your commitment to work your plan has to be formal. It has to be a real commitment, one that you never want to violate, because violating it will make you feel out of integrity.

As I said above, at this point any commitment to follow your plan has to be tentative, because you don't yet know what your plan might entail. I'll give you tips about making plans, but your plan and objectives will be yours and, consequently, acceptable to you. So please stay open to the idea that the plan will meet your approval, and make the commitment. You can change your mind later if you decide it's too hard or would be ineffective.

You might be wondering why I'm asking you to make the steps in this process so specific and formal. You may be asking yourself why the definition of your unwanted habit, your objective, and the decision to pause require so much ceremony; why you need to *formally* decide that you want to try and manage your unwanted habit; and why I'm asking you to be so formal about making the commitment to pause and choose what to do?

Ceremony—or in this case, explicit, formal commitments—are important because the Brain will take your commitments more seriously when you declare their significance, along with your intention and accountability for following through with them. Formalism empowers your Sentinel. Remember how seriously the subconscious takes your commitments to appropriate speech and manage your itching.

From what I can gather from the literature and have experienced myself, the planting of intentions and promises in the brain is not a casual thing. The brain—your Sentinel—has to know that the intention or promise is important, and it does that through repetition and clear expressions of intention. "I *might* work on that tomorrow," "*might* not cheat on you," or "*might* be kind" just don't measure up as clear expressions of intent. You have to talk to your

Sentinel as if you mean it and reaffirm your commitment periodically so that your Brain knows and remembers that your commitment is important.

So now, ask yourself, are you willing to turn intention into commitment? If so, take some action to convince your Brain that you mean it. If you're willing to make these commitments, decide that they are promises to yourself, and that you'll hold yourself accountable to acting in accordance with them.

Demonstrate the importance of your intentions to your Sentinel by saying them aloud or writing them down. Write them on sticky notes and posters, and put them where you will see them. (If you're concerned about letting others discover this bit of business about you, make the sign something you'll understand and others won't—a colored sticky note will do, even if you write nothing on it.) You could also look at yourself in the mirror and tell yourself about your commitment. For extra credit and a little insurance, tell someone—a friend, advisor, family member, or coach. Almost anyone with whom you have regular contact will do. I suspect it's possible to get some effect by telling a stranger. Telling someone increases the feeling of accountability and signals your Brain that you really do mean business.

Having expressed your commitments to yourself, periodically renew your intention by repeating some of the steps just described.

I leave this chapter assuming that you have made the commitments to pause and choose. Let's go now and see what the awareness step is all about.

CHAPTER 19

A Is for Awareness

We practice [mindfulness meditation] so that our
awareness can become faster than our habits.
—attributed to Jetsun Khandro Rinpoche

I know I've said it a lot, but it bears repeating: you have to become aware of the unwanted impulses as soon as possible, hopefully *before* it turns into action. (Waking to find yourself in the midst of the unwanted action is better than letting it complete; realizing that you've caught it early is better than realizing much later.) You have to train your subconscious awareness, Brain itself, to interrupt the Master Habit rather than let unwanted habits slip by unnoticed and turn into action. As I discussed in Part I, self-awareness breaks through the Master Habit and puts us in the Choosing Space knowing what has happened and what we're about to do. In this chapter I'll describe the technique for training your "unconscious awareness," specifically your Sentinel, to wake you when the impulse begins to appear. I'll also introduce you to a technique for bringing your motivation to consciousness more quickly.[191]

Remember that we and our Brains know how to do this, as the scratching and speech examples illustrate. The alarms that work in those cases were built up over time, and unintentionally. To plant them quickly, and intentionally, we need to enlist the help of our Sentinel. To see how that's done, let's visit Jackie and Ethel, her employee.

Jackie's Story

The Habit

Jackie is an experienced, highly regarded businesswoman. She serves on prestigious boards because they want her advice. Not so her daughter Angela, who's in her twenties. On the contrary, Jackie's habit of giving Angela unsolicited advice caused increasing resentment, straining their relationship. Jackie wanted, needed, to manage the habit—not all advice-giving, just giving unsolicited advice to Angela.

Managing the Habit

Jackie *hired* Ethel to help her. Jackie tells me Ethel is in her mid-fifties, has gray hair, always wears a sweater, and does this kind of work because she used to give advice to her adult children, causing the same problems for them. Ethel is with Jackie 24/7. She doesn't charge anything, but she's there full-time to monitor Jackie and figuratively tug on her sleeve when she detects the impulse that precedes Jackie giving Angela advice. Ethel simply draws Jackie's attention to the impulse Jackie is feeling, interrupting Jackie's Master Habit and opening the Choosing Space.

It's up to Jackie to pause and choose.

Ethel doesn't give advice. It's not her job. When Jackie feels Ethel's tug, she simply chooses in a hiccup-short pause. Sometimes she decides her advice is important enough to give, and she does—maybe more skillfully than before. But most of the time she chooses to keep the little gems to herself. Of course, sometimes the impulse is too strong and she gives the advice despite her better judgment, often regretting it later.

The Technique

Ethel's 24/7 availability is the spoiler in this story: Ethel is made-up. She's a Sentinel, just like the Sentinel you employ that wakes you to the need to adjust your speech or consider whether and how to scratch that mosquito bite. Ethel had to be made up deliberately and consciously. Jackie created her, gave her a name, an appearance, and a backstory, just like the imaginary friends children make up. Jackie trained Ethel by telling her exactly how the habit arises and plays out. She imagined Ethel listening intently as she recalled specific examples, and she pointed out where in the process she would have wanted Ethel to interrupt and remind her that she was on the verge of giving potentially unwelcome advice.

When Ethel misses one of these opportunities, Jackie patiently retrains her by recalling the situation and pointing out where interruption might have helped. (Sentinels are loyal and want to serve. When they fail it's because their training needs reinforcement or the situation is too heavily charged. It's bad form to get impatient with them.)

Sentinels

The Sentinel technique is *the* key tool for creating targeted mindfulness. Sentinels are used to train unconscious awareness to bring us to awareness—to the present, when specific circumstances occur.[192]

If you'll recall from Part I, when you work with your Sentinel, you're training the prefrontal cortex to come to awareness when impulses inconsistent with intention are present or just emerging.

So what exactly is a Sentinel? As mentioned several times previously, your brain keeps track of your intentions and lets you know when your actions contradict them. Your intention to avoid four-letter words around children is stored as an intention. When children are present and the impulse to swear arises, Brain lets you know that you want to be careful—to pay attention to what you're saying. That's an example of how the association between various elements brings us to attention: the presence of children plus the intention not to swear in their presence. Neither of those two standing by itself has the same power to warn us, because there's no need unless they're together. Similarly, Jackie doesn't need to be warned about advice-giving if her daughter isn't present.

A similar mechanism can help you remember to do something you want to do but might forget. Suppose a friend at work asks you to lend her a book, and you agree to do it. How are you going to remember your commitment? You could write yourself a note or tie a string around your finger. You could prop the book by the front door the night before so as not to miss it on your way out in the morning, but that only works if you remember to do that when you get home that evening. Instead, you could use this pretty reliable memory trick.[193] Take a moment to picture yourself leaving the house in the morning to go to work. Picture yourself at the door, hand on the doorknob, looking at your other hand in which you visualize the book you're to bring to your friend. Use that technique a few times and you'll probably find it works for you.

So how does that technique work exactly? It utilizes the Brain's associative memory system. You've planted your intention in your Brain and visualized your intention—you at the front door with the book in your hand. When you're at the door, it brings forward the intention you've coupled with the event. If you don't have the book as you're leaving in the morning, your subconscious will remind you of your intention. You'll look at your hand, remember something is missing, and then recall that you're missing the book.

Several elements that make this work: the few moments of effort to capture your intention, the intention to take the book to work, and, most powerfully, your visualization of you at your front door holding the book. That collection of associations and Brain's error-detection system make it all work.

The Sentinel technique works in the same way the memory trick does. The Sentinel will raise the alarms you've trained it to, alerting you to the need to pay attention to something that's going on then and there. The alarm breaks through Master Habit and cues you to pause and choose.

Creating Your Sentinel

When your Sentinel becomes aware that the conditions leading to an unwanted behavior or thought have arisen, it triggers you, figuratively tugging on your sleeve as Ethel does for Jackie, pushing you into the Choosing Space where you see the situation, know that an unwanted impulse is present or arising, and that this is the time to engage your commitment to pause and choose.

Design Your Sentinel

Design your Sentinel to suit yourself. Give your Sentinel a name, a gender, and a backstory, if you like. Design him or her in a way that's consistent with the role of simply pointing out that you're in a situation where you want to be alerted. You should like your Sentinel, be comfortable with, and even admire him or her so that you're willing to confess all, to hold back nothing when telling him or her about your habits.

You've already met Ethel. My Sentinel is named Paul after a college classmate whose demeanor I admired: rational, emotionally appropriate, pragmatic, impatient with useless emotion, but still able to express anger, disgust, and humor when the situation warranted. I've not constructed a backstory for Paul; it's enough for me to imagine his personality.

Common Misconceptions

There are a few things to keep in mind when you're designing your Sentinel. It **must not** be created in the image of a coach, parent, scold, muse, or some power figure—a person whose purpose is to keep you in line, catch you in error, and *make you do the right thing*. On first hearing about Sentinels, people often say something like, *Good, she'll keep me in line*. That's not what they're for. It's not what they do. Sentinels are not sentries. Sentries are armed and use their weapons to keep out invaders. Sentinels are unarmed and simply raise the alarm.

Sentinels only deal with facts. They're constantly on the lookout for the potentially dangerous situations you've trained them to recognize.

Sentinels are not, I repeat NOT, advisors. They will not tell you which habits you ought to manage, nor will they tell you what to *do or* choose when an unwanted impulse appears. They will only tell you it has appeared or is about to appear.

All Sentinels know how to do is let you know what's going on, because what you do with that information is entirely up to you and is your responsibility alone. Remember that Jackie's Sentinel, Ethel, simply notifies Jackie when she's about to give advice. Jackie chooses whether to give the advice. (If you are hearing advice from your Sentinel, it's not a Sentinel at all but some other source, possibly the habitual negative self-talk that so many people are subject to.)

Sentinels are not judges either. They have no stake in whether you engage in your habitual reactions or do something else. They are loyal and kind, but only perform their limited function. They are diligent at doing what you've trained them to do. If they have any emotion at all, it is compassion. No matter what you do, they know that you're doing your best, and that managing your unwanted habits is difficult. They are examples of the most trustworthy, reliable friends possible.

The Sentinel's role is limited to making you aware that the impulse you've trained them on is nigh. That's your cue to pause and choose. Your Sentinel will not even tell you to do that. Every aspect of how you respond to the Sentinel's warnings is your responsibility.

(As an aside, know that one of the most powerful assignments you can give your Sentinel is to warn you that you are listening to negative self-talk. There's more on this topic in the Resource Companion.)

Train Your Sentinel

The Sentinel's role is to watch for the impulse you're committed to be on guard against. The more detail you give your Sentinel the better. Tell him or her everything you know about the habit. Relive your experiences with it. Try to visualize those so that he or she experiences them too. It's especially important that you share with your Sentinel detailed recollections of the real, regretted, habitual outbursts you engaged in, and also the instances when you withdrew, didn't stand your ground, or say what you wanted to.

Recount it all in the imagined presence of your Sentinel. Just because you know what you did in the past and what you want to do in the future doesn't mean that your Sentinel also knows. Imagine talking to your Sentinel. He or she is right there, an eager friend, listening intently, wanting to serve. It may help to close your eyes. Recall the last time the unwanted impulse engaged: the time you lost your temper, held back, gave in to jealousy or pride, went too far in an inappropriate relationship, gossiped, lied, betrayed someone, wasted time or money, over-indulged, got captured by negative self-talk, allowed a mood to make everything bad when much was good—whatever your experience was of the habit you're trying to manage.

You have to relive your experiences in detail for your Sentinel to firmly plant the message in your subconscious as a high-value intention. Read over or recall the full description of the habit you were asked to describe in Chapter 14. Say it out loud as if you were talking to someone, which indeed you are. Remember that when training your Sentinel, you're training your subconscious.

Train to Your Objective

Be sure the training is consistent with the scope of your objective. For example, if all Pat wants to do is stop screaming at Alex when s/he hasn't done the dishes, Pat could train his/her Sentinel to look out for unwashed dishes. Pat would be specific about it: what the place looks like, the time of day, what s/he did right before she got angry, and, most importantly, the feelings that preceded his/her screaming at Alex. If Pat's choice of objective was to be kind instead of unkind, s/he would train the Sentinel to be sensitive to the impulse to act *unkindly*. S/He would do so by recalling several occasions when s/he was unkind, and reliving what that felt like.

Similarly, if the objective is concerned with unwanted attitudes or thoughts, say, self-doubt or judgment, train on the experience of being caught up in the attitude or thoughts so the Sentinel can alert you when you're indulging in those. Some of my unwanted habits involve negativity—feelings and attitudes like judgment, blame, and resentment—so my Sentinel, Paul, is trained to be aware of me having those negative feelings. He wakes me to the realization that I'm in a negative frame of mind, at which point I pause and choose to reframe the situation that brought it on. Having reframed it, I try to bring my attitude and behavior in line with my values and my reframed understanding of what's going on.

Be Accurate About the Facts

It's important to be as accurate as possible when describing the facts of the habit and how it starts, and to take responsibility for your reaction, not evade it. Remember that even if the trigger arises through someone else's actions, your reaction is your responsibility. It's important not to blame others because that will muddy your intention and make it difficult to choose a response that's consistent with your values.

Your description of what happens and what you do in response must be factual and free of judgment and self-justification. Recognize what you do, accept the causes and effects—stimulus, impulse and emotion, action—and take responsibility without blaming others and without shame or guilt. Regret is just fine. It's natural to regret that you caused a problem for yourself or someone else, and did something you didn't want to do. Guilt is an emotional response to the belief that we've violated our standards.[194] In and of itself guilt is not a destructive feeling, but in too many cases the standards we apply to ourselves are unrealistically high, in which case our feelings of guilt are often misguided self-aggression. (You'll find more about how to relate to guilt in the Resource Companion.)

Reliving situations that cause regret and pain are helpful tools for training your Sentinel because doing so works like confession. Maybe you cringe as you reveal what you did—even though you are confessing only to your Sentinel. First, of course, you have to be able to confess what you did to yourself. To do that, you have to break through denial and defensiveness to get at the un-ornamented facts, the truth of the situation. Don't worry about whether your Sentinel will forgive you; they don't judge.

After having relived the story and its consequences, replay it once more as if watching it on a screen, but this time pick the place in the scene where you would like to have been brought to attention. Tell your Sentinel, "This is the place where I'd like you to bring me to attention so I know to pause and choose. This is the place where I want you to interrupt me in the future." Again, like visualizing the book in your hand as you walk out the door, you are training your subconscious to call your attention to the fact that this is when you want to engage your commitment to pause and choose.

Support Your Sentinel

There are a number of things you can do to make your Sentinel more effective. Most important is to revisit your Sentinel occasionally. Repeating the training refreshes it so its effectiveness doesn't dwindle. Remember. Then remember some more. Memories are strengthened by repetition.[195] The scientific research is clear on that point: if you don't repeat training like this, or lose interest in managing the unwanted habit, it will return in full force.[196]

Training your Sentinel will also be more effective if you remain curious about what you do. It's not necessary to go all the way back to the specifics of what your father or mother said to you, where, and on what occasion. But curiosity about yourself and what you do will give you more insight into whether your habits might be misguided, misdirected, or useless. Increased understanding of your habits strengthens the prefrontal cortex's ability to override Reactive Brain's emotional action programs.

I've put a number of awareness practices in the Resource Companion. See what's there, and use what you think will help you. Experiment. If you're already a mindfulness practitioner or regular meditator, I'm confident these informal practices will increase your awareness when you are not formally practicing. I'm also particularly fond of working with slogans, which are like mantras and aphorisms. They efficiently transmit and help implant important principles.[197] Most Americans are acquainted with aphorisms like *a fool and his money are soon parted, a stitch in time saves nine,* and *the early bird catches the worm.* You've already encountered Tsoknyi Rinpoche's *real but not true,* a mantra that I have found extremely helpful in self-management, as have some of my clients. It is a master slogan for identifying faulty conditioning or misguided habits. I've put some more slogans in the Resource Companion (and at ActFromChoice.com).

What to Do When Your Sentinel Fails

Your Sentinel will fail from time to time. What should you do when that happens? If you were unaware of the impulse engaging, then either the Sentinel didn't notice (it failed) or the impulse or something else going on in or around you was so powerful that the Sentinel's priority wasn't high enough to bring you to attention.

When you or your Sentinel missed the onslaught of a habit, patiently retrain him or her by reviewing the circumstances he or she missed, again showing him or her where you would have liked to be alerted. Review the situation as you did previously, incorporating any new contextual features, feelings, and insights you've gained. Be kind to your Sentinel.

Remember that the Sentinel is loyal and wants to help. You did the best you could when you trained it, but now it might be time for a refresher to reinforce what you gave it earlier. Sentinels work like mnemonics—the more associations that are attached to the thing to be remembered, the more easily it's remembered.

Sometimes the Sentinel will do its job and you will fail to follow through. Even with the best of intentions, many of us choose to ignore the Sentinel's signal. If you were aware of the habit as it was building but failed to respond, the cause of failure was possibly the specific characteristics of the situation and/or the condition of your willpower. Your motivation has to be available to you when the Sentinel wakes you, and you try to do battle with Reactive Brain.

Knowing Mind

As described in Chapter 5, the self-awareness the Sentinel launches isn't always enough to arm Intentional Mind with the full power of your motivation, and in many cases it needs all of that to overcome Reactive Brain. You may remember that this is because the bodily changes brought about by the emotional action program need time to diminish. Until then, the lingering emotional state blocks your access to information that might help you countermand the impulse.

In that moment of choice, you need your mind to be as open and free of bias as you are capable of. You want to bring to bear a cognitive mind that can understand the conflict between Reactive Brain and Intentional Mind and be aware of everything you've discovered about the source of your motivation and its power. In Chapter 5 I called this Knowing Mind.

Knowing Mind is the best mind you can muster in the moment. You want to use that Mind to choose what to do. Consequently, I believe it is fair for you to accept decisions made in Knowing Mind even if you decide to accept Reactive Brain's impulse. As well, I urge you to do your best to resist unwanted impulses until you are able to evaluate the situation with your Knowing Mind.

So how do we do that? How do we jump out of Reactive Brain-besotted mind to Knowing Mind? The technique is called *Ask the Second Question*.

Ask the Second Question

You invoke Knowing Mind by asking yourself a question that Reactive Brain (Kahneman's System 1) can't answer. The question forces Brain [System 1] to bring Mind [Kahneman's System 2] into the situation. Even if your Sentinel has put you in a cognitive mind that is still under the influence of Reactive Brain, the Second Question will help turn your Mind into a more engaged and open Knowing Mind.

In Chapter 21 you'll meet Charlie, his chocolate chip cookie habit, and his choosing plan. Charlie has sworn off eating chocolate chip cookies until he loses a lot of weight, and the Second Question is part of his plan (as it should be in every plan). When confronted with temptation that he can't simply push past without help, Charlie will ask himself the Second Question, which will be "Are you willing to accept the consequences of eating the cookie?" or "Are you willing to eat the cookie?" (Either formulation works to invoke Knowing Mind.)

When confronted with temptation, we're first under the influence of Brain, which only knows what is directly in front of it and only the immediate benefits and costs of what it sees in that moment. It does not know about alternatives, your past commitments or consequences. In Charlie's case, Brain's entire world is a cookie and the desire to eat it, full stop. So naturally Reactive Brain tells Mind (Charlie), "Eat the cookie," and lazy Mind accepts the instruction. If you're wondering what the first question is, it's lazy, Reactive Brain-influenced Mind's acquiescence to the question "Do you want to do what Reactive Brain is telling you?" As long as Mind is lazy and in Master Habit, the question isn't asked and answered; there's just an implicit "yes" to whatever Reactive Brain wants.

Here's why the Second Question works. The Second Question asks Reactive Brain about consequences. Since it knows nothing about consequences, Reactive Brain asks Mind to help. Remember that Brain can answer the question $2 \times 2 = ?$ because the answer is stored knowledge. Reactive Brain can't and doesn't forecast or evaluate contingencies. Answering questions about consequences is like finding the answer to $35 \times 12 = ?$ Brain can't answer the question and calls on Mind. Mind, searching for the answer about consequences, brings onto the field everything you know and feel about the conflict between the respective desires of Reactive Brain and Intentional Mind, including the reasons you're motivated to manage the habit.

When Mind can't access all that you know about your motivation, it is nearly defenseless against Reactive Brain-induced desire, so you're effectively left with Reactive Brain calling the shots.

This is like using a scale to judge the worth of an alternative, when the scale has only one side. Ordinarily a scale has two sides. There's something on both sides and the scale tips toward the heavier one. But when only Reactive Brain is involved, there is only one side to the scale, and it always tips toward doing what Reactive Brain wants—in this case *eat the cookie*. Lacking input from Intentional Mind, the scale reflects a *Habit Mind* (Figure 7).

Figure 7

Habit Mind

To make the best choice you can, you need to put everything you know on the scale. You don't have to go to the Internet or open any books. When I say everything you know, I mean the results of all the thinking you've done about this habit. It's all there between your ears, ready for you to access in an instant. Everything you know comes to conscious Mind as a simple sense of *knowing*, without detail and without words. When simple *knowing* isn't enough for you, you have easy access to whatever detail you want, because Mind is now fully engaged.

Knowing Mind distributes what you know between the two sides of the scale appropriately, with as little bias as you're capable of in that moment. You get a scale with two arms, the balance you need to inform your decision, and the scale points where it points. You get something like what is shown in Figure 8 rather than the unbalanced Habit Mind shown in Figure 7.

Figure 8
Knowing Mind

The Second Question opens your Knowing Mind. The form of the Second Question is usually either "Are you willing to accept the consequences of _____ [following the impulse]?" or, more simply, "Are you willing to _____ [follow the impulse]?" For reasons I can't explain, the latter works better for me. Some people have more success with the former.

Whichever form you choose, both alert the Mind to the fact that there are important considerations other than desire or fear or anger to think about. You don't have to recite what those considerations might be. Motivation counts for a lot in this kind of decision making, and simply asking the question brings forward its full weight and places it on the appropriate side of the scale.

I, and others who have used this technique, have shared that when we invoke Knowing Mind by asking the Second Question, we overwhelmingly choose intention over the unwanted impulse. We feel the consequences of going with the habit, including the anticipated regret that would come from not doing what we intended. The Second Question is so powerful, and works so well for me, that I sometimes have to struggle to get myself to ask it. I realize that if I ask it, I'm almost certain to overcome the unwanted habit. As a result, when the impulse is powered by strong desire (cookies) or resistance (procrastination), it takes a separate, extra effort to ask the question. I have to force myself to ask it rather than give in to the impulse right then. And sometimes I fail. (Now there's a confession for you!)

Conclusion

Maybe you're angry and about to say something hurtful. You know it's hurtful, but you get carried away and blurt it out in spite of yourself. Sometimes we try to fool ourselves into thinking that we didn't realize what we're doing, or realizing it, we try to convince ourselves that stopping the habit isn't important, that this time it won't count: it's a calorie-free day! Or maybe we make up other excuses for not following through with intention. It's these tendencies that make the commitment to pause and choose so important.

If we don't pause, and instead say or think, *Oh never mind*, and do the @#$#$ regrettable thing, we suffer for it later. Whether it's eating a cookie or diving into something more consequential, the failure to follow through with intention can lead to subtle but pervasive feelings of being out of integrity—even of self-betrayal. Repeated failure to follow through can undermine confidence and reinforce any negative self-talk we might be subject to.

In contrast, when you pause with the intention to formally choose what to do—to go through each and every step you've planned—you're in charge. There's a feeling of competence, of self-efficacy no matter what final decision and action you choose.

No matter what, I hope you'll give a Sentinel the opportunity to help you. Creating a Sentinel may sound hokey or woo-woo, but keep in mind the powerful benefits of self-awareness and curiosity that this practice enhances. (Remember, since your relationship with a Sentinel happens "in the privacy of your own Mind," you don't have to tell anyone what you're doing.[198] So you really have nothing to lose.) Give it a try.

These practices work for many people. While some of their success comes from the effectiveness of the practices themselves, the secret sauce is often the increased curiosity created by reading or hearing about self-management and trying to do *anything* to increase self-awareness and self-efficacy.

And I'll let you in on a secret: if you have identified your unwanted habit, have a sense of your motivation, and mean to improve the way you manage yourself, you've already created a Sentinel. Naturally, this implicit Sentinel will not be as effective as one you consciously design and train. Knowing that, you might at least give it a name. Even that small act will impress your intention on your prefrontal cortex and strengthen your Intentional Mind.

Still, that alone will not sustain the effort over time, and it may not be enough to reliably trigger your brain's error circuits and break you free of Master Habit. Surely you are like the rest of us. You take on new projects with great enthusiasm, only to find your interest fades as you neglect to feed and water your initial motivation. Take advantage of the level of interest you're displaying by reading this book, and develop as much self-awareness as you can before letting your interest and effort fade.

Remember, too, to be prepared to ask the Second Question when you find yourself self-aware but can't immediately push through to assert your intention. Take a moment now to frame your Second Question so you have it at hand. Remember that it's usually enough to say, "Are you willing to accept the consequences of _____ [following the impulse]?" or, more simply, "Are you willing to _____ [follow the impulse]?"

Whether you use these methods or others, make the effort to choose what to do when you become aware that a habit is about to take over. The Sentinel has called your attention to the fact that it's time to pause, to open the Choosing Space and choose. It's up to you to keep it open. What will you do? How will you go about choosing? What tools in addition to the Second Question will you use? That is the focus of the next and final chapters as we move from developing awareness and training the subconscious to alert us to the impulse, to planning what to do when your Sentinel wakes you to an unwanted impulse in progress.

CHAPTER 20

P Is for Plan

You're aware of the habit you want to manage; you know your objective and the sources and extent of your motivation; you've made your commitment to pause at the first sign of the unwanted impulse; and you've begun to develop self-awareness. Now it's time to plan what you'll do when you become aware.

Your plan needs to describe your objective and how you'll wrestle with the unwanted impulses so you can choose what to do and try to make it happen. The plan needs to be aligned with the characteristics of the habit you're dealing with. But, regardless of the habit you're trying to manage, the commitments to pause and choose are essential, and part of every plan. You've committed to follow the plan. Now you have to design it so that you can believe in it and be willing to put it into action.

The Commitments

Your ability to assert Intentional Mind over Reactive Brain's demands will be decided by what happens when you first enter the Choosing Space. You deal with the first challenge of self-management by developing a Sentinel to make you aware of the unwanted impulse, which launches you into the Choosing Space. The next challenge is to maintain the pause in order to keep the Choosing Space open so you can choose. You will need a plan designed to your capabilities and preferences, and the characteristics of the unwanted habits you're trying to manage. As you'll see, the essential characteristics of the Choosing Space are pretty much the same for most habits. Intentional Mind and Reactive Brain are in conflict. The impulse that wakes us up, that Reactive Brain tries to sustain, is often accompanied and powered by emotions that are pushing us in habit's direction.

There are only three possibilities for what you'll find when your Sentinel wakes you to the situation (see Figure 9):

- **You've engaged intention**. If you are well practiced, your intention and willpower are strong, and the force of the habit is not overwhelming. It's possible you've immediately overridden the habit's impulse and are doing what you intended, or

- **Habit is carrying you away.** You didn't notice the impulse soon enough, and/or the forces of Reactive Brain are too strong, and/or Intentional Mind is not strong enough, and so you're performing the habitual action, or_

- **You're paused and can still choose,** even if you're heading toward executing the impulse. You haven't yet engaged intention, but there's still time to intervene. You might feel yourself *being of two minds*, needing to choose whether to go with the habit or intention. Will you eat the cookie, or will you reject it and stay on your diet?

Figure 9
Alternative Results When
Experiencing an Impulse

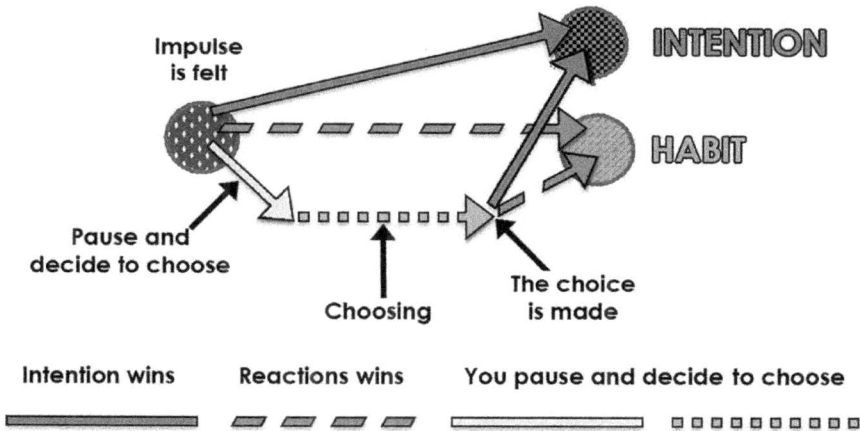

You might have gone directly to intention, in which case the choosing has been accomplished. Or you could have gone directly to habit, in which case the opportunity to choose has been lost, unless of course it's not too late to interrupt execution of the habit and choose to do something else.

But if neither of those has happened, and you're still in command of yourself but have not chosen either intention or habit, you have the opportunity to choose. You'll need to have your choosing plan ready. It describes the formal process which you've committed to go through, step by step, in fulfillment of the second commitment you made in Chapter 18, "Commitment."

Commit to a Formal Process

We don't just fall into the choosing process and flail around. We've decided on a process, and that's what we'll do when the impulse appears. You have to design your plan ahead of time. If you wait for the impulse to arrive before deciding how to manage it, you'll be under the influence of the unwanted emotion and have little capacity to figure out how to choose.

To illustrate using two of my favorite cold habit examples, suppose you are confronted by the legendary chocolate chip cookie you've resolved not to eat, or it's time to go to the gym and don't want to go. When you first feel the desire for the cookie or the resistance to exercising, you may not be able to execute your intention right away. Moreover, while you have time to work in opposition to Reactive Brain when dealing with cold habits, it's far more challenging to deal with hot habits. They tend to promote an immediate reaction. There's been a high-energy emotional reaction to something. The emotion is insistent. It's anger, jealousy, fear, or something else that requires you to do something you know you may regret. It's especially important in those time-limited, hair-triggered situations that you have a plan that tells you what to do when the impulse strikes.

Apart from the allure of the unwanted impulse—the cookie, the thing to buy, the *good excuse* for a towering, self-justifying rage—the real obstacle to overcome is the emotional force of the impulse, not the substance of the trigger's consequences. If you worked through the motivation chapter, you did a lot of work on motivation and have concluded that objectively, cognitively, the alternatives to the habit are more valuable to you than the habit is. So what else is driving you in the habit's direction? Your emotions of course.

So, in the Choosing Space, we battle with emotions. We need to know their strengths and weaknesses. What you're about to learn will show you how to create your plan to have as much success as you can in managing them. This is all about the *emotional profile*—the way emotions gain and lose strength over time.

Emotional Profiles

We've all experienced desire, resistance, aggression, and fear. Each feels different. And their force varies too. When Reactive Brain thinks a lot is at stake, emotions have a lot of force; when the stakes are lower, we may have no sense that emotions are involved at all.

Speaking about strong emotions, those that hit hard and fast—anger, for example—Paul Ekman, whom you met in Chapter 10, posits that as an emotion develops over time, the strength of feeling it produces looks much like a volcano. Immediately after the trigger, the feelings peak rapidly, stay there for some time, and then slowly diminish. Immediately after the trigger, we are in the grip of the emotion, blind to new information, unable to think clearly about what to do. He calls this the "refractory period" (darkest of the shaded area in Figure 10).[199] In the refractory period, we're on full autopilot with our habitual responses calling the shots. The length of the refractory period varies by individual. It can last for a few seconds or minutes. How rapidly we recover is a measure of *emotional resilience*."[200]

Figure 10

**The Emotional Profile
And Refractive Period
When Can Intervention be Effective?**

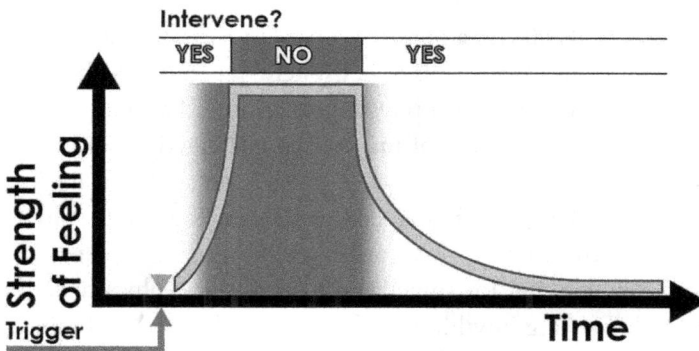

If Ekman is right about the refractory period—and I think he is—then the only places in the emotional profile where we can challenge the effects of the impulse are immediately—really *immediately*—after the trigger, or after the refractory period has collapsed enough for awareness and reason to return.[201] In general, the time between trigger and full-on refractory period is so very short that it takes an exceptionally well-trained Sentinel to interrupt initiation of the refractory period. Even so, the Sentinel will still be operating and is likely to plunge you into the Choosing Space during the refractory period. In that case, we have to battle to hold off the impulse until refraction has subsided enough that reason can intrude and intervention is possible.

There's every reason to believe that all strong emotions fit this profile that Ekman has proposed. If that's true, then the profiles of the emotions urging you to eat the chocolate chip cookie, to put off going to the gym, to buy the bauble, or to pound on your steering wheel in frustration at the traffic jam are the same, or very similar. The differences among emotional episodes lie in the actions the emotional action program wants you to perform, the emotion you feel, and its strength. Obviously, the emotional feeling that drives you to try to escape the tiger is not the same as the emotion that wants you to eat the cookie.

Another consequence of the emotional profile is this: when two people are angry with each other, and their emotional resilience is different, the one who recovers more slowly may prolong the upset—actually reigniting it after the other party thinks everything has been settled. Robert Sapolsky explains it this way: after being triggered, then agreeing to some resolution of the problem, the body of the person with greater resilience returns more quickly to normal and cools off. It's a matter of how fast the body can flush all those fight-or-flight hormones from his or her system, returning the body to a more neutral state.[202] This is simply a physical function; it has nothing to do with the person's character or sense of justice, though practice can help give you more control.

Even if the other party has agreed to the settlement, the physical state that came with the emotion may not have subsided completely. So his or her Brain keeps looking for something to justify the physical feelings that have lingered. Lacking anything in the present, his or her Brain dregs up something that caused a similar emotion in the past, reigniting the whole kerfuffle.[203] Obviously, the emotional profile is less important when the force of the unwanted impulse is weak compared to when it is strong. Still, it's important not to add to the emotional force of the impulse and make things worse. That's another habit to manage, even as we're trying to manage the unwanted impulse.

How We Make Things Worse

"Emotions love emotions," says Marsha Linehan, professor of psychology at the University of Washington and developer of Dialectic Behavior Therapy (DBT).[204] This statement refers to the common tendency to crank up and extend emotions in ways that continue the upset through a positive feedback loop. Surely you've seen people extend their emotions by digging deep to recall and rant about every emotional insult they've experienced that was anything like the stimulus that just set them off or that made them feel similar.

As I've said many times in this book, it often feels terrific to be angry; it can feel so right and righteous, and what's better than that? It feels good to let everyone know how much we've been injured, how much injustice we've endured, how bad the other guys are, and how we're going to get even. And when anger comes from feeling powerless, we'll do anything to feel powerful again. Is there any more direct way of feeling powerful than to attack, to retaliate, to show we're right, and to tell the world we'll wreak havoc on those who cross us? You may recall Pema Chödrön teaching that making emotional reactions bigger and worse is one of the four ways we try to escape discomfort.

And then there's *the story*. After being triggered—feeling insulted, mistreated, threatened, demeaned—we may want to tell a story, first to ourselves, then to anyone who'll pretend to listen. It sounds like this:

"[He, she, they] did _____, and then there was _____, and then _____. And if I do that [she, he, they] will _____, and then _____, and then _____ and then _____."

It goes on and on and on, sustaining the bad feelings and doing nothing toward addressing the feelings or what caused them. Ani Pema calls this the "story line"; it's partly an attempt to run away from what we're feeling, partly an attempt to justify what we did in reaction, partly a call for help, partly a need to put responsibility for the affair elsewhere, partly a way to recruit allies, and partly a way to let off steam. The main thing the story does is keep us from acknowledging or discovering the truth of the situation, which is mostly about what we're feeling. (If you tend to go into storytelling mode and don't want to do it anymore, train your Sentinel to tug at your sleeve when he or she hears you doing it.)

Telling the story to ourselves and others is another way we make the emotion bigger and last longer. It's usually a misdirected habit. We feel we're doing something that is totally justified, but in fact we're doing nothing at all to address the real problem—the original stimulus and its consequences. Often the best thing we could do is stop and get in touch with what we're feeling.

Validating Feelings Is Effective Medicine

Storytelling is often a response to feeling wounded. When we tend to the wound and our feelings, we feel healed and don't need to distract ourselves with misdirected, useless emotions. Getting in touch with the feelings, acknowledging them, and extending compassion to ourselves produces miraculous results. It can eliminate completely the need to act out in accordance with any secondary emotion, especially with anger. (Remember the reaction of the policeman whose son was about to go to jail, when the official helped him acknowledge his despair over the coming incarceration of the son he loved.)

When you acknowledge your feelings, you reduce the driving force behind misdirected outbursts. You don't have to do a lot. You just need to notice that you feel wounded, sad, angry—whatever you're feeling. You don't need to justify your feelings. That you have them and they make you feel bad is all the justification you need to extend compassion to yourself. At a deeper, more profound level, acknowledging what you feel and how it affects you, and making it okay to take care of yourself in this way, builds an intimate, caring relationship with yourself. It is you caring for you. No one and no thing can match the positive effects of such compassionate acknowledgment and self-caring. Stephen Levine writes, "Truly, we have been waiting our whole life to hear 'I love you' in our own voice."[205]

Putting it simply, strong emotions tend to take us over. At the start of the emotional build-up there is little if any ability to stop and decide. The strength of the emotion, including the time it takes to build and subside, determines how and when you have to intervene to manage yourself. You need to begin managing it as early as possible before you produce the actions that you'll regret, hopefully as soon as the subsiding refractive period permits.

Delaying Response

Reactive Brain always rushes us toward the action it prescribes. Consequently, when we arrive in the Choosing Space the emotion is often still in the refractory period. We may think we know what we should do, but while the emotion remains strong, we don't have access to all the reasons and force of our motivation. That is why we feel conflicting emotions that seem to emanate from two different and opposing minds.

Since thinking is distorted when we first experience a strong emotion, we need to include in our planning a set of tools for delaying our response to the stimulus and speed the reduction of the emotion's force. Your delaying tools could include techniques such as counting to ten, taking slow breaths, distracting yourself, say, by slowly reciting a prayer or mantra, or forcing yourself to think about something unrelated to the stimulus, say placing your attention on a neutral part of your body. More advanced techniques include dis-identifying from the unwanted thoughts or attitudes the emotion produces, reframing the situation and your reaction to it, and simply breaking off contact with whatever or whoever triggered your feelings. You could also try to stop preparing for any impulse-driven actions. If you anticipate that your emotions could be so strong as to make you ineffective, you could create a plan for leaving the room until the emotion is at a manageable level. (You'll find explanations for these techniques and others in the Resource Companion.)

However you do it, you have to hold the pause, forcing a delay in your reaction to the impulse's force, while you wait for the reactive period to wear itself out. The delay makes it possible for you to get to Knowing Mind so you can make your choice from its perspective. If you try to choose before you have Knowing Mind on your side, you're more likely to give in to the impulse.

You can improve your motivation and ability to hold the habit off if you incorporate in your plan a commitment, a rule, to not give in to the unwanted impulse until you've reached some specific point in your plan. When you read about Charlie's chocolate chip cookie plan, you'll see it includes such a commitment, specifically to hold off any decision to go along with the impulse until he's able to choose from the perspective of Knowing Mind. (Remember that you can invoke Knowing Mind by asking the Second Question.)

Next Steps

Your next task in the Act from Choice Method is to design your plan. The next three chapters present examples of plans that will give you ideas about how to build your own.

The next chapter, Chapter 21, "Simple Plans for Cold Habits," contains examples of plans for managing habits that give you plenty of time to respond to impulses, and habits that involve you dealing with you, or situations involving others where you have the time to figure out how to respond. The templates in the chapter include dealing with habits of desire (chocolate chip cookies) and resistance or aversion, specifically developing a routine like going to the gym. There's also a lot on dealing with procrastination, whether it involves putting off simple one-shot tasks or projects that take days to complete, such as doing your taxes, or working on longer-term multiple-session projects for work, home, or school.

The first of those templates, Charlie's chocolate chip cookie plan (Chapter 21), is a template on which all other templates can be based with minor modification. The templates in the final three chapters are based on and assume you know about Charlie's chocolate chip cookie plan, so be sure to check it out first, even if you think other templates may be more relevant to your interests.

Chapter 22, "Complex Plans for Hot Habits," gives examples of plans for habits characterized by strong emotions that come up in the presence of others, and are forcing you to respond right away, whether it's to hit someone or to leave the room in order to regain control. There are two examples in that chapter. The first is about a father who doesn't want to react as angrily as he does when his children spill milk or otherwise misbehave at breakfast; the other describes a very fraught relationship between a loving caregiver who is verbally abused by her partner who depends on her for everything.

Chapter 23, "To Cultivate Your Values, Manage Your Unwanted Attitudes," will help you use your unwanted habits to strengthen your values. Most of us experience attitudes, thoughts, and judgments that are contrary to our values, and thus are unwanted. These include attitudes like prejudice, judgment, stinginess, and narrowmindedness. They appear automatically, and when they do we may question whether we are who and how we mean to be. The chapter also describes how to use those unwanted attitudes to enhance and cultivate the attitudes their appearance contradicts.

I recommend you read through all three of these chapters. You may be reading this book because you have an unwanted habit that applies to only one of these chapters, but most of us have habits in each of these areas—cold, hot, and attitudinal habits. Moreover, you may find something in hot habits that will help with your cold ones or unwanted attitudes.

Again, be sure to read the chapter immediately following because of its description of the foundational template, Charlie's chocolate chip cookie plan.

Regardless of what you choose to read, use what you think will help. Regard these chapters and the Resource Companion as a toolbox; choose the tools you'll use based on their relevance to your unwanted habits, your comfort with using them, and most of all, on your sense that they can help you.

CHAPTER 21

Simple Plans for Cold Habits

My intention is that the plans presented in these three chapters are broadly applicable so that you can modify them to address your unique needs. As I've said above, in this chapter we're dealing only with cold habits—habitual reactions to situations in which only you are present, or if others are involved, an immediate response is not required and there is ample time to decide what to do. Figuring out how to react to an infuriating email is an example.

The first of the plans in this chapter, Charlie's chocolate chip cookie plan, contains elements that can be used in many different plans, including those for hot habits and unwanted attitudes. It is described in greater detail than you'll find in others. So this is the place to get the detailed understanding you'll need to apply these common-purpose tools to other habits.

There are two sections to this chapter. In the first we'll look at methods for managing unwanted habits of wanting or desire, specifically how to avoid that oh-so-wonderful chocolate chip cookie when you've sworn off them.

The second section is about unwanted habits of resistance and avoidance—procrastination, in particular.

Managing Unwanted Wanting

This first example can be used for managing pretty much any unwanted wanting: a bigger TV set, an extra drink, another pair of shoes, or that stranger sitting at the bar. (Consistent with other caveats you've seen in this book, if you have a habit or addiction that is dangerous to your health, relationships, livelihood, or fortune, I urge you to seek competent professional help to manage it, and rely on their advice as to whether you should work with this book. Do not rely on this book alone for problems of that significance.)

Now let's go meet Charlie and see how he develops and describes each element of his plan. We'll see it through his eyes. I'll introduce some new actions and concepts, and explain them after we've seen the entire plan.

The Situation and Plan

Charlie is overweight—very overweight. He frequently binges on chocolate chip cookies and wants to cut them from his diet until he reaches his target weight.

I'll set this up using the TOM-Decide-CAP structure in Charlie's voice as he employs the Act from Choice Method. I'm not using the forms (provided in previous chapters) in this example because I felt an informal presentation of the Method might be easier to follow. Chances are you'll gain additional insights that will more than justify the effort if you use the forms.

We'll start with the Preliminary Phase. There are three steps in this phase. The mnemonic is TOM, standing for Truth, Objective, and Motivation.

Here's what Charlie says.

PRELIMINARY PHASE
T—Truth

I'm gaining weight. Okay, I'm really overweight. I'm addicted to 500-calorie chocolate chip cookies and have decided that four of those beauties each day is too enriching for me, and the guys who sell me cookies and belts.

O—Objective

In addition to other dietary changes, I've decided I will not eat another chocolate chip cookie until I lose 125 pounds. At least that's what I'm thinking.

M—Motivation

Are you kidding? I can't fit in the furniture, much less my clothes. I think I lost a job promotion due to my appearance; my wife is threatening to leave me. And forget physical intimacy. What are the benefits and costs of managing this habit? On the benefits side, everything I've mentioned will improve. On the minus side, it's going to be really hard. I love my chocolate chip cookies. They're a great source of emotional comfort when I'm stressed. The benefit of not managing this habit is that I get to indulge. I don't have to control myself. The costs of not changing are losing all the benefits of change I mentioned, plus I'll continue to feel like a helpless, out-of-control addict.

When I look at it from a values perspective, I feel ashamed of what I've been doing. Eating these cookies means giving in to a very unhealthy habit just to fill some short-term nervous need for comfort, and that's not how I want to be or see myself. I can't keep doing this and still consider myself a self-sufficient, powerful person. I'll regain some self-esteem by controlling this habit. And knowing how hard this will be, I'll get an extra boost by knowing I've overcome this dreadful habit. This habit doesn't enhance any of my values, except that maybe I enjoy being self-indulgent. But is that really a value?

When I review what I've written, I see that I want to manage this habit, and I want to stick with the preliminary objective going forward.

DECISION
Yes. I will pursue this objective of not eating another chocolate chip cookie until I lose 125 pounds.

This brings us to the Committed Phase, for which the mnemonic is CAP, standing for Commitment, Awareness, and Plan.

Here's Charlie again.

COMMITTED PHASE
C—Commitment to Pause and Choose
I commit that whenever I feel the desire to eat a chocolate chip cookie before I've reached my weight goal, I'll pause and choose what to do using a formal procedure. I will develop a procedure that is clear about what I must do before giving up on my intention and giving in to eating the cookie. I will do whatever I can to keep from giving in until I can choose from the perspective of Knowing Mind.
A—Awareness
I've hired my Sentinel. His name is JoJo. He used to be tubby and a sugarholic. He lost over 200 pounds by managing his sugar addiction, and he wants to help others. He's my age (55) and he's skinny.

JoJo and I have long conversations in which I tell him how much I love my chocolate chip cookies. I describe how hungry I get every time I see or even think of one. The smell of freshly baked chocolate chip cookies really gets to me. I've taken him through many recent experiences, telling him what they were like, and asking him to experience my desire so he'll know when to alert me. I've asked him to alert me to what's going on when that desire starts, as soon as I experience the slightest whiff of cookie, see one, or when the thought of one enters my mind.

For my Second Question, I'll ask, "Are you willing to accept the consequences of eating the cookie?"

P—Plan

As soon as I experience the desire for a chocolate chip cookie or find I have one in my hand—it could happen(!)—I commit to pause and use this plan to choose whether to eat the cookie or not. This plan requires that I resist the urge until I've made a final decision in the Knowing Mind step (Step 3), below. I've considered whether I need to do any preparatory homework for how I'll deal with any cookies I encounter, and have concluded that I don't need any. So now for the action plan:

As soon as I become aware of the urge I will follow these steps:

Push through: I'll try to overcome the desire by pushing through it right away. If I find a cookie in my hand, I'll try to put it down. If that works, I'm done. If not, I have to move on to Step 2.

Apply tools: I'll try to wait a bit or distract myself in some other way. I'll try ten deep breaths, and I'll feel my stomach as a reminder of my intention. If that works, I'm done. If not, I'll move on to Step 3.

Invoke Knowing Mind by asking the Second Question, and then decide: I've committed to perform this step before accepting failure and giving in to the impulse. I'll ask the Second Question to give me a more global, cognitive-based perspective on the situation so that I'll remember why I want to manage this habit. I'll base my final decision on that perspective. If I decide to reject the cookie, I'm done. If not, I'll accept that I've failed this time, but I'll finish up as described in the next step before eating (and enjoying) the cookie.

Reflect/Recommit: If I choose to eat the cookie, there are two things I must do before eating it: first, tell myself what happened, why I couldn't succeed in meeting my objective of not eating the cookie. The rules are that I have to tell the truth. Examples of truthful statements might include, "I felt bad and sorry for myself," "I felt I needed the cookie," and "I was exhausted, it smelled so good, and I just didn't have the energy to fight the desire." I am not allowed to answer in a way that denigrates me, such as, "I am weak."

Second, I must ask myself if, in spite of this failure, I am still committed to this objective. If not, I'll stop pursuing it. Having completed both steps, I'm free to eat the cookie and enjoy it, guilt-free, because I've done what I committed to do. I'll keep a copy of the plan at hand and review it every Friday night so I'm prepared for the weekend's temptations.

Practice: I will have to renew JoJo's training from time to time or JoJo will forget, and the strength of the alarms I've planted will weaken. Whenever I fail, I'll retrain him. The only other thing I need to do is practice, to occasionally visualize a cookie confrontation and what I want JoJo and me to do in response.

There you have an illustration of a complete plan. It may look complicated, but it takes a minute or less to execute. Imagine that Charlie is confronted by a gorgeous, tempting cookie fresh from the oven. I hope you agree that having a plan like this would substantially increase his ability to resist eating the cookie.

The Plan in Detail—Commentary

Charlie's plan is the basic Act from Choice Method. It's as straightforward as it gets. I hope you find that the TOM and CAP steps prior to the P-Plan step are also straightforward. I simplified the Motivation step in this example to make it easier to read and understand, though I recommend you do all three motivational exercises described in Chapter 16, and complete all four boxes on the final two forms (Forms 3 and 4).

As I indicated above, most simple plans can use the steps Charlie outlined with only minor changes. What follows is an explanation of each step in the Committed Phase, with descriptions of how to tailor them to other cold-habit situations.

Charlie begins his plan with a summary statement: "As soon as I experience the desire for a chocolate chip cookie or find I have one in my hand—it could happen(!)—I commit to pause and use this plan to choose whether to eat the cookie or not. This plan requires that I resist the urge until I've made a final decision in the Knowing Mind step (Step 3), below."

Commitment is a crucial step to all programs. Charlie's commitment is to the entire procedure. He is committed 1) to pause so that he can choose; 2) to follow the plan he's devised, step by step; and 3) to keep from giving up until he's made a final decision in the Knowing Mind step (Step 3).

As to Preparatory Homework, he says: "I've considered whether I need to do any preparatory homework for how I'll deal with any cookies I encounter, and have concluded that I don't need any."

While Charlie doesn't see a need for any advance work, hot habits often require it, which includes practicing what you will do in stressful circumstances. Though Charlie's is a cold habit, he might benefit from periodically imagining a cookie confrontation and refusing to indulge it, and in fact he's included that in his practice step.

Here are Charlie's action steps.

Step 1. Push through: Charlie says, "I'll try to overcome the desire by pushing through it right away. If I find a cookie in my hand, I'll try to put it down. If that works, I'm done. If not, I have to move on to Step 2."

The idea is to strong-arm the impulse as directly and quickly as possible. If you can shut it down, just do it; there's no need to get fancy. The more often you succeed in overriding the impulse, the more likely you'll be able to do it without further ado, but if you can't, you go to the next step.

Step 2. Apply tools: Charlie says, "I'll try to wait a bit or distract myself in some other way. I'll try ten deep breaths, and I'll feel my stomach as a reminder of my intention. If that works, I'm done. If not, I'll move on to Step 3."

As discussed, emotions are most powerful immediately after they arise. If you can wait a few minutes, letting them and the conditions they've set up in your body calm down, the impulse may weaken enough to be easier to manage. Distraction, calming yourself, and recalling your motivation can be very effective in helping you wait out the calming-down period. You'll be better able to get through this period if you know in advance which tools you'll use, and how you'll use them.

Charlie has pre-selected three tools. First he will wait or distract himself. If that doesn't work, he'll try taking ten deep breaths. Finally, if necessary, he will try to recall his motivation by pressing his hand against his stomach.

Step 3. Invoke Knowing Mind by asking the Second Question: Charlie says, "I've committed to perform this step before accepting failure and giving in to the impulse. I'll ask the Second Question to give me a more global, cognitive-based perspective on the situation so that I'll remember why I want to manage this habit. I'll base my final decision on that perspective. If I decide to reject the cookie, I'm done. If not, I'll accept that I've failed this time, but I'll finish up as described in the next step before eating (and enjoying) the cookie."

Recall that in the Awareness step, Charlie chose for his Second Question, "Are you willing to accept the consequences of eating the cookie?"

The Act from Choice Method requires you to commit to a *formal process* of choosing. Integral to that commitment is deciding how much effort to expend before giving up—how far to go into the process before it's okay to give in to the habit if you can't overcome the impulse immediately.

A fair test to apply to the confrontation between Intentional Mind and Reactive Brain is to evaluate the situation using Knowing Mind; you want to make your choice of what to do from a Mind that is open and as free of bias as you can muster. You want to be aware of the conflict between Reactive Brain and Intentional Mind and be able to recall everything you've discovered about the source and power of your motivation. Asking the Second Question will give you the best mind you're capable of in that moment. Though it may not be the best you can do on a calm day, it's the best you'll have immediately available. Consequently, I recommend that you accept as final your answer to the Second Question. You've done what you committed to do and brought to your decision process the best Mind you're then capable of. And you paused and chose according to your plan.

Remember that the commitment to a formal procedure for choosing comes with permission to choose whatever you will. When you've become present, have roused Knowing Mind, and have brought to bear everything you know about your motivations, including the consequences of the habit, there is nothing further to do. If you can't overcome the impulse at that point or don't want to, you should congratulate yourself on having followed through with your commitment to pause and choose. But before eating (and enjoying) the cookie, complete Step 4.

Step 4. Reflect/Recommit: Charlie says, "If, after invoking Knowing Mind, I am unable or unwilling to follow through with my objective, I will accept my decision, at which point I'll be free to eat the cookie.

"If I choose to eat the cookie, there are two things I must do before eating it: first, tell myself what happened, why I couldn't succeed in meeting my objective of not eating the cookie. The rules are that I have to tell the truth. Examples of truthful statements might include, "I felt bad and sorry for myself," "I felt I needed the cookie," and "I was exhausted; it smelled so good, and I just didn't have the energy to fight the desire." I am not allowed to answer in a way that denigrates me, such as, 'I am weak.'

"Second, I must ask myself if, in spite of this failure, I am still committed to this objective. If not, I'll stop pursuing it. Having completed both steps, I'm free to eat the cookie and enjoy it, guilt-free, because I've done what I committed to do."

You require this step only when you decide to go along with the unwanted impulse. In that case, I've recommended that you answer two questions: Why did you give in to the impulse? Are you still committed to your objective?

The reasons you give to explain why you gave in must be the truth as far as you know it. You benefit from hearing yourself say those reasons. It will give you heightened awareness of what happened, and that will make it easier to resist in the future. If your answer seems weak and you repeatedly give yourself similar reasons, you may come to question whether you're really committed to your objective or need to try harder. You'll be the judge.

The more important question to answer for yourself is whether you're still committed to working on the objective you chose. Since you've just given yourself the permission to indulge your habit, this is an ideal time to test the strength of your commitment. Of course, there's danger in doing that. Having failed to follow through with your intention, there will be a tendency to feel guilty and not trust your judgment about how committed you are. I recommend that you do your best to judge your commitment as honestly as you can, and to trust the integrity of your judgment.

When you honor your commitment to choose formally, you've maintained your integrity no matter what your final decision is. Saying why you're going to eat it, and checking in with your commitment to your intention, maintains your intention and your commitment to managing your habit. Making a conscious choice to eat the cookie and then denying that you made that choice would damage your integrity more than eating the cookie could possibly do.

If you've followed the plan you've committed to—this or something else you've designed—and decided to eat the cookie, told yourself why you chose to eat it, and re-examined your commitment, you've done everything you've committed to do. Eat the cookie. Enjoy it guilt-free because you've met your commitments to yourself. Regret it if you must, but you've done the best you could do this time, and there's nothing better than doing your best.

Charlie's comments about **Step 5, Practice**, seem straightforward enough and do not require additional comment.

Recapping Habits of Wanting

This five-step plan for dealing with habits of wanting is the basic structure for working with all unwanted habits of action. (Habits of attitude—of thoughts that may not produce actions—require other techniques that are discussed in Chapter 23.)

Be sure to customize your plan to meet the requirements of your unwanted habit and the situations in which they occur.

To recap the basic structure incorporated in the plan, the initial steps are designed to execute your commitment to pause and choose, including, as Charlie's plan is designed, a commitment to not give up until you have chosen from the perspective of Knowing Mind.

So, one more time, the basic steps in the plan are these:

1. Immediately try to impose your intention.
2. If needed, use the tools you've selected in advance to delay action while the force of the impulse diminishes.
3. Invoke Knowing Mind by asking the Second Question; make your final decision from that perspective, and accept it.
4. Reflect/Recommit: If unable to resist the impulse, tell yourself why you chose to go along with the impulse; re-evaluate your commitment to your objective.
5. Practice the plan with your Sentinel.

And now for plans for a different kind of habit. Charlie's chocolate chip cookie plan is aimed at overcoming the desire to do something—to eat the cookie. These next plans are about overcoming habits of resistance and avoidance: procrastinating and avoiding things you feel you shouldn't put off.

Managing Unwanted Habits of Resistance and Avoidance

Habits of resistance and avoidance produce feelings like *I don't want to do that*, or *I don't want to be around that or engage with that—certainly not now*.

When "that" is something you need to do right now, delay can have serious consequences. Delay could impact you financially. If it's about delaying an interaction with someone, it can undermine the relationship.

Sometimes the consequences of delay are trivial. You dropped a piece of paper on the floor and walked by it a dozen times. So what? Except that you feel bad because you think you should act more quickly, and your home would look better if you'd attend to these inconveniences right away. Moreover, that piece of paper on the floor is an energy-draining, guilt-provoking reminder that you're not being the way you want to be, and it will continue playing that role until you pick it up.[206]

Habits of resistance and avoidance are similar in that we are resisting or avoiding someone or something we feel obligated to engage with. Simply put, we think we *should* do or engage with something, but don't want to. Someone may have placed the obligation on you, or you could have taken it on by yourself. The source of the obligation doesn't matter. The feeling is that you *should* be doing something, but you're avoiding it and wish you weren't.

Sometimes putting off something we think we should do can cause extreme, gut-grinding anxiety. Sometimes we avoid doing something for so long that the due date passes without having even started on it. Then it becomes pointless or embarrassing to do it, so we don't do it, and we suffer the consequences. Or we *must* do it (taxes!), and there's not enough time left to do it right. It seems that just about everyone has procrastinated or resisted their obligations from time to time. For those of us who procrastinate habitually and often, there are plenty of good reasons to work hard at managing the habit, whether the costs of delay and avoidance are material, psychological, or both.

Two Kinds of Triggers to Resistance

For the purpose of managing these habits, there are two types of triggers to consider because they require different plans. Some triggers of resistance appear unpredictably. There's the paper on the floor. Pick it up or not? Someone asks you to run an errand that was not what you planned to do right then. You don't want to do it so you *don't* do it, but you wrestle with the feeling that you should.

The other type of trigger is predictable or can be made so: there's something you have to do (or feel you should do). It could involve an obligation to others or only to yourself. Those that involve obligations to others include things like working on that big assignment for work, doing your taxes, calling a sick friend. Typical of those that are only between you and you are maintaining a regular exercise program, going to church, meditating, updating your résumé, or getting an estate plan done. Even if some of these have deadlines enforced by others, you can choose when to work on them. When you schedule your *work* you're scheduling when you will confront the habit and your resistance. The schedule becomes your Sentinel. When you realize the scheduled time has arrived, you're thrust into the Choosing Space.

Triggers That Occur Unpredictably

Resistance that comes up unpredictably can be managed just like Charlie's chocolate chip cookie habit with relatively minor tweaks. You go through the preliminary stage of the Method: Truth, Objective, and Motivation (TOM). The most interesting of these might be choosing your objective, because you'll want to choose between picking some huge, glorious, general objective, such as "I never want to give in to resistance (or avoidance)," to more narrowly focused and specific ones, such as "I always want to respond to requests for help," or even more specific: "I want to jump right on it when Alex asks me to help." As mentioned earlier, I recommend you work on the specific ones before taking on grander ones.

Your choice of objective may be influenced by how often and in how many different situations you resist. It's not as if resistance to picking things up off the floor, or to a regular exercise program, or to writing thank-you notes, might be the only things a person resists; for many of us, resistance appears in response to a great many obligations (my hand is raised). If that's you, you might want to set your objective on resistance in general, not your resistance to just one thing. On the other hand, you might want to develop that muscle by choosing one or two very specific objectives to work on to start. (You may want to review Chapter 15 to get a refresher on choosing your objective.)

After picking your preliminary objective, you do the Motivation exercise and keep revising your objective until you've settled on one you think is feasible and for which you have the required motivation. Then you go through the Decision step, and from there you move into the Committed Phase consisting, again, of CAP—Commitment, Awareness, and Plan. You'll commit to pause when you feel the resistance and to choose by going through the formal process you design.

Awareness is the next step. If you haven't already hired a Sentinel, you'll do that now and train him or her to the objective. If your objective is to manage all feelings of resistance, visualize previous occurrences and train your

Sentinel on them. If your objective is to respond to all requests for help, visualize those and train yourself on them. If you're Pat, and you only want to respond more quickly to Alex's requests, recall and visualize him/her asking for help and you not responding well to the request, and train your Sentinel on that. When practicing your plan, visualize responding right away.

Next, as part of the Awareness step, design your Second Question. In habits of wanting it's "Are you willing to accept the consequences of eating the cookie, buying that television set, or chatting up that person at the bar?" or, the other formulation, which is, "Are you willing to eat the cookie," and so on. In habits of resistance, instead of "Are you willing to accept the consequences of eating the cookie?" it will be "Are you willing to accept the consequences of not responding to Alex's request for help?" or "Are you willing to not respond to (or ignore) Alex's request?"

Finally, you get to the plan itself. For this kind of habit, you can use Charlie's chocolate chip cookie plan with only minor changes. You'll want to pick your own methods of delay or cooling off, if you need that step.

Scheduling When Habits Appear

You may feel anxious about what you'll do when faced with the need to work on something that isn't due for some time. But that can be a needless worry. Instead of letting those concerns badger you, you can eliminate the anxiety by scheduling when you'll work on them. If you do that, you'll find that your Brain won't keep reminding you that you need to complete the assignment because it will be satisfied that you've dealt with it, even if all you've done is to schedule the chore. Scheduling when you'll work on something not only relieves the intervening anxiety, it puts you in control of when you'll try to manage your resistance. You'll work on whatever you're avoiding according to a schedule of your choosing.

So the basic plan for managing your resistance, when the trigger is something you're trying to postpone or avoid, is to create your schedule as soon as you realize that you have to work on the task or routine. You set up the schedule on whatever calendaring system you prefer—the calendar on the refrigerator, an electronic calendar, or your smartphone. It's best if you use a system that has audible or visual alarms that can grab your attention when the scheduled time arrives. (If none of the systems I mentioned are reliable, ask a partner or friend to remind you, but make sure someone or something will shake your tree when the scheduled times arrive. If there's no other way to do it, consider signing up with FollowUpThen.com and use their system. They'll send you an email on any day and time you specify. It may cost you nothing.[207])

Routine and Simple Encounters

The first of these examples involves resistance to maintaining or beginning a routine, like going to the gym regularly—also doing simple, one-off tasks like calling a sick friend. We'll start with going to the gym.

To control your resistance to following a routine, tie it to a schedule. You don't decide that you'll go to the gym on Monday, Wednesday, and Friday, and every other Sunday. You decide that you'll go to the gym Monday, Wednesday, and Friday *at 5:30 p.m.* and every other Sunday *at 1:30 p.m.* It's essential to be specific as to day *and* time. It's like setting an alarm to wake up, and in fact you will set a physical alarm to remind you when the scheduled time arrives. Many of us use an alarm clock, and we set it for the hour and minute we want. I don't think anyone uses a clock that's supposed to wake them *sometime* during the day—whenever it's convenient for the clock.

You need to know precisely what time you want to be confronted with the obligation to do what you tend to resist. To a degree, the schedule reinforces the Sentinel. When it's 5:30, the alarm goes off. You've committed to go to the gym then. The time has come. You're automatically in the Choosing Space with the additional commitment to choose by following your formal plan, which is very close to Charlie's chocolate chip cookie plan.

The TOM-Decide-CAP procedure aimed at overcoming resistance to establishing a routine is simple. The Truth is that you resist going to the gym; your Objective is to go regularly. Those are simple steps, but you probably ought to spend some time on Motivation. The effort will pay you back many times over if you do. Assuming you have sufficient motivation to pursue the objective you've chosen, you decide to try to manage it. You move into the Committed Phase and make the commitments to pause and choose. Understand that the schedule you made helps the Sentinel by calling your attention to the fact that the day and time to confront the habit have arrived.

Here's a template for this and other plans of resistance that involve maintaining a routine. You've scheduled a time to go to the gym. When the time comes, as in the cookie example, the first thing is to try and push through—to simply assert your intention and turn it into action. If that doesn't work, you use some other tools you find useful. I know runners who are committed to putting on their running clothes and shoes before giving up on their intention to run, and that usually works, they say. Getting ready moves one into the stream of action, and that's often good enough to get through resistance. But suppose that tool, or others like it, don't work?

Then you move into Step 3, where you ask the Second Question. For going to the gym, your question might be, "Are you willing to *not* go to the gym?" or "Are you willing to accept the consequences of not going to the gym?" When resistance is the issue, asking "Are you willing to NOT go to the gym, to NOT go to church, to NOT practice the piano, to NOT work on the taxes" brings to mind all the motivational work you did in the Preliminary Phase. It's not that you think about everything you identified in the motivation step. Instead, it's as if you get an injection of the net motivational force as a wordless feeling that giving in to the resistance will deliver a ton of regret.

You ask and answer the Second Question, accept your decision, and go about your business free of guilt. If you've decided to give in to your resistance, before leaving the plan reflect and recommit: check in with yourself. Tell yourself why intention didn't win this time (no self-criticism allowed), and verify that you're still committed to manage the habit.

The technique just described works well for any routine task you tend to resist: brushing your teeth before bed, meditating, attending weekly prayer services, even making a weekly call to someone you want to stay in touch with. You can also use it for one-off activities you want to do but have been avoiding—for example, any conversation you've been avoiding, or the letter you've been meaning to write.

All of these work the same way. At some point you think to yourself, *I ought to call Charlie; he's having a bad time.* That's followed by feelings of resistance and avoidance: what to say, when is the best time to call, you're afraid of being awkward. To overcome these doubts, use the Act from Choice Method and schedule a time to call. Make sure you set some type of alarm so you don't fail to notice when the scheduled time arrives. If you think waiting a few days to call Charlie won't cause him additional suffering, or is otherwise immaterial, schedule the phone call for a few days later. In the intervening time between putting the call on the calendar and making the call, think about your motivation. Why do you want to call Charlie? What are the costs and benefits of calling and not calling? What are the values expressed and undermined if you do or don't call? You probably won't want to do a lot of detailed work for a one-off item you resist, but give your motivation some attention because it will help you manage the habit.

When the time comes to make a call you resist making, or to paint the garage door, approach it with the attitude that you intend to do it. See this as an opportunity to manage your resistance. Try to push through, use whatever other techniques you've selected, and, if those don't work, don't give up before asking the Second Question. If you give up, tell yourself why you're going to do something else instead, and—very important for this kind of task—*ask yourself if you're still going to call Charlie.* (How many times have you put off an obligation just like this one only to feel rotten after the opportunity has passed?) Presumably the reasons to call Charlie haven't changed. If you decide you're done trying to call, cross it off your list of obligations, but if you feel you still need to call, schedule it again, and soon.

Managing More Complex and Multi-Session Tasks

The call to Charlie is a simple task, a one-off that can be managed using a simple plan to overcome your resistance and/or procrastination. The plan works well for any simple task that you can finish in one session—phone calls, letter writing, and even painting the garage door. But what about when you have a large task to do, such as preparing your taxes, completing the project for your boss, or developing an estate plan? You need a slightly different approach to deal with complex undertakings, especially those requiring several work sessions to complete.

Taxes are an example of a large task that almost no one enjoys. Instead of thinking you can finish your tax return in one go, assume that you will need a number of sessions to complete it to your satisfaction. The key to reducing procrastination for multi-session resistance-producing projects is to make a schedule for when you'll work on them. Be very specific as to date and time, for example, every Sunday for two hours beginning at 4 p.m. starting with the first Sunday in March, except for the third Sunday in March when you're going to Bill and Lisa's wedding. If you're willing, commit to a minimum amount of time you'll spend on the project during each work session. When the scheduled times to begin the task arrive, use your plan to choose whether to work on your taxes or give in to your procrastination.

Before making that schedule, investigate and describe the source and amount of motivation you have to confront your procrastinating. Do the Motivation exercises in Chapter 16 to investigate and strengthen your motivation to do the project on time. You've failed at overcoming your procrastination before. If you don't discover and evaluate the sources of your motivation, and make a judgment as to whether your motivation is strong enough to overcome your procrastination, you'll probably do no better this time. So do all of the steps described in Chapter 16. Write down the consequences, the costs and benefits of managing and not managing procrastination on the project you'll be working on, and identify how procrastination supports or undermines your values. Then you'll be ready to make a schedule, and you'll have a good chance of following it.

Some additional steps will help you manage projects that require several sessions to complete. When the day and time arrive, engage with your plan. If you've committed to a minimum time for each session, remind yourself of that.

Once again, you try to push through and go to work on your taxes, say. If that doesn't work, you apply your tools. You could try waiting a moment or two for resistance to fade. You could also try taking up one small task that's easy to do. Often that will give you some momentum for continuing with the harder stuff. It's like putting on your shoes to help you go out for the daily run.

If you can't go directly to working on your taxes or starting one small task, shift your attention to figuring out what your very next step should be. See if you can bring yourself to start planning the work. Then you won't be so focused on doing the whole thing, but rather on where you would take the next step. If thinking about planning your next steps makes you feel you could tackle some of the work right away, stop the planning and do what you're motivated to do.

If you even resist making a plan for doing the work, take some tangible action that will feel like progress. Look at what you've done so far (if anything) and see if you're willing to do the next thing, something easy. That first step could be something as simple as putting your documents in a file, making an orderly stack of papers, scheduling a call to your accountant to make an appointment, or researching accounting software. In other words, do something, anything, to feel like you're working on the project, even if you think it's less than you *should* be doing.

Do not give up and go on to something else until you've asked the Second

Question. And always, whether you've worked a lot or a little, before stopping work entirely, figure out and write down the first step you think you should take when you go to work on the project the next time. Make it an action step. If you do that, the next time you're scheduled to work on the project your start will be much easier because you'll know exactly what you have to do to launch into it right away. There's even a good chance that, between sessions, you will have visualized carrying out that first step, making it easier to start again. When you return to the project, see where you left off the last time so you know where to begin. See if you can do at least the first thing you identified. If so, it's likely you'll be able to continue for a while.

It's also possible you won't be able to rouse yourself to do a single thing I've mentioned. If you've set a minimum time for each session, just sit there and do nothing. Let the feeling of boredom come over you, if not for the entire time you thought you should work, then at least for a set time, like fifteen minutes. (This minimum time commitment should be part of your plan.) See if your commitment to sit there doing nothing for the allotted time doesn't move you to do something on the project, however minor.

If that doesn't happen, go to Step 3 in which you'll decide from a Knowing Mind perspective. Ask the Second Question, something like "Are you willing to accept the consequences of not working on this right now?" Again, you can accept your answer to the Second Question as final.

If you've decided to give in, do so, but take a few moments to reflect and recommit. See when you're scheduled to work on the project again. Consider whether you'd be willing to revisit the project sooner than what you originally planned, and if you are, commit to that and set your alarm for that time and day.

Having gone through the labor of applying the tools, defining the next step, and then rejecting even that small step, you may feel down on yourself. Maybe you think you're constitutionally incapable of managing your impulses to procrastinate. If that's the case, use that feeling to motivate you to do better next time. You really can control procrastination.

If you feel bad enough that you want to make amends for disappointing yourself, go back and work on that next step—the step you decided to postpone. If that's not how you feel, see if you're willing to commit to take up the work and follow your plan at the next scheduled encounter.

Don't give up on your commitment until you've failed to follow through for at least three work sessions in a row. You know what will happen if you give up trying to manage your procrastination; it will be just like all the last times. You'll do nothing between now and the night before it's due, t hen go through the agony of getting it done, fearing the consequences of being late, and knowing that you'll be paying more taxes or turning in work that doesn't represent you at your best.

To summarize, here are the key features I recommend you include in your plans for dealing with cold habits of procrastination and resistance.

- Commit to pause, then to follow your plan, step by step.

- Your plan should include a commitment not to abandon your intention to meet your objective until you've tried to decide from the perspective of Knowing Mind.

- When working with procrastination or resistance, be sure to do the motivation investigations described in Chapter 16. If you want to proceed to manage your resistance, schedule the work you are likely to put off. Use the arrival of the scheduled time to force you to confront your reluctance to do what's required. Consider committing in advance to a minimum time for each work session.

- When the scheduled time arrives to work on the task or follow through with a routine you've been resisting, try to impose your intention immediately. If you want, you could jump immediately to Knowing Mind by asking the Second Question.

- For those occasions when you aren't able to impose your intention immediately, have in mind a number of tools to help you force your intention. When trying to manage procrastination for multisession projects, those tools could include doing one small thing, figuring out what you could do next, or simply sitting there for fifteen minutes or so to see what develops.

- As a final step, invoke Knowing Mind by asking the Second Question. Accept your answer as your final decision (except when dealing with procrastination over multisession tasks, where you might want to reconsider your answer).

- If habit wins, be sure to reflect on the challenges this situation raised, and then recommit to your goal of managing your resistance or procrastination the next time.

We'll move now from cold habits to looking at what to do in more fraught situations when we're reacting to hot habits—the feelings are strong, others are involved and present, and Reactive Brain is trying to get us to react immediately.

CHAPTER 22

Complex Plans for Hot Habits

There's no time to dither. If you're going to manage your hot, habitual reactions, you have to be ready for them. You have to plan your response in advance, rehearse it, and have the motivation, intention, and commitment to follow through with your plan.

The stimuli may be significant or trivial, but the intensity of your habitual response, the involvement of other people, and the need or impulse to respond instantly make hot habits much harder to manage than cold ones. You experience the trigger, are taken over by an emotion, and react immediately because the people and situation that created the trigger are right there, and you feel yourself propelled into an immediate response. Your emotions are obvious to everyone around you.

You don't have the inclination to pause and choose when hot habits strike. You're instantly caught up in the emotion, and the urge to act (or not act) is very powerful. The consequences of your actions can be very big: you might say or do something awful to someone important to you. There are often innocent bystanders present, only observers, but potential victims of your reactions. Consequently, a key objective for managing hot habits, including reducing collateral damage, is to get your behavior, thoughts, and attitudes under control very quickly.

The motivations for getting these types of habits under control are varied. Some people want to avoid the lasting damage to themselves and others that extreme emotions can cause. Some are made uncomfortable and even frightened by how extreme their reactions can be, whether or not they do something they later regret. Others find their reactions violate their personal standards of behavior, and want to moderate them for that reason.

There is a significant difference between emotional outbursts and the cold habits of wanting, resistance, and aversion. All are powered by emotions, to be sure, but the person wanting to overcome desire or aversion has to focus mostly on whether the action is good for them. The consequences of the habit, and the costs and benefits of managing it, usually affect only the individual. But the person who experiences big emotional outbursts involving other people has to manage their feelings as well as the feelings and consequences for others too.

I present two examples of habit management plans in this chapter. The first example describes a young father who wants to manage his angry reaction to his children's carelessness at the breakfast table. The second example is about high stakes confrontations between a caregiver and her invalid significant other who verbally abuses her, yet depends on her for everything.

What to Plan and Prepare

As with cold habits, you begin with the steps of the Preliminary Phase: you describe the truth of what you do, pick your preliminary objective, explore and describe the factors affecting your motivation—the consequences of the habit, the benefits and costs, and the personal values affected by managing and not managing it. If you decide to pursue your objective, you enter the Committed Phase, in which you make the commitment to pause and choose, and hire and begin training your Sentinel. Then you're at the Plan step.

Your plan will depend entirely on the specifics of the habit—the who, what when, where, and why of it—how you react, and how you want to react instead.

In the first example, the main character is Max, a father.

Max and the Boys

Max is the father of two very young, very energetic boys—great kids, but they argue and fight with each other a lot. They're also about as careless and clumsy as normal kids in the single digit age group. Max is usually very easygoing. He tells me he never gets upset when he finds himself stuck in traffic, and the elderly person blocking the supermarket aisle doesn't bother him at all. I've worked with him long enough to believe him. He's able to stay calm for a good while during the boys' typical living room fight, but if there's *any* misbehavior at the breakfast table, he gets angry and raises his voice. The most common affront is spilled milk. He hates the way he reacts. He's done enough introspection to figure out that his reaction is a gift from his own upbringing, but he keeps doing it.[208]

The TOM—Decide—CAP steps are pretty simple in Max's situation:

T—Truth

One or both boys spill milk at the breakfast table. Max gets furious and acts out by slamming his fist down on the table and yelling at them. The children are frightened. Max's wife is upset. Max feels guilty.

He feels his behavior is inconsistent with his values about how to be a good father. He feels that his boys' offenses are trivial and his own behavior is too big, too fast, and generally out of proportion to the cause. His boys are just being rambunctious and clumsy. He loves them, but his reaction hides his love. Max's recognition that his habit is a product of his own childhood makes it easier to let go of believing his reaction has some moral validity. He wants to make sure he doesn't pass this habit on to future generations, and that adds to his motivation.

O—Objective

Max wants his reaction to be more appropriate. He wants to remember his loving feelings for his children while still being able to correct their behavior. He wants his reaction to convey his standard of behavior (being careful and taking responsibility), without making them feel they're bad people. He means to be a loving father with reasonable standards of discipline, being both fair and effective in the way he responds to breaches of behavior. He wants to raise his children to feel loved and to be good citizens.

M—Motivation

The benefits and costs of getting his behavior under control are obvious. For Max, there is no alternative to making every effort to be a loving, good, and responsible parent. The benefits he'll gain from managing his anger better will far outweigh any benefit from yelling at the boys. No amount of effort is too high a price to pay to achieve his personal goal, he says.

Decision

He means to change his reaction. He's committed to it. And so he moves into the Committed Phase.

C—Commitment

He makes the commitment to pause and choose by using a plan of his own devising.

A—Awareness

He hired a Sentinel, Jason, and trained him to be sensitive to the breakfast table situation and other triggers common to a typical morning's upset. Max trained Jason to respond to the boys' carelessness and to Max's rising anger at one or more of the children—actually for any purpose, but particularly in the breakfast situation. (Max uses Jason in his business too.)

P—Plan

These are the methods and tools Max uses when feeling the impulse to get unreasonably angry with the boys.

- He uses the initial pause to remind himself of his unconditional love for the boys in the hopes that the slight delay will quash his anger and help him speak from a more balanced place without giving up his insistence that they be more careful.

- As his Second Question, he asks himself, "Are you willing to get so angry over this?"

- In addition, he designed some specific words to say to the boys when they're careless: words of correction, words of encouragement, words designed to meet the boys' needs rather than his own, because they're small and he's big and can take care of himself.

- He's committed to practice, practice, practice his reaction in anticipation of the real event. In his practice he imagines the boys spilling milk. He pictures himself first reframing the situation by remembering that healthy boys of their age don't have much self-discipline. He recalls his standards for himself as a father, and then applies to any anger he feels the antidote, which is his love for his sons.

When all goes right, Jason alerts Max to what's going on when the boys spill milk or otherwise trigger Max's anger. He pauses, reframes the situation, and reacts in a positive, firm way to correct them.

He's still likely to feel the rising anger and the impulse to yell at his boys when they're careless at the breakfast table. Jason will help him recognize that he's getting angry and the impulse to act out is working on him. There may be times when he gives in to anger because his willpower is impaired. Remember that what is important is what Max expresses to the boys, not the impulses he feels.

Max is compassionate to his core. A little bit of effort, and the plan was made and practiced. After not much time, Max was able to manage his reactions at the breakfast table.

Max's situation and his solution demonstrate that advance planning is critical when the habits are hot. Key to Max's success was motivation, pre-planning, and rehearsal. First he was clear about what was happening (Truth). Then he defined his Objective and Motivation. But even those steps would not have been enough to assure his objective. He needed a plan. He needed to define what he would do, and to plan and practice it so that he could respond immediately and appropriately when he was triggered to anger.

Max's situation turned out to be pretty simple to plan and ultimately to manage. Unfortunately, the situation for Rachel and Richard is anything but simple. Theirs is complicated and heartrending. It has many elements of a seriously unwanted situation—a difficult relationship, high energy, habitually negative interactions, hot feelings and reactions, followed by regret, anger, and mistrust—all caused by objectively difficult external circumstances that must be dealt with in a constructive way.

Rachel and Her True Love

As this story opens, it's eighteen months since Rachel's husband, Richard, fell off a roof, breaking his back and much more. Profoundly disabled as a result, he is almost totally paralyzed, bedridden, unable to work, and requiring 24/7 care and supervision. Rachel must now be Richard's case manager, housekeeper, part-time nurse, fundraiser, and cook too. Money is very tight. The prognosis is grim, probably years of living with his condition, which will only get worse. While they have nearly full-time care for Richard, Rachel often has the night shift.

Richard does not participate in his care as much as he's able to. He is non-compliant with his medications and diet. Additionally, he periodically disconnects sensors essential for raising the alarm when his situation becomes critical, which it often does. He constantly berates Rachel, yells at her, insults her, and shows little gratitude for her contributions to his care. Despite his self-defeating behavior, it is clear to everyone around him that Richard is determined to live.

When he's aggressive, demeaning, and noncompliant, Rachel gets furious and sometimes acts out to the fullest extent of her rage, which, as she describes it, sounds pretty Olympian. She feels betrayed, frightened, and powerless.

She is angry.

She says she wants to manage her anger at Richard. On the one hand, she feels guilty about getting angry with him, saying she wants to go to peace instead of anger when he acts out. But then she tells how good it feels to get angry at him. She says it makes her feel powerful when she otherwise feels powerless. She knows her anger creates a barrier between them.

Their anger is a vicious cycle, each one feeding off the other's anger, and it's often hours before they can communicate effectively. In addition to the damage to their relationship, these confrontations make it difficult for them to make critical health care and financial decisions.

Rachel remains very devoted to Richard, but her primary feelings are betrayal, powerlessness, and fear. She believes that her anger is probably a secondary emotion.

Here is the TOM—Decide—CAP process of the Act from Choice Method for this situation.

T—Truth

Rachel's feelings of hurt, betrayal, and powerlessness fuel her angry reactions toward Richard. Her anger is destructive to the relationship and inhibits her effective management of Richard's care and their finances. Rachel means to gain control of her anger. She feels it is a secondary emotion stemming from her feelings of powerlessness and fear about the future.

O—Objective

Rachel wants to work with Richard constructively to manage the challenges caused by his deteriorating health and their financial situation. She believes that objective requires her to stop going to anger and acting out. Secondarily, she would like to bring love back to the foreground of their relationship as a support for the difficult work of dealing with their situation. Finally, she wants to get past the feelings of hurt, betrayal, and powerlessness, to "go to peace," as she says; also, she wants to reclaim her feelings of self-worth. The bottom line is that she means to be a loving, competent caregiver and partner with a healthy sense of her own self efficacy. Her near-term, actionable objective is to engage with Richard without expressing anger in his presence, to leave the room and return later if she is unable to contain her anger.

M—Motivation

Her motivation is very clear. She means to be a loving, competent caregiver and partner who has a healthy sense of her own self-worth. Her inability to manage her anger has negative consequences for Richard, her effectiveness at managing their situation, and their relationship, and undermines all the values of loving, caregiving and self-efficacy that she cherishes. The only thing that offsets those costly consequences of her anger is the extremely short-term relief it gives her.

Decision

Something must be done. The decision to work on this situation is choiceless. There is no alternative. Solutions must be found, so she moves on to the Committed Phase.

C—Commitment

She commits to pause and choose her behavior by following her plan and not giving up until she has made her choice after asking the Second Question.

A—Awareness

Rachel trained her Sentinel, Marjory, to be particularly sensitive in the sickroom where most of Rachel's interactions with Richard take place. Marjory puts her on guard when Rachel thinks about going to the sickroom or finds herself going there. She's also trained Marjory on Richard's raised voice and her own rising anger.

P—Plan, Homework

When describing Charlie's chocolate chip cookie plan, I indicated homework might be important when managing certain habits. In Richard and Rachel's plan, homework is essential because Rachel has some healing to do, and almost no one can work on self-healing when they're trying to master their emotions on the spot. She needs to work on herself, preferably with a really good therapist. She recognizes that her love for Richard can be the antidote to her anger if she can keep the anger at bay while she figures out what to do. There's little doubt that Richard's anger is misdirected, a secondary emotion coming from his feelings of fear, powerlessness, and despair. These factors suggest that Rachel could help herself by periodically visualizing Richard's reactions to her, reframing them as his cry of despair, and using that recognition to rouse her feelings of compassion and love. She could repeat this visualization frequently, especially when preparing to enter his room.

Rachel committed to take time to sit with herself and acknowledge the situation, how hurt she feels, how much she's contributed to improving the situation and Richard's care, and how well she's done in the circumstances. She doesn't need to justify her feelings by telling a story. Far more important is that she acknowledge her feelings and understand that feeling the way she does is truth, not weakness.

My experience is that self comforting, validation, and self-care can reduce her need to run away from her feelings and turn despair into anger as a way to feel better. Extending compassion to herself will also help her see Richard more accurately, making her more willing to extend compassion to him when he lashes out.

In case there's any doubt about what I intend here, this self-validation is not meant to excuse, cover up, or promote denial about Rachel's part in this situation. It is simply an important step that Rachel needs to take in order to acknowledge herself as a person who is adequate, has intrinsic dignity, is worthy of respect and compassion, and is hurting.[209] She'll be better able to deal with Richard when she's able to support herself in that way.

Rachel also needs to develop the skills necessary to have difficult conversations. For this, I usually recommend two highly respected books: *Crucial Conversations: Tools for talking when stakes are high*, by Kerry Patterson and Joseph Grenny,[210] and *Non-Violent Communication: A language of life*, by Marshall B. Rosenberg, PhD.[211] These two highly acclaimed, practical, and well-respected books teach how to approach difficult topics by emphasizing the sharing of information and dealing with feelings, as well as facts, in non-threatening ways.

Plan—Actions

The following are the steps Rachel will follow when Richard sets her off:

Step 1. Push through: When she becomes aware of rising anger, his or hers, or of being in danger of being mistreated by Richard, she'll try to push through the anger and respond calmly.

Step 2. Apply her tools: It will take some practice before Rachel can quickly gain control of herself. (Remember that Rachel's anger is a hot emotion with a lot of history. Consequently, the refractive period is likely to last for quite a while—minutes, not seconds.) Therefore, she'll need tools to get past the refractive period, to wait it out until she's cool enough to speak purposefully, factually, and as free as possible of anger. Here are some of the tools she will prepare and practice in advance.

First, she'll do her best to pause and quiet herself. When she feels calm, she will decide whether she needs to leave the room or continue interacting with Richard. If she's aware she can't quickly calm herself, she will leave right away.

She can cool down using any of these methods:

- Becoming quiet and taking a few slow breaths, counting, if necessary
- Directing her attention to her body to ground herself
- Reframing Richard's behavior as a reflection of his despair and powerlessness rather than an attack on her
- Applying the antidote of loving kindness

She committed to leave the room without angry words if she loses control, or if her emotions don't subside enough to allow her to be in control after she's used those tactics— especially if she feels she wants to attack Richard. She's prepared the words she'll say when she's decided to leave the room to recover self-control: "I'm going to leave the room. I'll be back as soon as I can, and we can talk about this then." As part of her practice, she will visualize needing to leave, saying those words, then leaving the room.

Step 3. Invoke Knowing Mind/Second Question: The challenge in this situation is to maintain some semblance of self-control. When the despair and anger is in danger of breaking through, she will ask herself, "Are you willing to make this situation worse than it already is?" or "Are you willing to let your feelings stand in the way of making this situation better?" If asking the Second Question doesn't produce calm, she'll do her best to leave the room and recover her equanimity elsewhere.

Step 4. Reflect/Recommit: The stakes are very high, and this hot situation will come up repeatedly. Whether Rachel controls herself or not, she needs a period of post-encounter reflection to think about what went well and figure out how to do it better next time.

It takes courage, determination, and skill to manage situations like these. Practice is an essential part of making this plan work. Rachel has to practice with her Sentinel, Marjory, so she's able to anticipate her anger. She'll be helped by visualizing encounters with Richard in which she behaves the way she means to. She also needs to practice and hone the phrases she'll use with Richard. There is no alternative to these practice sessions. Without training and effort, Reactive Brain will have free rein.

This chapter concludes the discussion of the Act from Choice Method as it relates to habits of action—habits that cause us to act in ways that are not in our longer-term interests or consistent with our values. The focus in working with habits of action is management of the specific actions (or non-actions) the habits want us to perform. In the next chapter, we'll look at habits of Mind. In those, the unwelcome habit is the appearance in consciousness of attitudes, thoughts, and judgments that are contrary to the way we mean to be; that is, they are contrary to the values that we've chosen and want to claim as our own.

CHAPTER 23

How to Cultivate Your Values
by Managing Unwanted Attitudes

This chapter is about working with unwanted attitudes, thoughts, and judgments that are contrary to how we mean to be. I'll call them attitudes for brevity's sake. The mere appearance of these attitudes in our Minds is troubling because, whether or not they turn into action, we recognize that they are contrary to our values and, consequently, to who we think we are. Though they may reflect how you are in that exact moment, they feel nothing like who you *mean* to be. They feel like "not me," and that feeling creates the motivation to manage them instead of agree with them.

The important distinction between habits of Mind and habits of action, the principal focus of previous chapters, is where we put our attention when trying to manage them. With habits of action, we're intent on stopping or managing the action. With habits of Mind, we're concerned about the attitude itself. For example, suppose you value your open-mindedness, kindness, and compassion, but find yourself stereotyping people. You become aware that you harbor attitudes about certain kinds of people, even though that's not a conscious value or intention. You see that you sometimes think that people who look like *those* people are bad, weak, or inferior in some way. Maybe it's their shape, size, color, or ethnicity that triggers your attitudes. Regardless, it's your attitudes about them that make you question your commitment to open-mindedness, kindness, and compassion.

Or maybe you think you're generous, but find that the sieve of judgment through which you filter people and situations before they earn your acceptance is exceedingly fine—surprisingly and disturbingly so. Realizing you have such tendencies, you wonder whether you're generous, or if you're too judgmental to claim that value as your own.

This chapter describes methods for working with unwanted attitudes, particularly negative ones triggered by and aimed at situations, people, and things external to ourselves. (Another type of unwanted attitude is aimed at ourselves and is almost always negative, even to the point of aggression at times. You may know this as "negative self-talk." You'll find more about this in the Resource Companion.)

The unwanted attitudes I'll discuss in this chapter are mostly about those that don't turn into action and therefore, strictly speaking, are habits of Mind. But unwanted attitudes can influence habits of action too. What about them? What's the difference?

In action habits, the important thing is the action itself. The motivation for wanting to manage the habit, and the focus for managing them, is to manage the action, full stop. Usually we're trying to keep from performing the action (or acting instead of not acting), or at least mitigating the action's regrettable consequences. Consequently, plans for managing action habits are about just that: what do you do to control the action when you wake up to the impulse demanding you to act according to its wishes? In those situations, we give very little thought to managing or moderating any accompanying attitudes.

For example, in the story of Max and his boys, one of Max's highest values was to be a good father. That value motivates him to stop overreacting when his children are careless at the breakfast table. He knows that his reaction is fueled by an inappropriate judgment of their behavior, but he's not trying to fix that, at least not right now. For him, it is far more urgent to control his behavior than to stop feeling the judgment that drives his reaction. Consequently, he trained his Sentinel, Jason, on the morning table, the children's actions, and his rising temper. Those associations wake him to the danger of executing the unwanted impulse to overreact. For him, success is behaving calmly rather than angrily.

For an example of habit of mind, you may remember earlier I cited the civil rights leader Jesse Jackson saying, "There is nothing more painful to me at this stage in my life than to walk down the street and hear footsteps and start thinking about robbery. Then look around and see somebody white and feel relieved...." I understand him to be referring to the pain he experiences when finding himself stereotyping members of his own race. That was his unwanted habit of Mind.

We don't see the habits of Mind that come along with habits of action when there's no gap between impulse and action. In those situations, we discover the attitudes only later, if we try to understand what happened.

Unwanted Attitudes Are Gifts

Discovering unwanted attitudes in your Mind can feel like a rebuke, but noticing them and recognizing them as unwanted is very good news. The reason you notice and want to disown those attitudes is that you honor the values they contradict: you feel bad about your unkind thoughts because you value kindness. You are frustrated at your impatience because you see your upset as useless and maybe unfair to the focus of your impatience. You wish you could be more patient. So rather than feeling bad when you notice temptations to be unkind to someone, less generous than you think you should be, or impatient and frustrated for no good reason, celebrate the fact that you want to disown the emotions, attitudes, judgments, and thoughts that contradict and undermine your values. Use those occasions to buttress and more fully manifest the values you honor. You chose those values, and I hope you can agree that your choices are the measure of you more than your habits are.

The Method

Habits of attitude are like the cold habits discussed in Chapter 21, and the methods for managing them are similar. There's no hurry and no risk because they're about you reacting to yourself, and the tangible stakes are usually very small.

It's pretty clear what you'll do when you see that you're experiencing an unwanted attitude. You will have decided that the attitude undermines one or more of your personal values, and you'll try to manifest the preferred value, your Value Objective, instead of the unwanted one. Unwanted and wanted values will be paired in your mind and become visible when you experience the unwanted one: for example, your Value Objective for unkindness might be kindness, for judgment it might be compassion, openness, or curiosity; for impatience, patience. When the unwanted attitude appears, you'll recognize that it's the one you don't want to manifest. You'll do your best to drop it, then manifest the wanted one in your thoughts and any immediate action you undertake.

ACT FROM CHOICE

Preliminary Phase

The Preliminary Phase for managing habits of attitude are much the same as described for other habits: TOM—Truth, Objective, and Motivation.

T—TRUTH

In this step you identify the attitudes, thoughts, and judgments you experience that violate your values and that you want to work with. Do you laugh at jokes about or prejudge people of a disparaged class or appearance, and think you shouldn't? Do you get angry at the woman in the supermarket with the screaming child and think you shouldn't? Are you often impatient and wish you weren't?

O—OBJECTIVE

In this step you define the value you mean to manifest and enhance when the unwanted attitude appears. This is your Value Objective. Repeating unwanted-wanted value pairs from above, if the unwanted attitude is unkindness, your Value Objective could be kindness; if judgment, then compassion; if impatience, then patience.

You may remember that there were several alternative objectives Pat could choose when dealing with his or her anger over the unwashed dishes. Some were specific: don't get angry when Alex doesn't wash the dishes. Some were general: being compassionate toward everyone always.

There are a lot of objectives you could choose. Suppose you get annoyed, angry even, at the mother and her screaming children in the supermarket. You could decide this is an unwanted (and useless) habit of impatience, unkindness, lack of compassion, of taking yourself and your comfort too seriously, a lack of openness to what others are experiencing, or just of giving in to a useless habit. Your annoyance is an opportunity, an invitation to enhance a value that your Reactive Brain tends to undermine.

Take your time choosing your Value Objective. If your unwanted habit of Mind is impatience, your Value Objective might simply be to turn annoyance and impatience into patience. Patience is defined as the ability to overcome intolerance to situations—to endure the discomfort. If you could choose only one alternative Value Objective it might be to turn impatience, judgment, intolerance (you pick) into openness—to use your discomfort as an invitation to try to understand the causes and conditions that lead others to do the things you don't want to tolerate. You might also decide you'll use those situations to investigate whether they're worth your aggravation (and possibly aggression?).

You might determine that the slogan "Don't make things worse than they already are" is more appropriate than the energy you customarily expend on these experiences.

Before you choose your Value Objective, see if there's something you can learn about the negative emotions that accompany your unwanted attitudes. Perhaps you're suspicious of strangers, maybe only certain kinds of strangers—*others*. If that's the case, maybe you want to choose a Value Objective that is something like *Become more open to and curious about strangers, what they're doing or experiencing, and what causes them to be that way.*

To help you choose your objective, decide which of your values is most challenged by the unwanted attitude you're experiencing. Is it the value of openness? Compassion? Patience? Wanting to be helpful? Something else? When in doubt, choose the Value Objective that you think will give you the greatest boost toward being how you mean to be. Try to keep your objective simple, especially if you're just starting to work with a method like this.

M—MOTIVATION

Presumably, your desire to manifest your Value Objective was stimulated by motivation to live up to the values you've chosen for yourself. That in itself is powerful motivation to do this work, and it may be enough for you. Yet there might be something to learn by going through the motivation exercises in Chapter 16. Those exercises can reinforce your commitment to your value choices and give you further insight.

Attitudes you find unwanted today may have served an important purpose in your life when you were younger, or living in a different culture or environment. It might be useful to get curious about what purpose they served. See what needs they fulfilled for you, and whether you still have those needs. For example, negative attitudes about people and situations may be secondary reactions to primarily wanting to feel better about yourself, to feel less powerless, to have more control, to defend against or express certain fears, or to conform to your culture's demands. You can investigate the needs that produced the unwanted values by chasing down answers to questions like "What if anything do I get from these attitudes? Do I still need what I used to get from those unwanted judgments, from entertaining those unwanted thoughts, from holding on to those unwanted attitudes?" See what answers you get from asking those questions. You may want to talk this over with a friend or advisor.

When pursuing any exploration like this, be firm in believing that the value you want to enhance is a better picture of who you are than are the needs or emotions that produce the unwanted attitudes. But if you find that these attitudes continue to fill certain needs that would otherwise be unfulfilled, consider whether you're ready to give up those benefits. For example, if you want to choose empathy and openness as your Value Objectives, check whether you're willing to give up the annoyance you feel when strangers' appearance, or noise-making, disturb your tranquility. Are you willing to give up your righteous anger and feelings of superiority over the mother who can't keep her child quiet in public places? Are you willing to think sympathetically about her, to see her embarrassment and sense of powerlessness, rather than condemn her as an incompetent who can't control her child? Try to envision situations that challenge you. See if you can content yourself with more value-oriented reactions to those situations than the annoyance you customarily feel.

Of course, if your contemplations lead you to believe that your unwanted attitudes are essential to filling your needs, you'll have to go with that conclusion. You can always change your mind later.

Decision

The motivational investigation might lead you to rethink, redesign, or even abandon your Value Objective, and that's okay. But let's assume you've cycled through that process enough. You're satisfied with your Value Objective, want to claim it for yourself, and have decided to proceed.

Committed Phase

The Committed Phase is CAP—Commitment, Awareness, and Plan.

C—COMMITMENT

This is just like the commitment step in the other examples. You've decided to work with your unwanted attitudes and your Value Objective, so you commit to pause and choose what to do when you become aware of the unwanted attitudes, thoughts, or judgments you've identified.

A—AWARENESS

You train your Sentinel on the unwanted attitude. Your Sentinel will remind you to work your plan and enhance your Value Objective. See if you can pick a Second Question or slogans to help you remember the reasons you're motivated.

P—PLAN

As in the other examples I've presented, the purpose of plans is to guide you when you first realize you're experiencing the unwanted attitude or impulse.

There are two approaches to planning how to manage unwanted attitudes: an *extended* plan and an immediate or *spot* plan. Choose the extended plan when you want to enhance a particular Value Objective by working on it daily for a defined period of time. A month would be typical. You might choose to work at enhancing patience or generosity, for example. Rather than waiting for the opportunities that cause the unwanted attitudes to appear, you make a concerted effort to practice the Value Objective every day, and review your progress daily. The extended plan has its own procedures that I'll describe in a few pages. The spot plan does not involve that everyday focus on a particular value. It is simply what one has decided to do when and if the unwanted attitude arises.

At the heart of both the extended and spot plans is the procedure for attempting to drop the unwanted attitude and manifest the Value Objective when a contrary attitude appears. (The Preliminary Phase and Decide, Commit, and Awareness steps are the same for the spot and extended plans.)

I'll begin this discussion by describing what one does in the extended and spot plans when the unwanted attitude appears. After that I'll describe the features unique to the extended plan.

THE SPOT PLAN

When you become aware of attitudes contrary to your Value Objective, your goal is to drop the unwanted attitude and manifest your Value Objective as soon as you can. If your Value Objective is to manifest patience, when awakening to experiencing impatience you try to put aside, to drop, the impatient feelings, then deliberately pause and try to find patience in yourself. If action is called for, you do your best to make your action reflect patience.

Here are some examples.

EXAMPLE: PATIENCE

Your Value Objective is patience; the unwanted attitude is impatience.

You're late and in a hurry. You don't want to stop at the supermarket, but you have to pick up a box of cereal—a last-minute command from your partner. Rushing into the supermarket, you walk quickly to the cereal aisle and find your access blocked by an elderly gentleman who is moving very slowly. Impatience flares. Your Sentinel wakes you to the feelings. You remember your Value Objective. What's your plan?

- You pause. Literally stop in your tracks.

- You realize you're impatient and remember you've pledged to enhance and manifest patience. Though your intention is patience, your body is pushing impatience. Impatience is a useless habit in this situation, because though the way to your objective is blocked, you're no bully. You're not going to climb over the nice man, so you're just stuck.

- You need to unwind your impatience and drop it as soon and as best you can. You turn your attention to the situation. The elderly person seems okay but is moving so, so slowly, and you're in a hurry. Your impatience makes you angry at him. In a flash you realize you can wait for him to move, awkwardly try to squeeze by him, or give in to your impatience by hoofing it as fast as you can to the other end of the aisle and enter it from the other direction. But that would add fuel to your impatience. Of course, doing something rude is out of the question. And, besides, this is an opportunity to practice patience.

- You accept the situation. You reject your feelings of impatience, take a deep breath, maybe sigh (but not so loud as to make the old guy feel bad), and wait until he moves out of the way enough for you to turn to him, smile, and say, "Pardon me, can I get by?" (Maybe you realize that the delay cost you all of one minute!)

- With him out of the way, you move gracefully by, get your cereal, and leave.

Maybe after doing your best to manifest patience, you slow down, the tension leaves your body, and you feel better than you have since you received the command to stop at the supermarket. Regardless, you leave the supermarket feeling better about yourself because you tried to manifest your Value Objective. You overcame your impatience by accepting the situation as it was, and worked with it with a patient attitude—even if you were only faking it, even if you were seething with impatience as you waited for "the old geezer to move, dammit." No one got hurt or was bothered by the encounter, and you arrived at home one minute later than you would have if you had indulged your impatience.

Imagine—remember is more like it—that you're stuck in traffic, all alone, late for work. Your temper is rising. You feel your impatience. If you're trying to be patient, acknowledge that the situation is what it is and relax. You loosen your grip on the steering wheel, and when you're in a safe place, you call whoever is waiting for you and calmly tell them you're stuck in traffic and will be late. You're calm because there are no practical alternatives to the situation you're in, and you've accepted that. You apologize for being late, if that's appropriate.

Again, no one gets hurt. You don't do anything foolish that could endanger yourself or others, and you arrive at your destination at the same time you otherwise would have if you stayed impatient—maybe sooner. Since you stopped feeding your frustration, your mind and body are better coordinated; you drive better, more safely, make better choices about lane changes, and are in a better frame of mind when you arrive at work.

EXAMPLE: GENEROSITY AND OPENNESS

This is a more challenging situation

You've decided you're more judgmental than you mean to be, too in a hurry, too caught up with getting everything exactly your way. You want to be more open and generous to people. You've chosen kindness and generosity as your Value Objective. On the way home you pass a homeless person asking for money. She's disheveled, not the kind of person you want to see in that place. You catch yourself making up a story about her: you think she's an addict, homeless, maybe mentally ill. You feel put upon, offended even; you wish she weren't standing there, asking you for money. You feel challenged by her and that makes you angry. You certainly don't want to give her anything.

But then your Sentinel wakes you to what you're feeling. It was exactly these feelings you decided were unwanted—these feelings that made you want to choose openness and generosity as your Value Objectives.

- You pause. You do whatever you've planned in advance to allow time for your emotions to unwind.

- You remember your pledge to yourself to be generous and open. You try to look at this woman with genuine, open curiosity. You try to see her not as an imposition on you, but as whoever she is. You see that she is suffering and needs the help she's asking for. Still, you recognize that she probably is everything you assumed: addicted, homeless, possibly mentally ill, but those facts rather than your value-laden judgments will influence what you do. So what do you do?

- You could give her money. You could ask her what she wants, buy it, and bring it to her. You could just talk with her. You could simply look her in the eye, acknowledge her, and smile. Of course, you could turn away and hurry on by as you usually do.

You make the best choice you can make according to your values, judgment about what will help, and what is the most you can bring yourself to do in the circumstances, this time.

Every encounter calling on us to be generous is different. You might think that giving her money would enable her addiction or cause other unwanted consequences. Should you do the maximum: take her order, buy it for her, and bring it back to her? Short of that kind of effort, anything that acknowledges her would be better for her than ignoring her by turning away and hurrying on by. You do what you can do and what you're willing and motivated to do, from a Knowing Mind.

The Extended Plan

The spot plans just described show how you might plan to act when discovering you were experiencing an unwanted attitude, whether your commitment was to only respond to them when you encountered them, or you wanted to do the extended practice so as to focus on developing a specific value.

The extended plan begins with choosing a specific Value Objective that you want to enhance and manifest so much so that you're willing to work on it every day for an extended period, usually a month. The idea is that rather than waiting for unwanted attitudes to arise, you make a concerted effort to practice the Value Objective every day for the term of your commitment. In a sense, one is on the lookout for unwanted tendencies, rather than waiting for them to happen and hoping you'll notice them.

This is a practice many people use when they want to more fully develop values often thought of as spiritual: values such as patience, loving kindness, compassion, generosity, humility, and piety—values that one might find at the core of their most deeply held aspirations.

On a more mundane level, I've found the extended practice of patience is excellent for helping clients develop emotional intelligence. Occasionally I'll have a client who is considered by his or her colleagues to be insensitive to their needs and the norms of the workplace. Their work may be excellent, but their behavior endangers their acceptance and career advancement. In these situations, I'll suggest they practice patience for a month. Mind you, impatience is not an unwanted attitude that they'd normally think to work on. In these cases, it's their colleagues who object. The client is usually oblivious to the reactions they're causing.

I recommend patience in these situations because practicing patience requires one to slow down and become more aware of what others experience when we interact with them. Remember that self-awareness is the foundational requirement for emotional intelligence. Patience practice develops self-awareness. We begin to see whether impatience helps or hinders us in achieving our goals; whether manifesting impatience helps us get things done faster or better—in other words, whether it's useful. Finally, we begin to question whether the things that incite our impatience deserve the significance we attach to them. I have seen clients who were in danger of damaging their careers, due to their impatience, totally change their attitudes and behavior after as little as two weeks practicing patience. It's truly amazing how effective this practice and its rewards can be.

Here is a procedure that provides the structure needed to carry out the extended plan:

The practice lasts a pre-chosen number of days. As mentioned above, thirty days is about right; fourteen days can work, but sometimes is marginal.

First, choose the Value Objective you want to practice. You can choose something you like, or, if you're experiencing unwanted attitudes that conflict with a cherished value, choose the undermined value.

The fact that you're motivated to do this practice is probably all your Sentinel needs to spur you to awareness when the unwanted value appears, but it wouldn't hurt to talk with him or her from time to time to review those contrary experiences.

The Value Objective example I'm using for this explanation is patience. Impatience is the unwanted value. If that is what you were working on, you'd want your Sentinel to bring you to awareness when you're peeved at the slow pace of traffic, the person standing in your way when you're in a hurry, your impatience with those customer service folks, your partner taking too long in the bathroom, the difficulty you're having threading a needle, or doing anything where patience is the appropriate attitude.

Of course, you can choose to practice any Value Objective. If you want to be open, train your Sentinel on feelings you've had of being closed, resistant to new ideas, people, places, and activities. Want to be more compassionate? Train your Sentinel to alert you when you experience the attitudes and thoughts that make you feel you're not compassionate—when you're stereotyping people or indifferent to the needs of others, for example. For kindness, train your Sentinel to alert you to your unkindness; for diligence, to laziness; for generosity, to stinginess. Gratitude instead of feelings of poverty is a particular favorite, and one that's been shown to promote happiness.[212]

To start, choose only one Value Objective to work on. Otherwise, your lack of experience may lead to confusion. You're likely to be confused, or forget what's important when you're awakened to the need to manifest some Value Objective. Which one, you'll wonder.

Having chosen your Value Objective, follow these steps:

- Every morning during the practice period, renew your intention by reminding yourself that today you are going to practice patience (or whatever value you've chosen). Put sticky notes where you'll see them—a really big one over the sink where you brush your teeth.

- Your Sentinel will let you know when the attitudes that conflict with your Value Objective are trying to take over. Your challenge is to simply notice what's going on and do your best to practice your Value Objective rather than getting caught up in your disappointment at not being world-class at manifesting the value you've chosen to work on.

- Try to adopt and manifest your Value Objective, to *be* it instead of the unwanted attitude that triggered it. If you know that you're about to be in a situation that will tax your ability to manifest your Value Objective, prepare for it. Get yourself in the right mood before entering the situation.

- If you can't seem to drop the unwanted attitude, try to fake it. But never fool yourself into thinking you are patient, if that's not what came up for you. Try to simply notice and acknowledge what happens: you wanted to practice patience, impatience came up instead, and you were more or less successful at switching yourself to patience.

- If, after finding yourself being impatient, you find you're judgmental about your performance, try to drop that feeling,

242

but do notice the expectations and attitudes you have about yourself. All of these observations are just that, you judging you, and nothing more. Do not use them to characterize you.

- Every evening, take a few moments, as much as five minutes, to review the day. Recall the times during that day (and only that day) when you naturally manifested your Value Objective. Recall those times when you were challenged and the undermining values came out. Recall the challenges and benefits of noticing where you were impatient, what you did in response, and what attitudes you had toward yourself, not only when you succeeded but when you failed. Were there times when the undermining attitudes crept in and you didn't notice until much later? Were there times when you realized you were caught up in undermining attitudes and couldn't bring yourself to practice your Value Objective? Were there times when you criticized yourself for not being better at this practice? Listen to the tone of voice you use when you talk to yourself after you've been tempted by unwanted attitudes.

- See and recall. Accept and reject, but judge nothing. Be as honest and fair with yourself as you can be. Notice any difficulty you have accepting the truth of whatever happened. Notice those times when you judged yourself, when you tried to make excuses, to give yourself points or demerits for whatever you experienced. Notice those times when you were frustrated with yourself and turned your anger inward. Every attempt at honest self-appraisal of oneself requires bravery, no matter whether you succeed or not. Congratulate yourself on the bravery of your effort, and remind yourself to continue the practice the next day.

That is the extended practice. After completing the number of days you committed to, continue on if you wish, or simply remind yourself of your Value Objective from time to time so that you'll keep your Sentinel's connection to your intention fresh. If you've stopped using this as a daily practice—that is, giving yourself the daily reminders of your intentions—you will still use the same approach every time you recognize that the unwanted attitude or thoughts have entered your Mind.

Challenges

No matter what value you're trying to enhance, unwanted attitudes, like all other habits you want to manage, are powered by emotions, so it's not surprising that they present similar challenges as other unwanted habits.

Difficulty Dropping Unwanted Attitudes and Manifesting the Value Objective

When we become aware of the unwanted attitude and try to manifest the Value Objective, we come right up against the difficulty of banishing the unwanted attitude. It isn't easy to rouse patience when that child over there is screaming. You're fighting the fact that it feels good to be angry at the child and judgmental of the mother who can't control her child. Or does it feel good? Feelings that the unwanted attitude is justified lose their charm as soon as you recall your Value Objective. That's why it is so very important that you emphasize the need to manifest the Value Objective as soon as you recognize that the undermining values have appeared.

Still, like other emotions, we find it hard to simply switch the unwanted ones off and become the emotions and values we want to manifest. There will often be a residual hanging on to the unwanted attitude—the stronger the attitude, the longer it takes to dissipate. Consequently, as in the case of the strong emotions discussed in the hot habits chapter (Chapter 22), it's important to choose delaying tactics ahead of time so they are close by and ready to be engaged. You have to be prepared to use your delaying tools: take a breath, count to ten, let the energy of your frustration or impatience dissipate, then, as soon as you are in control, reframe the situation. If the child is having fun, appreciate that. If she's miserable about something, try to extend kindness and openness toward her. You don't have to approach mother or child. You only need to rouse in yourself feelings appropriate to your Value Objective. Try to see the mother as she is—helpless to stop the noise and still able to get her shopping done. She's under pressure at that moment. Above all she's embarrassed and feels helpless because she knows that everyone in the store hates her, and there's nothing she can do about it. Give a smile if you can.

Reframing is one of the most important tools you can learn if you're going to pursue this path of turning unwanted attitudes and thoughts into the values you want to manifest. If reframing doesn't come naturally to you, try asking yourself how someone like you, someone who wants to manifest your Value

Objective, would feel about the situation. Be creative. Find the good and positive in the situation that's triggered your unwanted attitude.

Another important strategy is to try and get perspective about the situation and what is bothering you. Question whether whatever triggered your unwanted attitude is worth the energy you're giving it. Does it matter that you can't move as quickly as you want behind the slow-moving crowd? Is there a way around? Are you enjoying your frustration so much that you want to hang on to it, or might you be willing to let go of the anger when you can't change the situation? Are the consequences of the situation worth the emotions you're contributing to it?

If you're doing the extended practice, when you review the day's performance, consider the alternatives—giving the trigger and its imagined consequences less importance, looking for alternative actions that could have reduced your frustration or whatever unwanted attitude you felt. Evaluate whether alternative approaches would have worked, whether the frustrated goal was that important, whether, in fact, the trigger was important enough to be worth your attention, anger, or effort. Could you have been more helpful to the situation?

Having said all this, I need to be clear that I'm not suggesting that you should overlook or tolerate the truly bad that you encounter, the lack of consideration, and the abuse of others that could lead to you having seriously negative attitudes, thoughts, and judgments about what's going on around you. By all means, deal with those situations as best you can.

Attributing Too Much to Individual Success

Another challenge is the tendency to decide that if you were able to manifest your Value Objective, you are that kind of person. Suppose you went to extremes to help the homeless woman who asked you for help. You really went out of your way, and you witnessed the benefit you produced. Even when you feel you can claim generosity as a value because you are exemplifying it, do not translate your successes to mean that you are generous. Take credit for having been generous that time, and for the fact that you're striving to be a generous person. Go a step further. Solidify your intention to be generous by acknowledging your desire to act similarly in the future. But know that you're working on this value, and that continuing the effort is your reward.

When working with unwanted attitudes in order to enhance your values, it is easy to confuse the practice and the results. In other words, it is tempting to think that by practicing patience and generosity (or whatever other quality you're practicing), you are that value. As Ken McLeod teaches in his book *Wake Up to Your Life,* "Everything that arises in the practice that [is contrary] to your intention is the operation of a habitual pattern[.]"[213] If you're to learn and ultimately embody a value, you must first see how you are often its opposite. You have to see the contradiction in order to work at eliminating it. Consequently, you must not suppress or deny those experiences, because you stop learning if you do. You want to know how you are, because those insights are the source of your motivation and define the targets of your training. Pretending to have achieved the results of the practice would deny you those benefits. Accept that there will always be challenges to your values, that in order to manifest your value goals you will have to remain on guard and keep working at it. It's a life's work. Is that so bad? Must there be a merit badge at some point? Or does the continuing effort validate your values and your integrity in pursuing them? You decide.

Judging Yourself Unfairly

Here it comes again—the reminder that you will fail to fulfill your intentions from time to time. Sorry about that.

The example involving the homeless person exposes a particularly important challenge that many of us face when trying to manifest our values, namely, did I do enough? Was I generous enough? Did I put myself out enough? Was I patient enough, kind enough? What if the maximum that you could bring yourself to do was not as much as you thought you should do. Suppose you decided that giving money to the homeless person would simply enable the habits that keep her in her situation. You think you should ask her what she wants and go buy it for her, but you just can't extend yourself that much. Is that because you're lazy or judgmental, or because you really do have to be somewhere very soon, or have set the standards for your performance too high? Only you know the answer.

When you decide the best you can do is turn to her and smile, maybe you feel guilty. You feel that you've let both of you down because you didn't do what you think your best should be. In addition to being disappointed in your performance, whether you've done enough or not, some causes and conditions will create situations in which your intentions aren't strong enough to overcome Reactive Brain. You won't be able to drop the unwanted attitudes and manifest your Value Objective, and you'll manifest unwanted ones. What to do about that?

As always, first make sure that you're judging yourself by valid standards. Should you go to the store, order a sandwich and coffee for the woman on the street, wait for it, take it back to her, and only then go on your way? Maybe that was reasonable in the circumstances, maybe not. Judge yourself fairly—that is, by standards that are no higher than you'd judge another person by. Be as accurate as possible when remembering the situation—how it felt, and what constraints were operating on you at the time. Factor those into your judgment. Instead of thinking about what you should have done, imagine you are judging a person who responded to the situation the way you did. If you think you would have expected that person to do more than you did, choose regret (not guilt), and commit to try harder next time.

Even more important, do your best to look at what happened through the lens of just noticing. That means seeing and remembering the situation as a series of unadorned facts before allowing yourself to judge what happened. See the facts as if they made up a sequence of steps in a dance. Your partner did something. You responded. He or she responded, then you did, and so on.

You can judge each fact separately. See which facts, which steps in the dance, were done well or poorly by your standards. This approach will give you some insight as to what "facts" were helpful or hurtful and what you could have done differently. Try to keep from making sweeping judgments about the individuals involved. Instead try to see what helped or hurt, and learn from those.

Try especially hard to refrain from making sweeping judgments about yourself or your performance. We start a program like this wanting to be good, to prove to ourselves that we're able to be in control of ourselves. No matter what you've read in the pages of this book, your reflex will be to think you should be in control, always disciplined, and disappointed with yourself when your performance is otherwise. Judge yourself fairly. The birthright of every one of us is a place on this earth, deserving of dignity and respect. In that connection, I would like to remind you of the words that began Chapter 1 of this book:

> *Each of you is perfect the way you are ... and you can*
> *use a little improvement.*
>
> —*Suzuki Roshi*[214]

ACT FROM CHOICE

And now, let me invite you to turn the page and join me in some final words of advice about being how you mean to be.

BE HOW YOU MEAN TO BE

I invite you once again to believe that you are who and how you mean to be when you're giving it your best. And that your best is plenty good enough.

Be how you mean to be.

Commitment and effort validate our claims to the values we hold dear. If your behavior doesn't always meet your standards, get curious about what it is that you do. Identify those things you do that fall short of your standards—the realistic ones that are attainable, not the heroic ones that almost no one can do. Choose to work on things that truly dismay you when your behavior fails to measure up. Be forthright in acknowledging that you do what you do. Know what you mean to do instead. Look for the sources of your motivation. Know them so that you can remember them when impulse and emotion want you to do or think something unwanted.

Keep these ideas in mind: every time you find yourself of two minds, torn between your intentions and reactive impulses, remember that you are the prize in a battle between Reactive Brain and Intentional Mind. Both are parts of you. One part, Reactive Brain, operates on automatic. It has only a short-term focus. The other part, Intentional Mind, is trying to honor your values, judgments, and priorities.

Both parts are trying to get you to execute their idea of what is best for you. But your Intentional Mind is aware of the longer-term consequences of your actions and is trying to enforce your choices, while Reactive Brain's singular concern is the next few moments. Disagreements between Reactive Brain and Intentional Mind are battles between old, automatically programmed, mindless habits and wisdom borne of experience. They are battles between automaticity and well considered intention, between immediate gratification and your longer-term priorities. The wisdom you've gained from experience has led you to choose how you mean to be.

Reactive Brain is trying to protect you, to get you the goodies it thinks you want, or to relieve immediately any discomfort you're feeling, regardless of the consequences. Its programs came from observing and remembering what you did when presented with threat and opportunity. When the immediate results were release from discomfort or instant gratification, it turned what you did into a habit. That the results were regrettable in some way, that the stimulus was misinterpreted, that what you did helped the discomfort but left you with the problem, or worse, was of no account to Reactive Brain. If it produced immediate pleasure or relieved discomfort, it became a lifelong habit that you're now trying to manage because of its regrettable consequences.

Reactive Brain is usually right in what it wants you to do. It alerts us to danger and opportunities continuously throughout every day. We'd be dead without it. But it's occasionally error prone, shortsighted, distracted, and plagued with unintended biases we're seldom conscious of. Worse, it operates on its own, out of reach and out of sight. It's these errors that cause unwanted habits.

In spite of everything I write about Reactive Brain's faults, I urge you to remember that it deserves your esteem and should never be disparaged. It's part of you, and it' s your true friend. And like every other part of you it deserves your gratitude and respect. So think kindly of it. Do not denigrate it. But when the material or psychological stakes are important, verify what it tells you. Question the impulses, gut feelings, and emotions it feeds you.

In some ways, the battle between Reactive Brain and Intentional Mind is unevenly matched. Intentional Mind has only wisdom and willpower on its side. Reactive Brain has the immense power of emotion at its disposal and doesn't stop its insisting. Intentional Mind has to overcome it.

While Reactive Brain is right most of the time and Intentional Mind agrees with it, at the root of those battles between them are disagreements about that programming that was created automatically, mostly when you were too young to be wise. You've learned a lot since then, have different opinions and values, are more nuanced in your thinking, and want different outcomes than Reactive Brain's emotional action programs will produce.

Willpower is the instrument you use to resist Reactive Brain, but it is a limited resource, as you've read here. Motivation helps you to engage the willpower resources you have, and priorities are a major source of motivation. On that subject, Antonio Damasio writes, "Willpower is just another name for the idea of choosing according to long-term outcomes rather than short-term ones."[215] In other words, willpower tries to enforce your priorities—giving greater priority to your wellbeing over unhealthy habits, to dealing with the causes of disturbing situations rather than lashing out at others just to feel better for a few moments, and to standing up for what is important to you rather than compromising your beliefs in order to fit in.

If you decide to commit to be how you mean to be, make the commitment to pause and choose every time you experience the unwanted impulses you've identified. Hire and train a Sentinel to help you train your subconscious. When you feel unwanted impulses or attitudes, don't allow yourself to think that it doesn't matter that time, that it's alright to give up or cave to the impulse right away. Work through the plan you devised by executing every step, step by step. Have ready a powerful Second Question to help you move from habit mind to Knowing Mind. And don't give in to the impulse until you've made your decision in Knowing Mind, able to feel the motivation that led to your commitment to manage the habit.

Remember, too, that the habits that produce those unwanted impulses and emotions were acquired by happenstance and innocently. Consequently, the mere existence of unwanted impulses is no cause for guilt, shame, or denial. Avoid the trap of thinking that experiencing unwanted impulses is a mark against character. Such beliefs can lead to guilt, shame, and feeling powerless, to denigrating ourselves—even to denying that we do what we do. Any of these feelings can make us reluctant to face the reality of what we do and make it nearly impossible to work on managing our unwanted habits.

Ultimately what we do is what matters, not the impulses we feel. We are innocent of our impulses, but not of our behavior. We are fully responsible to try our best to keep unwanted impulses from turning into behavior that conflicts with our values—especially those behaviors which harm others. No matter how hard we try, we will always be tested by habits that can lead to unwanted behavior. Therefore, we're obligated to learn how to interrupt them at the impulse stage and choose behavior consistent with our values and intentions.

In the Act from Choice Method we manage habitual unwanted impulses by being clear about our intentions, values, and motivations; by training our subconscious to warn us when we're in danger of acting contrary to our values and intentions; and by designing and executing an action plan that describes the specific steps we are committed to execute when we first feel the unwanted impulse.

Even so, as I've said repeatedly, if we follow these guidelines faithfully, there will be times when the impulses are stronger than our willpower and training, and Intentional Mind loses the battle. These failures are an opportunity to practice self-compassion and renew intention. They should never seem as acceptable excuses for self-denigration, or giving up the effort to manage ourselves.

If you're working with habits whose consequences are important, periodically review the last few occurrences of the habit as objectively as you're able. Then visualize the next occurrence and yourself reacting the way you want to behave, and feeling the way you want to be. If your habit produces fear, imagine yourself as brave—frightened, but leaning into the situation, as best you can, without hurting yourself.

Understand that there is no such thing as perfect. Learn from each experience of your unwanted habits, and use what you learn to modify your plan as appropriate. Then reaffirm your commitment to manage your unwanted habits as well as you can.

In some ways, the most important part of the Act from Choice Method is having a plan and following it, step by step, just as you designed it. Skip any step in the plan, give in before completing your plan, and you'll be less successful than you otherwise would be, and you'll question whether you gave the occasion all the effort you committed to.

So, when your Sentinel wakes you, or the time you committed to do the thing you've habitually procrastinated doing comes along, do what you planned. Remember that in the Act from Choice Method it's okay to choose habit over intention, just not before you've arrived at the point in the plan where you've decided it would be alright to give in. If you're feeling lazy or unmotivated, remember what's at stake. Remind yourself of your motivation, not just because you want to avoid a regrettable outcome, but because of your desire to be in integrity with the values you say you hold. You won't feel good if you ignore your plan.

There's a fine line here. On the one hand, it's important to accept that impulses will carry you away sometime, and to forgive yourself for that. On the other hand, know that if you ignore your plan, simply devour the chocolate chip cookie without attempting to overcome the habit, you'll feel you let yourself down. Keep in mind, too, that habits are changed by what you do. Execute the habit and you deepen the groove they run in, but every time you resist them you've made them weaker. Regardless of the outcome, effort is still important, and you are the only one able to judge fairly whether you gave enough to the effort. One of the great challenges for all of us is to learn to judge ourselves fairly, to have enough regard for ourselves to trust our judgment—to believe that the way we judge ourselves meets our standards of integrity.

No matter what happens, if you care about yourself, never let the occasional failure be an excuse for abandoning your efforts to manage your habits, your emotions, and yourself. Stay with it as long as there's even the slightest commitment to reach the objective you set for yourself. Don't count the failures. On this path, only effort and successes count.

———————————————

We've come to the end of the material that you might want to read in sequence. The Resource Companion which follows contains additional procedures, tips, tools, and perspectives that I hope you'll find useful in managing your habits. It contains specific tools for delaying your reactions when you can't simply push through to your objective; practices to help you increase your ability to become present; and techniques for managing certain difficult emotions, specifically anxiety, anger, fear, guilt, and shame. You will also find several slogans that can give you new perspectives on situations we all encounter—slogans like *Real but not true*, *Happiness is the absence of unhappiness*, and *Don't make things worse than they already are*.

You'll also find useful information at the Act from Choice website (www. ActFromChoice.com). It will grow as new techniques and articles are added to it. You'll also find forms for the motivation investigation described in Chapter 16, as well as other downloads. You're always welcome to email me with your questions. I'll answer all that I can.

ActFromChoice.com is the place to find information about telephonic group discussions of the Act from Choice Method that I'll lead. Call in and ask your questions, or just hang out and listen to what other people are asking and talking about. Check the website often, and please sign up for our mailing list. I'd be grateful, as well, if you'd drop me a note telling me what you liked and didn't like about *Act from Choice*, including corrections and ideas for improving it. RobertG@ActFromChoice.com will reach me.

In closing this part of the book, I extend my congratulations to you for deciding to work with yourself. It's a sign that you want to be more consistent with your values, to manage yourself so you can act from choice, and to be how you mean to be. Working with yourself, with your mind and your emotions, is a life's work. There is no such thing as being done. As we reach each new horizon we inevitably see new horizons ahead, horizons that offer us the opportunity to be more fully in our lives and our world.

ACT FROM CHOICE

As a final offering, you'll find a poem on the next page. It's there to remind you that the path to openness, generosity, and relationship with the world and ourselves is always there—that we can re-engage with it at any time, even after we've been away for a while.

I wish you good fortune in everything you do.

Begin Again, Again

Every day we wake again.

For a moment,
Maybe we are open—
Everything is clear.
We are wise,
Not confused,
Loving.
There is joy.
We can begin
Again.

Every day—

Perhaps
For a moment
Everything is fresh.
Gone are
Worries and prejudices
That closed
The open
Uncluttered mind.
The natural energy,
Fear,
Confusion,
Yearning,
Are what they are
And no thing more.
We can work with them
Fearlessly,
With joy—
In peace.
Again.

Every day
We can engage
In a different way
With those we love;
With those who discomfort us;
With those we ignore.

Every day
We can begin again;
With fresh mind;
With the energy
Always there, if only for a
moment—
Again.

In sacred moments
We remember
We can begin again.
We renew intention.
We promise we won't forget.
And we forget
Until the next sacred moment
When we remember—
Again,
That we can begin again.
Again.

My wish is
That you remember
What is always there
In you,
For you,
And for everyone you touch:
The loved,
The difficult,
The ignored.
And that every day,
And every moment
In every day
Can be sacred;
A time
To wake again,
And remember,
Again,
To begin again,
Again.

The Act from Choice
Resource Companion

CONTENTS

Introduction 259

Highlights of the Act from Choice Method...260

Tools to Use During Pause and Choose...263
    Find Your Center..263
    Cool Off...264
        Repeat Something Important to You 264
        Withdraw 264
    Get More Clarity...265
        Reframe 265
        Disidentify 266
        Investigate..266
        Accept What Is True 267
    Leverage Intentional Mind 267
        Acknowledge Pain and Console Yourself.......................................267
        "Drop the Storyline"..268
        Figure Out If You Have any Power...268
        Communicate and Negotiate 269
        Choose Principles and Sacred Values 269
        Renounce the Unwanted Action or Attitude 270
    When All Else Fails 270
        Tell Yourself Why...271
        Reexamine Your Commitment 271
        Choose Regret Instead of Guilt..272

About Certain Emotions...273
    Guilt and Shame 273
        Guilt 274
        Shame...275
    Anxiety..276
        Overwhelm: Too Much to Do 277
        Anxious That Bad Things Might Happen.......................................278
        Everything Accommodated, but Still Anxious?...............................280
    Negative Self-Talk 280
        Introducing Gremlins 281
        For Some, the Antidote for Negative Self-Talk 283

Slogans, Mantras, and Aphorisms...285

Developing Greater Awareness 291
    The Power of Awareness and Curiosity..291
    Knowing Mind..292
    Getting to Knowing Mind 294
    Tips for Increasing Awareness...294
        Tooth-brushing Practice...295
        Acceptance Training...297
        Practice Becoming Present 298
        Set Alarms to Bring You Present 299

Introduction

This Resource Companion is a collection of tools, tips, and perspectives to supplement the Act from Choice Method described in the main text of the book. It is not a replacement or digest of the book.

There are four main sections to the Companion.

Highlights of the Act from Choice Method shows the key elements of the Method, in a very few pages. It is meant to serve as a refresher for those who have read Part II of the book.

Tools to Use During Pause and Choose describes 16 things you can do to be more effective when choosing what to do, and, if necessary, after failing to withstand Reactive Brain. The tools are divided into five categories: Find Your Center, Cool Off, Get More Clarity, Leverage Intentional Mind, and When All Else Fails.

About Certain Emotions presents perspectives and approaches to working with guilt, shame, anxiety, and negative self-talk.

Slogans, Mantras, and Aphorisms discusses the use of these tools for remembering principles important to you. It lists several of the slogans described in the main text and ten new ones. You can find more slogans at ActFromChoice.com.

Developing Greater Awareness introduces new material on the power of awareness and curiosity and Knowing Mind. In addition, it presents five informal (non-meditative) practices for increasing your ability to become present and self-aware in the course of daily activities.

You'll find that some of these tools and perspectives can help you work with your unwanted habits. By no means is this meant to be a complete and exhaustive set of such tools, but these can significantly expand your capabilities to manage your habits and yourself. In time, you'll find still more at ActFromChoice.com. As always, investigate and try those approaches that interest you. Ignore those that don't.

Highlights of the Act from Choice Method

TOM-Decide-CAP

FOUNDATION

- Unwanted behavior, attitudes, and thoughts are stimulated by habitual patterns acquired as a result of genetics and experience, not conscious choice, and do not reflect on our character. They are the results of normal processing of the human brain which, while otherwise truly marvelous, is also error prone, shortsighted, distractible, lazy, and plagued with biases we're seldom conscious of.

- Habitual patterns are unwanted when we realize they produce undesirable consequences for oneself and/or others, and/or because the behaviors, attitudes, and thoughts they produce are antithetical to one's values and feelings of integrity.

- Failure to recognize that habitual impulses were acquired innocently can lead to feelings of guilt, shame, self-denigration, and powerlessness, and may result in reluctance to work on managing them, and even to denial.

- We can manage how we react to habitual unwanted impulses by 1) knowing what we do, 2) being clear about our intentions, values, and motivations, 3) training our subconscious to warn us when we're in danger of acting contrary to our intentions, and 4) making, committing to, and then following a formal step-by-step plan when first becoming aware of unwanted impulses.

- Even so, we will occasionally fail to follow through with our intentions because the stimulus is stronger than our willpower and training, or because willpower is temporarily depleted.

- Understanding the causes of such failures, they can become occasions for self-compassion, and renewal of intention.

THE METHOD

Preliminary Phase

TRUTH

What happens? What is the experience?
What is observed?
    Triggers, stimuli, reactions?
    Who, what, where, when?
Your reaction
    Feelings
    Action and/or attitudes felt, possibly expressed*
        Who, what directed at?
        Consistent with values?
Misdirected, misguided, useless?
        Is the feeling real but not true?
        Is the reaction aimed at solving the "problem" or feeling
        better?
        Is the reaction useful?
Are the feelings primary or secondary?
        If secondary, what should be managed?
  * Attitudes expressed (displayed): e.g. patience vs. impatience; felt: e.g.
understanding vs. judgment

T

OBJECTIVE

Choose preliminary objective: Outcomes desired during and
    resulting from managing the situation, as applicable **
        Generality of objective***
        Effects on relationships
        Importance of results or solution
        Actions and/or attitudes
        Attitudes toward others, situation, and self
    ** During: e.g. Be a loving father; resulting: e.g. Don't crash the
    plane or spend the money
    *** Aimed at improving a quality of being or more specific –
        dealing with the stimulus or unique situation

O

MOTIVATION

Consequences of the unwanted reactions to yourself and others
Costs and benefits of change and no change
Contribution of change and no change to your values
Revisit objectives—and reevaluate if necessary

M

DECIDE

Is your objective how you mean to be, or do you merely want it?
Are you committed to it, or is it an aspiration?

Committed Phase

COMMITMENT

Commit to pause when experiencing the unwanted impulse,   **C**
then to follow your plan step-by-step to formally choose what
to do.

AWARENESS

Hire and train your Sentinel   **A**
Prepare a Second Question
Investigate and train other awareness practices

PLAN

Decide whether this is a hot or cold habit
Be clear about desired result
Choose the tools you'll use to pause and choose   **P**
Choose when to ask the Second (final) Question
Select additional tools as appropriate*
> Examples: finding your center, cooling off, accepting what is
> true, reframing

ACT FROM CHOICE

Follow Your Plan

Tools to Use During Pause and Choose

Your Sentinel made you aware that you were about to do something that conflicted with how you mean to be. You feel the pull of the habit. Simultaneously you feel the intention-induced restraint, but you are not sufficiently in command to override the impulse. You're of two Minds. Maybe you're fully within the refractive period.

Good jazz musicians are ferociously competent technically and have accumulated the experience, tools, and skills that help them make wonderful music. If you're going to improvise with whatever life gives you, it would be best if you could master your instrument to manage your emotions and yourself so that you can be how you mean to be. Choose your tools. Practice with them and have them ready so you can play the tune your way when unwanted impulses make you want to play your part.

The tools in this section will help you stall your action, see what's going on in a different light, or get some leverage to assist Intentional Mind. With these tools you can create the space needed to experience and enhance your motivation as you're trying to choose what to do.

You'll see some repetitions from the book in this section. They're meant as reminders. Chances are you'll revisit this Resource Companion long after you've read the book, by which time you may have forgotten some of what you read.

Here are the tools.

Find Your Center

If your Mind is hot, or speedy, buzzing around like a crazed bumble bee, quiet it and find your center by bringing your attention to your body. You become present when Mind and body are together. Getting in your body is not a big-deal spiritual practice, but its effects are profound. No matter how you do it, when you direct your attention to your body, your Mind comes along, and you are more present; Mind can't go off on wild excursions while you're fixing your attention on your body.

There are many ways to do this. Some people get in their body by paying attention to their breath. For example: Take deep, slow breaths; maybe do some belly breathing. Pay attention to your body as it breathes. If you're feeling speedy, count your breaths. Three breaths work for some; sometimes ten are needed.

If breathing doesn't work for you, pay attention to a particular body part that you have no ordinary interest in. I like to use a knee or elbow because they're easy to identify and focus on.

If you're sitting you can feel the chair against your bottom. If you need to distract yourself from what's going on, get seriously curious about what's under the skin, but only if you want the distraction. You might want to keep some awareness on what's happening, including the emotions you're feeling while trying to pay attention to your body. But, to be clear, while you're torn between intention and reaction, hold tight to your body. Don't let go until your Mind and emotions settle down.

Cool Off

Cooling off means delaying action and/or distracting yourself while letting the emotional profile come down off its peak so that your Mind begins to open and rationality can return. The breathing exercises just mentioned can do that for you. Here are some others:

REPEAT SOMETHING IMPORTANT TO YOU

If you know a prayer, a mantra, a poem, or favorite slogan that has meaning for you, say it, and keep repeating it until you cool off. The Serenity Prayer works for some. (Reminder: "God grant me the serenity to accept the things I cannot change; courage to change the things I can; and wisdom to know the difference.") Some of my clients find *real but not true* to be very calming when they're feeling fearful or anxious about something that has no substance. The Serenity Prayer has a similar effect because it reminds one to be discerning about whether they can change whatever is triggering them. The upset seems to diminish when people recognize they're dealing with things they can't change.

When picking a prayer or poem to repeat, choose something uplifting, something that doesn't diminish you or require you to do anything.

WITHDRAW

If you're out of control, or if you or others you're engaging are in danger of losing it, get away. If the stimulus is in the room, leave. If this happens often, prepare what you'll say in advance. Acknowledge you're upset if you feel like it; then say you're leaving, and, if you're able, say that you'll be back, will talk about it later, or something similar.

Leave a little of yourself behind so the people you're dealing with know you're not running away from the issue or breaking off the relationship. (If you want to break off the relationship, come back and do it later when you're calm. You and they will respect you more if you handle it that way, rather than in anger.) If you're on the phone and want to hang up, do so. If possible, say something similar to what you'd say if the person you're talking with was physically present. If you can't do that without losing it, hang up while you're talking, not when they are. And don't answer the phone when they call back. That will give you time to collect yourself.

Get More Clarity

Habits may cloud thinking and judgment even beyond the lack of clarity we experience in the refractive period of an emotion. Here are some tools for getting clearer about what's going on, including ways to find interpretations more in line with your values.

REFRAME

Is there something you can gain from the trials you face? Thank everyone who makes you wake up to yourself, to your advantages, successes, and challenges. Reframing includes looking for the good, the bright side in what is causing you difficulties, and considering how you might make things better in difficult situations. Sometimes the only way you can make something better is to accept it for what it is and work with it. I'm not suggesting you overlook the harmful and try to make something nice and fuzzy out of something truly hateful. But is there something good, or an opportunity in what is bothering you?

Is there another way to see what's going on? Is the thing that triggered you good for someone else, like the delighted child in the supermarket who's shrieking with joy? See if you can appreciate someone else's pleasure rather than basking in annoyance and jealousy.

Is what's disturbing you someone else's suffering? Is the person you're angry with someone you could extend help and compassion to instead? Is there something in this situation you can learn from? Is this an opportunity to stretch yourself and manifest your values more powerfully? Remember the patience example from Chapter 23: every time you regret your impatience, for example, remember that it's your values that are calling your attention to your impatience. It's an opportunity to practice how you mean to be.

Notice how you solidify the importance of some situations, objects of desire, and prizes you want. Try to see through the filters placed there by desire, preconceptions, bias, prejudice, and wishing that things were different than they are.

DISIDENTIFY

Disidentifying means disowning the impulse (or self-talk) that you're feeling. Regard it as an artifact of Brain that has no legitimacy, and push back against it with Intentional Mind. To dis-identify means to recognize that what you're experiencing is simply an automatic emanation from Brain that doesn't represent your choice, your considered judgment, or some wisdom—divine, cultural, or otherwise. Like so many things Brain puts out, it's not an expression of your values or belief; it's not you.

A sense of humor helps. Noticing the feelings, you might say, "Oh, that again!" and brush them aside. You might ascribe them to some personality that has taken up residence in your Brain without your permission and gets its kicks by messing with you. For an advanced degree, take it a step further and extend compassion to that part of your Brain that can find joy in no other way. (See more about this in the discussion of negative self-talk, below.) In spite of what I've just written about a sense of humor, never diminish your feelings or make fun of yourself when you feel wounded.

INVESTIGATE

If the situation is manageable and you are able to be curious about it, take a moment to dive deeper into what's happening. Assess reality by asking yourself questions like these:

> Is the stimulus—the problem—real? True? Important?
>
> Do you really need to care about this? Does any of it matter?
>
> Is the person you're blaming responsible? Did they do what you think they did?
>
> What are the causes and consequences of what happened, or what you fear will happen?
>
> Could it be something good instead of bad?
>
> Are you telling yourself a story?

ACCEPT WHAT IS TRUE

Accept what is that can't be changed, and its likely consequences. Just dropped an egg on the floor? Don't want to pick it up? The situation will only get worse. The mess will harden and be difficult to clean. Accept that the egg is sitting there, and no one will pick it up for you. If you clean it up complaining all the while about the effort and inconvenience, and that you're clumsy, you will be guilty of making things worse than they already are. And cleaning up the mess will anger you more because emotions love emotion.

Use ideas like those to motivate yourself to deal with the situation as it is—to do it willingly and gracefully, because any deviation from that standard will just make things worse—for you. This is a practical rather than a moralistic observation. So just do it.

Nothing makes things easier than accepting what you must do with grace, and doing it without complaint. It's one of humanity's oldest and best labor-saving technologies.

Leverage Intentional Mind

Maybe you've decided you don't want to yell at the kids or eat too many chocolate chip cookies. You've set up your plan to restrain yourself when you're angry at the children, or want to eat the chocolate chip cookie. Then you find that such direct action isn't enough. You need leverage, something more than simple intention and resistance. *Something else* is like a lever you'd use to help you lift a weight rather than trying to lift it unaided. Here are some tools that can provide that leverage.

ACKNOWLEDGE PAIN AND CONSOLE YOURSELF

Suppose you believe that your anger at some loss was a secondary emotion to your feeling of loss. Suppose you come to believe that your chocolate chip cookie habit is an attempt to relieve pressures at work. Your lever in both cases is to acknowledge how you feel. Console yourself if that's what you need to do to relieve the discomfort. Then address the cause of the discomfort directly if you can. Even if you can't do anything to make the cause of the primary emotion better, the fact that you're dealing with the primary emotion—taking care of your emotional needs by extending compassion to yourself—will reduce the need to express anger when sad or disappointed or to binge when under pressure.

"DROP THE STORYLINE"[216]

In this context, stories are often about putting the blame elsewhere to justify what the storyteller did, or to call for attention and sympathy. We tell stories because they distract us from thinking about what we did or how bad we feel. We use blame as both defense and weapon.

If you find you tend to tell stories to relieve your discomfort and want to stop it, train your Sentinel to pull on your sleeve when you're doing it. Like the preceding examples, attend to the feelings—the primary emotions. Don't run away from them. Acknowledge what you're feeling, and tend to your needs accordingly.

FIGURE OUT IF YOU HAVE ANY POWER

This statement is aimed at reminding you of the Serenity Prayer and useless habits. If you don't have the power to change what is upsetting you, deal with the upset directly. Remember that useless anger is equivalent to taking poison hoping that someone else will die.

If you don't have the power to change what is causing you to be upset, deal with what you're afraid will happen—that you'll be late for work, that s/he won't love you, that you'll lose your job. These are not trivial upsets. And we have to work with what is. If you think the situation can be changed, try to change it. If it can't be changed, work with that. Nothing else makes sense.

If you recall your past, you'll remember that some things you were afraid would happen actually did happen. If you feared something might happen, you may have lived in fear until it did. Maybe you told yourself that you couldn't stand it if it happened. But when it happened, you stood it and dealt with it.

The fact is we deal with everything we experience, no matter how bad it is. We do in fact change what we can and work with what we can't—even though we sometimes struggle against what proves to be inevitable. It's up to us to decide how we will deal with the things we can't change and don't like. Will we kick and scream and let our emotions keep us working at the situation as if it were the way we wanted it to be when it can't be that? Or will we work with the situation as it is, using whatever bravery we can muster to be effective in the face of our disappointment and fear. The good life requires us to be brave, by which I mean trying our best even while afraid.

COMMUNICATE AND NEGOTIATE

Formal skills can be very useful in fraught situations: I recommended reading *Crucial Conversations*[217] and *Non-Violent Communication*.[218] Both books are million-copy sellers and are clear, accessible, and very useful.

With or without those tools, adopt the attitudes recommended by the cross-cultural anthropologist Angeles Arrien: Show up. Listen. Tell the truth. And don't be attached to the outcome.

That last item, don't be attached to the outcome, is a real shocker, isn't it? The way I understand it is to give up any idea that you have the right answer going into the confrontation. Leave space that allows you and those you're engaging with to co-create a different solution or outcome. Let that attitude of openness suffuse your interactions. My experience is that the outcomes you'll arrive at when you approach opportunities and problems this way are always better, richer, and more creative. They may not be anyone's favorite solution, but they will almost always be outcomes that all participants can endorse and execute willingly and with good conscience.

CHOOSE PRINCIPLES AND SACRED VALUES

I imagine that most of us, maybe you too, have seen something that we're not entitled to, felt a twinge of desire, and formed a foolproof plan for taking it for yourself. It was a Brain-born impulse. You instantly rejected the idea but might have felt ashamed that the thought even occurred to you. It was a selfish impulse, beneath you, contrary to your principles or sacred values, maybe even illegal. But, yes, it did happen. It was one of those impulses you really can't be responsible for, and you did the right thing instead.

You exercised principle. That is a perfect example of Pause and Choose. It's common for even the best of us to be tempted by Brain to act against our values; to lie, cheat, or steal to get something; to undermine a competitor, take the unguarded valuable, engage in clearly inappropriate sex, take advantage of others through deception or force. We feel the temptation that comes from Brain but choose principled action instead, and Intentional Mind wins again.

Principles and sacred values are powerful motivators. They help us leverage simple intention. The Second Question will usually bring those to Mind if you've done the motivation exercises in Chapter 16 and trained your Sentinel accordingly. But if they haven't come to Mind and you have even the slightest notion that your impulses are violating principles or sacred values, do your best to extend your pause so you can bring them to the foreground, where you're conscious of them and they can add power to your intention.

RENOUNCE THE UNWANTED ACTION OR ATTITUDE

Decide not to do that something anymore, no matter what. Make it a bright line rule. By bright line I mean that the alternatives are black and white: permitted and not permitted, this and that, with no place for gray or maybe.

For many Westerners renunciation conjures up the vision of making a great effort to push away something they want. It connotes enduring hardship to renounce something we want. We do it because our principles, culture, or something outside of us has told us we should. We may imagine that punishment will fall on those who don't succeed.

True renunciation occurs when we no longer want that thing, or we want it but see it as having no value, and that insight kills our desire for it. True renunciation does not require value language, like good or evil. We realize that we're not willing to indulge it anymore. Renunciation is the highest result one could achieve from doing the motivation exercises in Chapter 16.

Those exercises will not get you all the way there. It takes time; you have to revisit the reasoning supporting your judgment. Be patient. Desire for things that are bad for you are habits too. Let the lessons you've given yourself merge with your subconscious and bring you to a state of true renunciation. It is better to come slowly and patiently to understand that some things lack value than to cultivate hate toward them. Recall that Carl Jung said, "What you resist persists." Conviction and indifference are always better than having to rely on force.

When All Else Fails

Inevitably there will be times when you're unable to follow through with your intentions. It's better to face the fact of that with open eyes. I've written much of what you'll read in this section before, but it is very important and bears repeating.

If you asked the Second Question, you brought out all you can muster to counter the habit. If the answer was Yes, I'm willing to accept the consequences of eating the cookie, you were permitted to eat it, and do so joyfully, free of shame or guilt, and to be proud of yourself for going through your process.

Of course, sometimes you won't get to that Second Question moment. You'll eat the cookie right away. But there's always a next time, a time to begin again, again.

Remember that the Act from Choice Method recommends that you take two additional steps before you eat the cookie, or do that other thing you intended not to do.

TELL YOURSELF WHY

Tell yourself why you couldn't follow through with your intention. This is not about creating an excuse; these are reasons. Your attitude should be one of testifying to yourself, answering the question as factually and truthfully as you are capable of, "I'm feeling the need for comfort food, and this is it." Or, "I was so stressed out from work, I forgot to adjust my mood when I got home, and I took it out on my kids." If your reason is that resisting was too difficult, simply acknowledge that your willpower wasn't up to resisting the impulse.

Your reasons for violating your intention this time may give you useful insight for the next time. For example, the simple acknowledgment that you're eating the cookie because you're down will lead you to consider whether the cookie makes you feel better, for how long, and whether the feel-better benefit was enough to make it okay to eat the cookie. You may decide that it really helped to eat the cookie, or that it doesn't help enough to make it worthwhile to sacrifice intention.

REEXAMINE YOUR COMMITMENT

If you ate the cookie, ask yourself if you're still committed to your objective. Believe your answer. If yes, take about five seconds to renew your commitment. You could just say to yourself, "I'm still committed to managing this habit."

If you chose to give up the objective, hooray! You've applied the tests and come up with a realistic assessment of how important it is to manage the habit, and have decided it isn't worth it, or that you just aren't up for it. If you're not committed, or it's really too hard for you, acknowledge those facts and drop the whole thing. Put it in your aspiration box if you think you might take it up later.

You tried; you weren't ready, or it was not as important as you first thought. There is nothing to forgive. Move on feeling you've done your best. But if you decided to stop this effort and are feeling queasy about what happened . . .

CHOOSE REGRET INSTEAD OF GUILT

Acknowledge what you did. Consider what you might have done better. Stick to the facts. Evaluate your performance but not yourself. Avoid the trap of saying "I didn't do this well, therefore I'm not good, I'm incapable, so bad, so unworthy, so unlovable."

You did what you did. You did the best you were capable of in that moment. Your behavior showed strength and weakness, no doubt. But that's all there was to it. (See the discussion of choosing regret not guilt in the discussion of guilt and shame, below.)

Everyone experiences disturbing emotions from time to time: fear, anger, guilt, shame, and all their variations. As mentioned several times in the book, emotions are essential to our well-being. They're problematical when the reaction is stronger than can be objectively justified and they lead us to make decisions or behave counter to our interests and intentions.

As a result of personal experience, my work with clients, and study, I've chosen approaches to non-clinical manifestations of guilt, shame, anxiety, and negative self-talk that I present in this section. (As always, I urge you to consult with qualified professionals and discuss with them the advisability of using this book if you are subject to any emotions that are debilitating, dangerous, or could in any way be considered clinical in their severity.)

Fear and anger seem to get the most attention from all of us. You can find hundreds of books that suggest ways of dealing with those, and I've discussed them in the book itself. Guilt, shame, and anxiety are extremely valuable emotions when they are well founded. Guilt makes us aware that we've violated our own standards, and provides the motivation to improve. Shame makes us aware that we may be violating social norms, which could lead to ostracism and all its consequences. Anxiety is a very important emotion because it warns us to be wary. The difficulties arise with these when we've overreacted: when we feel guilty because we're judging ourselves against unreasonable standards—ours or someone else's; when we fear that what we do or think is unacceptable to people, and it isn't; when we're anxious for no good reason.

I can't find any value in negative self-talk because it is always, by definition, an attack against oneself, by oneself. It keeps us from being the best we can be.

Guilt and Shame[219]

We often conflate guilt and shame, though they have different causes. Guilt is caused by the belief that we've violated our own standards. Shame is produced by fear that people would think less of us, even ostracize us, if they knew certain things about us. Those certain things make us feel ashamed, and we want to keep them secret.

The things that make us feel guilty can trigger shame along with the guilt. You're addicted to chocolate chip cookies, or something worse. You can't control your chocolate chip cookie appetite but think you should be able to, and therefore feel guilty. You also feel that if people found out about

your addiction they would ostracize or shame you; at the least they would think less of you.

I know many people who consider themselves to be frauds—at least that's what they've told me. I can't know for sure whether that makes them feel guilty, but I'm certain it makes them feel shame, because the definition of being a fraud is to hide facts about oneself to keep from being found out!

Often feelings of guilt and shame are undeserved, in which case they can be corrosive. They undermine self-esteem. Guilt makes us feel we're not as good as we should be. We're bad, not worthy of our own regard. Shame makes us wary of exposing our true selves to the world for fear that it will reject us.

The first challenge when dealing with feelings that could be guilt and/or shame is to try to untangle them. Understand which is which, because the way you deal with them depends on what stimulated them: Are you feeling you're not entitled to your own regard, or is it the regard of others and the social consequences you fear? Are you afraid of being seen by others?

We'll start with guilt.

GUILT

Here's what I recommend for dealing with guilt.

First decide whether you violated your own values or moral codes. If you think you did, decide whether the values or moral codes you think you violated are yours or other people's. If the latter, consider whether you should be treating your emotion as shame, not guilt.

If you've decided the standards you violated are yours, consider whether they're legitimate standards to hold yourself to. I frequently find people holding themselves to standards that are totally unreasonable. When I suspect someone is judging themselves by standards that are too high (and have permission to work with them), I'll suggest they join me in the following role play.

I tell the person to imagine I'm a friend, and to listen to my story.

Then, speaking in the first person, I say that I did what they said they did. I cover all the facts including any mitigating factors they've mentioned. After repeating the person's story as if it were I who did it, I ask what the person thinks of what I did, and what they think of me. I may ask if the person thinks any less of me, whether my behavior was reasonable, and whether I tried hard enough to mitigate any ill-effects of what I did.

Invariably, the other person gives me a clean bill of health. At that point I ask the person why they should judge themselves by higher standards than they would apply to someone else.

Silence.

Then I point out that holding oneself to a higher standard than one would hold anyone else to is either arrogance or self-aggression.

Silence again.

The idea that holding oneself to a higher standard than one would hold others to is arrogance comes as a real shocker and is a great conversation starter. The conversation proceeds swiftly and deeply from there.

You can conduct this exchange with yourself. You don't need someone else to help you with it. When I do it with another person, they invariably leave the conversation with their guilt relieved. Of course the guilt returns later, because it's a habit. We repeat the role play each time guilt returns, and it takes less time to reduce the guilt each time we do it. Ultimately they get it and are able to mitigate their feelings of guilt without involving me or anyone else.

If, on the other hand, the person decides that their standards are legitimate, and they would judge anyone else the way they judge themselves, we go through the procedure for choosing regret rather than guilt.

The steps for choosing regret, not guilt, are:
- Acknowledge what you did.
- Apologize.
- Make amends. Better yet, make things even better than they would have been.
- Commit to avoiding the mistake in the future.
- Accept the consequences of what you did.
- Stand up straight.
- Forgive yourself.
- Let it go.

SHAME

Remember, this is about being afraid that if people knew something about you they would ostracize you or think badly of you.

Shame is another corrosive emotion when it is unfounded. If you are doing something you think is right, but hiding it from others, you are hiding your true nature. This is tantamount to saying to yourself and the world, "What I think doesn't matter. It's only what they think that does." In other words, one is discounting their importance to themselves. They are making what they believe, their way of being, and their feelings subservient to the judgment of others. There are times when that might be appropriate—for example, when one is hiding an unhealthy or illegal addiction, chemical or behavioral. Absent that kind of situation, one needs to be able to own who they are and display it to the world without fear.

Here's what to do if you are feeling shame—and you're hiding something important about yourself.

First check your judgment. Would people reject you if they discovered your secret? If you decide they would not, then work with your fear of discovery by exposing your secret little by little. Do it proudly—maybe not all at one time or to everyone, but whatever you disclose, disclose it without apology. If you get clues that your assumption was wrong, pull back and regroup.

If you believe people would reject you if they discovered your secret, you have a couple of choices. The first is this. If you are not willing and able to give up the secret thing, your alternatives would be to leave the group or to stay while continuing to hide your secret. You would stay and hide if you decided that the benefits of continuing with the activities, beliefs, or possessions that comprise the secret, and staying with the group, outweigh the costs of continuing the deception and feeling afraid of discovery, with its accompanying feelings of shame.

If you feel you would be rejected, but are able to stop doing what you're hiding, you could give up what you're doing and do whatever is necessary to hide your secret past.

In thinking about what it is about you that could be cause for rejection, you could decide that the real cause of your emotions is guilt—that what you're keeping secret violates your own standards but no one else's. If that's the case, review what you're keeping secret under the guilt procedure before looking at the shame aspects.

Anxiety

Anxiety covers a very broad range of emotional experiences from mild unease that not everything is right, to clinical panic reactions and worse. Sometimes the cause of the anxiety is known. Sometimes it is free-floating and unnamable. (I am addressing here feelings that are uncomfortable but still tolerable, certainly not debilitating, nor anything that could be considered clinical.)

The two causes of anxiety that I encounter in my coaching practice (and experience) are 1) the feeling that there is too much to do, or that 2) something bad is going to happen in the person's family, their business, or in the world.

Whatever the source of anxiety, even if the source is unknown, I ask the person to make a list—to get whatever is bothering them out of their Minds and onto paper (or computer). For the person feeling there is more to do than they can do, I ask them to make a list of everything they think they have to do and when it needs to be done. For the person who thinks that bad things are going to happen in the business, family, or world (on a trip, when they buy the car, throw a party—whatever), I ask them to make a list of outcomes they're concerned about.

OVERWHELM: TOO MUCH TO DO

There is some evidence that the subconscious remembers and creates emotional tension when tasks have been started and not completed. In psychology, this is known as the Zeigarnik effect. It's alleged that people typically remember work undone better than completed. I suspect there's a similar tension caused when we think there is something we should do, but haven't even started. If true, it could contribute to feelings of overwhelm.

Try this out. When you're feeling overwhelmed, make a list on paper (or computer) of all the things you think you must do. Include the things you think you should do as well. Much of the time you'll find there is less on the list than you thought, and that the list is quite manageable, especially if you assign priorities and dates to each item.

My favorite priority system is

1. Important and urgent
2. Important, not urgent
3. Not important but urgent
4. Not important, not urgent

Ignore the items in the bottom category on that list (#4) and concentrate on two important categories (#1 and #2). Use any leftover energy on the not important but urgent category (#3). It's essential to work on things that are important and not urgent (#2) rather than not important but urgent items—even though the sense of urgency makes us want to attend to them before working on things that are not urgent. The reason for giving more attention to important, not urgent items (#2) is that if you don't, they will become urgent and jump to a #1 priority; moreover, if you've been wasting time on the two unimportant ones, you won't have enough time to work on the important ones.

It may turn out that not important but urgent (#3) and not important, not urgent items (#4) are your favorite things to do. You'll discover that if you arrange your tasks by priority.

You'll have to figure out what the trade-offs are between being anxious about important things you can't get to and having unimportant things that must wait. That's not always an easy call. If that's your situation, consider that you might be happier if you act according to your priorities rather than letting others dictate yours.

Seeing when things need to be done, you may find that not important but urgent items (#3) are trying to grab more attention than important ones—causing more tension than the lower-priority items are worth. If so, park them. Decide when you'll work on them, and commit to take them up at that time.

Say you need a new car, but not tomorrow. It's important, not urgent. But you want to get on it right away because it will be fun, and you've got to replace that clunker you're driving. There just isn't the time right now. Nevertheless, it will tug on you like a two-year-old that wants a toy until you do something about it. You can quiet that tension by deciding when you'll take your next action on the task. Figure out what that action will be—online research or visiting car dealers, say. Figure out what date you'll start on the task. Enter it in your calendar system, and you're done.

If you're like just about everyone else, your commitment to pick the task up at a specific later date is all the Brain needs to be satisfied until that day arrives. Try it. It really works. It even works if you don't know what your next action will be. You can simply say to yourself that you can't deal with this until the first of next month, then write on your calendar "revisit car purchase," and the tension will most likely stop.

The most important thing: get your list out of your head. It makes trouble in there. Put it on paper.

ANXIOUS THAT BAD THINGS MIGHT HAPPEN

When you're anxious about the future—concerned with the country's direction, afraid that the new product won't sell, that people won't sign up, or that the children won't come home for Christmas—any of that—try this.

- Make a list. Specifically, what are you anxious about?
- Rank them, with the ones that disturb you most at the top.

At this point I like to keep these two slogans in Mind:

The first slogan is Don't know. Can't know. Anxieties about the future are invariably about fear that something we don't want to happen will. But unless the future is walking up your front steps right now, you simply don't know and can't know what will happen. Yet the anxiety we feel is caused by forecasting that it will happen, or that the probability it will happen makes it almost certain to happen. So we're anxious.

Don't know. Can't know is a reminder that we are ignorant of the future, that we are caught up in hope or fear and can't know what will happen.

The second slogan is *Contingencies, yes. Forecasting, no.* This slogan is about what is reasonable to do in the face of anxieties about the future. Rather than fight your anxiety, work with the idea that what you're anxious about could really happen. Make a contingency plan for every occurrence that concerns you—a description of what you'll do if the feared results come about. That's the *contingency* part of the slogan.

Just don't allow your Brain to make you nuts by thinking it *will* happen, that your anxiety is a forecast. That's the *Forecasts, no* part of the slogan.

Instead of accommodating that forecasting state of Mind, treat your concerns as possibilities and make contingency plans for each one. Start at the top of your list and make a contingency plan for the first one. Write what you'd do if what you're afraid of happened. This may sound a little strange to you, but consider this. As I wrote above, we humans deal with every single thing we encounter: the good and the bad, the delightful and the unthinkable, the exquisite and the awful. We deal with everything we encounter and usually come out the other end pretty much okay. So why spend time in nameless fear?

For each concern, write down what you'd do if it occurred. These are your contingency plans. Write each on a separate piece of paper, and put each in a separate envelope with the name of the event on the front. Then put the plans where you keep your fire insurance policy. If you don't have one, put it where you put other insurance policies or some other place that's easy to remember and access. Insurance policies are contingency plans. Your contingency plans should live with them, not with you.

Now you're prepared. Your Brain knows you're prepared; it may trust your contingency plans more than you do.

You may find your anxiety lessening as you work at creating your contingency plans. Keep going even if it lessens. Complete this assignment or those fears will probably come right back, and you'll have to start again.

By the way, don't seal those envelopes. Make it easy to get to the contents so you can look them over for reassurance and change them if you get a better idea.

EVERYTHING ACCOMMODATED, BUT STILL ANXIOUS?

The anxious feelings left after you've identified what you're anxious about and have recorded your contingency plans is you being anxious for no reason you can identify. Maybe it's just the way you are. Anxiety has a strong genetic component. You've identified everything that you think could or should cause you anxiety in your view. Maybe what's left is free-floating anxiety.

If that's the way you are, see if you can habituate yourself to those anxious feelings. Knowing that there's no objective basis for the feelings, as far as you know, you can think of them as just *those feelings*—feelings in your body that make you uncomfortable; a sense that something is wrong, though you can't identify what it is.

You can try to get used to those feelings or ignore them. Certainly they're uncomfortable. Compassionately reject the idea that there's something there to worry about. Remind yourself that everything is all right as far as you know, and you have plans to deal with the things you're anxious about.

Then train yourself to tolerate the feelings of anxiety in your body. When you become aware of them, breathe into them. Take some slow deep breaths and imagine that the breath is flowing into the tight spaces. A strong, relaxing stretch might be good. Of course it's not, but that little visualization will help relax the feelings in your body. Remember too that emotions are feelings in the body and nothing more. When you know there's no reason for having the emotions, you can work with them to build your ability to tolerate the sensations. If and when you discover things to be anxious about that you haven't handled already, create their contingency plans to accompany the others.

Also, if you haven't already done so, begin the tooth-brushing practice described below. It will give you daily practice in overcoming Reactive Brain's unwanted commands.

Negative Self-Talk

Strictly speaking this is a habit, not an emotion. And it's common. Negative self-talk may manifest as feelings rather than words. Either way there's a belief that one is not good, skilled, deserving, or lovable enough. It's the feeling that you shouldn't do *that* because you don't deserve for it to work out the way you want, and you'll probably fail at doing it because you don't know what you're doing. For extra credit, the gremlin in your head may tell you someone will take it away from you if you manage to get it—whatever *it* is.

I labeled that voice your gremlin because that is what it is. It is a habit of self-critical voices and feelings that have no other purpose than to make us feel bad. Not everyone has them, but my experience is that most do.

INTRODUCING GREMLINS

The guru of gremlins is Rick Carson, author of *Taming Your Gremlin*. I was given my first copy over 30 years ago and have given away maybe a hundred copies to people who rave about it. If you'll promise yourself to buy a copy of his current edition (for about $14 currently), you could skip what I write here about gremlins. But since I can't know that you'll get Carson's book, here's a brief summary of his method, followed by something from me describing an antidote to negative self talk.

The basic idea is that gremlins are the accumulation of all the bad news you've ever heard or thought about yourself. It's as if you have living in your head (the attic of your house) a crank whose only purpose is to make you feel terrible and keep you from reaching your full potential.

Picture gremlins as unwanted live-in relatives who are there to interfere and give you an uninterruptible stream of wrong-headed advice. They are know-it-alls, simple-minded, opinionated, self-important, have nowhere else to go, will never move out, and don't like you. (For extra credit you could decide that their lives are so miserable they should be objects of compassion. That would be highly desirable, but truly advanced practice.)

Carson recommends that you give gremlins a solid identity apart from your own. Visualize them. Decide how big they are, what they wear, their color and general appearance. Draw them, if you're up for that. Don't make your gremlins scary; make them funny and pitiful looking. Imagine their voice as squeaky. Nothing about gremlins should suggest they have authority. Make them funny like clowns that make you laugh because they show their incompetence as they try to deliver on their grandiose promises. It's important that you fully embrace the idea and feeling that what the gremlin says is not your opinion, is not competent advice, and certainly is not wise. Nothing a gremlin says has any value—none!

Give your gremlin a name, and always use it when referring to him or her. When you refer to them by name you're pinning the blame for the negative self-talk on them, not you, and not the universe. Whenever you hear negative self-talk, say to yourself, "That's Marty," or "That's Mary."

Do not pick a name that reminds you of a real authority figure or someone you admire. Don't name your gremlin after someone you're afraid of, or want to punish. Just pick a name that makes them inconsequential.

Listening to gremlins and following their advice are habits. Repetition makes them stronger. Doing what you want instead weakens them. But don't expect they'll ever move out.

Never argue with or resist your gremlins. It makes them more stubborn. Gremlins can't be killed or banished. Frontal assault—arguing with them or disagreeing with them—doesn't work. *What you resist persists.*

Inevitably you either deal with your gremlin or do what they say. What can you do if arguing with them doesn't work? Whenever you hear gremlin-speak, say, "Thanks. But I'll do this my way," and then execute your choice. There's a specific attitude to hold as you talk to your gremlin. You hear him or her (not the same as listening) but you remain, as Carson puts it, "*at choice.*" You're in control. You can choose, and you will, and it doesn't matter what the gremlin thinks.

My experience is that the biggest obstacle to working with gremlins is the habit of not noticing they're speaking, and accepting their advice. You doubt your ability to do what you want to do, and so you do something else, something you didn't want to do instead, never realizing that you were following your gremlin's orders.

Listening to your gremlin, thinking its voice is your voice, is a costly habit. Some people grasp the idea enthusiastically, create and name their gremlin, and try to work with the concept, but continue to be influenced by their gremlin because they don't recognize that they're listening to gremlin-talk.

Give the assignment to watch out for gremlin-talk to your Sentinel. Still, there's a problem. Because gremlin speech frequently slips by Mind's defenses, most people have difficulty recalling examples of listening to the gremlin that they can use to train their Sentinel. If that's your situation, periodically recall the recent past. Set up a schedule to spend ten minutes or so looking for evidence of having taken gremlin advice. Look for times when you pulled back from doing something you wanted to do in life or livelihood because you thought you weren't good enough to do it, or that people wouldn't let you do it or like you if you tried. Use your judgment about how often to do the review. Use examples you recall to train your Sentinel.

If you're strongly and frequently affected by your gremlin, you might want to do your gremlin search every day, or three times a week. You be the judge. Use what you experience as a guide to adjusting the frequency. If you do your search every other day and don't find anything each time, you may want to drop back to every three days. Keep track of the number of gremlin events you find when you do your review. You may find the number increases, and that may discourage you. But you may be finding more incidents because practicing makes it easier to recognize the gremlin events. That would be good news.

Remember: visualize and create that gremlin persona. Be clear that it is him or her speaking, not some advisor you should trust, and certainly not your own intuition or wisdom. Picture the gremlin as someone whose appearance discourages confidence in what he or she says. Hear but don't listen to the squeaky voice, and always refer to your gremlin by name.

Notice that I've never capitalized *gremlin*; they're not due that much respect.

FOR SOME, THE ANTIDOTE FOR NEGATIVE SELF-TALK

Some people have such low regard for themselves that they find it hard to work with gremlins. It happens often to people from families or cultures that tie love or esteem to objective achievements. Don't get all A's, don't get elected class president, and you're just not what they had in mind. Still worse, in those environments, the rewards for achievement are often skimpy and short-lasting. Seemingly, the principal reward for achievement was greater expectations. Those kinds of experiences, repeated over and over again, create gremlins that are very powerful and difficult to ignore, because the person they're tormenting can't identify with the dignity, lovability, and competence that each of us has.

The antidote is self-love. Not self-absorption. Not conceit. Simply love.

Chances are you have or had children, a pet, and beloved relatives who made problems for you. If a pet, they chewed things, soiled the floor, threw up on your couch, clawed your furniture. Yet you loved them unconditionally. If you have young children, you know that their stubbornness and failure to listen, to be respectful, to do the dishes or their homework unless you beg, plead, or blow your top, are often trying beyond description. But you love them unconditionally, of course.

So why can't you feel that way about yourself? Why are you so undeserving that you can't love yourself as much as you love your pets or your children? Imagine some of your friends. You might think it would be laughable if they didn't love themselves as much as they love their children.

One of the most important teachings I've received came from Stephen Levine, whom I quoted previously in this and other connections. It came in these two quotations from his book *Healing into Life and Death*:

> Turning gently within, begin to direct toward yourself feelings of loving kindness relating to yourself as though you were your only child.[220]

And

> Truly we have been waiting our whole life to hear "I love you" in our own voice.[221]

I came across those sentences in 1988. Just previously I had wrecked something very important to me, and was desolate. I had no good words for myself. When friends told me I should love myself, I spit out a long list of errors, inadequacies, and other failings, as if their suggestion was outrageous, even stupid. I had no idea what it meant to love oneself. I felt, as many do, that one had to be perfect to love oneself, even though the demands on me for performance when growing up were nowhere near as tough as I described above. Nor was love lacking in my family. Still, I had the bug. (Isn't this the same kind of standard that leads to inappropriate guilt discussed above?)

Levine's words made the definition clear. As a father of girls who survived the teen years, I knew exactly what it meant to love something like an only child. If I could love my children and pets, surely I could love myself. Taking him literally, I began then the habit of saying as I roll over to go to sleep, "I love you, Robert." It works wonders. Try it. It will help you stand up for yourself and recognize that your gremlin has nothing worthwhile to contribute to your life.

Slogans, Mantras, and Aphorisms

You've met some slogans in the book's main text. Call them whatever you're comfortable with. I prefer slogans, but you might think of them as mantras or aphorisms. Some that you're already familiar with are part of folk wisdom—A fool and his money are soon parted, The early bird catches the worm. Others are more profound, even sacred—Love your neighbor as yourself, Do unto others as you would have them do unto you.

Slogans remind us of teachings. Something happens, and the right slogan appears in your Mind. It says just the right thing, giving context to the situation and guidance about what to do next. It's because they work so well that I recommend using them to help connect you ever more solidly to your values and intentions.

Many people I know find particularly helpful Tsoknyi Rinpoche's Real but not true. It comes up when conditioning has produced an irrational emotional reaction. It's an especially powerful slogan, and here's how it works.

- First, one realizes that there are no grounds for thinking the situation would produce the consequences the emotion is preparing us for. Brain is trying to protect us, but it's mistaken.

- Next, the slogan validates your reaction. It acknowledges that though there's no *objective reason* for the reaction, you are in fact reacting that way and it feels bad.

- Finally, the fact that there's a slogan acknowledging what you're going through is evidence that this happens to other people as well. That simple fact is comforting.

Real but not true validates your experience and eliminates most if not all of the guilt or shame you would feel if you thought your reaction was wrong and unique to you. Thus, the slogan frees you to try to address the truth of the situation, rather than let the illogical, not-true emotion direct your behavior.

You've come across a number of other slogans in the book, including these:

Beneath anger there is fear. Beneath fear there is a tender heart. Pema Chödrön

Don't make things worse than they already are.

Pain is inevitable. Suffering is optional. Anonymous

Ask the Second Question.

Emotions love emotions. Marsha Linehan

Drop the storyline. Pema Chödrön

Choose regret, not guilt. Pema Chödrön

Earlier in this Resource Companion you were introduced to *Contingencies, yes. Forecasting, no,* and *Don't know. Can't know.*

If you want to work with slogans, here's my suggestion: put the slogans you'd like to work with on individual index cards, place a stack of them in a conspicuous place, and expose a new card every day. When doing so, take a moment or two to consider the slogan's message. See if there's something in that day's slogan that you might want to use during the day.

If you take up this practice, don't expect immediate results. Just keep doing it. If you've chosen slogans that mean something to you, they'll ultimately have their way with you. Choose slogans that speak to you because they're relevant to what you're experiencing in your life, you wholeheartedly agree with the sentiment or philosophy, and you want to make them part of you.

Here are ten more slogans with their interpretations. I offer them as a sampler. You will find more at ActFromChoice.com that you can download and print, or buy pre-printed ones, if you prefer. If you'd like to receive slogans periodically on your computer or smartphone, follow me on Twitter at #ActFromChoice. You may notice that several slogans may point to the same principles. Choose the ones that work best for you.

(Slogans are attributed to their authors where known. Slogans without an identified author, that I haven't written myself, are attributed to *Anonymous*. Slogans I've written are unattributed. Each slogan is accompanied by a short interpretation. I take full responsibility for any misinterpretations of the authors' intentions.)

- **Validate what is true**. Try to understand and validate your feelings. Get curious about them. Is Brain motivated by something that is true, or not? Has it created a secondary emotion that wants to guide your actions? Learn to recognize and deal with the primary emotion. Very often the only purpose served by secondary emotions is to make you ignore the primary one. Truth is usually in the primary emotion, not the secondary one.

- ***Catharsis is fun, but so expensive.*** The psychological research says that catharsis doesn't work. It doesn't relieve feelings; it only makes the emotion bigger and last longer, creating greater opportunity to stimulate regrettable behavior.

- ***Judge behavior, not the actor.*** Don't judge people by what they do. Identify the behavior you object to and do whatever you can to make it better or deal with the consequences. This slogan is especially germane to parenting. Children feel more loved and secure when they don't interpret a parental outburst as meaning they are bad and their parents don't love them. Parental anger can make it difficult to follow through with this distinction. It is also hard to do in the adult world when we decide people are good or bad depending on whether they agree with us. That attitude denies us the opportunity to work with them to make things better. Besides, what makes us think we can divine someone's intention or motivation from their behavior?

- ***Happiness is the absence of unhappiness.***[222] Almost nothing we strive to get from outside of us can give us authentic lasting happiness. The last promotion, new car, television set, graduation, larger home, and stupendous vacation didn't do it. Pleasures—good conversation, a glass of wine, hearty sex, a walk in the sun, a massage—might make us happy, but the happiness lasts only as long as the activity lasts. They do not fulfill us. They do not give us lasting happiness. Search out the sources of your unhappiness and work with them. Reframe them if you can. Form a new relationship with them; question the importance you give them. Transform your attitude toward them so they no longer produce unhappiness. You can do this with almost everything in your life, even terminal illness and pain. Eliminate the sources of unhappiness one way or another and you will experience equanimity. Then choose activities and goals that will have you feeling that your life is fulfilled, and enjoy those pleasures as something extra, not as the whole game.

- ***Do not do to yourself what you would not do to others.*** What possible excuse could there be for treating yourself worse than you would treat others? Are you so undeserving of common decency, consideration, compassion, and love? If this slogan is difficult for you, reread the sections on guilt and negative self-talk in this Resource Companion.

- ***Work with what is.*** We give enormous energy to wanting, hoping, and pretending things are not the way they really are or fearing the future that we cannot know. Of course we want to make things be the way we want. This slogan, and many like it, do NOT recommend that you accept what is without trying to make it better. But after we've done all that we can do to change things, we're left with an (at present) unchangeable reality, and there's nothing to do but work with what is, as it is. Working with things as if they were different than what they really are; expending useless effort in trying to change the unchangeable; withholding effort waiting for change that will not happen—those activities turn pain into needless suffering. (See, *Pain is inevitable, suffering is optional.*) This slogan also recommends that we accept that some things really are the way they are and should not be denied—that the abusive husband really is an abusive husband, and unable to change. Maya Angelou, the late, renowned poet, said, "When a person shows you who they are, believe them the first time." She also said, "*If you don't like something, change it. If you can't change it, change your attitude,*" all of which falls within the meaning of *work with what is.*

- ***Welcome discomfort.*** Failure and discomfort are our primary teachers. Fortunately they can't be wholly avoided. Discomfort is the doorway to growth and wisdom. We find what our values are when we realize we've done something we don't approve of, or someone calls us out on our behavior. We realize what we're attached to when we're in danger of losing it. It may take separation to make us realize how much we love. We learn more from the weaknesses we discover than we do from our achievements. After you've gotten over the pain that accompanies discomfort or coming up short in your estimation of yourself, be grateful for your failures.

- ***Everything teaches. Give more attention to the lessons than the tuition.*** Bad things happen to good people, good things too. All produce lessons. We celebrate the lessons we learn from things we enjoy. But we tend to focus more on the pain than the lessons when they've been taught by misfortune. After the misfortunate events, we are how we are. Validate pain, resentment, disappointment, and feelings of poverty. Let the feelings go when you've grieved enough so you can get to using the lessons.

- ***God lives on the other side of the armor around your heart.*** The love we want to receive and give needs a path to the heart that is open not only to the world but to our own tenderness. Whether your conception of God is a metaphysical presence or simply everything the universe has to offer with no consideration of deity, it can speak to us only when we are able to hear. The armor we've acquired is possibly too thick, welded in place and multi-layered. If so, it developed that way to protect us from what happened around and to us. It would be too painful to suddenly rip it away as if it were an adhesive bandage. Still, we can poke little holes in it to ventilate us a bit, then more. Ultimately, maybe all but a small patch of it could go. Look for that time when you can begin to open up. There's always further to go.

- ***When you look, you will see. When you see, you will know what to do.*** Cynthia Kneen.[223] For me, this slogan summarizes the motivation for and fruition of mindfulness practices. The slogan sounds easy, but there is much to it, and its fruition can take a lifetime. *Looking* requires us to have curiosity and bravery—the willingness to discover anything and everything that might be there to see. *Seeing* refers to the practice of just seeing and allowing oneself to understand. It implies being awake to what is present, non-conceptually, without bias or preconception; having the discernment to know what is acceptable and not, but without the judgment of good and bad. *Knowing what to do* implies that one has truly seen. It implies panoramic awareness, knowing the situation, the alternatives, their consequences, and the resources one has available to effect their choice. The reward for such clarity is captured in this ancient Buddhist teaching, "Where there is no obscuration of mind there is no fear."[224]

You'll find more slogans at ActFromChoice.com. Contribute your favorite slogan by emailing me at RobertG@ActFromChoice.com, if you'd like. Include your interpretation, if its meaning isn't obvious. And let me know how to refer to you if I post it on the site.

Developing Greater Awareness

The Power of Awareness and Curiosity

Picking up this book and thinking about what it is you do gets you a long way into learning to manage your habits, because you've started to deepen your self-awareness. That will make you more alert to yourself and strengthen your Sentinel too.

When we think about something that has some importance, the Brain takes it seriously. It even looks for things we've heard about recently whether we're actively curious or not.

Imagine you're at a party and someone you don't know and will never see again tells you he heard that Chrysler 300 sedans are improving. He finds them attractive and is thinking about buying one, maybe (as if you care!). I chose Chrysler 300 series cars for this example, not because I recommend them, know anything about them, or think you should, but because there are so few of them where I live that I can use them to make a point.

Before the party, you never thought about Chrysler 300 sedans, maybe wouldn't know one if you saw one. As I said, there aren't that many out there compared to other brands and models. Nevertheless, I'll wager that after talking to this guy you'd see Chrysler 300s everywhere, even though you were not consciously looking for them, even though you were not interested in cars, or in buying one now. But after that conversation you'd see them a lot, be amazed at how many there are, and surprised you'd never noticed them before. (Reading this example could be enough to make you notice them.)

The Brain's like that. You may doubt whether your Sentinel will trigger your awareness of a rising habit, but if the Brain can look out for Chrysler 300s, it can and will look out for your unwanted habits. But it has to know you're interested, even if only a little.

In his book *Emotional Intelligence*, Daniel Goleman emphasizes that self-awareness is the bedrock requirement for self-management. Your desire to manage yourself better, and reading this far in this book (even if you're skipping around), will naturally increase your curiosity about yourself. Chances are you didn't pick this book up because you want to improve your posture, but you're more likely now to steal glances of yourself in mirrors and windows you pass. You'll begin to think about regrettable episodes your habits have caused and will find other habits you'll want to manage. Everything you do that increases self-awareness will make you more effective at managing yourself, so cultivate curiosity about yourself. Don't squelch it.

Remember that the goal of awareness practice is to simply notice non-judgmentally what is going on in the present moment.[225] The value of self-awareness increases to the extent curiosity, insight, an open mind, lack of judgment, and self-forgiveness (self-compassion) are present. The effort to cultivate those attitudes yields amazing returns.

It is essential that you are included in your awareness, that you are aware of what you're doing and feeling.

Knowing Mind

You were introduced to the concept of Knowing Mind in Chapter 5. It is a Mind that knows and understands much more than our less potent Mind states do. It is not distracted, nor is it focused too narrowly. When we're in Knowing Mind we are aware of what's going on around us, what we're feeling and believing, and what our higher aspirations are. We know all that without needing words to tell us what we know. We just know.

Knowing Mind is a Mind-space in which we tap into all the wisdom we can have at our disposal in the moment. It can influence us profoundly, resulting in decisions more in line with how we mean to be.

See if this metaphor helps to illustrate the awareness that Knowing Mind is capable of. See if you recognize the difference between a Mind that is spacious and aware of current experience, and one that is either completely distracted or narrowly focused on doing something without appreciation of its necessity, its usefulness, and its relationship to our intentions.

Imagine a small steel ball and a balloon fresh from the package with no air in it. Imagine that you poke the ball into the balloon so that the uninflated balloon is now tight around the ball. In this metaphor the balloon represents your Mind in Master Habit. The ball is an emotion, thought, or attitude.

When you're in Master Habit, your Mind is entirely filled by its contents, just like the balloon, uninflated tight around the ball. It's not that there's a lot occupying that Mind. It's simply flitting from one thing to another. Or it could be intent on something but avoiding the context of what it's working with and within. That is Mind [Kahneman's System 2] when it's resting and accepting of whatever Brain [System 1] sends it.

When we're taken over by highly charged thoughts, emotions, and attitudes, the Mind grips them, like the balloon grips the steel ball. There's no air in that Mind, no space for greater awareness (Figure 11). When in that state, the Mind is the thought or emotion that's captured it. There's no self-awareness. There's no so-called observer-self. If we're joyful, we're joy. If we're walking, we walk without any idea of I'm walking. We may know that we're walking and where we're going, but without awareness of ourselves, of our posture, whether we're pleased or sad, for example. We're on automatic.

Figure 11

Master Habit
Distraction and Narrowly Focused Experience

When the Mind is small like that, any awareness we have is not the knowing awareness of the athlete, artist, or improvising jazz musician. Theirs is focused but open to possibilities. When Mind is focused so narrowly on carrying through with impulses, there's no past, no future, no alternatives, no sense of higher-level intentions, goals, or broader objectives; no sense of consequences. There are no alternatives to consider, no questions to be asked, no information it needs to get. It's just what's going on now in the narrowest sense.

Now imagine that instead of settling for that tiny, narrowly focused Mind of limited awareness, you inflate the balloon (Figure 12). Create an enormous amount of space in that balloon that represents your Mind; step back from the action, from yourself, and see what's going on. You're now awake with expanded awareness; you see yourself. You see how you are in that moment.

Figure 12

Knowing Mind
Expanded Awareness

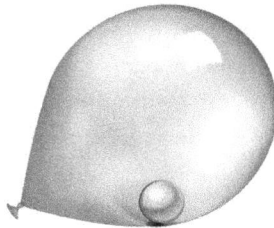

There's room for much more now than there was in your narrowly focused or distracted Master Habit Mind. Instead of simply experiencing the emotion or thought, and being intent on performing the impulse to the best of your ability, you see yourself and know what you're feeling and doing. Instead of that steel ball being all that you experience, instead of being focused solely on what emotions want you to do, you now see them as simply the contents of your Mind. You have the possibility of being in Knowing Mind, where you can bring into focus all the considerations that bear on influencing your next actions. It's no longer a matter of how to be angry, or sad, or jealous; how to satisfy your blood-lust, or your need for revenge or ego reinforcement.

In Knowing Mind the decisions are about how to be—whether and what to do: whether to let go of the emotion or modify it, to be enraged or negotiate, maybe to just let go of whatever stirred you up.

Getting to Knowing Mind

You will stay in Master Habit until something knocks you out of it by directing your attention to something specific. It takes an internal or external event to move us out of Master Habit. An external event will do it, a loud noise or bumping into something. Brain chooses which internal stimuli to pay attention to, which is why it's important to train your Sentinel to be alert to them. If your intentions about how to act in a particular type of situation are well planted, and your behavior contradicts that, your Sentinel will wake you up to the mismatch between intention and action.

Remember that when you first become aware of yourself in the grips of impulse you may not be fully in Knowing Mind. The balloon may be only slightly inflated, in which case you can get to Knowing Mind more quickly by asking the Second Question.

Tips for Increasing Awareness

The practices in this section will help bring you to the present more often whether you are an experienced mindfulness practitioner, someone just exploring meditation, or someone who does not now and never will take up meditation. It is quite common for people who are regular, even long-term meditators to make a cocoon of meditation: they practice in order to feel better, which presumably gives them great benefit. While that's excellent if that is their intention, it's not what is generally meant by mindfulness practice.

Mindfulness meditation practices are not meant to make us more comfortable or peaceful. Those benefits often are the byproducts of mindfulness practices, but they are not the goal. Mindfulness practices are meant to train one to stabilize the Mind and create a different relationship with Mind's contents, not only in the quiet of formal meditation practice, but, more importantly, when one is out in the world. But it's quite common to see people who are terrific meditators—who have very stable Minds when formally meditating—have little self-awareness when not formally meditating.

The practices I suggest below will make you more likely to become self-aware when you're simply out in the world. They are things to do in the course of the day, without the formality of meditation. These will work for you whether you meditate or not. Doing them in ordinary situations helps plant the intention to become aware in the present moment when you're just doing what you do—walking around; engaging with family, friends, and business associates; or washing the dishes when all alone.

The practices that follow will help you blow up that balloon of awareness and get present.

TOOTH-BRUSHING PRACTICE[226]

When you first wake up in the morning, having nothing to measure the condition of your Mind, you don't know if it, and you, are slow or speedy. This practice will do three things for you. First, it will tell you how settled or unsettled your Mind is. Second, it will help you learn to recognize Reactive Brain's attempts to move your Mind around and keep you in Master Habit. Third, it is a way to train yourself to override Reactive Brain's impulses. All you have to do to get these benefits is brush your teeth the way, and for the time, your dentist told you to.

When you brush your teeth in the morning, spend 30 seconds on each quadrant of your mouth. Try to do the quadrants in the same order every morning. (You might do outside of bottom teeth, then inside, inside top, finishing at outside top. The quadrants defined that way have boundaries that are easy to identify and enforce.) Do not leave one quadrant for another before the full 30 seconds have passed.

This practice is best done with an electric toothbrush that signals you every 30 seconds, but you can do reasonably well by watching a clock instead.

The first thing you'll experience when doing this practice is that the time you're taking on each quadrant seems to vary a lot from day to day, and the amount it varies may surprise you. Somedays it feels as if 30 seconds on the clock passed in ten seconds. Somedays each quadrant seems to take two minutes or more.

Those differences in felt-time indicate how your Mind is: if each quadrant seems to take too long, you're speedy, likely to be uptight and anxious. When time passes quickly, you're more relaxed and open. (It's also possible that you lost attention to what you were doing and, for that reason, didn't notice the time passing.) Observe also how easy or difficult it is to keep your attention on what you're doing.

These observations about the condition of your Mind may come as a surprise. To get some more insight, before starting to brush, tell yourself how you think your Mind will be when brushing: fast or slow, easily distracted or not?

After you've brushed your teeth take what you've learned about that day's early morning Mind, and see if you want to do anything about it.

The second thing to learn from this practice is how to recognize when Reactive Brain is interfering with you. That's what's going on when you feel compelled to rush on to the next quadrant before you've spent 30 seconds on the one you're on.

So, while you're trying to resist those feelings, pay attention to what that impatient insistence feels like in your body. That is Reactive Brain trying to take charge. See if Brain is also speaking to you, saying, You better hurry up, complaining that you're taking too long, or that the practice is silly. (Remember you're doing this for all of two minutes, no more.)

The third thing to learn from this practice is how to resist and tolerate Reactive Brain's impulses. Of course, that's what you're doing when you stick with those quadrants that feel like they're taking too long.

Pay close attention to what that compulsion to move ahead, to stop doing what you're doing and do something else, feels like. The more you resist Reactive Brain the more uncomfortable you may feel. Get into those feelings; become intimate with them. While continuing to follow your intention by staying on the quadrant, allow those impatient feelings to be there. Try to relax into acceptance of your commitment to the full 30 seconds per quadrant. Acceptance usually leads to the impatient feelings diminishing on their own. Keep at this and you'll find you're able to resist Reactive Brain by simply allowing the feelings while holding to and executing your intentions.

So do what you intend. Stay with the 30-second program. In doing so you will learn that you can stand whatever discomfort remains. You'll learn that you can win, and that the discomfort of resisting Reactive Brain is manageable.

The lasting results are first that you will become more sensitized, more alert when Reactive Brain is trying to take over. Second, you will increase your ability to tolerate the discomfort. An additional benefit from this practice is that you get a daily reminder of how Brain and Mind work—that the demands made on you by your unconscious Mind do not represent anything wise, and that the Brain, while truly wonderful, is not always reliable.

You get all this training by simply spending the two minutes brushing your teeth that you ought to spend anyway, by paying attention to what you're doing, and by working with your Mind as you do so. Two minutes a day. That's all it takes.

ACCEPTANCE TRAINING

You can use the tooth-brushing technique every time you're impatient. Impatience is Reactive Brain saying no more, get on with it, not this, I'm bored. It's Reactive Brain's version of the child's Are we there yet? repeated over and over and over.

Suppose you're driving somewhere. You've been on the road for three hours, and there are two more to go. You want to be there already, dammit! That feeling is Reactive Brain, again, only this time there's nothing to do but either give in to the impatience or manage it. You are at that Serenity Prayer point. You could drive off the road, distract yourself, and thereby lengthen the trip. You could make up stories about how it's the other drivers, or that you never should have started on this journey. Or you could accept that you're going to finish the trip and it will take that long no matter what you're feeling. All negative emotions at that point are making things worse than they already are. I find it helps me, at these times, to say to myself, "It takes that long. There's nothing to do about it." Or, "Don't make things worse than they already are." Either works. Telling myself that I'm dealing with things that cannot change seems to turn my negative emotions way down.

What about when what I'm doing is optional? There are times when I'm meditating and it's taking too long, or my Mind is so jumpy that I'm uncomfortable.

Reactive Brain is telling me to stop, get up, and do something different. Like most meditators, I've set the timer for the time I want to meditate, and it hasn't gone off yet. So I remind myself of my commitment to stay until it goes off, and that I'm going to stay until it does. I may let out a big (inaudible) sigh, and that's the end of it. For some reason, after that exchange with myself, Reactive Brain leaves me alone for the balance of the meditation session. Try that technique with any task that Reactive Brain wants to interrupt. Simply tell yourself that you're going to stick with your commitment to work to a certain point before stopping, and see if Reactive Brain doesn't leave you alone until then.

If that doesn't work, ask the Second Question. Ask if you're willing to violate your commitment. I don't recommend starting with that when you first hit resistance. It's better to just push through the resistance by restating your intention. That's the better habit. Asking the Second Question presents the alternative of going with the impulse to give up. Try to push your way through to following your intention before opening up that possibility and you'll be less likely to give up on your intention. (In over 30 years, I have never once ended a meditation before the time I set on the timer at the start.)

PRACTICE BECOMING PRESENT

Take a few moments each day to get present. Use things that happen in the environment to remind you to do it. I'll tell you about the alarms when I've finished telling you about getting present.

Here's what I mean. Simply take a moment to detach from Master Habit. Become aware of yourself, check in to see what you're doing, how you feel, what emotions, if any, you're aware of, and what's going on around you. There are a number of ways to do this. Feel free to modify these instructions to suit yourself. This *getting present* is meant to take about two minutes, no more.

To begin, gently let go of what is going on for you: your activities, thoughts, emotions.

Become present.

Next, take a few relaxing breaths. If you're agitated, take more. You might want to breathe with your abdomen instead of your chest. Pay attention to your body as it breathes. If that's too general, if you have trouble disengaging from your thoughts and directing your attention to your body, put your attention on some part of your body that you have little attachment to or concern about—a shoulder, elbow, or knee, for example.

Focus your attention there for a few moments. Be curious about what that part of your body feels like. Feel the clothing on your skin if any covers it.

That focus will help you let go of anything that caught your attention when you began to get present. After a little time with the body part, you'll have enough calmness to direct your attention to your body as it breathes.

If you're highly agitated, it might help to place your palm over your heart-center (on your sternum) and breathe slowly and mindfully.

Having made yourself ready, simply open up. Take a relaxed breath, and as it goes out gently drop whatever is in your Mind. Let your mind expand. See what you see without words. Don't search for anything. Just see what comes to you from outside or inside you. Notice what you're feeling. Drop any thoughts that intervene and want to take you away. Use no words. Just let yourself be open. Visualize your mind as that balloon of awareness if you think that metaphor will help you. When you've had enough, take another relaxing breath or two, and then return to whatever you want to do.

Some teachers recommend analyzing what you've just felt or seen, and the experiences you've had of yourself. If that's what your teacher tells you to do, stick with it. For myself I recommend that you simply content yourself with the nonverbal knowing. Take in whatever you experience and try not to put words on your experience. Labeling things and experiences takes away the uniqueness of our experiences. Too much analysis can solidify the experience for all time, which eliminates the possibility that it can take on new and different meanings over time.

For example, if you've just been admiring a flower, you deprive it of its uniqueness when you name it. Call it a rose and it becomes a stereotypical rose, rather than that particular flower that engaged you. You will never feel the same about a flower after you name it. (Even calling it a flower diminishes it.) See if it is true that taking in what you experience in these moments of openness to the present gives you more than you get when you name what you've experienced. As with everything I recommend, try it if you want. Use it if you find it of value. Otherwise, forget it.

SET ALARMS TO BRING YOU PRESENT

As with all changes of mind-states such as from not present to present, you'll need to set some alarms to break you out of Master Habit so you'll remember to get present. The basic idea is to decide in advance that you'll stop what you're doing and become present when you experience the situations you've chosen as alarms. Here are some examples.

- When hearing specific sounds (I like to use nasty, obnoxious ones like police and fire truck sirens, bad, and/or loud music, dogs barking, and the start of TV commercials).

- Before picking up the phone to make or answer a call

- Before pressing send (email)

- When seeing or thinking about particular people

- Upon entering a room, especially one you're not familiar with, or when others are present; when walking through any doorway

- During particular times of day, e.g. noon or when first waking, or sitting on the side of the bed before getting into or out of it

- Showering

- Eating

- Having to wait for anything

- Stopping the car at a stoplight (don't do this at stop signs because you'll be holding up the people behind you)

- Arriving home, before opening the door

- Upon arriving at, sitting down, or leaving your workplace

Start by picking just a few alarms; just one will do to start. When the event comes, do your best to get present. Remember that you're only going to do this for a minute or so. For extra credit, forgive yourself, or chuckle when you realize an alarm has slipped by and you missed it. As with other applications of the Act from Choice Method, renew your intention when you failed to follow through with your intentions.

This concludes the tips and practices included in the Resource Companion. More will be added to ActFromChoice.com in time. If you have practices you would like to share, please email me with your suggestions: RobertG@ActFromChoice.com

Acknowledgments

Acknowledgment doesn't say enough. *Gratitude* says it better.

I started this book 14 years ago. It has taken much support and encouragement from others to bring it to publication, and I am grateful for every single bit of it. Several people have discussed it, reviewed it, commented on it, and provided substantive input and advice, all of it valuable. If any of it were missing, the book would be different. Some people have helped in each of those 14 years.

First among the helper-contributors is Victoria Self, my life partner since 1999. There is no counting the number of meals dominated by discussion of various aspects of the book. A longtime meditator and committed Buddhist, she was often able to see how something I had written could lead to a deeper place with broader applicability than I had envisioned, not to mention a bit of nudging that led to more felicitous language in places. More important than her substantive input was her unflagging belief in the project. Imagine, if you will, sitting across the table from someone who spoke of his book, continuously, for 14 years. Imagine being able to maintain your belief that the book would someday be finished, and would help people live fuller and happier lives. So much easier to lose faith, which she never did. Or she hid it well.

Next in importance are a few hundred clients. We try to teach our clients, and then discover that we're there to learn, and we do. I've learned much from them. Their challenges and opportunities showed me some of what we need to feel fulfilled, and they gave me the opportunity to suggest approaches that might work. The techniques that survived are in the book. Some of my clients are in there too, disguised, of course.

A number of friends and colleagues have given me input over the years. Most read all or parts of one or more manuscripts. Their reactions and inputs were important, and their encouragement was and continues to be essential. These stalwarts include Regina Blakeley, Hank Burgoyne, Laird Durham, Gwen Essex, Clyde Grossman, Doug Hamilton, Doug Jarvis, Michael Kay, Sara MacDwyer, Georgianna Marie, Jonathan Maslow, Steve McElfresh, Bob Schwartz, Sita and Jamie Sherman, Mike Smith, and my dear friend, and our dharma brother, John Bright, recently deceased and so sorely missed.

Another important source of support over these years was First Tuesday, a (mostly) monthly gathering of business people, hosted by the Clausen Law Group and Mechanics Bank, in Point Richmond, California. For 13 years I gave the end-of-season talk with the aim of giving folks something to think about over the summer hiatus. The time spent preparing and delivering the talks turned out to be extremely valuable to me—probably a good deal more so than the benefits the audience and sponsors got from the talks.

As the bibliography of this book might indicate, my self-study of psychology, neurobiology, and biology of behavior has been extensive. I am neither a scholar nor a scientist. Consequently, before undertaking this work I had no knowledge or appreciation of researchers in this field or others.

We do indeed stand on the shoulders of giants. As a lay-person I have been awe-struck by the diligence and devotion of the scientists who spend their lives trying to understand our bodies, minds, and behavior. A few citations here and there, a few listings in a bibliography, don't begin to convey how vast the body of research performed by scientists is, nor its importance. To mention one or many contributors to the research in these fields is to slight hundreds more. Nevertheless, with apology to those I won't list here, I want to mention the researchers whose work most influenced me: John Bargh, Roy Baumeister, Antonio Damasio, Richard Davidson, Paul Ekman, Michael Gazzaniga, Daniel Kahneman, Joseph LeDoux, Marsha Linehan, Steven Pinker, Martin Seligman, and Robert Zajonc.

Then there are the writers and teachers who transmit and explain the work of others. Their writings are essential to making the work of scientists accessible, and give the public a way to touch the mysteries they teach and write about. The work of two in particular were most helpful. Daniel Goleman writes much about the mind. He's deservedly famous for describing emotional intelligence. But he's written much more of benefit. Especially important for me are his books about and written in conjunction with His Holiness, the Dalai Lama, and the Mind and Life Institute.

I am especially indebted to Robert Sapolsky at Stanford University. He is not cited frequently in Act from Choice, but his teachings have profoundly influenced my thinking about how and why we behave the way we do. A much-honored research scientist and teacher, Sapolsky's teachings on just about anything are illuminating, accessible, and captivating. He, perhaps better than anyone else, describes the constellation of factors that influence human behavior, daring us to oversimplify and thus hide the complexity of the interactions among those factors that shape what we do. I can recommend anything he presents, sight unseen. I recommend especially his 25-lecture series on Human Behavioral Biology, available on YouTube. com (http://tinyurl.com/Sapolsky-HB-lectures). Particularly helpful to me early in my literature studies were two series of Sapolsky lectures offered by The Teaching Company: Biology and Human Behavior: The Neurological Origins of Individuality, 2nd Edition, and Being Human" Life Lessons from the Frontiers of Science.

With it all, closer to my heart than the scientists and the reporters and teachers of science are the spiritual teachers, such as those listed in the Dedication that begins this book: Pema Chödrön, Stephen and Ondrea Levine, John Kabat-Zinn, and my principal teacher, Tsoknyi Rinpoche.

Ani Pema appears in numerous places in the book. Her manner, her devotion to teaching and to her own spiritual development in the spirit of the Indian mahasiddha, Atisha, stand as models of compassion, effort, and sanity for me and thousands more.

Pema's teachings have been very important to me. Her teachings on *shenpa*, were one of the main stimuli for my work leading to this book. *Shenpa* is the experience of being caught up in emotions that are unwanted and lead to behavior contrary to one's values and intentions (my interpretation of *shenpa*, not necessarily hers). Looking at myself in the mirror, and at my dharma brothers and sisters, it was obvious that while we have the necessary training and are well practiced in mindfulness, we are not as proficient at managing ourselves—our *shenpa*—as one would hope or imagine.

Daniel Goleman's book Emotional Intelligence made the point that self-awareness is essential to emotional intelligence. Pema's teachings on *shenpa* and Goleman's observations set me on the path of trying to find methods to target mindfulness to wake us to specific unwanted habitual patterns—our *shenpa*—earlier in their arising, before the damage is done.

For those not already familiar with the work of Stephen and Ondrea Levine's work, know that they have spent their lives tending to the needs of the dying. No less have they taught for the benefit of the rest of us who, thankfully, have yet to arrive that state, but certainly will and be better off for their teachings. They demonstrated mercy, compassion and unselfish devotion to relieving the suffering of others, always putting us ahead of themselves spiritually, physically and materially. Their constant refrain, "Have mercy," will continue to be with us. If only we would not forget.

I suspect that if we had a way to keep score it would be obvious that the mindfulness movement sweeping the US was sparked to a great extent by Jon Kabat-Zinn, beginning with the creation of the entirely secular Mindfulness Based Stress Reduction (MBSR) program he developed at the University of Massachusetts Medical School, albeit with the help of many others including, most particularly, Sakti Santorelli.

I am a huge fan of the MBSR program and recommend it to everyone I meet who is interested in learning more about mindfulness. The scientific evidence is clear that people who take the eight_week program experience lasting benefits. Jon is tireless in his promotion of mindfulness and is free of dogma. He is generous in his encouragement of all who want to transmit the benefits of mindfulness training.

Tsoknyi Rinpoche is my teacher. In the Tibetan tradition, the student-teacher relationship is a special one that needs no elaboration here. But in addition to that, we who know of his work find particularly remarkable the scope and number of Rinpoche's projects. In addition to maintaining a nearly continuous schedule of teachings in North and South America, Europe, and Asia, he started and maintains numerous monastic centers in Asia. Especially noteworthy is his work to bring modern education and the highest, most advanced Buddhist training and practices to women and girls. These few words don't begin to describe the number, breadth and importance of his projects. Rinpoche undertakes all of this with an energy, effectiveness and modesty of style devoid of ostentation, that is remarkable and humbling to witness. (You can find out more about Rinpoche's projects at www.tsoknyirinpoche.org. To learn more about his work with nuns in Nepal and Tibet, see www.tsoknyine-palnuns.org and watch http://tinyurl.com/TsoknyiNuns on YouTube.)

My appreciation of heroes like these, my attempts at developing myself, and working with others were spurred by two transformational experiences. The first of these was the privilege of being a volunteer facilitator at the Center for Attitudinal Healing in Marin County. The center was founded by Jerry Jampolsky, author of the bestselling *Love Is Letting Go of Fear*. From its founding, the center was well known for its work with children with life-threatening illnesses—cancer mostly—and with their parents. It served people who were in many trying situations of other sorts, who came to the Center, mostly weekly, to share their experience and caring with others having similar challenges. I volunteered there as a facilitator of groups of caregivers. We didn't really know anything, except how to be quiet, listen, and to help others speak and learn from each other. It might have seemed a little too new-agey for some, but those who came and stayed were helped and grateful. We, the facilitators, were helped even more than they, because of what participants taught us as we tried to be with them in a non-judgmental way, sharing our own experiences too, and trying hard to accept that we knew nothing. As with other of my experiences, I'm reluctant to mention the names of any who were part of the volunteer staff because my memory is so selective. Nevertheless I do want to mention, with gratitude, Janet Rostad, my co-facilitator for most of my time at the center.

The second of the transformational experiences in time, but first in importance, was my introduction to Buddhism, which started when I was introduced to Shambhala Training and Vajradhatu International in 1992. The founder, Chögyam Trungpa, had passed on in 1987; his successor, the Vajra Regent Ösel Tendzin had passed in 1992, causing much turmoil.

The teachings I received then and since have changed me. But it is not those I mean to praise here; everyone rightly thinks the spiritual traditions they have adopted are precious and sacred. I wish to praise instead those students of Rinpoche who worked so hard, so diligently, and with such impressive devotion to their teacher to preserve the teachings and make them available to all comers. It is to them, no less than the teachings, to whom I offer my profound gratitude.

Mostly volunteers, they served with energy and commitment, which was apparent in Halifax, Nova Scotia, the seat of what was then Vajradhatu, but more importantly at centers throughout North and South America, Europe and Asia; old-dogs, we called them. They took me in in San Francisco, Berkeley and other practice centers and offered me everything I could learn. It was a display of great generosity for which I will be forever grateful. Though for reasons entirely personal I am no longer associated with the successor organization, Shambhala International, I maintain my affection and esteem for those who helped me and others so much, and continue to do so.

If you've never tried to get a book to market you may not know how much help authors need to get their words to the published page. Ingrid Emerick of Girl Friday Productions was my first advocate and did the original developmental edit, in the process teaching me more about writing than I thought I needed to learn. Angie Kiesling of The Editorial Attic took up the editing chores and was extremely helpful in arranging and coordinating other aspects of the book's completion and publication.

The book cover is the work of Mary Schuck, a genius of design. It is based on a photo recommended and supplied by Sita Sherman, a good friend. Interior design and typesetting is the work of Pamela Trush of Delaney-Designs, a professional of extraordinary patience. Illustrations were made by the indefatigable Nick Heitzman. Nancy Kopper did the index. (How do they do that?) Champion Fleming, of Champion Designs, designed the Act from Choice website, and Anita Goodman of AgoodgirlDesign, a true partner in creation, contributed crucial designs and support for both book and website. Julie Mikos made the picture of me.

NOTES

(Endnotes)

1   From an interview with Dave Iverson on the radio program "Forum," broadcast on KQED-FM, San Francisco, October 29, 2010.

2   Freudians might think of separate subconscious forces as similar to the interactions of Freud's ego, superego, and id; Buddhists could see in this a reference to the five skandhas; and some others might see this as a reference to the devil or other dark forces.

3   The subconscious functions of the brain are very extensive, of course. In this book, I deal only with the functions involved with producing reactions to what is going on in the immediate environment, including attempts to carry out our intentions.

4   For more on how we acquire those habitual reactive impulses very early in life, even before we have language, see Goleman (2006). Chapter 11 of this book describes how we acquire our unique reactions.

5   See in particular Bornstein & Pittman (1992), a collection of essays about Perception Without Awareness, which is the title of the book. Many other journal articles in the bibliography describe this phenomenon—for example, papers by Robert Zajonc and John Bargh, discussed in Chapter 7.

6   Witness some of the debate in Baer (2008), Rigoni (2012), Sarot (2013), and Harris (2012).

7   Free will and free won't are prosocial values; the maintenance of civilized society requires us to believe in the personal responsibility inherent in the idea of both, but in free will in particular. Still, it's likely that conscious choices that lead us to want to do something different from our habitual reactions are influenced by similar unconsciously acquired causes and conditions in the same way that automatic ones are. In that case, one could argue that there isn't free won't either. But our values, preferences, and personalities do indeed change with time, making it likely that the current ones are based on conscious judgment to some degree, and if not that, at least on more recent experience. So, if there isn't free won't, maybe there's sorta free won't. In any case, it's important that we take responsibility for what we do, and that requires us to accept that we have choice and are responsible to ourselves and others. The alternative is societal chaos.

8   See, for example, Sapolsky (2010) and Wang (2010).

9   Chadwick (2001).

10   Simon, Paul, "Crazy Love, Volume II" (1986).

11   Remarks at a meeting of Operation PUSH in Chicago (27 November 1993). Quoted in "Crime: New Frontier - Jesse Jackson Calls It Top Civil-Rights Issue" by Mary A. Johnson, 29 November 1993, Chicago Sun-Times. Partially quoted in "In America: A Sea Change On Crime" by Bob Herbert, 12 December 1993, New York Times. The rest of the quote, which to me seems off the main point, is "...after all we have been through, just to think we can't walk down our own streets, how humiliating." This information sourced from https://en.wikiquote.org/wiki/Jesse_Jackson

12   Maureen Dowd quoting Patty Stonesifer, CEO of the Bill and Melinda Gates Foundation, recalling a conversation with Nelson Mandela. "She's Getting Her Boots Dirty," 2 June 2013, New York Times, Sunday Review section.

13   Tskonyi (2012), Chapter 1.

14 See Table 3.

15 Bushman (2002).

16 While the philosophy of the Serenity Prayer appears reflected in the ancient texts of many traditions, the modern version is attributed to the Protestant theologian Reinhold Niebuhr. It has been adopted by many groups, most particularly by Alcoholics Anonymous. I understand it's quite all right to start the prayer at "Grant," if you prefer.

17 Some claim this to be a Cherokee saying: "...hate wears you down, and does not hurt your enemy. It is like taking poison and wishing your enemy would die." Source: http://www.firstpeople.us/FP-Html-Legends/TwoWolves-Cherokee.html, accessed 5-23-2016.

18 "Philosophy in Psychotherapy" with Albert Ellis, Ph.D. Transcript of an interview with Dr. Ellis conducted by Dr. Jeffrey Mishlove, in the series Thinking Allowed. Conversations on the Leading Edge of Knowledge and Discovery. Retrieved from www.intuition.org/txt/ellis.htm.

19 Baumeister (1996).

20 Goleman (2006).

21 The idea for using the Apostle Paul in this way came from seeing how John Bargh used him in virtually the same way (Bargh 2008A in Baer 2008).

22 Romans 7:18-19, New International Version, obtained at http://www.biblegateway.com/passage/?search=Romans+7&version=NIV> accessed July 25, 2013.

23 Sapolsky (2010).

24 Baruchin (2011).

25 Interviewed by Barkha Dutt on NDTV, updated July 6, 2010, obtained at http://www.ndtv.com/article/india/in-conversation-with-the-dalai-lama-35955> accessed July 27, 2013 (URL now expired)

26 Time Magazine interviewed His Holiness in May 2010 for an interview titled "10 Questions for the Dalai Lama," retrieved from <http://www.dalailama.com/messages/transcripts/10-questions-time-magazine> July 27, 2013.

27 From the ABC News show Beliefs that aired April 18, 2011, retrieved from http://abcnews.go.com/GMA/video/dalai-lama-angry-13400561, July 27, 2013.

28 Damasio (1994).

29 Bornstein (1992).

30 LeDoux (1996).

31 Principally the hypothalamus, which controls actions of the autonomic nervous system, as described in Chapter 10.

32 Schachter (1962); Sapolsky (2012).

33 I owe this example to Pema Chödrön. She uses scabies for her itch.

34 Remarks delivered at the end of a traditional Tibetan Buddhist three-year retreat at Kyogle, Australia, April 2008, quoted in Dick (2008).

35 See Table 3, which describes the triggers for seven basic emotions, including a description of the results the emotions are trying to achieve. See also Linehan (2014), 328.

36 Viktor E. Frankl. BrainyQuote.com, Xplore Inc., 2015. http://www.brainyquote.com/quotes/quotes/v/viktorefr160380.html, accessed December 20, 2015.

37 An important purpose of mindfulness training is learning to place attention where you want and keeping it there. See the exercises at the end of Chapter 6.

38 The most concise description I've found of how attention is directed is ". . . attention is not 'deployed' but rather is an ongoing competition among information processing hierarchies vying for access to working memory" (Knudsen, 2007, 73.) He continues, "Top-down bias signals can selectively enhance representations of certain information so that the information continues to have a high probability of gaining entry into working memory." "Top-down" signals are those that come from competition among brain structures arguing about what has the greatest priority for the organism—that's us. External stimuli are called "bottom-up" signals; they compete with top-down signals and among themselves. Working memory contains the information we're conscious of. As long as we're conscious of something, paying attention or not, it's in working memory. When something is outside of working memory, it's not available to consciousness unless and until something causes the brain to put it in working memory.

39 Erik's flash of anger is an example of the so-called "refractory period" that appears at the very beginning of strong emotions, as proposed by Ekman (2008). See Chapter 20.

40 Retreat at Spirit Rock, April 12, 2008.

41 Found at http://www.shareguide.com/Goleman.html.

42 The reaction is thought to be an "emotional conflict due to the suppression of the honest response." It is associated with activation of the dorsolateral prefrontal cortex, the anterior cingulate cortex, and the amygdala (Baumgartner, 2009).

43 Maslow's need hierarchy is a theory that humans attend to their needs in a hierarchical fashion. In other words, we do not address higher-ranking needs until lower-ranking needs are satisfied. Membership needs—that is, belonging and social acceptance—rank third, just after physiological and security needs. Ego satisfaction and self-actualization needs are above membership needs in the hierarchy, which is to say that we tend to ignore our ego and self-actualization needs until our membership needs are satisfied. How much it takes to satisfy each level of needs is highly individual. For some, membership needs seem to be insatiable. If you wonder how significant membership needs are for some, consider how much time they devote to their social media accounts.

44 Linehan (2014), 328.

45 The definition of limbic system is controversial and varies among writers. Some question whether the term has any validity at all. I'm referring to the functions performed in perceiving and responding to threats and opportunities, and instigating emotional action programs. Robert Sapolsky and others include the frontal cortex when talking about the limbic system. There's good reason for that position. I don't include it because I am focused on managing the competition between Intentional Mind and Reactive Brain. The brain structures that support Intentional Mind are predominantly in the prefrontal cortex and are crucially involved in willpower and intention formation, while the rest of the limbic system is more reactive and habitual. I find it useful to talk about the frontal cortex as separate from the rest of the limbic system so one can focus on the opposing forces rather than bury them within a single structure.

46 This example is from Sapolsky (2005A).

47 On a personal note, I'm somewhat concerned that persistence (willpower sustained over time) is often described as a mark of character, and diminished persistence or weakened willpower a lack of it. Surely more important for determining character are the characteristics of the goal that is persistently pursued. Any number of persistent monsters come easily to mind—Hitler, Pol Pot, and Stalin, for example—never mind your local

serial killer and bank robbers.

48   An excellent summary of Baumeister's work, written for the general public, is Baumeister (2011). Though older, and somewhat less up to date, a more detailed and analytical presentation source is Baumeister (1994). In addition to the Baumeister listings in the bibliography, you might want to check out works by Muraven and Tice, his frequent collaborators, and works by Brass, Duckworth, Dweck, Filevich, Kuhn, Ochsner, Rigoni, Roberts, and Walsh, also listed in the bibliography.

49   The first widely reported case connecting brain (prefrontal cortex) damage to specific behavioral changes is the case of Phineas Gage, a miner working in California in 1848. An explosion propelled a steel rod through Gage's skull, entering his cheek and exiting through the top of his head, taking out most of his left prefrontal cortex. Prior to the accident he had been diligent, well spoken, hardworking, and respected, but afterward he was, according to his doctor, "fitful, irreverent, and grossly profane, showing little deference for his fellows." These changes in personality were attributed entirely to the loss of brain tissue. There are many places one can read about Gage. He's mentioned in Damasio (1994) and Davidson (2012) and in many other places describing neurophysiology of behavior. The most complete and authoritative source of information about Gage is probably Macmillan (2012).

50   Research done by Carol Dweck (2006, 2008) at Stanford University and Angela Duckworth (2016) at the University of Pennsylvania shows that several factors beyond exercising willpower, particularly motivation and belief, can make it stronger. In my opinion, while these findings are important in showing how baseline willpower can be increased, they do not change the fact that at any moment, the amount of willpower is limited and subject to reduction from baseline caused by recent use.

51   From Stephen Levine workshops given in San Francisco in the late 1980s or early 1990s.

52   I owe this concept to Pema Chödrön and her principal teacher, Dzigar Kongtrul Rinpoche. See *Realizing Guiltlessness, Tricycle*, Winter 2004, also available at http://www. tricycle.com/dharma-talk/realizing-guiltlessness See the bibliography listing as *Tricycle* Magazine Editors.

53   Linehan (2014), 328.

54   Dweck (2006 and 2008).

55   Duckworth (2016).

56   As I understand the work of Dweck and Duckworth, the focus is on long-term persistence. Their work is not meant to address management of impulses as discussed in this book. Nevertheless, the conditions that develop Duckworth's "Grit" or Dweck's equivalent—specifically commitment, practice, and values-based motivation—are also critical in creating the motivation that is essential for success in self-management. The techniques for marshalling those qualities are presented in the description of the Act from Choice Method presented in Part II.

57   Prochaska (1992), 1104-5.

58   In Goleman (1984), Emmanuel Donchin, director of the Laboratory for Cognitive Psychophysiology at the University of Illinois, is quoted as saying, "An enormous portion of cognitive activity is nonconscious. Figuratively speaking, it could be 99 percent; we probably will never know precisely how much is outside awareness." George Lakoff, cognitive scientist, linguistics professor, and co-director of the neural computation laboratory at the University of California, Berkeley, says, "Most thought is unconscious; only 2 percent is conscious." Source: Philosophy Talk, a radio program broadcast May 14,

2013, on KALW-FM.

59 Purves (2001).

60 What follows is a description of the creative process as taught by Robert S. Hartman in a course on Value Theory at MIT, 1955-1956.

61 See Zajonc (1980) for theories and evidence about how Brain develops preferences about things it encounters before we know they're there; see also LeDoux (1996) for a short history of the development of interest in emotions by the psychology community.

62 This experiment is a variation of one taught by Reginald A. Ray at the 2002-2003 Winter Dathun (retreat) held at Shambhala Mountain Center.

63 I learned this technique from B. Alan Wallace at a weeklong seminar in April 2009.

64 Bargh (2008).

65 Depending on which Web-based pronunciation guide you consult.

66 Zajonc (1980), 151 and 31.

67 Zajonc (2000) in Forgas (2001), Chapter 2, p. 31.

68 Damasio (1994).

69 This quote and the list that follows of ways we might develop preferences are from Zajonc (2001), 224.

70 Zajonc (1968).

71 A number of sources led me to the priming examples in this chapter, in particular Kahneman (2011) and numerous papers by Joseph Bargh. I've read most of the sources Kahneman cited and have included some of them in the notes and bibliography.

72 Bargh (1996).

73 Many philosophers and psychologists seem fascinated by the Trolley Experiment. You can find books and papers describing it from every possible angle. For example, see Cathcart (2013) and Kamm (2015).

74 This and preceding variation and data from DeSteno (2011).

75 Shu (2012).

76 Kahneman's citation is to Bateson (2006).

77 Steele (1995).

78 Vohs (2006).

79 Zhou (2009).

80 Kahneman (2011), 55-56.

81 Solomon (2015). If you have any concerns about your own reactions to world events that make you feel afraid, this is the book to read, as are many of the individual papers on this subject.

82 Arndt (2002).

83 Landau (2004).

84 Greenberg (1990).

85 Pyszczynski (2006).

86   Rosenblatt (1989).

87   Ibid.

88   Ibid.

89   Schimel (1999).

90   Ibid.

91   Landau (2004). WTC is the abbreviation for World Trade Center.

92   Ibid.

93   Greenberg (1990); Harmon-Jones (1997).

94   Tversky died before the Nobel was awarded, and it is never awarded posthumously. Kahneman is clear that Tversky, had he lived, was more than deserving of sharing the prize.

95   Ariely (2009).

96   Kahneman (2011), 56-57.

97   Bargh (1992).

98   Kahneman (2011).

99   Example and comments based on Kahneman (2011), 73.

100   Kahneman (2011).

101   Of course, biases are also unwanted habits, except that they can't be unwanted when we're not aware that we have them.

102   To reiterate, "emotional action program" is terminology coined by Antonio Damasio (1994).

103   I take full responsibility for any misunderstanding of Kahneman's work and any other faults arising from equating System 1 and System 2 with Brain and Mind, respectively, in the context I'm writing about.

104   Kahneman (2011), 73.

105   Kahneman (2011), 24.

106   This and the following example are based on Kahneman (2011).

107   Kahneman (2011), 25.

108   Ibid., 21.

109   Ibid., 90.

110   Ibid., 25.

111   Frederick (2005). The test consists of three problems. The third problem (actually second in the order given in the test) is, "If it takes 5 machines 5 minutes to make 5 widgets, how long would it take 100 machines to make 100 widgets?" The intuitive answer is 100 minutes. The actual answer is 5 minutes, because it takes one machine 5 minutes to make one widget.

112   Kahneman (2011), 45. Kahneman had access to and quotes detail not in Frederick (2005).

113   Frederick (2005), Table 1, 29; the median number of correct answers was 1.25 out of 3.

114 Ibid.

115 Sorry, Subaru owners. I don't mean to pick on you. Subarus may be fine cars, but love does not adequately describe any car's relative value, performance, or quality compared to other makers' offerings.

116 Listing is titled "Cognitive Biases."

117 The Sutra of the Heart of Transcendent Knowledge, translated by the Nalanda Translation Committee.

118 Pratchett (2010), 48-49.

119 An excellent summary of the evolution of research on emotions and the brain is the introductory portion of Joseph LeDoux's groundbreaking book *The Emotional Brain* (1996), about his discoveries concerning the role of the amygdala.

120 Damasio (1994).

121 Ibid., Chapter 3, "A Modern Phineas Gage," summarizes stories of Elliot, an otherwise unidentified patient, which follow. Quoted material is from the same source.

122 Damasio (1994), 192-194.

123 This is an example of a misdirected habit rather than a misguided one. The panic is for good cause. Its purpose is to get you out of a dangerous situation; hence, it is a well-guided habit. But the impulse to steer away from the skid is exactly the wrong thing to do, so it is misdirected.

124 Zajonc (1980), 156, paraphrased for readability and clarity. The original is, "Affective reactions are inescapable. Unlike judgments of objective stimulus properties, affective reactions that often accompany these judgments cannot always be voluntarily controlled. Most often, these experiences occur whether one wants them to or not. One might be able to control the expression of emotion but not the experience of it itself. It is for this very reason that law, science, sports, education, and other institutions of society keep devising ever new means of making judgments 'objective.' We wish some decisions to be more independent of these virtually inescapable reactions."

125 Gladwell (2007).

126 Sources for these numbers: Hollywood figures are my best recollection of research in this area I was privy to in the late 1980s. Presumably, the demand for DVDs, new television series, and foreign distribution has improved these returns since then. But still, monumental flops come out of Hollywood all the time. Studio executives asked about the possible benefits of pre-production research openly referred to their "golden guts," even in the face of their very low number of successful pictures compared to their flops.

127 Kahneman (2011), 213.

128 Lovallo (2003).

129 Sapolsky (2011).

130 See discussion and sources under Brain's Early Warning System, later in this chapter.

131 Goleman (1995), 291.

132 The first stop of visual signals is the superior colliculus, which is responsible for keeping track of things in the visual field and directing our gaze to them immediately when there's a sudden change. Some anatomists regard the superior colliculus as part of the thalamus.

133 Part of the processing of sensory data is actually done in nuclei generally considered to be in the thalamus, the pretectum which adjusts the pupils, and the superior colliculus, which maps the location of stimuli and directs the eyes toward quickly moving objects, among other functions. There are two superior colliculi, one for each brain hemisphere. Some anatomists have them as a separate structure.

134 Sensory processing is complex and not fully understood. For a simple description of visual processing, see http://tinyurl.com/HowSight, which will take you to a BrainHQ page on the Posit Sciences website. See also Li (2002), Schmolesky (2007), Thorpe (1996), and Vanrullen (2001) for sight, Shepherd (2005) for smell (olfaction).

135 Emotional processes involve many brain structures in addition to the amygdala. For example, the insula, another structure in the limbic system, is heavily involved in the emotion of disgust, along with the brain stem.

136 LeDoux (1996) describes his discovery of the short, fast path from the thalamus to the amygdala. Sapolsky (2012) names LeDoux as its discoverer.

137 Quotes in this paragraph and discussion of the connections between sensory information and the amygdala and its nuclei are from LeDoux (2008).

138 Sapolsky (2005). As mentioned earlier, Sapolsky includes the prefrontal cortex in the limbic system.

139 James (1890), 449.

140 Nummenmaa (2014).

141 Ekman (1993).

142 Kahneman (2011), and many others.

143 The prefrontal cortex's connection to the amygdala that's referred to here is to its central nucleus. This interaction among the prefrontal cortex, amygdala, its central nucleus, and the hypothalamus is described in most of the LeDoux papers listed in the bibliography.

144 According to LeDoux (2003), information from higher centers farther along in the processing of sensory data also project to the lateral nucleus of the amygdala. That sensory data is more complete than what the amygdala gets from the thalamus, but arrives later than data from the thalamus.

145 LeDoux (1996), 63.

146 Damasio (1994), 179.

147 The table is based on Barondes (2011), an excellent guide if you'd like to pursue this subject further.

148 Davidson (2012).

149 This table is based on material in Davidson (2012).

150 According to Davidson and Begley, the right hemisphere of our brain is more stable (Davidson, 2012). Therefore, to be more open, we must work on making the left hemisphere stronger.

151 Barondes (2011).

152 Davidson (2012).

153 Barondes (2011), Davidson (2012), Pinker (2003), and Sapolsky Stanford lectures.

Notes

154 The factual assertions in this paragraph are supported by numerous scientific papers. Pinker (2003) does an excellent job of bringing together the arguments for and against.

155 Davidson (2012).

156 Sapolsky (2010) and Wang (2010), among others.

157 Pinker (2003).

158 Pinker (2003), 34-5.

159 You can read more about the twins Oskar Stohr and Jack Yufe in numerous articles online, in particular Grimes (2015).

160 Pinker (2003), 47.

161 For information about patterns of change in personality, values, and preferences, see Quoidbach (2013) and Barondes (2011).

162 The factual statements in this section are based on many sources, but Pinker (2003) in particular.

163 Damasio (1996), 117. Damasio uses the term organism instead of brain.

164 LeDoux (1996), 267. If you have difficulty crediting evolution, think genetics.

165 Damasio (1994) calls the reaction to a learned association (a bear is a predator and thus to be feared) a secondary emotion. I use "secondary emotion" to refer to an emotion triggered by a more basic one, as in "misdirected habits."

166 Ekman (1971, 1969). Experiments took place in the US, Japan, Brazil, Argentina, Chile, and in two locations in New Guinea.

167 Paul Ekman defines an emotion as "a bio-psycho-social reaction to events that have immediate consequences for our welfare."

168 If you're interested in the psychology of positive emotions, you can learn more from the International Positive Psychology Association (www.ippanetwork.org).

169 Table 3 is based on the workbook and presentations made by Paul Ekman Group for the Emotional Awareness Workshop, San Francisco, October 18, 2008, and Ekman (2008A).

170 Heard during retreats conducted by Ani Pema, probably in the late 1990s.

171 Damasio (1994).

172 Norden (2007), Sapolsky (2005A), among many others.

173 Sapolsky (2005A).

174 Medline Plus Editors, Post-traumatic stress disorder, accessed at https://medlineplus.gov/ency/article/000925.htm, March 15, 2016.

175 Editors, Encyclopedia of Mental Disorders, Post-traumatic stress disorder, accessed at http://www.minddisorders.com/Ob-Ps/Post-traumatic-stress-disorder.html, March 15, 2016.

176 Chödrön (2002). "Nonaggression and the Four Maras" is the chapter title.

177 From an interview with Terry Gross on "Fresh Air" in 2001, rebroadcast on May 12, 2008.

178 Quoidbach (2013).

179 Remarks about the durability of conditioned reactions and mechanisms and limitations of extinction are supported by research reported in Quirk (2006 and 2008) and Sotres-Bayon (2004 and 2006).

180 Bouton (2006).

181 Quoidbach (2013).

182 Barondes (2011).

183 Chödrön (2007), 34.

184 Barondes (2011).

185 Ibid.

186 Tsoknyi (2012).

187 Ani is an honorific used with Buddhist nuns, much like Sister is used with Catholic nuns.

188 Bushman (2002).

189 Source unknown.

190 Quoidbach (2013).

191 For simplicity's sake, I've couched this chapter in terms of detecting the *impulse* rather than the stimulus. It's even better if you can teach your unconscious awareness to detect the stimulus and thus act faster than waiting for the impulse to appear. However, that requires that the stimulus is unique and can be anticipated, for example, if you want to be on guard when someone specific is around.

192 I developed the Sentinel technique over ten years ago to give my clients (and me) a tool for catching unwanted impulses early in their development. Though original to this book, I believe the idea was inspired in me by thinking about the words "mind protection," and Protectors and Protector Principle, concepts present in Tibetan Buddhist practice and teachings.

193 I learned this technique from a memory improvement course many years ago. The specific reference is lost (poor memory!). Search the Web for "memory trick, visualization" and you'll find a long list of sites with information about using visualization as a way to memorize very long lists of unrelated objects. This example is not the same technique as remembering long lists of unrelated things, as in the Memory Palace technique. The example I use brings the memory to consciousness even when you're not trying to remember. There are many books with Memory Palace in the title that aim to teach the technique. The website http://www.mostlymaths.net/2011/03/learn-to-remember-everything-memory.html claims the technique came about in the fifth century BCE. It has easy-to-understand examples and instructions.

194 Linehan (2014), 328.

195 The research findings are that memories themselves can actually be changed and distorted by repetition because they're rewritten every time we access them. But that is a different matter than what is meant here. This training is more like "reminding" the Sentinel what happened.

196 Bouton (2006), Ji (2007), Quirk (2006, 2008), Rauch (2006), Sotres-Bayon (2004, 2006).

197 My motivation for presenting these slogans comes from the use of lojong slogans, an important practice in Tibetan Buddhism.

Notes

198   I owe "privacy of your own mind" to Charlotte Linde, an especially gifted Buddhist teacher.

199   Ekman (2008, 2008A, 2007). The term "refractory period" as used to describe a period of male impotence after a sexual experience is unrelated to the emotional refractory period that Ekman describes.

200   Davidson (2012).

201   Figure 10 is based on Ekman (2008A).

202   Sapolsky (2012).

203   Sapolsky (2012) states that the recovery rate from strong emotions is typically slower for women than for men.

204   The quote is from remarks Linehan made at a workshop that took place in San Francisco, March 2010, titled "Dialectical Behavior Therapy: Updates to Emotion Regulation and Crisis Survival Skills." At the time of this writing, DBT is the only therapy shown to be effective for Borderline Personality Disorder, a mental disorder characterized by extreme emotional variability. Prior to the development of DBT, there was no therapy shown to be effective in helping people with this disorder. Even today, many therapists are unable or unwilling to work with patients who have it.

205   Levine (2010), 89.

206   Some in the coaching community label the failure to address things like the paper on the floor "tolerations." Tolerations are anything you think you should take care of but haven't. They include things like changing the burned-out lightbulb at the bottom of the cellar stairs, tightening the loose knob on the silverware drawer, and being without a will, estate plan, and current résumé.

207   I disclose any financial or other interest I have in you doing what I recommend. If there's no such disclosure, I have no such financial or other interest in what you do with the suggestion, as is the case with FollowUpThen.com.

208   Max's observation that his reactions come from the way he was brought up is useful but not decisive. As mentioned previously, looking for the cause of one's habit can be a diversion from getting at managing it right away. If you want to go searching for the underlying cause, with or without professional help, that's okay. Just don't wait to complete your search before starting to work on managing the habit.

209   The term self-adequacy is shorthand for the idea that one is able, equipped, and can fully participate as a normally endowed human being. Self-esteem is often interpreted to mean that one is better than something or someone. Self-adequacy means that one is more than enough than is needed to meet any situation. See Barasch (2005).

210   McGraw-Hill (2012).

211   Second Edition, Puddle Press, Encinitas, CA, 2003.

212   See Seligman (2005). This study reported that people who recorded daily for only one week "three good things" that happened each day had increased levels of happiness even six months later. On the other hand, people who were asked to write and deliver a letter of gratitude to someone who helped them had an initial increase in happiness that lasted only one month. Clearly, the impacts varied depending on what type of gratitude expression was tested, and the way it was expressed—to oneself as receiver or to the giver.

213   McLeod (2001), 251.

214   Chadwick (2001).

215   Damasio (1994), 175.

216   An instruction from Pema Chödrön.

217   Patterson (2011).

218   Rosenberg (2015).

219   My approach to guilt and shame is a synthesis of several approaches, these in particular. The definitions of shame and guilt and the approach I use to figure out which is which, and which emotional factors need to be addressed, come from Marsha Linehan's approach to guilt and shame as part of Dialectical Behavior Therapy (Linehan, 2009). The role play exercise is my own but is based on Reggie Ray's teachings that holding oneself to standards higher than one would judge others by is arrogance or self-aggression. Asking people to choose regret not guilt comes from an article by Pema Chödrön and her principal teacher, Dzigar Kontrol, Rinpoche (*Tricycle* magazine editors, 2004).

220   Levine (1987), 23. Page numbers for this endnote and the next are from the 2010 edition.

221   Ibid., 89.

222   Many, though not all, of the thoughts expressed here are reflections of the work of Martin E.P. Seligman, particularly his *Authentic Happiness* (Seligman, 2004). I believe that Seligman is the prime instigator of the Positive Psychology movement, a founder of the International Positive Psychology Association, of which I am an associate member. In *Authentic Happiness* Seligman lays out a remarkably clear and comprehensive structure for understanding different forms of happiness, from simple pleasures to those that are more fulfilling, from happiness about the past to happiness about the future. I cannot recommend the book highly enough.

223   Cynthia Kneen is a longtime student of Chögyam Trungpa, Rinpoche, and many other eminent teachers. She is the author of the audio book *Shambhala Warrior Training* and the prize-winning book *Awake Mind, Open Heart: The Power of Courage and Dignity in Everyday Life*. This slogan came from a teaching she gave at a Level 5, Shambhala Training weekend in Berkeley, California, sometime during the late 1990s.

224   From the Sutra of the Heart of Transcendent Knowledge (The Prajnaparamita Sutra) translated by the Nalanda Translation Committee.

225   This definition is similar to the definition of "mindfulness" used by Jon Kabat-Zinn, the founder of Mindfulness Based Stress Reduction (MBSR), which is that mindfulness is "paying attention on purpose, in the present moment, and non-judgmentally, to the unfolding of experience moment to moment." I support and am a fan of the MBSR program. Self-awareness is best when accompanied by non-judgment and an open Mind, but the term self-awareness does not imply any specific attitude one has about what is seen.

226   This practice is based on one introduced by Reggie Ray at the 2002-3 Winter Dathun held at Shambhala Mountain Center that I was privileged to staff. Ray identifies this feeling in the body I'm referring to as "The blood of ego," which is mentioned in a Tibetan Buddhist chant.

BIBLIOGRAPHY

The sources noted below provided the research findings, integrative perspectives, and provocative speculations on which much of this book is based. Whether or not they are cited herein, they are all invaluable resources for me—and might be for you as well. If you want to delve more deeply into topics discussed in this book, a scan of the titles below may lead you on fascinating journeys and amazing discoveries, as they did me.

Aamondt, S, and Sam Wang. "Welcome to Your Brain: Why You Lose Your Car Keys but Never Forget How to Drive and Other Puzzles of Everyday Life." NY: Bloomsbury, 2008.

Ajzen, Icek. "Behavioral Interventions Based on the Theory of Planned Behavior." (2006). https://www.researchgate.net/publication/245582784_Behavioral_Interventions_Based_on_the_Theory_of_Planned_Behavior.

———. "From Intentions to Actions: A Theory of Planned Behavior." In *Action Control*, 11-39: Springer, 1985.

———. "Nature and Operation of Attitudes." *Annual Review of Psychology* 52, no. 1 (2001): 27-58.

Alford, John R, Carolyn L Funk, and John R Hibbing. "Are Political Orientations Genetically Transmitted?" *American Political Science Review* 99, no. 02 (2005): 153-67.

Allman, John M, Atiya Hakeem, Joseph M Erwin, Esther Nimchinsky, and Patrick Hof. "The Anterior Cingulate Cortex." *Annals of the New York Academy of Sciences* 935, no. 1 (2001): 107-17.

Ariely, D. *Predictably Irrational Revised and Expanded Edition: The Hidden Forces That Shape Our Decisions.* New York, N.Y.: Harper Collins, 2009.

Armstrong, Karen. *Twelve Steps to a Compassionate Life.* Random House, 2011.

Arndt, Jamie, Jeff Greenberg, Jeff Schimel, Tom Pyszczynski, and Sheldon Solomon. "To Belong or Not to Belong, That Is the Question: Terror Management and Identification with Gender and Ethnicity." *Journal of Personality and Social Psychology* 83, no. 1 (2002): 26.

Arndt, Jamie, Sheldon Solomon, Tim Kasser, and Kennon M Sheldon. "The Urge to Splurge: A Terror Management Account of Materialism and Consumer Behavior." *Journal of Consumer Psychology* 14, no. 3 (2004): 198-212.

Arnold, Carrie. "Diss Information: Is There a Way to Stop Popular Falsehoods from Morphing into 'Facts'." *Scientific American (October 4, 2012)*, 2012.

Arnold, Magda B. *Emotion and Personality.* Vol. I, Psychological Aspects, New York: Columbia University Press, 1960.

Avila, Irene, and Shih-Chieh Lin. "Motivational Salience Signal in the Basal Forebrain Is Coupled with Faster and More Precise Decision Speed." *PLoS Biology* 12, no. 3 (2014)

Azrin, NH, and RG Nunn. "Habit-Reversal: A Method of Eliminating Nervous Habits and Tics." *Behavior Research and Therapy* 11, no. 4 (1973): 619-28.

Banaji, Mahzarin R, and Anthony G Greenwald. *Blindspot: Hidden Biases of Good People.* Delacorte Press, 2013.

Bandura, Albert. "Self-Efficacy Mechanism in Human Agency." *American Psychologist* 37, no. 2 (1982): 122.

———. "Self-Efficacy: Toward a Unifying Theory of Behavioral Change." *Psychological*

Review 84, no. 2 (1977): 191.

Bandura, Albert, and Karen M Simon. "The Role of Proximal Intentions in Self-Regulation of Refractory Behavior." *Cognitive Therapy and Research* 1, no. 3 (1977): 177-93.

Bao, A. M., G. Meynen, and D. F. Swaab. "The Stress System in Depression and Neurodegeneration: Focus on the Human Hypothalamus." *Brain Research Reviews* 57, no. 2 (Mar 2008): 531-53.

Barasch, Marc. *Field Notes on the Compassionate Life: A Search for the Soul of Kindness.* Rodale, 2005.

Bargh, J. A. "Being Unaware of the Stimulus Versus Unaware of Its Interpretation: Why Subliminality Per Se Does Not Matter to Social Psychology." In *Perception without Awareness*, edited by R. F. Bornstein and T. S. Pittman, 236-55: New York: Guilford Press, 1992.

Bargh, John A. "Free Will Is Un-Natural." Chap. 7 In *Are We Free?* 128-54, 2008.

Bargh, John A, and Tanya L Chartrand. "The Mind in the Middle." In *Handbook of Research Methods in Social and Personality Psychology*, 253-85, 2000.

———. "The Unbearable Automaticity of Being." *American Psychologist* 54, no. 7 (1999): 462.

Bargh, John A, Mark Chen, and Lara Burrows. "Automaticity of Social Behavior: Direct Effects of Trait Construct and Stereotype Activation on Action." *Journal of Personality and Social Psychology* 71, no. 2 (1996): 230.

Bargh, John A, Peter M Gollwitzer, Annette Lee-Chai, Kimberly Barndollar, and Roman Trötschel. "The Automated Will: Nonconscious Activation and Pursuit of Behavioral Goals." *Journal of Personality and Social Psychology* 81, no. 6 (2001): 1014.

Bargh, John A, and Ezequiel Morsella. "The Unconscious Mind." *Perspectives on Psychological Science* 3, no. 1 (2008): 73-79.

Barker, Jane E., and Yuko Munakata. "Time Isn't of the Essence: Activating Goals Rather Than Imposing Delays Improves Inhibitory Control in Children." *Psychological Science* (November 5, 2015).

Barkley, Russell A, and Paul J Lombroso. "Genetics of Childhood Disorders: Xvii. Adhd, Part 1: The Executive Functions and Adhd." *Journal of the American Academy of Child and Adolescent Psychiatry* 39, no. 8 (2000): 1064-68.

Barlow, David H, Laura B Allen, and Molly L Choate. "Toward a Unified Treatment for Emotional Disorders." *Behavior Therapy* 35, no. 2 (2004): 205-30.

Barnes, Jessica JM, Angela J Dean, L Sanjay Nandam, Redmond G O'Connell, and Mark A Bellgrove. "The Molecular Genetics of Executive Function: Role of Monoamine System Genes." *Biological Psychiatry* 69, no. 12 (2011): e127-e43.

Barondes, Samuel. *Making Sense of People: Decoding the Mysteries of Personality.* FT Press, 2011.

Baruchin, Aliya. "Stigma Is Toughtest Foe in an Epilepsy Fight." *New York Times*, August 29, 2011.

Bateson, Melissa, Daniel Nettle, and Gilbert Roberts. "Cues of Being Watched Enhance Cooperation in a Real-World Setting." *Biology Letters* 2, no. 3 (2006): 412-14.

Baumeister, Roy F., Ellen Bratslavsky, Catrin Finkenauer, and Kathleen D. Vohs. "Bad Is Stronger Than Good." *Review of General Psychology* 5, no. 4 (2001): 323-70.

Baumeister, Roy F, Lauren E Brewer, Dianne M Tice, and Jean M Twenge. "Thwarting the Need to Belong: Understanding the Interpersonal and Inner Effects of Social Exclusion." *Social and Personality Psychology Compass* 1, no. 1 (2007): 506-20.

Baumeister, R. F., C. N. DeWall, N. J. Ciarocco, and J. M. Twenge. "Social Exclusion Impairs Self-Regulation." *Journal of Personality and Social Psychology* 88, no. 4 (Apr

Bibliography

2005): 589-604.

Baumeister, Roy F, Matthew Gailliot, C Nathan DeWall, and Megan Oaten. "Self-Regulation and Personality: How Interventions Increase Regulatory Success, and How Depletion Moderates the Effects of Traits on Behavior." *Journal of Personality* 74, no. 6 (2006): 1773-802.

Baumeister, Roy F, and Todd F Heatherton. "Self-Regulation Failure: An Overview." *Psychological Inquiry* 7, no. 1 (1996): 1-15.

Baumeister, Roy F, Todd F Heatherton, and Dianne M Tice. *Losing Control: How and Why People Fail at Self-Regulation.* Academic Press, 1994.

Baumeister, Roy F., and Mark R. Leary. "The Need to Belong: Desire for Interpersonal Attachments as a Fundamental Human Motivation." *Psychological Bulletin* 117, no. 3 (1995): 497-529.

Baumeister, Roy F, and John Tierney. *Willpower: Rediscovering the Greatest Human Strength.* Penguin, 2011.

Baumeister, Roy F, and Kathleen D Vohs. "Self-Regulation, Ego Depletion, and Motivation." *Social and Personality Psychology Compass* 1, no. 1 (2007): 115-28.

Baumeister, Roy F, Kathleen D Vohs, and Dianne M Tice. "The Strength Model of Self-Control." *Current Directions in Psychological Science* 16, no. 6 (2007): 351-55.

Baumgartner, Thomas, Urs Fischbacher, Anja Feierabend, Kai Lutz, and Ernst Fehr. "The Neural Circuitry of a Broken Promise." *Neuron* 64, no. 5 (2009): 756-70.

Baumgartner, T., D. Knoch, P. Hotz, C. Eisenegger, and E. Fehr. "Dorsolateral and Ventromedial Prefrontal Cortex Orchestrate Normative Choice." *Nature Neuroscience* 14, no. 11 (Nov 2011): 1468-74.

Bazerman, Max H, and Ann E Tenbrunsel. *Blind Spots: Why We Fail to Do What's Right and What to Do About It.* Princeton University Press, 2011.

Bechara, Antoine, Hanna Damasio, Antonio R Damasio, and Gregory P Lee. "Different Contributions of the Human Amygdala and Ventromedial Prefrontal Cortex to Decision-Making." *Journal of Neuroscience* 19, no. 13 (1999): 5473-81.

Bechara, A., D. Tranel, H. Damasio, R. Adolphs, C. Rockland, and A. Damasio. "Double Dissociation of Conditioning and Declarative Knowledge Relative to the Amygdala and Hippocampus in Humans." *Science* 269, no. 5227 (1995): 1115-18.

Beer, Jennifer S, Oliver P John, Donatella Scabini, and Robert T Knight. "Orbitofrontal Cortex and Social Behavior: Integrating Self-Monitoring and Emotion-Cognition Interactions." *Journal of Cognitive Neuroscience* 18, no. 6 (2006): 871-79.

Begley, Sharon. *Train Your Mind, Change Your Brain.* Constable, 2007.

Bem, Daryl J. "Self-Perception Theory." *Advances in Experimental Social Psychology* 6 (1972): 1-62.

Benforado, Adam. "Opinion | Flawed Humans, Flawed Justice." *The New York Times*, June 13, 2015.

Berthoz, S, JL Armony, RJR Blair, and RJ Dolan. "An fMRI Study of Intentional and Unintentional (Embarrassing) Violations of Social Norms." *Brain* 125, no. 8 (2002): 1696-708.

Berthoz, S, J Grezes, JL Armony, RE Passingham, and RJ Dolan. "Affective Response to One's Own Moral Violations." *Neuroimage* 31, no. 2 (2006): 945-50.

Bertini, Caterina, Roberto Cecere, and Elisabetta Làdavas. "I Am Blind, but I 'See' Fear." *Cortex* 49, no. 4 (2013): 985-93.

Bishop, S. J. "Trait Anxiety and Impoverished Prefrontal Control of Attention." *Nature Neuroscience* 12, no. 1 (Jan 2009): 92-8.

Blair, I. V., C. M. Judd, and J. L. Fallman. "The Automaticity of Race and Afrocentric Facial Features in Social Judgments." *Journal of Personality and Social Psychology* 87, no. 6 (Dec

2004): 763-78.

Blair, R. J. "The Amygdala and Ventromedial Prefrontal Cortex in Morality and Psychopathy." *Trends in Cognitive Sciences* 11, no. 9 (Sep 2007): 387-92.

Block, Martin P, and Bruce O Vanden Bergh. "Can You Sell Subliminal Messages to Consumers?" *Journal of Advertising* 14, no. 3 (1985): 59-62.

Bornstein, Robert F, and Paul R D'Agostino. "Stimulus Recognition and the Mere Exposure Effect." *Journal of Personality and Social Psychology* 63, no. 4 (1992): 545.

Bornstein, Robert F, Dean R Leone, and Donna J Galley. "The Generalizability of Subliminal Mere Exposure Effects: Influence of Stimuli Perceived without Awareness on Social Behavior." *Journal of Personality and Social Psychology* 53, no. 6 (1987): 1070.

Bornstein, Robert F, and Thane S Pittman. "Perception without Awareness: Cognitive, Clinical, and Social Perspectives." Paper presented at the "Perception Without Awareness: Cognitive, Clinical and Social Perspectives," held in Mar, 1–2, 1991 at Gettysburg College, Gettysburg, PA., 1992.

Bos, Maarten W., Ap Dijksterhuis, and Rick B. van Baaren. "The Benefits of "Sleeping on Things": Unconscious Thought Leads to Automatic Weighting." *Journal of Consumer Psychology* 21, no. 1 (2011): 4-8.

Botvinick, Matthew M, Todd S Braver, Deanna M Barch, Cameron S Carter, and Jonathan D Cohen. "Conflict Monitoring and Cognitive Control." *Psychological Review* 108, no. 3 (2001): 624.

Bouton, M. E., R. F. Westbrook, K. A. Corcoran, and S. Maren. "Contextual and Temporal Modulation of Extinction: Behavioral and Biological Mechanisms." *Biological Psychiatry* 60, no. 4 (Aug 15 2006): 352-60.

Braitenberg, Valentino. "Brain." *Scholarpedia* 2, no. 11 (2007): 2918.

Brass, M., and P. Haggard. "To Do or Not to Do: The Neural Signature of Self-Control." *Journal of Neuroscience* 27, no. 34 (Aug 22 2007): 9141-5.

Brooks, Arthur C. "Opinion | a Formula for Happiness." *The New York Times*, December 14, 2013.

———. "Opinion | Love People, Not Pleasure." *The New York Times*, July 18, 2014.

Brooks, David. "Opinion | the Heart Grows Smarter." (2012). https://www.nytimes.com/2012/11/06/opinion/brooks-the-heart-grows-smarter.html.

———. "Opinion | the Mental Virtues." (August 28, 2014).

———. "Putting Grit in Its Place." *New York Times*, May 10, 2016.

Brown, Kirk Warren, and Richard M. Ryan. "The Benefits of Being Present: Mindfulness and Its Role in Psychological Well-Being." *Journal of Personality and Social Psychology* 84, no. 4 (2003): 822-48.

Bush, George, Phan Luu, and Michael I Posner. "Cognitive and Emotional Influences in Anterior Cingulate Cortex." *Trends in Cognitive Sciences* 4, no. 6 (2000): 215-22.

Bushman, Brad J. "Does Venting Anger Feed or Extinguish the Flame? Catharsis, Rumination, Distraction, Anger, and Aggressive Responding." *Personality and Social Psychology Bulletin* 28, no. 6 (2002): 724-31.

Caccavale, John G, C Wanty Thomas III, and Julie A Edell. "Subliminal Implants in Advertisements: An Experiment." *NA-Advances in Consumer Research Volume 09* (1982).

Campbell, John. *Campbell's Physiology Notes.* Lorimer, 2009.

Cardinal, Rudolf N, John A Parkinson, Jeremy Hall, and Barry J Everitt. "Emotion and Motivation: The Role of the Amygdala, Ventral Striatum, and Prefrontal Cortex." *Neuroscience & Biobehavioral Reviews* 26, no. 3 (2002): 321-52.

Carretié, Luis, Francisco Mercado, Manuel Tapia, and José A Hinojosa. "Emotion, Attention, and the 'Negativity Bias', Studied through Event-Related Potentials." *International*

Bibliography

Journal of Psychophysiology 41, no. 1 (2001): 75-85.

Carson, Richard David, and Rick Carson. *Taming Your Gremlin: A Surprisingly Simple Method for Getting out of Your Own Way.* Harper Paperbacks, 2003.

Carter, Rita, and Christopher D Frith. *Mapping the Mind.* Univ of California Press, 1998.

Caspi, A., B. W. Roberts, and R. L. Shiner. "Personality Development: Stability and Change." *Annual Review of Psychology* 56 (2005): 453-84.

Cathcart, Thomas. *The Trolley Problem, or Would You Throw the Fat Man Off the Bridge? A Philosophical Conundrum.* Workman Publishing, 2013.

Chadwick, David. *To Shine One Corner of the World: Moments with Shunryu Suzuki: Stories of a Zen Master Told by His Students.* Broadway Books, 2001.

Chödrön, Pema. *Comfortable with Uncertainty: 108 Teachings on Cultivating Fearlessness and Compassion.* Shambhala Publications, 2008.

———. *The Places That Scare You: A Guide to Fearlessness in Difficult Times.* Shambhala Publications, 2007.

———. *Taking the Leap: Freeing Ourselves from Old Habits and Fears.* Shambhala Publications, 2009.

———. *When Things Fall Apart: Heart Advice for Difficult Times.* Shambhala Publications, 2000.

Christensen, Riddoch, and Kimberly Christensen. *Dialectical Behavior Therapy Skills, 101 Mindfulness Exercises and Other Fun Activities for Children and Adolescents: A Learning Supplement.* AuthorHouse, 2009.

Coates, John. "Opinion | the Biology of Bubble and Crash." *The New York Times*, June 10, 2012.

Cohen, Jonathan D, and Kenneth I Blum. "Reward and Decision." *Neuron* 36, no. 2 (2002): 193-98.

Cohen, Jonathan D, Matthew Botvinick, and Cameron S Carter. "Anterior Cingulate and Prefrontal Cortex: Who's in Control?" *Nature Neuroscience* 3 (2000): 421-23.

Correll, Joshua, Geoffrey R. Urland, and Tiffany A. Ito. "Event-Related Potentials and the Decision to Shoot: The Role of Threat Perception and Cognitive Control." *Journal of Experimental Social Psychology* 42, no. 1 (2006): 120-28.

Creswell, J David, William T Welch, Shelley E Taylor, David K Sherman, Tara L Gruenewald, and Traci Mann. "Affirmation of Personal Values Buffers Neuroendocrine and Psychological Stress Responses." *Psychological Science* 16, no. 11 (2005): 846-51.

Csikszentmihalyi, Mihaly. *Flow-the Psychology of Optimal Experience.* Harper Perennial, 1991.

Cunningham, William A, Kristen A Dunfield, and Paul E Stillman. "Emotional States from Affective Dynamics." *Emotion Review* 5, no. 4 (2013): 344-55.

Dahl, JoAnne, Kelly G Wilson, and Annika Nilsson. "Acceptance and Commitment Therapy and the Treatment of Persons at Risk for Long-Term Disability Resulting from Stress and Pain Symptoms: A Preliminary Randomized Trial." *Behavior Therapy* 35, no. 4 (2004): 785-801.

Damasio, Antonio. "Neural Basis of Emotions." *Scholarpedia* 6, no. 3 (2011): 1804.

Damasio, Antonio R. *Descartes' Error: Emotion, Reasoning, and the Human Brain.* GP Putnam. 1994.

Davidson, Richard. "Richard Davidson Uncut." By Steve Paulson. *To the Best of Our Knowledge* (November 1 , 2012).

Davidson, Richard J, Sharon Begley, and Francesca Amari. *The Emotional Life of Your Brain.* Brilliance Audio, 2012.

de Vries, Hein, Margo Dijkstra, and Piet Kuhlman. "Self-Efficacy: The Third Factor Besides Attitude and Subjective Norm as a Predictor of Behavioral Intentions." *Health*

Education Research 3, no. 3 (1988): 273-82.

DeSteno, David. "Opinion | Stop Trusting Yourself." *The New York Times*, January 17, 2014.

DeSteno, David, and Piercarlo Valdesolo. *Out of Character: Surprising Truths About the Liar, Cheat, Sinner (and Saint) Lurking in All of Us.* Harmony, 2011.

Devine, Patricia G, E Ashby Plant, David M Amodio, Eddie Harmon-Jones, and Stephanie L Vance. "The Regulation of Explicit and Implicit Race Bias: The Role of Motivations to Respond without Prejudice." *Journal of Personality and Social Psychology* 82, no. 5 (2002): 835.

Dijksterhuis, Ap, Henk Aarts, John A. Bargh, and Ad van Knippenberg. "On the Relation between Associative Strength and Automatic Behavior." *Journal of Experimental Social Psychology* 36, no. 5 (2000): 531-44.

Dijksterhuis, A., M. W. Bos, L. F. Nordgren, and R. B. van Baaren. "On Making the Right Choice: The Deliberation-without-Attention Effect." *Science* 311, no. 5763 (Feb 17 2006): 1005-7.

Dreifus, Claudia. "A Macarthur Grant Winner Tries to Unearth Biases to Aid Criminal Justice." January 5, 2015.

Druckerman, Pamela. "Opinion | Learning How to Exert Self-Control." *The New York Times*, September 12, 2014.

Duckworth, Angela. *Grit: The Power of Passion and Perseverance.* Simon and Schuster, 2016.

Dweck, Carol. *Mindset: The New Psychology of Success.* Random House, 2006.

Dweck, Carol S. "Can Personality Be Changed? The Role of Beliefs in Personality and Change." *Current Directions in Psychological Science* 17, no. 6 (2008): 391-94.

Ekman, Paul. "Are There Basic Emotions?" *Psychological Review* 99, no. 3 (1992): 550-53.

———. "Emotional Awareness Workshop Manual." San Francisco: Paul Ekman Group, 2008A.

———. *Emotional Awareness: Overcoming the Obstacles to Psychological Balance and Compassion.* Macmillan, 2008.

———. *Emotions Revealed: Recognizing Faces and Feelings to Improve Communication and Emotional Life.* Macmillan, 2007.

———. "Facial Expression and Emotion." *American Psychologist* 48, no. 4 (1993): 384.

Ekman, Paul, Richard J Davidson, Matthieu Ricard, and B Alan Wallace. "Buddhist and Psychological Perspectives on Emotions and Well-Being." *Current Directions in Psychological Science* 14, no. 2 (2005): 59-63.

Ekman, Paul, and Wallace V Friesen. "Constants across Cultures in the Face and Emotion." *Journal of Personality and Social Psychology* 17, no. 2 (1971): 124.

Ekman, Paul, E Richard Sorenson, and Wallace V Friesen. "Pan-Cultural Elements in Facial Displays of Emotion." *Science* 164, no. 3875 (1969): 86-88.

Erhard, Werner, Michael C Jensen, and Steve Zaffron. "*Integrity: A Positive Model That Incorporates the Normative Phenomena of Morality, Ethics and Legality* (March 23, 2009). *Harvard Business School NOM Working Paper No. 06-11* . No. 06-03. ." Barbados Group Working Paper, 2008.

Ewbank, M. P., P. J. Barnard, C. J. Croucher, C. Ramponi, and A. J. Calder. "The Amygdala Response to Images with Impact." *Social Cognitive and Affective Neuroscience* 4, no. 2 (Jun 2009): 127-33.

Falk, E. B., E. T. Berkman, D. Whalen, and M. D. Lieberman. "Neural Activity During Health Messaging Predicts Reductions in Smoking above and Beyond Self-Report." *Health Psychology* 30, no. 2 (Mar 2011): 177-85.

Fehr, E., and B. Rockenbach. "Human Altruism: Economic, Neural, and Evolutionary Perspectives." *Current Opinion in Neurobiology* 14, no. 6 (Dec 2004): 784-90.

Felitti, Vincent J, Robert F Anda, Dale Nordenberg, David F Williamson, Alison M Spitz,

Valerie Edwards, Mary P Koss, and James S Marks. "Relationship of Childhood Abuse and Household Dysfunction to Many of the Leading Causes of Death in Adults: The Adverse Childhood Experiences (Ace) Study." *American Journal of Preventive Medicine* 14, no. 4 (1998): 245-58.

Fellous, Jean-Marc. "Models of Emotion." *Scholarpedia* 2, no. 11 (2007): 1453.

Fernbach, Philip M, Steven A Sloman, Robert St Louis, and Julia N Shube. "Explanation Fiends and Foes: How Mechanistic Detail Determines Understanding and Preference." *Journal of Consumer Research* 39, no. 5 (2013): 1115-31.

Filevich, E., S. Kuhn, and P. Haggard. "Intentional Inhibition in Human Action: The Power of 'No'." *Neuroscience and Biobehavioral Reviews* 36, no. 4 (Apr 2012): 1107-18.

Finch, David. "Dealing with Asperger's Syndrome, with the Help of His Wife." *The New York Times*, May 15, 2009.

Fiske, Susan T, Amy JC Cuddy, Peter Glick, and Jun Xu. "A Model of (Often Mixed) Stereotype Content: Competence and Warmth Respectively Follow from Perceived Status and Competition." *Journal of Personality and Social Psychology* 82, no. 6 (2002): 878.

Forgas, Joseph P. *Feeling and Thinking: The Role of Affect in Social Cognition.* Cambridge University Press, 2001.

Fox, Stuart Ira. *Human Physiology 9th Edition.* McGraw-Hill Press, New York, 2006.

Frederick, Shane. "Cognitive Reflection and Decision Making." *The Journal of Economic Perspectives* 19, no. 4 (2005): 25-42.

Friedman, Naomi P, Akira Miyake, Susan E Young, John C DeFries, Robin P Corley, and John K Hewitt. "Individual Differences in Executive Functions Are Almost Entirely Genetic in Origin." *Journal of Experimental Psychology: General* 137, no. 2 (2008): 201.

Friedman, Richard A. "Opinion | a Natural Fix for A.D.H.D." (2014). https://www.nytimes.com/2014/11/02/opinion/sunday/a-natural-fix-for-adhd.html.

Friedman, Richad A. "Why_Teenagers_Act_Crazy." *New York Times*, June 28, 2014 2014.

Fries, Mason. "Mindfulness Based Stress Reduction for the Changing Work Environment." *Journal of Academic and Business Ethics* 2 (2009): 1.

Fugelsang, JA. "On the Reception and Detection of Pseudo-Profound Bullshit." *Judgment and Decision Making* 10 (2015): 549563.

Gafford, Richard. "The Operational Potential of Subliminal Perception>." *Studies in Intelligence* 2, no. Spring, 1958 (1958).

Gilbert, Daniel. "What You Don't Know Makes You Nervous." *The New York Times* 21 (2009).

Ginges, J., S. Atran, D. Medin, and K. Shikaki. "Sacred Bounds on Rational Resolution of Violent Political Conflict." *Proceedings of the National Academy of Sciences of the United States of America* 104, no. 18 (May 1 2007): 7357-60.

Gladwell, Malcolm. *Blink: The Power of Thinking without Thinking.* Back Bay Books, 2007.

Goldenberg, Jamie L, Tom Pyszczynski, Jeff Greenberg, Sheldon Solomon, Benjamin Kluck, and Robin Cornwell. "I Am Not an Animal: Mortality Salience, Disgust, and the Denial of Human Creatureliness." *Journal of Experimental Psychology: General* 130, no. 3 (2001): 427.

Goleman, Daniel. *Destructive Emotions: A Scientific Dialogue with the Dalai Lama.* Bantam, 2008.

———. *Emotional Intelligence.* Bantam, 1995.

———. *Healing Emotions: Conversations with the Dalai Lama on Mindfulness, Emotions, and Health.* Shambhala Publications, 2003.

———. "How to Mind Your Feelings." On-line magazine, *Lion's Roar* (2015). Published electronically June 23, 2015. http://www.lionsroar.com/how-to-mind-your-feelings/?utm_source=Shambhala%2BSun%2BCommunity&u

tm_campaign=84d887f177-+Sf_Weekly_June_30_20156_30_2015&utm_
medium=email&utm_term=0_1988ee44b2-84d887f177-21419333. .

———. "New View of Mind Gives Unconscious an Expanded Role." *The New York Times*, November 6, 1984.

———. "Rich People Just Care Less." *The New York Times*, 2013.

Goyal, Madhav, Sonal Singh, Erica MS Sibinga, Neda F Gould, Anastasia Rowland-Seymour, Ritu Sharma, Zackary Berger, *et al.* "Meditation Programs for Psychological Stress and Well-Being: A Systematic Review and Meta-Analysis." *JAMA Internal Medicine* 174, no. 3 (2014): 357-68.

Grant, Adam. "Raising a Moral Child." *New York Times*, April 11, 2014.

Gray, Jeremy R, Todd S Braver, and Marcus E Raichle. "Integration of Emotion and Cognition in the Lateral Prefrontal Cortex." *Proceedings of the National Academy of Sciences* 99, no. 6 (2002): 4115-20.

Graybiel, A. M. "Habits, Rituals, and the Evaluative Brain." *Annual Review of Neuroscience* 31 (2008): 359-87.

Greenberg, Jeff, Tom Pyszczynski, and Sheldon Solomon. "The Causes and Consequences of a Need for Self-Esteem: A Terror Management Theory." In *Public Self and Private Self*, 189-212: Springer, 1986.

Greenberg, Jeff, Tom Pyszczynski, Sheldon Solomon, Abram Rosenblatt, Mitchell Veeder, Shari Kirkland, and Deborah Lyon. "Evidence for Terror Management Theory II: The Effects of Mortality Salience on Reactions to Those Who Threaten or Bolster the Cultural Worldview." *Journal of Personality and Social Psychology* 58, no. 2 (1990): 308.

Greenberg, Jeff, Sheldon Solomon, Tom Pyszczynski, Abram Rosenblatt, John Burling, Deborah Lyon, Linda Simon, and Elizabeth Pinel. "Why Do People Need Self-Esteem? Converging Evidence That Self-Esteem Serves an Anxiety-Buffering Function." *Journal of Personality and Social Psychology* 63, no. 6 (1992): 913.

Greene, Ciara M, Wouter Braet, Katherine A Johnson, and Mark A Bellgrove. "Imaging the Genetics of Executive Function." *Biological Psychology* 79, no. 1 (2008): 30-42.

Greene, Deanna J., Jonathan M. Koller, Amy Robichaux-Viehoever, Emily C. Bihun, Bradley L. Schlaggar, and Kevin J. Black. "Reward Enhances Tic Suppression in Children within Months of Tic Disorder Onset." *Developmental Cognitive Neuroscience*.

Greenwald, Anthony G, and Mahzarin R Banaji. "Implicit Social Cognition: Attitudes, Self-Esteem, and Stereotypes." *Psychological Review* 102, no. 1 (1995): 4.

Greenwald, Anthony G., Mahzarin R. Banaji, Laurie A. Rudman, Shelly D. Farnham, Brian A. Nosek, and Deborah S. Mellott. "A Unified Theory of Implicit Attitudes, Stereotypes, Self-Esteem, and Self-Concept." *Psychological Review* 109, no. 1 (2002): 3-25.

Greenwald, Anthony G, Debbie E McGhee, and Jordan LK Schwartz. "Measuring Individual Differences in Implicit Cognition: The Implicit Association Test." *Journal of Personality and Social Psychology* 74, no. 6 (1998): 1464.

Grewal, Daisy. "A Happy Life May Not Be a Meaningful Life." *Scientific American*, February 18, 2014.

Grezes, J., S. Berthoz, and R. E. Passingham. "Amygdala Activation When One Is the Target of Deceit: Did He Lie to You or to Someone Else?" *Neuroimage* 30, no. 2 (Apr 1 2006): 601-8.

Grimes, William. "Jack Yufe, a Jew Whose Twin Was a Nazi, Dies at 82." *New York Times*, November 13, 2015.

Gross, James J. "The Emerging Field of Emotion Regulation: An Integrative Review." *Review of General Psychology* 2, no. 3 (1998): 271.

Guenther, Corey L., and Mark D. Alicke. "Self-Enhancement and Belief Perseverance."

Journal of Experimental Social Psychology 44, no. 3 (2008): 706-12.

Gusnard, D. A., E. Akbudak, G. L. Shulman, and M. E. Raichle. "Medial Prefrontal Cortex and Self-Referential Mental Activity: Relation to a Default Mode of Brain Function." *Proceedings of the National Academy of Sciences of the United States of America* 98, no. 7 (Mar 27 2001): 4259-64.

Gyurak, A., M. S. Goodkind, A. Madan, J. H. Kramer, B. L. Miller, and R. W. Levenson. "Do Tests of Executive Functioning Predict Ability to Downregulate Emotions Spontaneously and When Instructed to Suppress?" *Cognitive, Affective & Behavioral Neuroscience* 9, no. 2 (Jun 2009): 144-52.

Hagemann, T., R. W. Levenson, and J. J. Gross. "Expressive Suppression During an Acoustic Startle." *Psychophysiology* 43, no. 1 (Jan 2006): 104-12.

Haggard, P. "Human Volition: Towards a Neuroscience of Will." *Nature Reviews: Neuroscience* 9, no. 12 (Dec 2008): 934-46.

Haidt, Jonathan. "Elevation and the Positive Psychology of Morality." Chap. 12 In *Flourishing: Positive Psychology and the Life Well-Lived*, edited by C. L. M. Keyes and Jonathan Haidt, 2003.

———. "Reasons Matter (When Intuitions Don't Object)." *New York Times* (2012). https://opinionator.blogs.nytimes.com/2012/10/07/reasons-matter-when-intuitions-dont-object/.

———. *The Righteous Mind: Why Good People Are Divided by Politics and Religion*. Vintage, 2012.

Hamm, Alfons O, Almut I Weike, Harald T Schupp, Thomas Treig, Alexander Dressel, and Christof Kessler. "Affective Blindsight: Intact Fear Conditioning to a Visual Cue in a Cortically Blind Patient." *Brain* 126, no. 2 (2003): 267-75.

Harmon-Jones, Eddie, Linda Simon, Jeff Greenberg, Tom Pyszczynski, Sheldon Solomon, and Holly McGregor. "Terror Management Theory and Self-Esteem: Evidence That Increased Self-Esteem Reduced Mortality Salience Effects." *Journal of Personality and Social Psychology* 72, no. 1 (1997): 24.

Harris, Jennifer L, John A Bargh, and Kelly D Brownell. "Priming Effects of Television Food Advertising on Eating Behavior." *Health Psychology* 28, no. 4 (2009): 404.

Harris, L. T., and S. T. Fiske. "Dehumanized Perception: A Psychological Means to Facilitate Atrocities, Torture, and Genocide?" *Zeitschrift für Psychologie* 219, no. 3 (Jan 1 2011): 175-81.

Harris, Sam. *Free Will*. Simon and Schuster, 2012.

Hatemi, P. K., and R. McDermott. "The Genetics of Politics: Discovery, Challenges, and Progress." *Trends in Genetics* 28, no. 10 (Oct 2012): 525-33.

Hayward, Jeremy W. *Gentle Bridges: Conversations with the Dalai Lama on the Sciences of Mind*. Shambhala Publications, 2001.

Henig, Robin Marantz. "Understanding the Anxious Mind." *New York Times Magazine*, October 4, 2009.

Himle, M. B., D. W. Woods, J. C. Piacentini, and J. T. Walkup. "Brief Review of Habit Reversal Training for Tourette Syndrome." *Journal of Child Neurology* 21, no. 8 (2006): 719-25.

Hinshaw, Stephen P. *Origins of the Human Mind*. Teaching Company, 2010.

Hölzel, Britta K, James Carmody, Mark Vangel, Christina Congleton, Sita M Yerramsetti, Tim Gard, and Sara W Lazar. "Mindfulness Practice Leads to Increases in Regional Brain Gray Matter Density." *Psychiatry Research: Neuroimaging* 191, no. 1 (2011): 36-43.

———. "Mindfulness Practice Leads to Increases in Regional Brain Gray Matter Density."

Psychiatry Research: Neuroimaging 191, no. 1 (2011): 36-43.

Horowitz, Seth S. "Opinion | Why Listening Is So Much More Than Hearing." November 9 2012 2012.

Houshmand, Zara, and Alan B. Wallace. *Consciousness at the Crossroads: Conversations with the Dalai Lama on Brain Science and Buddhism.* Shambhala, 1999.

Howard, Ron. "A Beautiful Mind." 135 minutes. Culver City, CA: Universal Pictures, 2001.

Huber, Cheri. *How to Get from Where You Are to Where You Want to Be.* Hay House, Incorporated, 2005.

———. *The Key: And the Name of the Key Is Willingness.* Keep It Simple Books, 2005.

Huber, Cheri, and June Shiver. *That Which You Are Seeking Is Causing You to Seek.* Keep It Simple Books, 2006.

———. *There Is Nothing Wrong with You: Regardless of What You Were Taught to Believe.* Keep It Simple Books, 2001.

Huet, Ellen. "Bay Area Native Awarded Medal of Honor." *San Francisco Chronicle*, August 26, 2013.

Hutson, Matthew. "Opinion | How Firm Are Our Principles?" (2013). https://www.nytimes.com/2013/03/31/opinion/sunday/how-firm-are-our-principles.html.

Immordino-Yang, M. H., A. McColl, H. Damasio, and A. Damasio. "Neural Correlates of Admiration and Compassion." *Proceedings of the National Academy of Sciences of the United States of America* 106, no. 19 (May 12 2009): 8021-6.

Interlandi, Jeneen. "The Brain's Empathy Gap." Marcy 19, 2015.

———. "Can Mapping Neural Pathways Help Us Make Friends with Our Enemies." *New York Times Magazine*, March 19, 2015.

Ito, Tiffany A, Jeff T Larsen, N Kyle Smith, and John T Cacioppo. "Negative Information Weighs More Heavily on the Brain: The Negativity Bias in Evaluative Categorizations." *Journal of Personality and Social Psychology* 75, no. 4 (1998): 887.

Jacoby, Larry L, Jeffrey P Toth, D Stephen Lindsay, and James A Debner. *Lectures for a Layperson: Methods for Revealing Unconscious Processes.* Guilford Press, 1992.

Jacowitz, K. E., and D. Kahneman. "Measures of Anchoring in Estimation Tasks." *Personality and Social Psychology Bulletin* 21, no. 11 (1995): 1161-66.

James, William. *Principles of Psychology.* 2 vols. Vol. 1: Dover Publications, 1890.

Ji, J., and S. Maren. "Hippocampal Involvement in Contextual Modulation of Fear Extinction." *Hippocampus* 17, no. 9 (2007): 749-58.

Jones, J. T., B. W. Pelham, M. Carvallo, and M. C. Mirenberg. "How Do I Love Thee? Let Me Count the Js: Implicit Egotism and Interpersonal Attraction." *Journal of Personality and Social Psychology* 87, no. 5 (Nov 2004): 665-83.

Jung, Carl Gustav. *Memories, Dreams, Reflections.* Vintage, 2011.

Kabat-Zin, Jon. *Wherever You Go, There You Are.* Hyperion, 1994.

Kabat-Zinn, Jon, and Thich Nhat Hanh. *Full Catastrophe Living: Using the Wisdom of Your Body and Mind to Face Stress, Pain, and Illness.* Delta, 2009.

Kahan, Dan M, Ellen Peters, Erica Cantrell Dawson, and Paul Slovic. "Motivated Numeracy and Enlightened Self-Government (Preliminary Draft)." In *Cultural Cognition Project*: Yale Law School, 2013.

Kahan, Dan M., Ellen Peters, Maggie Wittlin, Paul Slovic, Lisa Larrimore Ouellette, Donald Braman, and Gregory Mandel. "The Polarizing Impact of Science Literacy and Numeracy on Perceived Climate Change Risks." *Nature Climate Change* 2, no. 10 (2012): 732-35.

Kahneman, Daniel. *Thinking, Fast and Slow.* Macmillan, 2011.

Kamm, FM. *The Trolley Problem Mysteries.* Oxford University Press, 2015.

Kandel, Eric R, James H Schwartz, Thomas M Jessell, Steven A Siegelbaum, and A James

Bibliography

Hudspeth. *Principles of Neural Science*. Vol. 4: McGraw-Hill New York, 2000.

Kaplan, Marty. "The Most Depressing Discovery About the Brain, Ever." *Alternet.org* (2013). http://www.alternet.org/media/most-depressing-discovery-about-brain-ever.

Kappas, Arvid. "Appraisals Are Direct, Immediate, Intuitive, and Unwitting... and Some Are Reflective...." *Cognition and Emotion* 20, no. 7 (2006): 952-75.

Kemeny, Margaret E, Carol Foltz, James F Cavanagh, Margaret Cullen, Janine Giese-Davis, Patricia Jennings, Erika L Rosenberg, *et al.* "Contemplative/Emotion Training Reduces Negative Emotional Behavior and Promotes Prosocial Responses." *Emotion* 12, no. 2 (2012): 338.

Kennerley, S. W., M. E. Walton, T. E. Behrens, M. J. Buckley, and M. F. Rushworth. "Optimal Decision Making and the Anterior Cingulate Cortex." *Nature Neuroscience* 9, no. 7 (Jul 2006): 940-7.

Kneen, Cynthia. *Awake Mind, Open Heart: The Power of Courage and Dignity in Everyday Life*. Marlowe & Company, 2002.

Knudsen, E. I. "Fundamental Components of Attention." *Annual Review of Neuroscience* 30 (2007): 57-78.

Koch, Christof, and Florian Mormann. "Neural Correlates of Consciousness." *Scholarpedia* 2, no. 12 (2007): 1740.

Koch, C., and N. Tsuchiya. "Attention and Consciousness: Two Distinct Brain Processes." *Trends in Cognitive Sciences* 11, no. 1 (Jan 2007): 16-22.

Koechlin, Etienne, Chrystele Ody, and Frédérique Kouneiher. "The Architecture of Cognitive Control in the Human Prefrontal Cortex." *Science* 302, no. 5648 (2003): 1181-85.

Koerner, Kelly. *Doing Dialectical Behavior Therapy: A Practical Guide*. Guilford Press, 2012.

Konnikova, Maria. "Opinion | the Power of Concentration." December 15, 2012.

———. "Walter Mischel, the Marshmallow Test, and Self-Control." *The New Yorker*, October 9 2014.

Kruger, Justin, and David Dunning. "Unskilled and Unaware of It: How Difficulties in Recognizing One's Own Incompetence Lead to Inflated Self-Assessments." *Journal of Personality and Social Psychology* 77, no. 6 (1999): 1121.

Kuhn, S., P. Haggard, and M. Brass. "Intentional Inhibition: How the "Veto-Area" Exerts Control." *Human Brain Mapping* 30, no. 9 (Sep 2009): 2834-43.

Kunst-Wilson, William, and RB Zajonc. "Affective Discrimination of Stimuli That Cannot Be Recognized." *Science* 207 (1980): 557-58.

Landau, Mark J, Sheldon Solomon, Jeff Greenberg, Florette Cohen, Tom Pyszczynski, Jamie Arndt, Claude H Miller, Daniel M Ogilvie, and Alison Cook. "Deliver Us from Evil: The Effects of Mortality Salience and Reminders of 9/11 on Support for President George W. Bush." *Personality and Social Psychology Bulletin* 30, no. 9 (2004): 1136-50.

Lau, Hakwan C, Robert D Rogers, and Richard E Passingham. "Manipulating the Experienced Onset of Intention after Action Execution." *Journal of Cognitive Neuroscience* 19, no. 1 (2007): 81-90.

Leary, Mark R. "Making Sense of Self-Esteem." *Current Directions in Psychological Science* 8, no. 1 (1999): 32-35.

Leary, Mark R, Ellen S Tambor, Sonja K Terdal, and Deborah L Downs. "Self-Esteem as an Interpersonal Monitor: The Sociometer Hypothesis." *Journal of Personality and Social Psychology* 68, no. 3 (1995): 518.

Leckman, James F, and Mark A Riddle. "Tourette's Syndrome: When Habit-Forming Systems Form Habits of Their Own?" *Neuron* 28, no. 2 (2000): 349-54.

LeDoux, Joseph. "The Emotional Brain, Fear, and the Amygdala." *Cellular and Molecular Neurobiology* 23, no. 4-5 (2003): 727-38.

———. "Finding Clues in the Fearful Brain." *The New York Times*, March 25, 2012 2012.

———. "Searching the Brain for the Roots of Fear." (2012). https://opinionator.blogs.

nytimes.com/2012/01/22/anatomy-of-fear/.

LeDoux, Joseph E. "The Amygdala Is Not the Brain's Fear Center, Separating Findings from Conclusions." In *I got a mind to tell you*. Psychology Today, 2015.

LeDoux, J. E. "Amygdala." In *Scholarpedia*, 2008.

LeDoux, Joseph E. "Emotion Circuits in the Brain." *The Science of Mental Health: Fear and anxiety* 259 (2001).

———. "Emotion: Clues from the Brain." *Annual Review of Psychology* 1995, no. 46 (1995): 209-35.

LeDoux, Joseph E. *The Emotional Brain: The Mysterious Underpinnings of Emotional Life*. Simon and Schuster, 1996.

LeDoux, Joseph E. "Sensory Systems and Emotion: A Model of Affective Processing." *Integrative Psychiatry* (1986).

Lehrer, Jonah. *Proust Was a Neuroscientist*. Houghton Mifflin Harcourt, 2008.

Leu, Lucy. *Nonviolent Communication Companion Workbook: A Practical Guide for Individual, Group, or Classroom Study*. PuddleDancer Press, 2015.

Levenson, Robert W. "Autonomic Specificity and Emotion." In *Handbook of Affective Sciences*, 212-24, 2003.

Levenson, Robert W. "Blood, Sweat, and Fears." *Annals of the New York Academy of Sciences* 1000, no. 1 (2006): 348-66.

Levine, Stephen. *Healing into Life and Death*. Anchor, 2010.

Li, Fei, Rufin VanRullen, Christof Koch, and Pietro Perona. "Rapid Natural Scene Categorization in the near Absence of Attention." *Proceedings of the National Academy of Sciences* 99, no. 14 (2002): 9596-601.

Libet, Benjamin. "Reflections on the Interaction of the Mind and Brain." *Progress in Neurobiology* 78, no. 3 (2006): 322-26.

Libet, Benjamin, Curtis A Gleason, Elwood W Wright, and Dennis K Pearl. "Time of Conscious Intention to Act in Relation to Onset of Cerebral Activity (Readiness-Potential)." *Brain* 106, no. 3 (1983): 623-42.

Lieberman, M. D. "Social Cognitive Neuroscience: A Review of Core Processes." *Annual Review of Psychology* 58 (2007): 259-89.

Linder, Douglas O, and Nancy Levit. "The Law According to Darwin: Evolution Neuroscience and Justice." *Salon*, May 25, 2014 2014.

Linehan, Marsha M. *DBT® Skills Training Handouts and Worksheets*. Guilford Publications, 2014.

———. *DBT® Skills Training Manual*. Guilford Publications, 2014.

Linehan, Marsha M. *Dialectical Behavior Therapy Skills Handouts (in Press)*. Guilford Publications, 2009.

Linehan, Marsha M. *Skills Training Manual for Treating Borderline Personality Disorder*. Guilford Press, 1993.

Lippincott, Will. "No Longer Wanting to Die." *The New York Times*, May 16, 2015.

Locke, Edwin A. "It's Time We Brought Introspection out of the Closet." *Perspectives on Psychological Science* 4, no. 1 (2009): 24-25.

Lord, Charles G, Mark R Lepper, and Elizabeth Preston. "Considering the Opposite: A Corrective Strategy for Social Judgment." *Journal of Personality and Social Psychology* 47, no. 6 (1984): 1231.

Lovallo, Dan, and Daniel Kahneman. "Delusions of Success." *Harvard Business Review* 81, no. 7 (2003): 56-63.

Ludlow, Peter. "The Banality of Systemic Evil." *The New York Times*, 2013.

Luhrmann, T. M. "Opinion | Why Are Some Cultures More Individualistic Than Others?"

Bibliography

The New York Times, December 3, 2014.

Lutz, Antoine, John D Dunne, and Richard J Davidson. "Meditation and the Neuroscience of Consciousness." In *Cambridge Handbook of Consciousness*, 499-555, 2007.

Lyubomirsky, Sonja. *The How of Happiness: A Scientific Approach to Getting the Life You Want.* Penguin, 2008.

———. *The Myths of Happiness: What Should Make You Happy, but Doesn't, What Shouldn't Make You Happy, but Does.* Penguin, 2013.

Macdonald, G., and M. R. Leary. "Why Does Social Exclusion Hurt? The Relationship between Social and Physical Pain." *Psychological Bulletin* 131, no. 2 (Mar 2005): 202-23.

MacLean, K. A., S. R. Aichele, D. A. Bridwell, G. R. Mangun, E. Wojciulik, and C. D. Saron. "Interactions between Endogenous and Exogenous Attention During Vigilance." *Atten Percept Psychophys* 71, no. 5 (Jul 2009): 1042-58.

Macmillan, Malcolm. "The Phineas Gage Information Page." Center for the History of Psychology, www.uakron.edu/gage/.

Marshall, Rosenberg, and Ph D Rosenberg. *Nonviolent Communication: A Language of Life.* Encinitas, Ca: A Puddle Dancer Press Book. 2003.

Maslow, Abraham Harold. "A Theory of Human Motivation." *Psychological Review* 50, no. 4 (1943): 370.

Mattis-Namgyel, Elizabeth. "An Invitation – Lion's Roar." *Buddhadharma: The Practitioner's Quarterly*, November, 2014.

Maxfield, David. *Silence Kills: The Seven Crucial Conversations for Healthcare.* VitalSmarts, 2005.

Mayse, Jeffrey D., Geoffrey M. Nelson, Irene Avila, Michela Gallagher, and Shih-Chieh Lin. "Basal Forebrain Neuronal Inhibition Enables Rapid Behavioral Stopping." *Nature Neuroscience* 18, no. 10 (10//print 2015): 1501-08.

McDonough, Kate. "Science: Divorce Could Be Contagious!" (2017). http://www.salon.com/2013/10/21/science_divorce_could_be_contagious/.

McGregor, Holly A, Joel D Lieberman, Jeff Greenberg, Sheldon Solomon, Jamie Arndt, Linda Simon, and Tom Pyszczynski. "Terror Management and Aggression: Evidence That Mortality Salience Motivates Aggression against Worldview-Threatening Others." *Journal of Personality and Social Psychology* 74, no. 3 (1998): 590.

McGuire, J. F., J. Piacentini, E. A. Brennan, A. B. Lewin, T. K. Murphy, B. J. Small, and E. A. Storch. "A Meta-Analysis of Behavior Therapy for Tourette Syndrome." *Journal of Psychiatric Research* 50 (Mar 2014): 106-12.

McGuire, Joseph F, Emily J Ricketts, John Piacentini, Tanya K Murphy, Eric A Storch, and Adam B Lewin. "Behavior Therapy for Tic Disorders: An Evidenced-Based Review and New Directions for Treatment Research." *Current Developmental Disorders Reports* (2015): 1-9.

McLeod, Ken. *Wake up to Your Life: Discovering the Buddhist Path of Attention.* Harper San Francisco, 2001.

Medical Express, Editors. "More to Facial Perception Than Meets the Eye." (2012). https://medicalxpress.com/news/2012-06-facial-perception-eye.html.

———. "Remembering to Forget." (2012). https://medicalxpress.com/news/2012-06-remembering-to-forget.html.

Medline Plus, Editors. "Post-Traumatic Stress Disorder." In *Medline Plus*, edited by Editors. Bethesda, MD: NIH National Library of Medicine, 2016.

Mental Disorders, Encyclopedia of Editors. "Post-Traumatic Stress Disorder." Advameg, Inc., http://www.minddisorders.com/Ob-Ps/Post-traumatic-stress-disorder.html.

Miller, Earl K, and Jonathan D Cohen. "An Integrative Theory of Prefrontal Cortex

Function." *Annual Review of Neuroscience* 24, no. 1 (2001): 167-202.

Miller, Greg. "How Our Brains Make Memories." (2010). http://www.smithsonianmag.com/science-nature/how-our-brains-make-memories-14466850/.

Mipham Rinpoche, Sakyong. *Turning the Mind into an Ally*. Penguin, 2004.

Miyake, Akira, and Naomi P Friedman. "The Nature and Organization of Individual Differences in Executive Functions Four General Conclusions." *Current Directions in Psychological Science* 21, no. 1 (2012): 8-14.

———. "The Nature and Organization of Individual Differences in Executive Functions: Four General Conclusions." *Current Directions in Psychological Science* 21, no. 1 (2012): 8-14.

Moll, J., R. De Oliveira-Souza, and R. Zahn. "The Neural Basis of Moral Cognition: Sentiments, Concepts, and Values." *Annals of the New York Academy of Sciences* 1124 (Mar 2008): 161-80.

Moll, Jorge, Roland Zahn, Ricardo de Oliveira-Souza, Frank Krueger, and Jordan Grafman. "The Neural Basis of Human Moral Cognition." *Nature Reviews Neuroscience* 6, no. 10 (2005): 799-809.

Monahan, Jennifer L, Sheila T Murphy, and Robert B Zajonc. "Subliminal Mere Exposure: Specific, General, and Diffuse Effects." *Psychological Science* 11, no. 6 (2000): 462-66.

Monterosso, John, and Barry Schwartz. "Did Your Brain Make You Do It." *New York Times. Retrieved from http://www. nytimes. com/2012/07/29/opinion/sunday/neurosci ence-and-moral-responsibility. html* (2012).

Morewedge, Carey K, Haewon Yoon, Irene Scopelliti, Carl W Symborski, James H Korris, and Karim S Kassam. "Debiasing Decisions Improved Decision Making with a Single Training Intervention." *Policy Insights from the Behavioral and Brain Sciences* (2015).

Morris, J. S. "Differential Extrageniculostriate and Amygdala Responses to Presentation of Emotional Faces in a Cortically Blind Field." *Brain* 124, no. 6 (2001): 1241-52.

Most, Steven B, and Daniel J Simons. "Attention Capture, Orienting, and Awareness." Chap. 7 In *Attraction, Distraction and Action: Multiple Perspectives on Attentional Capture*, edited by C. Folk and B. Gibson, 2001.

Muraven, Mark, and Roy F Baumeister. "Self-Regulation and Depletion of Limited Resources: Does Self-Control Resemble a Muscle?" *Psychological Bulletin* 126, no. 2 (2000): 247.

Murphy, Sheila T, Jennifer L Monahan, and Robert B Zajonc. "Additivity of Nonconscious Affect: Combined Effects of Priming and Exposure." *Journal of Personality and Social Psychology* 69, no. 4 (1995): 589.

Murphy, Sheila T, and Robert B Zajonc. "Affect, Cognition, and Awareness: Affective Priming with Optimal and Suboptimal Stimulus Exposures." *Journal of Personality and Social Psychology* 64, no. 5 (1993): 723.

Natterson-Horowitz, Barbara, and Kathryn Bowers. "Our Animal Natures." (2012).

Nisbett, Richard E, and Timothy D Wilson. "Telling More Than We Can Know: Verbal Reports on Mental Processes." *Psychological Review* 84, no. 3 (1977): 231.

Norden, Jeannette. *Understanding the Brain: Course Guidebook. Parts 1-3*. Teaching Company, 2007.

Nummenmaa, Lauri, Enrico Glerean, Riitta Hari, and Jari K Hietanen. "Bodily Maps of Emotions." *Proceedings of the National Academy of Sciences* 111, no. 2 (2014): 646-51.

O'Malley, Patrick. "Getting Grief Right." *The New York Times*, January 10, 2015.

Oatley, Keith, Dacher Keltner, and Jennifer M Jenkins. *Understanding Emotions*. Blackwell Publishing, 2006.

Ochsner, Kevin N, Silvia A Bunge, James J Gross, and John DE Gabrieli. "Rethinking Feelings: An fMRI Study of the Cognitive Regulation of Emotion." *Journal of Cognitive*

Neuroscience 14, no. 8 (2002): 1215-29.

Ochsner, K. N., R. D. Ray, J. C. Cooper, E. R. Robertson, S. Chopra, J. D. Gabrieli, and J. J. Gross. "For Better or for Worse: Neural Systems Supporting the Cognitive Down- and up-Regulation of Negative Emotion." *Neuroimage* 23, no. 2 (Oct 2004): 483-99.

O'Connor, Kieron. *Cognitive-Behavioral Management of Tic Disorders.* John Wiley & Sons, 2005.

Olesen, P. J., H. Westerberg, and T. Klingberg. "Increased Prefrontal and Parietal Activity after Training of Working Memory." *Nature Neuroscience* 7, no. 1 (Jan 2004): 75-9.

Ouellette, Judith A, and Wendy Wood. "Habit and Intention in Everyday Life: The Multiple Processes by Which Past Behavior Predicts Future Behavior." *Psychological Bulletin* 124, no. 1 (1998): 54.

Parens, Erik. "The Benefits of 'Binocularity'." *The New York Times*, September 28, 2014.

Park, Nansook, Christopher Peterson, and Martin EP Seligman. "Character Strengths in Fifty-Four Nations and the Fifty Us States." *The Journal of Positive Psychology* 1, no. 3 (2006): 118-29.

Patterson, Kerry, Joseph Grenny, Ron McMillan, and Al Switzler. *Crucial Conversations: Tools for Talking When Stakes Are High, Second Edition.* McGraw-Hill Companies, 2011.

Pelham, Brett W, Mauricio Carvallo, and John T Jones. "Implicit Egotism." *Current Directions in Psychological Science* 14, no. 2 (2005): 106-10.

Pessoa, Luiz. "Cognition and Emotion." *Scholarpedia* 4, no. 1 (2009): 4567.

Peterson, Christopher, and Martin EP Seligman. *Character Strengths and Virtues: A Handbook and Classification.* Vol. 1: Oxford University Press, 2004.

Phelps, Elizabeth A, and Joseph E LeDoux. "Contributions of the Amygdala to Emotion Processing: From Animal Models to Human Behavior." *Neuron* 48, no. 2 (2005): 175-87.

Philips, Tim. "Can Neuroscience Help Settle the Gun Control Debate?" (2014). http://www.salon.com/2014/01/09/missing_from_the_gun_control_debate_sacred_values_partner/.

Piacentini, John, Douglas W Woods, Lawrence Scahill, Sabine Wilhelm, Alan L Peterson, Susanna Chang, Golda S Ginsburg, *et al.* "Behavior Therapy for Children with Tourette Disorder: A Randomized Controlled Trial." *JAMA* 303, no. 19 (2010): 1929-37.

Piff, Paul K, Daniel M Stancato, Stéphane Côté, Rodolfo Mendoza-Denton, and Dacher Keltner. "Higher Social Class Predicts Increased Unethical Behavior." *Proceedings of the National Academy of Sciences* 109, no. 11 (2012): 4086-91.

Pinker, Steven. *The Blank Slate: The Modern Denial of Human Nature.* Penguin, 2003.

Posner, Michael I. "Attention: The Mechanisms of Consciousness." *Proceedings of the National Academy of Sciences* 91, no. 16 (1994): 7398-403.

Pratchett, Terry. *I Shall Wear Midnight.* Harper, 2010.

Prior, Markus, Gaurav Sood, and Kabir Khanna. "You Cannot Be Serious: The Impact of Accuracy Incentives on Partisan Bias in Reports of Economic Perceptions." *Quarterly Journal of Political Science* 10 (2015): 489-518.

Prochaska, James O, Carlo C DiClemente, and John C Norcross. "In Search of How People Change: Applications to Addictive Behaviors." *American Psychologist* 47, no. 9 (1992): 1102.

Purves, Dale, George J Augustine, David Fitzpatrick, Lawrence C Katz, Anthony-Samuel LaMantia, James O McNamara, and S Mark Williams. "The Association Cortices." Chap. 26 In *Neuroscience. 2nd Edition.* Sunderland, MA: Sinauer Associates, 2001.

Pyszczynski, Tom, Abdolhossein Abdollahi, Sheldon Solomon, Jeff Greenberg, Florette Cohen, and David Weise. "Mortality Salience, Martyrdom, and Military Might: The Great Satan Versus the Axis of Evil." *Personality and Social Psychology Bulletin* 32, no. 4

(2006): 525-37.

Quirk, G. J., R. Garcia, and F. Gonzalez-Lima. "Prefrontal Mechanisms in Extinction of Conditioned Fear." *Biological Psychiatry* 60, no. 4 (Aug 15, 2006): 337-43.

Quirk, G. J., and D. Mueller. "Neural Mechanisms of Extinction Learning and Retrieval." *Neuropsychopharmacology* 33, no. 1 (Jan 2008): 56-72.

Quoidbach, Jordi, Daniel T Gilbert, and Timothy D Wilson. "The End of History Illusion." *Science* 339, no. 6115 (2013): 96-98.

Rauch, S. L., L. M. Shin, and E. A. Phelps. "Neurocircuitry Models of Posttraumatic Stress Disorder and Extinction: Human Neuroimaging Research-Past, Present, and Future." *Biological Psychiatry* 60, no. 4 (Aug 15 2006): 376-82.

Ray, Rebecca D, Kevin N Ochsner, Jeffrey C Cooper, Elaine R Robertson, John DE Gabrieli, and James J Gross. "Individual Differences in Trait Rumination and the Neural Systems Supporting Cognitive Reappraisal." *Cognitive, Affective, & Behavioral Neuroscience* 5, no. 2 (2005): 156-68.

Rescorla, Robert. "Rescorla-Wagner Model." In *Scholarpedia*, 2008.

Ricard, Matthieu. *Happiness: A Guide to Developing Life's Most Important Skill.* Hachette UK, 2008.

Rigoni, D., S. Kuhn, G. Gaudino, G. Sartori, and M. Brass. "Reducing Self-Control by Weakening Belief in Free Will." *Consciousness and Cognition* 21, no. 3 (Sep 2012): 1482-90.

Roberts, B. W., and D. Mroczek. "Personality Trait Change in Adulthood." *Current Directions in Psychological Science* 17, no. 1 (Feb 1 2008): 31-35.

Roberts, B. W., K. E. Walton, and W. Viechtbauer. "Patterns of Mean-Level Change in Personality Traits across the Life Course: A Meta-Analysis of Longitudinal Studies." *Psychological Bulletin* 132, no. 1 (Jan 2006): 1-25.

Rogers, Robert D, Adrian M Owen, Hugh C Middleton, Emma J Williams, John D Pickard, Barbara J Sahakian, and Trevor W Robbins. "Choosing between Small, Likely Rewards and Large, Unlikely Rewards Activates Inferior and Orbital Prefrontal Cortex." *Journal of Neuroscience* 19, no. 20 (1999): 9029-38.

Ronquillo, Jaclyn, Thomas F Denson, Brian Lickel, Zhong-Lin Lu, Anirvan Nandy, and Keith B Maddox. "The Effects of Skin Tone on Race-Related Amygdala Activity: An fMRI Investigation." *Social Cognitive and Affective Neuroscience* 2, no. 1 (2007): 39-44.

Rosenberg, Paul. "Secrets of the Right-Wing Brain: New Study Proves It — Conservatives See a Different, Hostile World." *Salon* (2014). Published electronically July 29, 2014. http://www.salon.com/2014/07/29/secrets_of_the_right_wing_brain_new_study_proves_it_conservatives_see_a_different_hostile_world/.

Rosenberg, Paul H. "White Rage and White Lies: How the Right's Language About Race Created Michael Dunn and George Zimmerman." *Salon* (2014).

Rosenblatt, Abram, Jeff Greenberg, Sheldon Solomon, Tom Pyszczynski, and Deborah Lyon. "Evidence for Terror Management Theory: I. The Effects of Mortality Salience on Reactions to Those Who Violate or Uphold Cultural Values." *Journal of Personality and Social Psychology* 57, no. 4 (1989): 681.

Ross, Lee, David Greene, and Pamela House. "The "False Consensus Effect": An Egocentric Bias in Social Perception and Attribution Processes." *Journal of Experimental Social Psychology* 13, no. 3 (1977): 279-301.

Russell, James A. "Core Affect and the Psychological Construction of Emotion." *Psychological Review* 110, no. 1 (2003): 145.

Ruttan, Rachel L, Mary-Hunter McDonnell, and Loran F Nordgren. "Having "Been There" Doesn't Mean I Care: When Prior Experience Reduces Compassion for Emotional

Bibliography

Distress." *Journal of Personality and Social Psychology* 108, no. 4 (2015): 610.

Ruz, Maria, and J Lupianez. "Attentional Capture." *Psicologica* 23 (2002): 283-309.

Ruz, María, and Juan Lupiáñez. "A Review of Attentional Capture: On Its Automaticity and Sensitivity to Endogenous Control." *Psicológica* 23, no. 2 (2002): 283-309.

Ryan, Richard M, and Kirk Warren Brown. "Why We Don't Need Self-Esteem: On Fundamental Needs, Contingent Love, and Mindfulness." *Psychological Inquiry* 14, no. 1 (2003): 71-76.

Rydell, Robert J, Allen R McConnell, Diane M Mackie, and Laura M Strain. "Of Two Minds: Forming and Changing Valence-Inconsistent Implicit and Explicit Attitudes." *Psychological Science* 17, no. 11 (2006): 954-58.

Saletan, William. "'The Righteous Mind,' by Jonathan Haidt." (2012). https://www.nytimes.com/2012/03/25/books/review/the-righteous-mind-by-jonathan-haidt.html.

Sambataro, F., S. Dimalta, A. Di Giorgio, P. Taurisano, G. Blasi, T. Scarabino, G. Giannatempo, M. Nardini, and A. Bertolino. "Preferential Responses in Amygdala and Insula During Presentation of Facial Contempt and Disgust." *European Journal of Neuroscience* 24, no. 8 (Oct 2006): 2355-62.

Santorelli, Sakti F., Kabat-Zinn, Jon, ed. *Mindfulness-Based Stress Reduction Professional Training, Curriculum Guide and Supporting Materials*: Center for Mindfulness in Medicine, Health Care and Society, University of Massachusetts Medical School, 2007.

———, ed. *Mindfulness-Based Stress Reduction Professional Training-Scientific Papers from the Stress Reduction Clinic and the Center for Mindfulness in Medicine, Health Care, and Society 2008-1982*, 2008.

Sapolsky, Robert M. *Being Human: Life Lessons from the Frontiers of Science*. Teaching Company, LLC, 2012.

———. *Biology and Human Behavior: The Neurological Origins of Individuality*. Teaching Company, 2005A.

Sapolsky, Robert. "Human Behavioral Biology.25 Lectures - Youtube." Stanford University, http://bit.ly/2fVlpYP.

Sapolsky, Robert M. "The Influence of Social Hierarchy on Primate Health." *Science* 308, no. 5722 (2005): 648-52.

———. "A Natural History of Peace." *Foreign Affairs* (2006): 104-20.

Sapolsky, Robert M, and Lisa J Share. "A Pacific Culture among Wild Baboons: Its Emergence and Transmission." *PLoS Biology* 2, no. 4 (2004).

Sarot, Marcel. "Christian Faith, Free Will and Neuroscience." *Ars Disputandi Supplement Series* 6 (2013): 105-20.

Sarter, Martin, Ben Givens, and John P Bruno. "The Cognitive Neuroscience of Sustained Attention: Where Top-Down Meets Bottom-Up." *Brain Research Reviews* 35, no. 2 (2001): 146-60.

Schachter, Stanley, and Jerome Singer. "Cognitive, Social, and Physiological Determinants of Emotional State." *Psychological Review* 69, no. 5 (1962): 379.

Schall, Jeffrey D, Veit Stuphorn, and Joshua W Brown. "Monitoring and Control of Action by the Frontal Lobes." *Neuron* 36, no. 2 (2002): 309-22.

Schel, M. A., S. Kuhn, M. Brass, P. Haggard, K. R. Ridderinkhof, and E. A. Crone. "Neural Correlates of Intentional and Stimulus-Driven Inhibition: A Comparison." *Frontiers in Human Neuroscience* 8 (2014): 27.

Schimel, Jeff, Jamie Arndt, Tom Pyszczynski, and Jeff Greenberg. "Being Accepted for Who We Are: Evidence That Social Validation of the Intrinsic Self Reduces General Defensiveness." *Journal of Personality and Social Psychology* 80, no. 1 (2001): 35.

Schimel, Jeff, Linda Simon, Jeff Greenberg, Tom Pyszczynski, Sheldon Solomon, Jeannette Waxmonsky, and Jamie Arndt. "Stereotypes and Terror Management: Evidence

That Mortality Salience Enhances Stereotypic Thinking and Preferences." *Journal of Personality and Social Psychology* 77, no. 5 (1999): 905.

Schmerler, Jessica. "The Secret to Cracking Writer's Block." (2015). http://www.salon.com/2015/05/31/the_secret_to_cracking_writers_block_partner/.

Schmolesky, Matthew. "The Primary Visual Cortex." In *Webvision: The Organization of the Retina and Visual System,* edited by Helga Kolb, Eduardo Fernandex, Ralph Nelson and Bryan Jones Valencia Spain: Universitas Miguel Hernandez, 2011. http://webvision.umh.es/webvision/VisualCortex.html.

Schonert-Reichl, K, Eva Oberle, M Lawlor, David Abbott, Kimberly Thomson, T Oberlander, and Adele Diamond. "Enhancing Cognitive and Social Emotional Development through a Simple to Administer School Program." *Manuscript submitted for publication* (2011).

Schultz, Wolfram. "Reward." In *Scholarpedia*, 1652, 2007.

Seligman, Martin. *What You Can Change... And What You Can't.* Nicholas Brealey Publishing, 2011.

Seligman, Martin E.P. *Authentic Happiness: Using the New Positive Psychology to Realize Your Potential for Lasting Fulfillment.* Simon and Schuster, 2004.

———. *Helplessness: On Depression, Development, and Death.* WH Freeman/Times Books/ Henry Holt & Co, 1975.

———. *Learned Optimism: How to Change Your Mind and Your Life.* Vintage, 2011.

Seligman, Martin E.P, Tracy A Steen, Nansook Park, and Christopher Peterson. "Positive Psychology Progress: Empirical Validation of Interventions." *American Psychologist* 60, no. 5 (2005): 410.

Seligman, Martin E. P., and Mihaly Csikszentmihalyi. "Positive Psychology: An Introduction." *American Psychologist* 55, no. 1 (2000): 5-14.

Shapiro, Shauna L, Linda E Carlson, John A Astin, and Benedict Freedman. "Mechanisms of Mindfulness." *Journal of Clinical Psychology* 62, no. 3 (2006): 373-86.

Shepherd, Gordon M. "Perception without a Thalamus: How Does Olfaction Do It?" *Neuron* 46, no. 2 (2005): 166-68.

Sherman, David K, and Geoffrey L Cohen. "The Psychology of Self-Defense: Self-Affirmation Theory." *Advances in Experimental Social Psychology* 38 (2006): 183-242.

Shermer, Michael. "Free Won't." *Scientific American* 307, no. 2 (2012): 86-86.

Shiota, M. N., and R. W. Levenson. "Effects of Aging on Experimentally Instructed Detached Reappraisal, Positive Reappraisal, and Emotional Behavior Suppression." *Psychology and Aging* 24, no. 4 (Dec 2009): 890-900.

Shu, L. L., N. Mazar, F. Gino, D. Ariely, and M. H. Bazerman. "Signing at the Beginning Makes Ethics Salient and Decreases Dishonest Self-Reports in Comparison to Signing at the End." *Proceedings of the National Academy of Sciences of the United States of America* 109, no. 38 (Sep 18, 2012): 15197-200.

Silverstein, Jason. "Why White People Don't Feel Black People's Pain." *Slate.com* (2013). http://www.slate.com/articles/health_and_science/science/2013/06/racial_empathy_gap_people_don_t_perceive_pain_in_other_races.html.

Sinclair, Stacey, Elizabeth Dunn, and Brian Lowery. "The Relationship between Parental Racial Attitudes and Children's Implicit Prejudice." *Journal of Experimental Social Psychology* 41, no. 3 (2005): 283-89.

Solomon, Sheldon, Jeff Greenberg, and Tom Pyszczynski. *The Worm at the Core: On the Role of Death in Life.* Random House, 2015.

Sotres-Bayon, Francisco, David EA Bush, and Joseph E LeDoux. "Emotional Perseveration: An Update on Prefrontal-Amygdala Interactions in Fear Extinction." *Learning & Memory* 11, no. 5 (2004): 525-35.

Sotres-Bayon, F., C. K. Cain, and J. E. LeDoux. "Brain Mechanisms of Fear Extinction:

Bibliography

Historical Perspectives on the Contribution of Prefrontal Cortex." *Biological Psychiatry* 60, no. 4 (Aug 15 2006): 329-36.

Speeth, Kathleen Riordan. *The Gurdjieff Work.* Berkeley, California: AND/OR PRESS, 1989.

Stahl, Bob, and Elisha Goldstein. *A Mindfulness-Based Stress Reduction Workbook.* New Harbinger Publications, 2010.

Stanley, Damian, Elizabeth Phelps, and Mahzarin Banaji. "The Neural Basis of Implicit Attitudes." *Current Directions in Psychological Science* 17, no. 2 (2008): 164-70.

Steele, Claude M, and Joshua Aronson. "Stereotype Threat and the Intellectual Test Performance of African Americans." *Journal of Personality and Social Psychology* 69, no. 5 (1995): 797.

Stins, J. F., G. C. van Baal, T. J. Polderman, F. C. Verhulst, and D. I. Boomsma. "Heritability of Stroop and Flanker Performance in 12-Year Old Children." *BMC Neuroscience* 5 (2004): 49.

Stokes, Timothy B. *What Freud Didn't Know: A Three-Step Practice for Emotional Well-Being through Neuroscience and Psychology.* Rutgers University Press, 2009.

Strahan, Erin J, Steven J Spencer, and Mark P Zanna. "Subliminal Priming and Persuasion: Striking While the Iron Is Hot." *Journal of Experimental Social Psychology* 38, no. 6 (2002): 556-68.

Sytsma, Justin, and Edouard Machery. "Two Conceptions of Subjective Experience." *Philosophical Studies* 151, no. 2 (2010): 299-327.

Talhelm, T, X Zhang, S Oishi, C Shimin, D Duan, X Lan, and S Kitayama. "Large-Scale Psychological Differences within China Explained by Rice Versus Wheat Agriculture." *Science* 344, no. 6184 (2014): 603-08.

Tamietto, Marco, and Beatrice Gelder. "Affective Blindsight." *Scholarpedia* 2, no. 10 (2007): 3555.

Tanaka, James W, and Lara J Pierce. "The Neural Plasticity of Other-Race Face Recognition." *Cognitive, Affective, & Behavioral Neuroscience* 9, no. 1 (2009): 122-31.

Tart, Charles. *Living the Mindful Life: A Handbook for Living in the Present Moment.* Boston: Shambhala, 1994.

Taylor, S. E., J. S. Lerner, D. K. Sherman, R. M. Sage, and N. K. McDowell. "Are Self-Enhancing Cognitions Associated with Healthy or Unhealthy Biological Profiles?" *Journal of Personality and Social Psychology* 85, no. 4 (Oct 2003): 605-15.

Taylor, Shelley E, William T Welch, Heejung S Kim, and David K Sherman. "Cultural Differences in the Impact of Social Support on Psychological and Biological Stress Responses." *Psychological Science* 18, no. 9 (2007): 831-37.

Terrell, John Edward. "Evolution and the American Myth of the Individual." *The New York Times*, November 30, 2014.

Thaler Richard, H, and R Sunstein Cass. *Nudge: Improving Decisions About Health, Wealth, and Happiness.* New Haven, CT: Yale University Press, 2008.

Thompson, Ross A. "Emotion Regulation: A Theme in Search of Definition." *Monographs of the Society for Research in Child Development* 59, no. 2-3 (1994): 25-52.

Thorpe, Simon, Denis Fize, and Catherine Marlot. "Speed of Processing in the Human Visual System." *Nature* 381, no. 6582 (1996): 520-22.

Tice, Dianne M., Ellen Bratslavsky, and Roy F. Baumeister. "Emotional Distress Regulation Takes Precedence over Impulse Control: If You Feel Bad, Do It!". *Journal of Personality and Social Psychology* 80, no. 1 (2001): 53-67.

Tolle, Eckhart. *The Power of Now: A Guide to Spiritual Enlightenment.* New World Library, 2010.

Toplak, Maggie E, Richard F West, and Keith E Stanovich. "The Cognitive Reflection Test as a Predictor of Performance on Heuristics-and-Biases Tasks." *Memory & Cognition* 39, no. 7 (2011): 1275-89.

Tricycle Magazine, Editors "Realizing Guiltlessness, the Venerable Dzigar Kongrul Rinpoche Speaks with Pema Chödrön." *Tricycle Magazine*, Winter 2004.

Trungpa Rinpoche, Chogyam. *Shambala: The Sacred Path of the Warrior*. Boston: Shambala Press, 1988.

Trungpa Rinpoche, Chogyam *Training the Mind and Cultivating Loving-Kindness*. Boston: Shambhala, 1993.

Tsoknyi, Rinpoche. *Fearless Simplicity*. Boudhanath: Rangjung Yeshe Publications, 2003.

Tsoknyi, Rinpoche, and Eric Swanson. *Open Heart, Open Mind: Awakening the Power of Essence Love*. Harmony, 2012.

Tsoknyi Rinpoche, Drubwang, Erik Pema Kunsang, and Marcia Binder Schmidt. *Carefree Dignity: Discourses on Training in the Nature of Mind*. Edited by R. M. Sage: Rangjung Yeshe Publications, 1998.

University, Bangor. "Developing 'Mental Toughness' Can Help Footballers Cope with High Pressure Penalty Shoot Outs." *Medical Express* (2017). Published electronically June 22, 2012. https://medicalxpress.com/news/2012-06-mental-toughness-footballers-cope-high.html.

Uylings, Harry B. M., Henk J. Groenewegen, and Bryan Kolb. "Do Rats Have a Prefrontal Cortex?" *Behavioural Brain Research* 146, no. 1-2 (2003): 3-17.

van de Griendt, J. M., C. W. Verdellen, M. K. van Dijk, and M. J. Verbraak. "Behavioural Treatment of Tics: Habit Reversal and Exposure with Response Prevention." *Neuroscience and Biobehavioral Reviews* 37, no. 6 (Jul 2013): 1172-7.

van den Brand, R., J. Heutschi, Q. Barraud, J. DiGiovanna, K. Bartholdi, M. Huerlimann, L. Friedli, *et al.* "Restoring Voluntary Control of Locomotion after Paralyzing Spinal Cord Injury." *Science* 336, no. 6085 (Jun 1 2012): 1182-5.

Vanrullen, Rufin, and Simon J Thorpe. "The Time Course of Visual Processing: From Early Perception to Decision-Making." *Journal of Cognitive Neuroscience* 13, no. 4 (2001): 454-61.

Verdellen, C, J van de Griendt, S Kriens, and I van Oostrum. "Tics. Workbook for Parents." Amsterdam, the Netherlands: Boom Publishers. Retrieved from http://www. uitgeverij-boom. nl/upload/Tics_Workbook_for_parents_EN. 2011.

Vogeley, Kai, Martin Kurthen, Peter Falkai, and Wolfgang Maier. "Essential Functions of the Human Self Model Are Implemented in the Prefrontal Cortex." *Consciousness and Cognition* 8, no. 3 (1999): 343-63.

Vohs, Kathleen D, and Roy F Baumeister. *Handbook of Self-Regulation: Research, Theory, and Applications*. Guilford Publications, 2016.

Vohs, Kathleen D, Nicole L Mead, and Miranda R Goode. "The Psychological Consequences of Money." *Science* 314, no. 5802 (2006): 1154-56.

Wallace, B Alan. *The Attention Revolution: Unlocking the Power of the Focused Mind*. Simon and Schuster, 2006.

———. *Genuine Happiness: Meditation as the Path to Fulfillment*. John Wiley & Sons, 2005.

Wallace, B. A., and S. L. Shapiro. "Mental Balance and Well-Being: Building Bridges between Buddhism and Western Psychology." *American Psychologist* 61, no. 7 (Oct 2006): 690-701.

Wallace, B Alan, and Shauna L Shapiro. "Mental Balance and Well-Being: Building Bridges between Buddhism and Western Psychology." *American Psychologist* 61, no. 7 (2006): 690.

Walsh, E., S. Kuhn, M. Brass, D. Wenke, and P. Haggard. "EEG Activations During Intentional Inhibition of Voluntary Action: An Electrophysiological Correlate of Self-Control?" *Neuropsychologia* 48, no. 2 (Jan 2010): 619-26.

Walton, G. M., and G. L. Cohen. "A Question of Belonging: Race, Social Fit, and Achievement." *Journal of Personality and Social Psychology* 92, no. 1 (Jan 2007): 82-96.

Walton, G. M., G. L. Cohen, D. Cwir, and S. J. Spencer. "Mere Belonging: The Power of Social Connections." *Journal of Personality and Social Psychology* 102, no. 3 (Mar 2012): 513-32.

Wang, D. J., H. Rao, M. Korczykowski, N. Wintering, J. Pluta, D. S. Khalsa, and A. B. Newberg. "Cerebral Blood Flow Changes Associated with Different Meditation Practices and Perceived Depth of Meditation." *Psychiatry Research* 191, no. 1 (Jan 30 2011): 60-7.

Wang, Sam. *The Neuroscience of Everyday Life*. The Great Courses, 2010. DVD lecture series, Course 1540.

Wang, Sam, and Sandra Aamodt. "Your Brain Lies to You." *The New York Times*, 2008.

Warneken, Felix, and Michael Tomasello. "Altruistic Helping in Human Infants and Young Chimpanzees." *Science* 311, no. 5765 (2006): 1301-03.

Weaver, Janelle. "How Motivation Triggers Speedy Decisions." *PLoS Biology* 12, no. 3 (2014): e1001812.

Welberg, Leonie. "The Moral Brain." *Nature Reviews Neuroscience* 8, no. 5 (2007): 326-26.

Welwood, John. *Challenge of the Heart: Love, Sex, and Intimacy in Changing Times*. New York: Shambhala Publications, 1985.

———. *Journey of the Heart: Path of Conscious Love, The*. Harper Collins, 1996.

———. *Ordinary Magic: Everyday Life as Spiritual Path*. Shambhala, 1992.

———. *Perfect Love, Imperfect Relationships: Healing the Wound of the Heart*. Shambhala Publications, 2005.

Wheeler, Mary E, and Susan T Fiske. "Controlling Racial Prejudice Social-Cognitive Goals Affect Amygdala and Stereotype Activation." *Psychological Science* 16, no. 1 (2005): 56-63.

Wikipedia, Contributors. "Bias."

———. "Prefrontal Cortex."

———. "Anterior Cingulate Cortex."

Wile, D. J., and T. M. Pringsheim. "Behavior Therapy for Tourette Syndrome: A Systematic Review and Meta-Analysis." *Current Treatment Options in Neurology* 15, no. 4 (Aug 2013): 385-95.

Wiley, Maya. "Inside Our Racist Brains." *Salon.com* (2013). http://www.salon.com/2013/07/18/inside_george_zimmermans_brain/.

Wilhelm, Sabine, Thilo Deckersbach, Barbara J Coffey, Antje Bohne, Alan L Peterson, and Lee Baer. "Habit Reversal Versus Supportive Psychotherapy for Tourette's Disorder: A Randomized Controlled Trial." *American Journal of Psychiatry* 160, no. 6 (2003): 1175-77.

Willcutt, Erik G, Alysa E Doyle, Joel T Nigg, Stephen V Faraone, and Bruce F Pennington. "Validity of the Executive Function Theory of Attention-Deficit/Hyperactivity Disorder: A Meta-Analytic Review." *Biological Psychiatry* 57, no. 11 (2005): 1336-46.

Williams, Lawrence E., Julie Y. Huang, and John A. Bargh. "The Scaffolded Mind: Higher Mental Processes Are Grounded in Early Experience of the Physical World." *European Journal of Social Psychology* 39, no. 7 (2009): 1257-67.

Wilson, Edward O. "The Riddle of the Human Species." *The New York Times*, February 24, 2013.

Wilson, Timothy D, and Nancy Brekke. "Mental Contamination and Mental Correction: Unwanted Influences on Judgments and Evaluations." *Psychological Bulletin* 116, no. 1 (1994): 117.

Wolman, David. "A Tale of Two Halves." *Nature* 483, no. 7389 (2012): 260.

Woods, Douglas W, Michael P Twohig, Christopher A Flessner, and Timothy J Roloff. "Treatment of Vocal Tics in Children with Tourette Syndrome: Investigating the Efficacy of Habit Reversal." *Journal of Applied Behavior Analysis* 36, no. 1 (2003): 109-12.

Wrzesniewski, Amy, and Barry Schwartz. "Opinion | the Secret of Effective Motivation." *The New York Times*, July 4, 2014.

Wrzesniewski, Amy, Barry Schwartz, Xiangyu Cong, Michael Kane, Audrey Omar, and Thomas Kolditz. "Multiple Types of Motives Don't Multiply the Motivation of West Point Cadets." *Proceedings of the National Academy of Sciences* 111, no. 30 (2014): 10990-95.

Yang, Y., and A. Raine. "Prefrontal Structural and Functional Brain Imaging Findings in Antisocial, Violent, and Psychopathic Individuals: A Meta-Analysis." *Psychiatry Research* 174, no. 2 (Nov 30, 2009): 81-8.

Yearley, Lee. "The Virtues in Christian and Buddhist Traditions in Healing Emotions." Chap. 8 In *Healing Emotions: Conversations with the Dalai Lama on Mindfulness, Emotions, and Health*, edited by Daniel Goleman: Shambhala Publications, 2003.

Zajonc, Robert B. "Attitudinal Effects of Mere Exposure." *Journal of Personality and Social Psychology* 9, no. 2p2 (1968): 1.

Zajonc, Robert B. "Feeling and Thinking: Closing the Debate over the Independence of Affect." Chap. 2 In *Feeling and Thinking, the Role of Affect in Social Cognition*, edited by Joseph P. Forgas: Cambridge University Press, 2000.

Zajonc, Robert B. "Feeling and Thinking: Preferences Need No Inferences." *American Psychologist* 35, no. 2 (1980): 151.

———. "Mere Exposure: A Gateway to the Subliminal." *Current Directions in Psychological Science* 10, no. 6 (2001): 224-28.

Zajonc, Robert B, and Donald W Rajecki. "Exposure and Affect: A Field Experiment." *Psychonomic Science* 17, no. 4 (1969): 216-17.

Zhou, Xinyue, Kathleen D Vohs, and Roy F Baumeister. "The Symbolic Power of Money: Reminders of Money Alter Social Distress and Physical Pain." *Psychological Science* 20, no. 6 (2009): 700-06.

Zimbardo, Philip G. *Lucifer Effect*. Wiley Online Library, 2007.

Zola-Morgan, Stuart, Larry R Squire, Robert P Clower, and Pablo Alvarez-Royo. "Independence of Memory Functions and Emotional Behavior: Separate Contributions of the Hippocampal Formation and the Amygdala." *Hippocampus* 1, no. 2 (1991): 207-20.

A

Accept what is true, 267

Acceptance training, 297–298

Act from Choice Method. *See also specific phase*
  Committed Phase, 137–139, 262
  Decision Phase, 136, 262
  highlights, 260
  overview, xxiv–xxvi
  Preliminary Phase, 136, 139, 261
  targeted mindfulness, xxv–xxvi

Action
  habits, 231, 232
  renouncing unwanted actions, 270
  from stimulus, 13–14
  subconscious, 12–14

Affective reactions, 81 n.124

Age and willpower, 30

Agitated opposition, 53

Alarms set to bring you present, 299–300

Amygdala
  emotions, development of, 92–94
  motivation to act, 94–95
  role of, 77 n.119
  self-awareness of unwanted impulses, 23 n.42
  senses, 92
  unprocessed information, 98

Angelou, Maya, 288

Anger
  The Dalai Lama, 9
  dealing with, 273
  frustration causing, 19
  refractory period, 22 n.39, 195 n.199, 195–196
  triggers, 114
  usefulness of, 5
  as useless habit, 149–150

Anterior cingulate cortex, 23 n.42

Anxiety
  causes of, 276–277
  controlling, 121–122, 280

genetic component of, 280
  importance of, 273
  overwhelm, too much to do, 277–278
  priority listing, 277–279
  stereotype threat, 58–59
  that bad things might happen, 278–280

Aphorisms, 285–290

Apostle Paul. *See* Paul the Apostle

Ariely, Dan, 62

Aronson, Joshua, 58–59

Arrien, Angeles, 269

Ask the Second Question
  Charlie's chocolate chip cookie plan, 205, 207–208, 213
  complex and multi-session tasks, 217–218
  Knowing Mind, 187–189
  Rachel and her true love, 229
  routine and simple encounters, 215–216
  useless habits, 122–123

Attention
  bottom-up bias signals, 21 n.38
  directed, 21 n.38
  mindfulness training, 21 n.37
  to the present, 21–22
  top-down bias signals, 21 n.38

Authentic Happiness (Seligman), 287 n.222

Avoidance. *See* Resistance and avoidance as unwanted habits

Awareness. *See also* Self-awareness
  acceptance training, 297–298
  conscious and unconscious, 11, 14
  increasing, 294–300
  Knowing Mind, 292–294
  overcoming impulses, 28–29
  power of, 291–292
  practice becoming present, 298–299
  self-management and, xxv, 135

set alarms to bring you present, 299–300
tooth-brushing practice to increase, 295–297
training, 138
Awareness (in Committed Phase)

accuracy of the facts, 184
Charlie's chocolate chip cookie plan, 204
creating your Sentinel, 181–184
Jackie's story, 178–179
Knowing Mind, 186–189
managing unwanted attitudes, 236
Max and the boys, 223–224
method highlights, 262
overview, 141, 190–191
Rachel and her true love, 227
routine and simple encounters, 214
Sentinel failure, 185–186
Sentinel technique, 180–181
supporting your sentinel, 185
train to your objective, 183
training your Sentinel, 182–183
triggers, 212–213

B
Bad habits as unwanted, not bad, 4–5
Balloon example, 292–293
Bargh, John, 8 n.21, 52, 55–56, 63
Bat-and-ball problem, 69–70
Baumeister, Roy, 7, 30
Be how you mean to be, 249–255
Begin Again, Again (Goldmann), 255
Begley, Sharon, 104–106
Behavior and realistic expectations, 32–33, 131–132
Behavioral economics, 62
Belief and willpower, 30 n.50
Beneath anger there is fear. Beneath fear there is a tender heart (Chödrön)., 115, 285
Benjamin Franklin balance sheet, 163
Betancourt, Ingrid, xix
Betrayals, Large and Small, 1
Bias
to avoid pain, 102
bias blind spot bias, 72–73, 74

confirmation bias, 73, 82
fundamental attribution error bias, 73
halo effect, 72
implicit, 147
loss aversion bias, 73, 83
Reactive Brain and Intentional Mind, interaction of, 72–74
representativeness bias, 73
social projection bias, 73
unwanted habits and, 65 n.101
Big Five personality dimensions, 103–104, 106, 145
The Blank Slate: The Modern Denial of Human Nature (Pinker), 108–110
Blink (Gladwell), 82
"The blood of ego," 295 n.226
Borderline Personality Disorder, 197 n.204
Brain
amygdala. See Amygdala
anterior cingulate cortex, 23 n.42
capital-B Brain defined, 43
defined, 43
development of preferences, 47 n.61
dorsolateral prefrontal cortex, 23 n.42
early warning system, 91–94
emotion production, 87–90
frontal cortex, 26 n.45
functions, 85–87
hippocampus, 92
injury, 42–43
insula, 92 n.135
interaction with Mind, 65–74
left hemisphere, 106
limbic system, 26 n.45, 92, 95
neurons, 27
prefrontal cortex. See Prefrontal cortex
Reactive Brain. See Reactive Brain
right hemisphere, 106
small-b brain defined, 45
subconscious. See Subconscious

superior colliculus, 92 nn.132, 133
thalamus, 92, 92 n.133
understanding of, 41
Buddhism
    biases, 74
    "The blood of ego," 295 n.226
    lojong slogans, 185 n.197
    Protectors and Protector Principle,
        xxvi, 180 n.192
    subconscious, beliefs about, xxii n.2
Burrows, Lara, 55–56
Bush, George W., 61

C
CAP (Commitment, Awareness, and
    Plan), 139, 141
Carson, Rick, 281–283
Cat and pneumosilicosis example, 67–68
Catharsis is fun, but so expensive, 287
Center, finding your, 263–264
Charlie Hebdo terrorist attack, 61
Charlie's chocolate chip cookie plan
    detail and commentary on the plan,
        206–209
    overview, 200, 202
    situation and plan, 203–206
Chen, Mark, 55–56
Cherokee saying, 6 n.17
Chinese proverb, 101
Chödrön, Pema
    awareness, 142
    misdirected habits, 121, 148, 197
    secondary emotions, 115, 148
    self-management failure, 32, 33
    When Things Fall Apart, 121
Choices, you are what you choose, not
    your habits, 7–10
Chose regret, not guilt (Chödrön)., 33,
    132, 286
Choose what to do and follow through,
    137
Choosing Space
    commitment to choose by using a
        specific procedure, 175–176
    defined, 20

emotions and decision-making, 98–99
impulse results, 192–193
overcoming impulses, 28–29
purpose of, 22
Reactive Brain vs. Intentional Mind,
    25–29
self-awareness, 20–22, 37
self-management, 20
tools, 263–272
Chrysler 300 example, 291
Classical conditioning, 118–119
Cognition as brain function, 52–53
Cognitive Reflection Test (CRT), 69–70
Cold habits
    complex and multi-session tasks,
        216–219
    dealing with, 138–139
    defined, 138
    habits of wanting, 210
    managing unwanted wanting,
        202–209
    plans, 200, 206–209
    procrastination and resistance,
        219–220
    resistance and avoidance, 210–220
    routine and simple encounters,
        214–216
    scheduling when habits appear,
        213–214
    situation and plan, 203–206
    triggers, 211–213
Commitment, reexamination of, 271
Commitment vs. aspiration, 172
Committed Phase of the Act from Choice
    Method. *See also* Reflect/recommit
    CAP (Commitment, Awareness, and
        Plan), 139, 141
    Charlie's chocolate chip cookie plan,
        204–206
    choose by using a specific procedure,
        175–176
    commitment, 137–138
    formal commitments, 176
    managing unwanted attitudes, 236
    Max and the boys, 223

overview, 141, 262
pausing the action, 175
plan, 138–139
Rachel and her true love, 227
routine and simple encounters, 214
train your awareness, 138
triggers, 212
Commitments, ceremony of 176
Communication, 228, 269
Competition
in the brain, 27
judge yourself fairly, 35
Conditioning
classical, 118–119
faulty, 185
misguided habits, 118–120, 146–147
Pavlov's dogs, 5–6, 118
preferences created by, 53
PTSD, 119–120, 124
Confirmation bias, 73, 82
Conscious awareness
habitual impulses, 11
Mind exercises, 50
sensory information processing, 14
Consequences
Ask the Second Question, 187–188
dealing with failure, 136
Form 2: Consequences of the Unwant-
ed Habit, 162
of unwanted reactions, 161
Console yourself, 267
Contingencies, yes. Forecasting, no., 279,
286
Contingency plans, 279–280
Cool down methods, 229, 264–265. See
also Pausing
Creative process, 46–47
CRT (Cognitive Reflection Test), 69–70
Crucial Conversations: Tools for talk-
ing when stakes are high (Patterson &
Grenny), 228, 269
Cultural norms, violations of, 147
Curiosity, power of, 291–292

D
The Dalai Lama, 9
Damasio, Antonio
bias to avoid pain, 102
emotional action program, 11
emotions and decision-making research, 76, 77–80, 82, 127–128
good or bad events, 111
learning and its effects, 116
willpower, 250–251
Davidson, Richard, 104–106, 108
DBT (Dialectic Behavior Therapy), 197,
273 n.219
Death, causes of, 30
Decision Phase of the Act from Choice
Method
Charlie's chocolate chip cookie plan,
204
commitment, 171–173
commitment vs. aspiration, 172
managing unwanted attitudes, 236
Max and the boys, 223
overview, 141, 262
purpose of, 136, 139
Rachel and her true love, 227
routine and simple encounters, 214
Decision-making. See Emotions and
decision-making
Declarative memory, 124
Delaying response, 198–199
Denial of unwanted impulses, 8
Descartes, René, 46
Dialectic Behavior Therapy (DBT), 197,
273 n.219
Discipline
motivation and, xx–xxi
willpower, 30, 36
Discomfort, escaping, 121–122
Disgust as an emotion, 92 n.135
Disidentify, 266
Distracted Mind exercise, 48–49
Distraction from self, 17–20, 37
Distraction-caused ignorance of experi-
ences, 18

Index

Do not do to yourself what you would not do to others, 288

Don't know. Can't know, 279, 286

Don't make things worse than they already are
  planning, 197–198
  with useless habits, 122, 149–150

Don't trust. Question then verify
  feelings and values, 47
  gut feelings, 63, 83
  Mind/Brain unreliability, 66

Dorsolateral prefrontal cortex, 23 n.42

Doubting the subconscious, 62–64

Drop the storyline (Chödrön)., 268, 286

Duckworth, Angela, 36

Dweck, Caroline, 36

Dzigar Kongtrul Rinpoche, 33 n.52, 273 n.219

Dzongsar Jamyang Kyentse Rinpoche, 17

E

Early warning system of the Brain, 91–94

Economic decisions and gut feel, 83

Ego depletion, 30

Ego satisfaction, 24 n.43

Ekman, Paul
  basic emotions, triggers, and goals, 113, 114
  human emotions study, 5
  refractory period, 195–196

Ellis, Albert, 7

Emotional action program
  defined, 11
  emotions and decision-making, 76, 127–128
  importance to survival, 12
  purpose of, 37
  sensory information processing, 14
  System 1 Brain functions, 65–66

Emotional habits, forming, 118–123
  conditioning for misguided habits, 118–120
  misdirected habits, 118, 121–122
  useless habits, 122–123

Emotional Intelligence (Goleman), 7–8, 291

Emotional memory, 86, 124

Emotional resilience, 195–196

Emotional styles
  changing emotional habits, 124–125
  conditioning produces misguided habits, 118–120
  definition and examples, 104–106
  early childhood personality and adult reactions, 110, 123
  emotions, 112–115
  fears, 111–112
  genetic influences, 106–110
  memory of events causing extreme reactions, 124
  misdirected habits, 121–122
  personality and, 123
  reactions, 112
  secondary emotions, 115
  useless habits, 122–123

Emotional toolbox, 114

Emotions
  anger, 273. *See also* Anger
  anxiety, 273. *See also* Anxiety
  basic emotions, 112–114
  as Brain function, 52–53
  Brain production of, 87–90
  defined, 39, 113 n.167
  development of, 91–99
  disgust, 92 n.135
  driving habits, 4–6
  fear, 111–112, 273
  feeling of, 95–97
  goals, 113
  guilt, 273. *See also* Guilt
  linkage of body and, 97
  primary, 148–149
  secondary, 112 n.165, 115, 148–149
  shame, 273. *See also* Shame
  triggers, 113

Emotions and decision-making, 75–84
  brain research, 74, 76–77
  emotions as deciders and motivators, 75–76
  gut feelings are mostly right, 81–84

required for making decisions, 76–81
patient who could not decide or
    choose, 77–81
Reactive Brain and, 127–128
Emotions Love Emotions (Linehan)., 197,
286
Error mechanism of Sentinel, 23, 37
*Everything teaches. Give more attention to
    the lessons than the tuition.*, 289
Executive functions, 26–27, 43
Exercises
    distracted Mind, 48–49
    experience your Mind, 48, 50–51
Expectations, realistic, 32–33, 131–132
Experience your Mind exercise, 48, 50–51
Experiences
    actions and, 13–14
    habits and, 7, 101
    willpower and discipline, 36
Explicit memory, 124
Extended plan, 240–243
External stimulus, 12–13

F
Failure
    dealing with consequences of, 136
    pausing to deal with, 270–272
    self-management, 32–34, 38, 136
    Sentinel, 179, 185–186
    when all else fails, 270–272
    willpower, 29–31
Fears, 111–112, 273
Feelings, validating, 198
Figure-skating competition, 35
Five Factor Model, 103–104, 106
Form 1: This Is My Unwanted Habit,
    153–154
Form 2: Consequences of the Unwanted
    Habit, 162
Form 3: Benefits and Cost of Self-Man-
    agement, 163–164
Form 4: My Values Manifested/My Values
    Undermined, 166
Formal commitment, 176, 194
Frankl, Viktor E., 20

Frederick, Shane, 69–70
Free will
    Free won't xxiii, xxiii n.7
    generally, xxiii n.7
    personality and emotional styles, 107
    subconscious, beliefs about, xxiii
Free won't, xxiii, xxiii n.7
Freud, 46
Freudian ego, superego, and id, xxii n.2
Frontal cortex, 26 n.45
Frustration as a useless habit, 149–150
Frustration response to anger, 19
Fundamental attribution error bias, 73

G
Gage, Phineas, 30 n.49
General mindfulness, xxv
Generosity and openness Value Objective,
    239–240, 245
Genetics
    actions and, 13–14
    anxiety and, 280
    habits and, 7, 101
    personality and emotional styles and,
        102–103, 106–110, 128
    reactions and, 102
    twins separated at birth and reunited
        as adults, 109–110
    unwanted habits and, 3
    willpower and discipline, 30, 36
Getty Museum statue purchase as real or
    fake, 82
Gladwell, Malcolm, 82
Goals
    achieving, xxi
    of impulses, 113
    self-management, xx
    targeted mindfulness, xxv–xxvi
    values and, xxi
*God lives on the other side of the armor
    around your heart*, 289
Goldmann, Robert, *Begin Again, Again*,
    255
Goleman, Daniel
    Emotional Intelligence, 7–8, 291

emotional mind vs. rational mind, 91
    pausing, 23
Goode, Miranda, 59
Great Recession (2008), 117
Greenberg, Jeff, 60
Gremlins, 281–283
Grenny, Joseph, 228, 269
Group, conforming to norms, 24
Guilt
    awareness, 184, 273
    causes of, 273
    choosing regret instead of, 272, 275
    consequences of, 273–274
    dealing with, 274–275
    defined, 33
    from unwanted impulses, 130–131
Gut feelings
    Decision Phase of the Act from Choice
      Method, 136
    emotions and decision-making, 80
    intuition, 69–70, 81–82
    as mostly right, 81–84
    preferences and, 75
    Reactive Brain producing of, 47
    skepticism about, 63–64

H
Habits
    cold. *See* Cold habits
    emotions driving, 4–6
    hot. *See* Hot habits
    misdirected. *See* Misdirected habits
    misguided. *See* Misguided habits
    procrastination, 2
    of reaction, 13
    source of, 151
    stereotypes, 3 n.11
    unwanted. *See* Unwanted habits; Un-
      wanted impulses
    useless. *See* Useless habits
    what you do or don't do, 2–3
Habits of Mind, 3, 231, 232
Habitual impulses, 11–14
    emotional action program, 11, 12, 14,
      37

stimulus, impulse, action, 12–14
    subconscious and awareness, 11–14
Halo effect, 72
Happiness is the absence of unhappiness,
    287
Happiness levels, 242 n.212
Healing into Life and Death (Levine), 284
Heatherton, Todd F., 7
Hippocampus, 92
Hollywood decisions from gut feel, 83,
    83 n.126
Honesty change caused by priming,
    57–58
Hot habits, 221–230
    complex plans, 221–222
    dealing with, 139
    defined, 139
    Max and the boys, 222–225
    planning and preparing, 200, 222
    Rachel and her true love, 225–229
Hypothalamus, 13 n.31, 94–95

I
Implicit bias, 147
Impulses
    detection of, 178 n.191
    habitual, 11–14, 37
    management of, 15–16
    unwanted. *See* Unwanted impulses
Insula, 92 n.135
Intentional Mind
    Brain functions, 26 n.45
    defined, 25-28
    development of, 160
    early childhood personality and adult
      reactions, 110
    interaction with Reactive Brain, 65–74
    leveraging, 267–270
    mechanics of, 26
    Reactive Brain vs., 25–29, 249–250
Intentions
    choices reflecting, xix
    commitment and, 176–177
    impulse control, 192
    memory techniques, 180–181

when violating, tell yourself why, 271

Intuition. *See also* Gut feelings
    Cognitive Reflection Test (CRT),
      69–70
    as mostly right, 81–82

In-utero experiences and reactions, 102,
    107

Investigation, 266

Iraq War, 61

Itch and scratch impulses, 15, 23

J

Jackson, Jesse, 3, 232

James, William, 96

Judge behavior, not the actor, 287

Judge yourself fairly
    be how you mean to be, 252
    learning to, 34–36, 38
    managing unwanted attitudes,
      246–247

Judgment and values, 3

Jung, Carl, 4

K

Kahneman, Daniel
    emotions and decision-making, 80, 83
    no rational people, 159
    Reactive Brain and Intentional Mind,
      interaction of, 65–74
    Thinking, Fast and Slow, 62–63, 65

Kekulé, Friedrich August, 46

Kerry, John, 61

Khandro Rinpoche, Venerable, 178

Kneen, Cynthia, 289–290

Knowing Mind
    Ask the Second Question, 187–189
    defined, 292
    developing awareness, 292–294
    unwanted impulses, 29, 186

L

Lake problem, 69–70

Landers, Ann, 109–110

Learning and its effects, 116–117

LeDoux, Joseph, 93, 99, 111

Left hemisphere of the brain, 106

Levine, Ondrea, 32

Levine, Stephen
    Healing into Life and Death, 284
    managing negative self-talk, 32
    self-management, 33, 131
    validating feelings, 198

Limbic system, 26 n.45, 92, 95

Linehan, Marsha, 197, 273 n.219

Lojong slogans, 185 n.197

Loss aversion bias, 73, 83

Lovallo, Dan, 83

Loving yourself, 283–284

M

Making it worse
    planning, 197–198
    with useless habits, 122, 149–150

Management of habits, xx, 135. *See also*
    Self-management

Managing impulses, 15–16

Mandela, Nelson, 5

Mantras, 285–290

Masking techniques, 55

Maslow's need hierarchy, 24 n.43

Master Habit
    distraction and narrowly focused expe-
      rience, 292–294
    distraction from self, 17–20, 37
    freedom from, 20
    impulsive actions, 19

Max and the boys, 222–225, 232

MBSR (Mindfulness Based Stress Reduc-
    tion), 292 n.225

McLeod, Ken, 246

Mead, Nicole, 59

Mean, defined, xx

Meditation, mindfulness, xxv

Membership needs, 24 n.43

Memory
    declarative, 124
    emotional, 86, 124
    explicit, 124

Index

Memory Palace technique, 180 n.193
    reminding the Sentinel, 185 n.195
    strengthening, 185
    techniques for, 180–181
Mere exposure and preference, 53–54
Mind
    capital-M Mind defined, 43
    conscious experiences, 44
    executive functions, 43
    exercises, 48–51
    interaction with Brain, 65–74
    protection, xxvi, 180 n.192
    understanding of, 41
Mindfulness
    attention and, 21–22
    defined, 292 n.225
    general, xxv
    purpose of training, 21 n.37
    targeted, xxv–xxvi
Mindfulness Based Stress Reduction
    (MBSR), 292 n.225
Mipham Rinpoche, Sakyong, 8
Misdirected habits
    consequences of, 5
    defined, 5
    forming of, 118, 121–122
    reaction to skidding on a slippery road,
        79, 79 n.123
    Truth in Act from Choice Method,
        147–148
Misguided habits
    consequences of, 5–6
    defined, 5
    forming of, 118–120
    Truth in Act from Choice Method,
        146–147
Mnemonic for the Method, 139, 141
Monahan, Jennifer, 53–54
Money
    $9.99 feels like $9.00, 72
    as prime, 59
Mortality as prime, 59–62
Moses and the ark, 65, 66–67
Moses Illusion, 66
Motivation

for decisions, 28–29
    discipline and, xx–xxi
    willpower and, 30 n.50
Motivation (in Preliminary Phase)
    Charlie's chocolate chip cookie plan,
        203–204
    consequences of habitual reactions,
        161–162
    evaluation, 167–169
    Form 2: Consequences of the Unwant-
        ed Habit, 162
    Form 3: Benefits and Cost of Self-
        Management, 163–164
    Form 4: My Values Manifested/My
        Values Undermined, 166
    managing unwanted attitudes,
        235–236
    Max and the boys, 223
    method highlights, 261
    overview, 141
    Rachel and her true love, 226–227
    routine and simple encounters, 214
    self-management benefits and costs,
        159, 161, 163–164
    sources of, 160, 161–167
    triggers, 212
    values, 165–167
Murphy, Sheila, 53–54

N
National Library of Medicine definition
    of PTSD, 119
National Vital Statistics System, 30
Negative self-talk
    antidote for, 283–284
    causes of, 280–281
    gremlins, 281–283
    managing, 32
    Sentinel's warnings, 182
Neurons, 27
Noah and the ark, 65, 66–67
Non-Violent Communication: A language
    of life (Rosenberg), 228, 269
Norms, violations of, 147
Nummenmaa, Lauri, 97

O

Objective (in Preliminary Phase)
  Charlie's chocolate chip cookie plan,
    203
  managing unwanted attitudes,
    234–235
  Max and the boys, 223
  method highlights, 261
  motivation, 155–156
  narrow vs. broad, 156
  overview, 141
  questions, 157–158
  Rachel and her true love, 226
  reconsidering, 170
  routine and simple encounters, 214
  stating your preliminary objective, 158
  training to, 183
  triggers, 212
  Value Objective. *See* Value Objective
Observer self, 50
O'Faolain, Nuala, 122
Open Heart, Open Mind (Tsoknyi), 146
Openness and generosity Value Objective,
  239–240, 245
Operation PUSH, 3 n.11
Overcoming impulse's momentum,
  135–136

P

Pain, acknowledging, 267
Pain is inevitable. Suffering is optional
  (Anonymous)., 150, 285
Panic, 79
Patience Value Objective, 237–243
Patriot Act, 61
Patterson, Kerry, 228, 269
Paul the Apostle
  doing the opposite of what I should
    do, 40, 107
  unwanted habits, 8 n.21, 8–9
Pausing
  accept what is true, 267
  center, finding your, 263–264
  commitment to pause the action, 137,
    175, 193
  cool off, 229, 264–265
  failure, dealing with, 270–272
  get more clarity, 265–266
  leverage Intentional Mind, 267–270
  overcoming challenges, 135
Pavlov's dog conditioning, 5–6, 118
Perception without awareness, 11
Perception Without Awareness (Bornstein
  & Pittman), xxii n.5
Persistence
  defined, 29 n.47
  long-term, 36 n.56
  as mark of character, 29 n.47
Personality style
  Big Five dimensions, 103–104, 106,
    145
  changing emotional habits, 124–125
  conditioning produces misguided
    habits, 118–120
  early childhood personality and adult
    reactions, 110, 123
  emotional styles and, 112–115, 123
  fears, 111–112
  genetic influences, 106–110
  learning and its effects, 116–117
  memory of events causing extreme
    reactions, 124
  misdirected habits, 121–122
  reactions, 112
  secondary emotions, 115
  useless habits, 122–123
Perspective about situations, 245
Pinker, Steven, 108–110
Plan (in Committed Phase)
  Charlie's chocolate chip cookie plan,
    205
  for cold habits, 202–220
  delaying response, 198–199
  emotional profiles, 194–196
  formal process, 194
  making things worse, 197–198
  managing unwanted attitudes, 236
  Max and the boys, 224–225
  method highlights, 262

Index

overview, 138–139, 141, 192–193
Rachel and her true love, 227–229
routine and simple encounters, 214
spot plan, 237
triggers, 212
validating feelings, 198
Political position change caused by mortality prime, 59–60
Positive Psychology, 287 n.222
Post-traumatic stress disorder (PTSD)
conditioning for misguided habits, 119–120, 124
defined, 119
military injuries, 31
as misguided habit, 6, 146
Power to change, 268
Practice, Charlie's chocolate chip cookie plan, 205–206
Pratchett, Terry, 74
Predictably Irrational (Ariely), 62
Preferences
biased to avoid pain, 102
brain development of, 47 n.61
development of, 53–55, 62
gut feelings, 75
mere exposure and, 53–54
Prefrontal cortex
damage causing behavioral changes, 30 n.49
emotions and decision-making, 77–80, 97
learning can shut down amygdala's response, 124
social mores, 117
willpower muscle, 30
Prejudice and values, 3
Preliminary Phase of the Act from Choice Method
Charlie's chocolate chip cookie plan, 203–204
highlights, 261
purpose of, 136
steps, 136
TOM (Truth, Objective, and Motivation), 139, 141

Preprogrammed reactions, 99
Present
attention to the present, 21–22
practice becoming present, 298–299
set alarms to bring you present, 299–300
Primary emotions, 148–149
Priming, 55–64
change from dishonest to honest, 57–58
defined, 55
doubting, 62–64
experiments, 55–57
money images, 59
mortality, consciousness of shifts political positions, 59–62
over- or under-performance, 58–59
subliminal exposure, 54, 55–57
Principles, choosing, 269
The Principles of Psychology (James), 96
Problem solving, 65–74
Procrastination
dealing with cold habits, 219–220
as a habit, 2
as misdirected habit, 148
scheduling tasks, 216–217
Project Implicit, 147
Protectors and Protector Principle, xxvi, 180 n.192
PTSD. *See* Post-traumatic stress disorder (PTSD)
Push through
Charlie's chocolate chip cookie plan, 205, 207
Rachel and her true love, 228
Pyszczynski, Tom, 60

Q

Questions. *See also* Ask the Second Question
objective, preliminary, 157–158
Second Question technique to bring motivation to awareness, 138
truth, 151–154

R
Rachel and her true love, 225–229
Reactions, individual, 101–126
    automatic reactions, 112
    changing emotional habits, 124–125
    childhood-influenced reactions, 110
    conditioning produces misguided
        habits, 118–120
    creation of, 101–103
    emotional styles, 104–110
    emotions, 112–115
    fears, 111–112
    genetics and, 107–110
    learning and its effects, 116–117
    memory of events causing extreme
        reactions, 124
    misdirected habits, 121–122
    personality and emotional styles, 123
    personality changes, 125–126
    personality styles, 103–104, 106–110
    secondary emotions, 115
    useless habits, 122–123
    validity and usefulness of, 151
Reactive Brain
    acceptance training, 297–298
    Brain functions, 26 n.45
    conditioning for misguided habits, 119
    defined, 25-28
    development of, 160
    emotions and decision-making, 81, 96,
        127–128
    first reactions, 47
    habitual reactions and, 101, 102
    Intentional Mind vs., 25–29, 249–250
    interaction with Intentional Mind,
        65–74, 129–130
    interruption of the impulse, 174
    mechanics of, 26
    momentum, 98
    preference development, 62
    responses to threats, 87–90
    subconscious processes, 39–40, 46
    temptation and, 187–188
    tooth-brushing practice to recognize
        interference, 296

    willpower to overcome, 31
Real but not true
    emotions and conditioned responses,
        120
    guilt and shame, 285
    identifying faulty conditioning or
        misguided habits, 185
    misguided habits, 6, 146–147, 150
    source of habits, 151
Reasons for decisions, 28–29
Recollections are unreliable, 98
Reflect/recommit
    Charlie's chocolate chip cookie plan,
        205, 208–209, 210
    Rachel and her true love, 229
Refractory period, 22 n.39, 195 n.199,
    195–196
Reframing, 244–245, 265–266
Regret
    awareness, 184
    choosing instead of guilt, 272, 275
    defined, 33
Reliving situations causing regret, 184
Renounce unwanted action or attitude,
    270
Representativeness bias, 73
Research
    emotions and decision-making, 76–81,
        127–128
    identical twins, 109–110
Resistance and avoidance as unwanted
    habits, 210–220
    complex and multi-session tasks,
        216–219
    dealing with cold habits, 219–220
    routine and simple encounters,
        214–216
    scheduling when habits appear,
        213–214
    triggers, 211–213
Responses to threats, 87–88
Responsibility shifting, 143–144
Right hemisphere of the brain, 106
Rosenberg, Marshall B., 228, 269

Index

S

Sacred values, 269

San Bernardino, California, terrorist attack, 59–60, 61

Sapolsky, Robert
emotional resilience, 196
execution of epileptics, 9
frontal cortex and limbic system, 26 n.45, 95
prefrontal cortex functions, 117

Scheduling
complex and multi-session tasks, 216–217
importance in managing habits of resistance and avoidance, 212-217
when habits appear, 213–214

Scripture, Romans 7:18-19, 8–9

Second Question technique to bring motivations to awareness, 138

Secondary emotions, 112 n.165, 115, 148–149

Self-actualization, 24 n.43

Self-adequacy, 228 n.209

Self-awareness
Choosing Space, 20–22, 37
defined, 292 n.225
purpose of, 129

Self-blame for unwanted impulses, 130–131

Self-editing for speech control, 16

Self-esteem
defined, 228 n.209
fear-based priming and, 62

Self-judgment, judge yourself fairly, 34–36, 38, 246–247

Self-love, 283–284

Self-management
awareness and, xxv
benefits and costs of, 159, 161, 163–164
challenge of, xx, 135
Choosing Space, 20, 22, 25–29, 37
disagreement of you and your subconscious, xxi–xxii
failure of, 32–34, 38, 136

goals, xx
improving, xxi
itching and scratching, 15, 23
judging yourself fairly, 34–36, 38
Master Habit, 17–20
self-awareness for, 291–292
Sentinel, 23–25
speech control, 15–16
underlying cause of reactions, 222 n.208
unwanted attitudes, 139
willpower, 29–32. *See also* Willpower

Self-talk, negative. *See* Negative self-talk

Seligman, Martin E.P., 287 n.222

Senses
Brain functions, 92
functions, 85
response to threats and, 89–90
sight. *See* Sight
smell, 92

Sentinel
cold habits, 212–213
creating your Sentinel, 181–184
defined, 180
designing, 181
error mechanism, 23, 37
examples of use for, 23–24
failure of, 179, 185–186
formalism as empowering, 176–177
gremlins, 282
impulse results, 192–193
intention and behavior mismatch, 160, 192
managing conditioned habits, 120
memory techniques, 180–181
misconceptions, 181–182
overview, xxvi, 129
purpose of, xxvi, 23
training, 138, 182–183

September 11, 2001, terrorist attack, 61

Serenity Prayer
antidote for useless habits, 6, 122
philosophy, 6 n.16
power to change, 268
used to cool off, 264

Shame
  awareness, 273
  causes of, 273, 275–276
  consequences of, 273–274
  dealing with, 276
  fear of ostracism, 33
  from unwanted impulses, 130–131
Sight
  data processing in the Brain, 92 n.133
  mechanics of, 92
  sensory processing, 92 n.134
  stimulus, 91
Sins, unwanted impulses, xxv
Slogans, 285–290
Smell, sense of, 92
Smoking cessation, 121
Snaky-shaped something
  emotions and decision-making, 91,
    92, 94
  lessons, 98–99
Social acceptance and the Sentinel func-
    tion, 23–24
Social injustice, 3
Social projection bias, 73
Social systems, 116–117
Solomon, Sheldon, 60
Speech control, 15–16
Spot plan, 237
Steele, Claude, 58–59
Stereotype
  mortality prime, 61
  social injustice, 3
  threat, 58–59
Stimulus
  emotions, birth of, 91
  external, 12–13
  subconscious, 12–14
Stokes, Timothy, xxii
Storyline, 197, 268
Storytelling, 198
Subaru automobiles, 72
Subconscious
  cognitive activity, 42 n.58, 45
  emotions and cognition are separate,
    52–53

free will, xxiii
functions, xxii, xxii n.3, 46–47
habitual impulses, 11–12
Mind vs. Brain, 43–45
preference development, 53–55
priming, 55–64
programming, xxii
Reactive Brain processes, 39
Subliminal exposure, 54, 55–57
Superior colliculus, 92 nn.132, 133
Surgical procedure survival rate, 72
Survival as highest priority, 111
Suzuki Roshi, 1, 247
System 1 and System 2
  biases, 72–74
  Brain functions, 65–74
  emotions and decision-making, 80, 81
  overview, 65–66
  roles and interactions, 67
  unreliability examples, 66–71

T
Taming Your Gremlin (Carson), 281–283
Targeted mindfulness, xxv–xxvi
Tell yourself why, 271
Temptation, Ask the Second Question,
  187
Terrorism
  Charlie Hebdo attack, 61
  San Bernardino, California attack,
    59–60, 61
  September 11, 2001, World Trade
    Center, attack, 61
Thalamus, functions, 92, 92 n.133
Thinking, Fast and Slow (Kahneman),
  62–63, 65
Threats, responses to, 87–88
To be how you mean to be, xx
Tolerations, 211 n.206
TOM (Truth, Objective, and Motiva-
  tion), 139, 141
Tools
  Charlie's chocolate chip cookie plan,
    205, 207
  emotional toolbox, 114

pause and choose, 263–272
Rachel and her true love, 228
Tooth-brushing practice to increase
awareness, 295–297
Top-down bias signals, 21 n.38
Train awareness, 138
Traumatic brain injury, 31
Triggers
anger, 114
basic emotions, 113
predictable, 211–212
resistance and avoidance, 211–213
unpredictable, 211, 212–213
for unwanted behavior, 144–145
Trolley Experiments, 56 n.73, 56–57
Trump, Donald, 59–60
Truth (in Preliminary Phase)
Charlie's chocolate chip cookie plan,
203
Form 1: This Is My Unwanted Habit,
153–154
managing unwanted attitudes, 234
Max and the boys, 223
method highlights, 261
misdirected habits, 147–148
misguided habits, 146–147
overview, 139, 141
primary or secondary emotions,
148–149
questions, 151–154
Rachel and her true love, 226
responsibilities, 143–144
routine and simple encounters, 214
source or habits, 151
triggers, 144–145, 212
useless habits, 149–150
validity and usefulness of reactions,
151
what you do or don't want to do,
142–143
Tsoknyi Rinpoche
lack of attention, 22
Open Heart, Open Mind, 146
Real but not true, 6, 120, 185, 285
Tversky, Amos, 62

Twins separated at birth and reunited as
adults, 109–110

U
Unconscious awareness, 11
Unwanted attitudes, 231–248
action habits, 231, 232
challenges, 244–247
dropping unwanted attitudes,
244–245
as gifts, 233
habits of Mind, 231, 232
judging yourself unfairly, 246–247
manifesting the value objective,
244–245
the method, 233–243
Unwanted habits
defined, 3
Form 1: This Is My Unwanted Habit,
153–154
Paul the Apostle, 8–9
Reactive Brain vs. Intentional Mind,
69
truth of what happens, 142–143
unwanted, not bad, 4–5
Unwanted impulses
alternative results, 193
beliefs about, 251
management of, xxiii–xxiv
overcoming momentum, 135–136
problem of, 7–8
as sins, xxiv–xxv
unwanted, not bad, 4–5
Unwanted wanting, 202–210
committed phase, 204–206
decision, 204
managing, 202–209
plan details, 206–209
preliminary phase, 203–204
resistance and avoidance, 210–220
steps in the plan, 210
want, defined, xx
Useless habits
antidote for, 6
forming of, 122–123

power to change, 268
Truth step in Act from Choice
   Method, 149–150

V

Validate what is true, 286
Validating feelings, 198
Value Objective
   attributing too much to individual
     success, danger of, 245–246
   choosing, 234–235
   committed phase, 236–237
   defined, 234
   dropping unwanted attitudes,
     244–245
   extended plan, 240–243
   generosity and openness example,
     239–240, 245
   judging yourself unfairly, 246–247
   motivation to act, 235–236
   patience example, 237–239
   spot plan, 237
   unkindness, 233
Values
   defining, 165
   Form 4: My Values Manifested/My
     Values Undermined, 166
   goals and, xxi
   managing unwanted attitudes, 200
   manifested or undermined, 161,
     165–167
   prejudice and judgment, 3
   sacred, 269
   values claimed, xix
van Buren, Abigail, 109–110
Vision. *See* Sight
Vohs, Kathleen, 59

W

Wake Up to Your Life (McLeod), 246
Want, defined, xx
Wanting. *See* Unwanted wanting
Watchfulness, 63–64
Websites

personality profile, 104
   Project Implicit, 147
Welcome discomfort, 288–289
What You See Is All There Is (WYSIATI),
   71, 72
When Things Fall Apart (Chödrön), 121
*When you look, you will see. When you
   see, you will know what to do* (Kneen).,
   289–290
Widget problem, 69 n.111
Wikipedia, 72
Willpower
   a limited resource, 127
   be how you mean to be, 250–251
   ego depletion, 30
   failure of, 29–31
   giving importance to long-term out-
     comes over short-term ones, 250
   like a muscle, xxiii
   mechanics of, 29–30
   motivation and belief, 30 n.50
   not a measure of character, xxiii
   overcoming Reactive Brain, 31, 38
   persistence, 29 n.47
   purpose of, 29
   strength factors, 29–31
   weakness of, xxiii
Withdraw to cool off, 229, 264–265
Word arrangement experiment, 55–56
Work with what is, 288
World Trade Center terrorist attack, 61
*The Worm at the Core: On the Role of
   Death in Life* (Solomon), 60
WYSIATI (What You See Is All There Is),
   71, 72

Z

Zajonc, Robert
   Brain knows and decides before we do,
     52–55
   emotions and decision-making, 76,
     80–81
   Reactive Brain and Intentional Mind,
     interaction of, 68
Zeigarnik effect, 277

THE AUTHOR

Act from Choice is the result of Robert Goldmann's experience helping people see themselves and their situations more clearly in order to manage their lives more effectively. *Seeing clearly* means seeing with a clarity that cuts through the biases and filters we're subject to. Though each of us has this skill, and uses it frequently, it's not a skill we're aware of or use consciously. With training and practice we can call on it to bring ourselves to a mind-state from which we can more easily make decisions closer in line with our value-driven intentions and goals.

Though he has extensive experience in business, when talking about this book, Robert points to his years as a mindfulness practitioner and meditation instructor, as a business and life coach and mentor, and as a facilitator of groups dealing with life-threatening illness and bereavement. Those experiences informed and motivated his self-study of psychology and neurobiology that produced the perspectives and techniques he presents in *Act from Choice*.

His coaching practice, now in its 15th year, has given him a firsthand view of how habitual patterns stand in the way of achieving effectiveness, happiness, and fulfillment. And it's been a proving ground for many of the techniques in the book.

As to formal training, Robert has a degree in mechanical engineering from MIT, and a MBA from Harvard Business School. He has formal training as a coach, having graduated from CoachU. In addition he has attended numerous retreats and workshops led by teachers such as Pema Chödrön, Jon Kabat-Zinn, Stephen and Ondrea Levine, Reggie Ray, Sakyong Mipham, Alan Wallace, and Robert's principal teacher, Tsoknyi, Rinpoche.

He speaks on personal and professional growth, life balance, corporate strategy, and Buddhist topics and has led seminars and retreats on these and other subjects.

Before undertaking a career in coaching, mentoring, and consulting for executives, business owners, and professionals, Robert was CEO of three technology and financial services companies, the largest of which had over $100 million in sales and 1,100 employees. Prior to becoming a CEO he held senior management positions in large public companies where he was responsible for corporate strategy, acquisitions, and marketing.

He says this about *Act from Choice*—

> This book is about teaching people to be more effective at self-management. It's not about changing them. It's about learning to do more often and consciously what we now do only occasionally, in order to keep ourselves from acting against our values and interests.
>
> Our regrettable behavior and attitudes—resistance, denial, bias and prejudice, shutting down, and acting out, for example—are habit-driven. Most of these habitual reactions were acquired innocently, in childhood, even before we had language. They are instigated by automatic and rapid reactions the subconscious prescribes to avoid short-term discomfort and fear, even though the reactions do not always address the underlying cause of the discomfort.
>
> Habitual impulses turn into action before we notice we're in their grip. It takes both self-management and willpower to manage them. If you want to manage them, you have to wake up and choose what to do. Therefore, self-management is the foundation of self-management. My goal is to make available simple tools for training the subconscious brain to interrupt unwanted impulses and bring us to awareness, able to choose how to react so we can be how we mean to be.

Robert is a business and life coach with an international practice. He coaches and mentors executives, business owners, professionals and others, mostly by phone. He lives in the San Francisco Bay Area, with his partner, Victoria Self, close to his two daughters, their husbands and two grandchildren. He can be reached by email at RobertG@ActFromChoice.com.

www.ingramcontent.com/pod-product-compliance
Lightning Source LLC
Chambersburg PA
CBHW061753260326
41914CB00006B/1086